D0857590

CRITICAL INSIGHTS

Harlem Renaissance

CRITICAL INSIGHTS

Harlem Renaissance

Editor
Christopher Allen Varlack
Loyola University

SALEM PRESS
A Division of EBSCO Information Services, Inc.
Ipswich, Massachusetts

GREY HOUSE PUBLISHING

Publisher's Cataloging-In-Publication Data
(Prepared by The Donohue Group, Inc.)

Harlem Renaissance / editor, Christopher Allen Varlack, Loyola
  University. -- [First edition].

   pages ; cm. -- (Critical insights)

   Edition statement supplied by publisher.
   Includes bibliographical references and index.
   ISBN: 978-1-61925-822-8 (hardcover)

   1. American literature--African American authors--20th century--History and criticism. 2. African American authors--20th century. 3. Harlem Renaissance. 4. Harlem (New York, N.Y.)--Intellectual life--20th century. I. Varlack, Christopher Allen. II. Series: Critical insights.

PS153.N5 H37 2015
810.9/896073

First Printing

Contents _____

Critical Contexts _____

Critical Readings _____

About This Volume

Christopher Allen Varlack

Largely noted for its unparalleled growth in the art and literature of the African American community, the period of cultural rebirth known as the New Negro movement, also known as the Harlem Renaissance, has been a consistent source of interest for readers and scholars alike. With its production of key authors, from Langston Hughes to Claude McKay, among others, the Harlem Renaissance saw the rise in creative endeavors by black artists and writers eager to celebrate the unique characteristics of black life and to challenge the institutionalized racial hierarchy pervasive within twentieth-century American society. These creative thinkers, certainly intellectuals in their own right, used their poetry, short stories, novels, and plays as a vehicle to critique the longstanding issues within society that limited socioeconomic mobility for blacks while perpetuating startling stereotypes about a community too long oppressed. Because of its undeniable impact in shaping the American cultural imagination regarding blacks and on the larger American literary canon, the Harlem Renaissance has since been heavily studied as the most significant period of artistic as well as cultural explosion the African American community has ever experienced. With a series of past studies on this vital period, including Australia Tarver and Paula C. Barnes' 2006 *New Voices on the Harlem Renaissance* and Jeffrey O. G. Ogbar's 2010 *The Harlem Renaissance Revisited,* this volume finds its place within an expansive, yet constantly growing, field of scholarship seeking to trace the core themes (intra- and extra-racial color politics, passing, the concept of the New Negro, etc.) that remain the lasting legacy of an era so important to American life.

Though the field of scholarship surrounding the Harlem Renaissance is so extensive, there are noticeable voids that *Critical Insights: Harlem Renaissance* seeks to correct, offering not only expanded readings of the central themes that have long captivated the attention of scholars across time, but also providing valuable insight into the texts, authors, and critical perspectives too often overlooked. Early reviews of Jean Toomer's *Cane* (1923), for instance, criticized its fragmentary nature, citing it as the source of the novel's poor reception among both black and white readers rather than recognizing its application of modernist principles akin to the style of Irish novelist and fellow modernist, James Joyce. Similarly, Claude McKay's *Home to Harlem* (1928) has suffered from its early criticism, too often described through the lens of primitivism that has since clouded other critical views. As J. Martin Favor notes in *Authentic Blackness: The Folk in the New Negro Renaissance*, "By privileging certain African American identities and voices over others, the critic of African American literature often restricts too severely his or her scope of intellectual inquiry" (3)—a flaw that has contributed to the perpetuation of these (and other) past oversights. With Jean-Christophe Cloutier's 2009 discovery of an unpublished manuscript by Claude McKay, *Amiable with Big Teeth*, and the renewed interest in the Harlem Renaissance that such a discovery brought with it, this volume is all the more important in filling in some of those persistent gaps, opening the scope of intellectual inquiry, and adding to the necessary conversations the era advances about race, class, and gender identity.

In the introduction, "The Harlem Renaissance: The New Negro Intellectual and the Poetry of the Sociopolitical Imagination," Christopher Allen Varlack, for example, examines poetry of the time and the ways in which authors, from Sterling Brown to Claude McKay, engage the overarching political motivations the progenitors of the movement set in place. Through works such as "He Was a Man" and "America" respectively, these authors responded to the hostile racial climate of the early to mid-twentieth century, most evident through the rise in lynchings as well as membership in the Ku Klux Klan. Here, Varlack traces the political impulse of the era's poetic works as a starting place for much larger conversations about the Harlem Renaissance and its effort to add a new dimension to the American racial debate. From there, the collection introduces four critical contexts essays that expand these key themes by tracing the history of the era in addition to introducing valuable critical and comparative perspectives necessary to understanding the spirit of the time. In "Dawn in Harlem: Exploring the Origins of the Harlem Renaissance through Image and Text," Carolyn Kyler, for instance, examines the intersections of visual and literary works in the era's most noted print publications, from the Harlem issue of *Survey Graphic* to *Fire!!*. In an attempt to probe the ways in which art and poetry combine to usher in a new dawn for the African-American community, Kyler emphasizes the multiplicity of artistic visions that comprised this diverse and celebrated period.

In his essay, "Apathetic Critiques Revisited: Jean Toomer's *Cane* and Its Importance to the Harlem Renaissance," Gerardo Del Guercio highlights the history of apathetic criticism regarding the novel *Cane* by Jean Toomer. Now considered an important modernist work, *Cane* was heavily criticized upon publication for what critics perceived as artistic missteps and inconsistencies within Toomer's work. Del Guercio seeks to trace that history of criticism and the overall importance of the novel as a unique undertaking in the Harlem Renaissance. Focusing on another author who often defied traditional artistic and racial conventions, in "Sugar Cane and Women's Identity in Selected Works of Zora Neale Hurston," Allyson Denise Marino calls attention to Hurston's short fiction and *Their Eyes Were Watching God* with a particular emphasis on the presence of sugar cane in these works. For Marino, sugar cane represents a history of racial and economic oppression for women that is a core theme across many of the era's most noteworthy texts. She thus expounds upon a materialist, feminist, and postcolonial lens in order to present this critique. This final critical contexts essay, "Mobile Subjects in Faulkner, Larsen, and Thurman: Racial Parody and the White Northern Literary Field" by Cheryl Lester, examines the urban North as an invaluable setting for the exploration of racial anxieties and the reconfigurations of a national identity in early twentieth century texts. Focusing on three novels with an emphasis on nation and race—Thurman's *The Blacker the Berry*, Faulkner's *The Sound and the Fury*, and Larsen's *Quicksand*—Lester provides a comparative perspective that helps us better understand the intersecting artistic and intellectual threads of the time. Together, the four essays in this section offer a framework for understanding the Harlem Renaissance, its criticism, and the overarching goals that its authors sought to achieve.

In its endeavor to explore the key themes and directions of the Harlem Renaissance period, *Critical Insights: Harlem Renaissance* then engages fourteen critical readings essays across four sections, with the first entitled, The New Negro: The Politics and Aesthetics of the Harlem Renaissance. These essays introduce the core artistic and political movements that shaped the literature of the time and inform our understanding of its central themes. In his essay, "'Hectic Rhythms': Unseen and Unappreciated Knowledge in Harlem Renaissance Fiction," for example, Jericho Williams examines Claude McKay's *Home to Harlem* and Wallace Thurman's *The Blacker the Berry* as a response to the Du Boisian concept of the talented tenth. Essentially arguing that these works posit an alternative to classical education, he interrogates the era's debate regarding the educated elite and the merits of the "low down" folk. In "Toward a Theory of Art as Propaganda: Re-Evaluating the Political Novels of the Harlem Renaissance," Christopher Allen Varlack also seeks to examine the ideology of W. E. B. Du Bois, discussing how Walter White's *The Fire in the Flint* anticipates the notion of art as propaganda, while George Schuyler's *Black No More* provides a clear political response to the history of lynching rampant in the twentieth century. Finally, Seretha D. Williams in "'The Bitter River': Langston Hughes and the Violent South," traces the ways in which the poet laureate of the Harlem Renaissance, Langston Hughes, uses his poetry to call attention to the oppression and exploitation of blacks. In doing so, Williams expands the timeframe of the Harlem Renaissance, noting the much farther-reaching discussion of lynching that continues well into the 1940s. Together, these essays provide insight into the purposeful intellectual and political projects of the Harlem Renaissance literary intelligentsia.

The next section, Across the Color Line: Racial Passing and the Harlem Renaissance, offers a look into one of the central topics explored in much of the era's literature: passing and the notion of racial indeterminacy. In Holly Simpson Fling's essay,

"Racial Connections in 'Time Space': A Chronotopic Approach to Johnson's *The Autobiography of an Ex-Colored Man*," she uses M. M. Bakhtin's notion of the chronotope as a vehicle to explore racial passing in one of Johnson's most celebrated works. For Fling, the journey of the unnamed protagonist in the novel parallels the very real experience of the nineteenth and twentieth centuries, calling attention not only the impulses that drive one to pass, but also the fears of white society that gave life to the color line. Charlotte Teague, in "Framing Racial Identity and Class: Magnifying Themes of Assimilation and Passing in the Works of Johnson and Hughes," then expands upon this present discussion, exploring the ways in which literature of the time probes the very real difficulties of the Negro question and the pervasive color line. For Teague, Johnson and Hughes integrate issues of assimilation and passing within *The Autobiography of an Ex-Colored Man* and *Not Without Laughter* in order to reach a better sense of conclusions about racial identity and class. Like Teague, Holly T. Baker also addresses the complications of passing in one of the era's most noteworthy texts. In her essay, "'Why Hadn't She Spoken That Day?': The Destructive Power of Racial Silence in Nella Larsen's *Passing*," she examines the trend of intra- and extra-racial silence or silencing that proves destructive in American society. Under this lens, racial passing is not only a source of discomfort for the white community, but also for those in passing—a fact that reinforced the need for more open conversations about race and racial indeterminacy as the American racial landscape continued to change. The final essay of this section, "Just Passing Through: The Harlem Renaissance Woman on the Move" by Joshua M. Murray, offers a comparative perspective on the era's passing novels, including White's *Flight*, Jessie Redmon Fauset's *Plum Bun: A Novel Without a Moral*, and Nella Larsen's *Quicksand*. By tracing the racial and geographical shifts that each protagonist explores, Murray highlights themes of liminality and transition as authors of the Harlem Renaissance sought to probe the experiences of black women in the United States.

Section three, entitled Black Woman/Black Mother: Toward a Theory of the New Negro Woman, is a particularly important section in expanding the definition of the New Negro, typically a figure gendered male. These essays trace the vital role of female characters and female-authored texts in shaping the discourse of the Harlem Renaissance. Lisa Elwood-Farber, for instance, in her essay, "Grimké's Sentimentalism in *Rachel:* Subversion as an Act of Feminism," traces Rachel's refusal to marry and have children— the traditional norms for women at the time—as an apparent form of protection for her unborn children, given the era's hostile racial climate, but also as a move toward social change for the black mother. Elwood-Farber highlights the unique concerns of black women far different from the concerns of their white counterparts. Similarly, in "'Where is that Ark uv Safty'?: Tracing the Role of the Black Woman as Protector in Georgia Douglas Johnson's Plays," Brandon L. A. Hutchinson also centers her discussion around the mindset of the black mother at a time of rampant lynchings. Hutchinson explores three works by Johnson, each tracing the ways in which the black mother responded to this consistent threat. Similarly, in her essay "'Don't knock at my door, little child': The Mantled Poetics of Georgia Douglas Johnson's Motherhood Poetry," Michelle J. Pinkard highlights the shifting conceptions of black motherhood and the complications with that definition during the Harlem Renaissance era. In the process, she foregrounds the role of the New Negro female poets in pursuing a type of sociopolitical agency otherwise denied them twofold as a result of their gender and race.

The final section, The New Negro Revisited: New Readings of the Harlem Renaissance, attempts to move beyond what Miriam Thaggert describes as the worn-out themes and approaches to the Harlem Renaissance, offering new insights into the era's most controversial, as well as under-examined, texts (16). In "Writing Across the Color Line: Carl Van Vechten's *Nigger Heaven* and the Insatiable Hunger for Literature of Black American Life," Christopher Allen Varlack attempts to review this text outside its traditional primitivist lens. Here, he focuses on the often-ignored discussion that the black intellectual Van Vechten incorporates into his text and his engagement of one of the core discussions of the time—how the black intellectual finds (or fails to find) harmony between the life of the folk and the life of the mind. In "Dancing Between Cultures: Claude McKay and the Harlem Renaissance," Lisa Tomlinson strives to explore those intersections of McKay's early Caribbean poetry and his later work after emigrating to the United States or travelling abroad. As Tomlinson argues, scholarship insisting on isolating these works vastly misrepresents McKay's artistic and intellectual project, as McKay expounds upon his themes of class and race oppression in his most celebrated post-emigration texts. In "'Blue Smoke' and 'Stale Fried Fish': A Decadent View of Richard Bruce Nugent," Tiffany Austin reintroduces the work of the only openly gay Harlem Renaissance figure, placing particular emphasis on *Salome* and a short story published in the only issue of the Niggerati's *Fire!!* Austin resurrects an author largely forgotten in Harlem Renaissance scholarship, his novel, *Gentleman Jigger*, only published decades after his death. The final essay in this section, "Going Back to Work Through: The Return to Folk Origins in the Late Harlem Renaissance" by Karl Henzy, then continues the work of resurrecting and revisiting. Here, Henzy focuses on four key novels from Hurston's *Jonah's Gourd Vine* to Arna Bontemps' *God Sends Sundays*. Henzy focuses on the novels' return to folk origins, the intellectual underpinnings of these works, and the ways in which these authors reflect on the Harlem Renaissance at large.

This volume concludes with an extensive chronology of the Harlem Renaissance era—one that attempts to call attention to key literary and artistic works that best define the spirit of the age. Few past studies on this period include a detailed chronology—David Levering Lewis' 1994 *The Portable Harlem Renaissance Reader* and George Hutchinson's 2007 *The Cambridge Companion to the Harlem Renaissance,* for instance—and so, with recent discoveries and publications in the field, including several posthumous works, it is long overdue for an updated timeline to accurately reflect the era's continued and evolving work. In its endeavors to push the boundaries of critical thought regarding the Harlem Renaissance, *Critical Insights: Harlem Renaissance*, we believe, is a valuable and much-needed contribution, which seeks to expand our understanding of an era that fundamentally resists boundaries to the core. "Like any complex cultural movement in which persons learn from each other, the Harlem Renaissance (and its continuing study) must be seen as a series of interrelated events, which reverberate down into our present consciousness. It is for such reasons that we [too] return to this project" (Kramer 1), as many have done before, in hopes of offering a few new points of consideration on an era that continues to heavily resonate in the American spirit and culture even today.

Works Cited

Favor, J. Martin. *Authentic Blackness: The Folk in the New Negro Renaissance.* Durham: Duke UP, 1999.

Kramer, Victor A. "Introduction to the New Edition." *Harlem Renaissance Re-Examined.* Troy, NY: Whitston, 1997. 1–2.

Thaggert, Miriam. *Images of Black Modernism: Verbal and Visual Strategies of the Harlem Renaissance.* Amherst: U of Massachusetts P, 2010.

The Harlem Renaissance: The New Negro Intellectual and the Poetry of the Sociopolitical Imagination

Christopher Allen Varlack

In his 1947 essay, "My Adventures as a Social Poet," Langston Hughes, often described as the "Poet Laureate of the Harlem Renaissance," declares that "[s]ome of my earliest poems were social poems in that they were about people's problems—whole groups of people's problems—rather than my own personal difficulties" (9). Though the Harlem Renaissance is arguably more renowned for its fiction, the poetry, in this sense, is perhaps the most important, speaking to the diverse range of real-world social and political issues that contributed to the racial wasteland of the United States in the early to mid-twentieth century. Tied to the era's black liberation struggle, these poems of the political imagination challenged the racial hierarchy and the limited opportunities for social mobility provided to a growing population of blacks. At the same time, these works called attention to the history of lynching and racial violence nationwide. In offering a much different perspective on the nation's increasingly hostile racial climate than cemented in the minds of many Americans by Thomas Dixon, Jr.'s *The Clansman: An Historical Romance of the Ku Klux Klan* (1905) and the heavily skewed media accounts, such poems exposed the stereotypes of the brute and sexually deviant black figure, in turn highlighting the history of lynching, castration, and miscarriage of justice of which many Americans were simply ignorant or willfully unaware.

Because of its overarching political insights, the poetry of the Harlem Renaissance speaks to one key intellectual project of the time—what W. E. B. Du Bois describes as propaganda in his 1926 essay, "Criteria of Negro Art"—and is, therefore, an appropriate vantage point for approaching and understanding the Harlem Renaissance at large. Here, through their individual works, the poets of the time inherently provided readers "overlapping social and intellectual circles, parallel developments, intersecting groups, and competing visions—yet all loosely bound together by a desire for racial self-assertion and self-definition in the face of white supremacy" (Hutchinson 1). The rebel sojourner Claude McKay, for instance, incensed by the Red Summer of 1919 and the rise in brutal lynchings of blacks, wrote his infamous poem, "If We Must Die," conveying the universal struggle for survival and legitimacy in a society where blacks were then second-class citizens at best. Langston Hughes, tackling the stereotypical depictions of blacks enacted upon the minstrel stage, wrote poems such as "Minstrel Man" and "The Jester" as a way to call attention to the silent and silenced figure beneath the minstrel mask. In doing so, these authors, among others, sought to usher in that era of cultural awakening from the centuries-long slumber of the antebellum and Civil War days. As a result, the Harlem Renaissance, also known as the New Negro movement, "signif[ied] a . . . moment of recognition—both self-recognition (for it was a very self-conscious phenomenon) and recognition from 'without'" (Hutchinson 2).

In honing in on the poetry of the era, we can then begin to highlight the socio-political project proposed by the Harlem literary intelligentsia—those same souls that "have been put out of or barred from quite a number of places, all because of [their] poetry—not the roses and moonlight poems (which [they] write, too) but because of poems about poverty, oppression, and segregation" (Hughes, "My Adventures" 11) that threatened the existing racial order as well as the one-sided propaganda—an issue with which Du Bois is disturbed—that kept that racial order in place. From Langston Hughes to Sterling Brown, Countee Cullen to Claude McKay, these poets evoked the spirit of a tumultuous, but also celebratory age, providing necessary insight not always into the New Negro that the progenitors of the movement attempted to create, but rather into the everyday Negro fighting against an oppressive American culture, while celebrating his unique dark-skinned self. While the "[s]ocial forces [of the 1900s] pull backwards or forwards, right or left, and social poems [certainly] get caught in the pulling and hauling" (9), it is there, too, in that interplay of these social forces and the poets' artistic responses, that Hughes, Brown, Cullen, and McKay—just a mere sampling of a much larger poetic tradition—unveil their central critiques.

"Christ in Alabama": Langston Hughes and a Theory of Social Responsibility

"I am sure none of these things would ever have happened to me had I limited the subject matter of my poems to roses and moonlight" (15), writes Hughes in "My Adventures as a Social Poet," addressing his aforementioned barring for engaging topics too sensitive and too political for a public stage. The African American writer, after all, had long been told what he could and could not write from white and black society alike. As he declares in "The Negro Artist and the Racial Mountain" (1926), "'Oh, be respectable, write about nice people, show how good we are,' say the Negroes. 'Be stereotyped, don't go too far, don't shatter our illusions about you . . .,' say the whites" (3). Under this lens, Hughes criticizes the narrowing of African American expression into predetermined types—a politics and aesthetics wildly inconsistent with his personal artistic goals, eager to shed light on the multiplicity of figures and experiences that define black life. For this reason, Hughes severed his relationship with his patron, Charlotte Osgood Mason, in 1930 to preserve creative control over his own writing. As he openly declares, "[U]nfortunately, I was born poor—and colored—and almost all the prettiest roses I have seen have been in rich white people's yards—not in mine. That is why I cannot write exclusively about roses and moonlight, for sometimes in the moonlight my brothers see a fiery cross and a circle of Klansmen's hoods" (Hughes, "My Adventures" 15).

This artistic and intellectual philosophy Hughes then realizes within his most renowned poetic works—poems such as "Christ in Alabama" (1931) that ultimately tackle the controversial subjects headfirst without tightened lips or limiting reserve. In the poem, Hughes responds to the Scottsboro case of the same year, in which nine African American teenagers were accused and convicted of raping two white women and thus were sentenced to death—an event that stirred the already mounting discontent of the black community. The opening lines of the poem reveal Hughes' refusal to turn from such highly politicized subjects, instead engaging that same social responsibility that he acknowledges in his nonfiction works. Here Hughes writes, "Christ is a Nigger, / Beaten and black— / *O, bare your back*" (lines 1–3). Essentially caught between the era's political and aesthetic trends, Hughes "responded," as evidenced by this work, "by assuming the task of redefining the artistic function in new social and political terms" (Graham 213)—a type of intellectual work vital to the Harlem Renaissance and its redefinition of the image of the black. For Hughes, the poetic form offered a mirror for the larger American public, casting a much more detailed image of the nation's racialized state than the prevailing distortions would allow. Through equating Christ, a revered figure in the largely Christian United States, with a nigger, an inferior creature abhorred in the same United States, Hughes seeks to highlight the depravity and the moral degradation pervasive in an American society known for its lynching culture and the assumption of black guilt.

His intention here ultimately seems quite purposeful. Hughes, after all, truly believed that "[c]ontemporary white writers can perhaps afford to be utterly irresponsible in their moral and social viewpoints. Negro writers cannot" ("The Task" 28). With this in mind, his juxtaposition of the nation's most respected white figure with the most heavily dejected black—"*Nigger Christ / On the cross of the South*" (lines 12–13)—is certainly intended to provoke: to break not only the perception of complacency that some readers mistakenly associated with blacks, but also to help provoke the black community itself. For Hughes, it is clear that "[t]here is today no lack within the Negro people of beauty, strength and power— world shaking power" ("The Task" 28) and while under-recognized at the time, it had the ability to stir the American racial landscape. His art, then, moves toward that goal, pointing out the disconnect between the ideal (the notion of the American dream) and the reality (a veritable nightmare, at least for blacks). Through some of the era's strongest and most biting images—like that of the "*Nigger Christ*" (line 12)—Hughes thus foregrounds a social and cultural critique. Like Christ before his death, the Negro in America is the scapegoat for the ills that plague society, rejected and dejected as the dregs of a proud and powerful nation. At the same time, however, Hughes foreshadows the future acceptance sure to come. Though currently splayed "*[o]n the cross of the South*" (line 13), the African American, too, will rise from his neglected position and be revered.

In his conclusion to "My Adventures as a Social Poet," Hughes contends, "Sometimes in the moonlight a dark body swings from a lynching tree—but for his funeral there are no roses" (15). Is it possible, then, that his poems take their place, offering the type of remembrance, a eulogy of sorts, for the hundreds of black bodies left swinging? The italics throughout "Christ in Alabama" are important in that act of remembering. Central to the aesthetic and cultural impulses that drove the works of the Harlem Renaissance's most celebrated poets was the oral storytelling tradition—the evoking of black voices in text far beyond just the author's minute persona. These voices reflected a collective black consciousness— an echoing of the greatest joys and deepest sadness of the black community. As Karen Ford notes in "The Commodification of Langston Hughes," the italics are essential to Hughes' artistic endeavors in this text. Altered when reprinted in *The Panther and the Lash* (1967), the once italicized lines are no longer in italics—a fact that Ford posits as significant. In the original text, after all, moving toward that collective consciousness, the typographical feature suggests the presence of multiple layers of discourse—a call and response, perhaps, between the speaker and the society his words address. Works such as "Christ in Alabama" are, therefore, essential milestones in the development of the Harlem Renaissance, suggesting that the era—contrary to relatively recent contentions— was not a failure and that in this, the New Negro age, the New Negro began to successfully find his voice.

"He Was a Man": Engaging the Black Folk Ethos in the Work of Sterling Brown

Like Hughes, noted critic and poet, Sterling Brown, also sought to challenge those deeply rooted stereotypes that cast perpetual dark clouds over the image of the black community—each based upon the "hardening [of] racial character into fixed moulds . . . dangerous when applied to the entire group" ("Negro Character" 84). In his 1933 critical essay, entitled "Negro Character as Seen by White Authors," he ultimately contends that "[t]he Negro has met with as great injustice in American literature as he has in American life. The majority of books about Negroes merely stereotype Negro character" (56). Though his essay does not resolve the widely debated topic of who should carry the Negro's tale, Brown does acknowledge a startling misrepresentation of the Negro figure in text, describing the literary development of the stereotypical contented slave and tragic mulatto figures, among others, intended by their white creators as a defense of slavery for the antebellum South. In response, Brown strived to evoke the black folk ethos in his individual poetic works, using the multiplicity of artistic and expressive forms unique to the black people as a vehicle to deconstruct those very same stereotypes that were integral to the plantation myth. To Brown, black writers combated that "easy pigeonholing of an entire race" (56) by unearthing a much more expansive image of the race—one to foreground its humanity.

Following in the footsteps of his literary predecessors—now celebrated authors, like Paul Laurence Dunbar—Brown attempted to revisit "the language and tropes he has inherited in order to explore the inventive ways in which African Americans [can] articulate their own presence and modernity" (Sanders 9), as in much of his Slim Greer cycle. As a result, an overwhelming majority of existing criticism focuses on Brown's dialect work, tracing his use of dialect—once limiting—as a vehicle to allow his African American characters to speak their own presence free from the stereotypical masks. These works are considered to have "tapped the black folk ethos . . . [and to have] captured the essence of black folk life and culture, without the distortion and sentimentality of earlier American writers" (Rowell, "Sterling" 336). Still, it is Brown's non-dialect works, arguably lesser known, that prove most vital to challenging the myopic view held of the African American community. Poems including his 1932 "He Was a Man" illustrate the face beneath that mask—a face far different from the stereotypical banjo-plucking, brute Negro often depicted on the screen and stage. Like Hughes, Brown also responds to the constant threat of lynching in this particular work, writing about the 1931 hanging of Mack Williams outside of a courthouse in Maryland.

"It wasn't about no woman / It wasn't about no rape" (Brown, "He Was" lines 1–2), he writes in the poem's opening lines, challenging the brute Negro caricature that had steadily permeated the American cultural imagination with films such as the 1915 *Birth of a Nation* and the frequent depictions of razor-wielding black men who were waiting to strike, which followed. In contrast to this exaggerated image, the poem instead posits that Williams' assertions of his humanity (despite years of dehumanizing oppression and forced silence) as well as the rising discomfort with the changing racial order all around are what ultimately instigate his death. Williams "wasn't crazy, and he wasn't drunk, / An' it wasn't no shooting scrape, / He was a man, and they laid him down" (lines 3–5). Through these lines, Brown reverses the dehumanization, proclaiming Williams' humanity and, by nature, asserting the lack of humanity evident in his hanging. This, however, is only one aspect of the poem's critique. In the closing stanza, Brown speaks to the innocence of Williams—one among many in the 1930s—and to the true underlying motivations of the society that "laid him down" (line 5). He writes, "The mob broke up by midnight. / 'Another uppity Nigger gone— / He was a man, an' we laid him down'" (lines 58–60).

In his use of the blues ballad form, Brown engages, as a conscious artistic and intellectual project, "the multifarious traditions and verbal art forms indigenous to [the] black folk" (Rowell, "Sterling" 336) in order to celebrate a unique black art, but also "to give voice to the common black man" (336) too often silent or silenced in text. Through the ballad form, Brown evokes the all-important tradition of storytelling vital to the African American community, repeating that phrase "He was a man" in all of its shifting manifestations to represent the communal black voice set against a backdrop of the heroic narrative that Brown constructs. What Brown cements here is not only a record of the interracial violence and inequality that kept the United States consistently divided, but more importantly, his words record the legacy of this otherwise unidentified and forgotten man—"a po' boy [who] tried to get from life / What happiness he could" (Brown, "He Was" lines 18–19). And the voice he uses to communicate that is the lamentations of the black community at large—a song in unison, declaring both Williams and the Negro a man. Brown, after all, believed that "[t]he blues are full of consciousness of the ugly situation. They talk about it with irony" (Rowell, "'Let Me Be'" 289)—an irony that leaps from the page in its critique of white morality, the American racial hierarchy finally shifting.

"Scottsboro, Too, Is Worth Its Song": Activism in the Work of Countee Cullen

In his extension of the Harlem Renaissance critique, Countee Cullen also challenged the racialized social system throughout the United States, foregrounding the complex issues of race, discrimination, and racial identity in several of his most noteworthy works. Though Cullen was once widely criticized for aspiring to what Hughes perceived as whiteness and for his controversial declaration that "[i]f I am going to be a poet at all, I am going to be POET and not NEGRO POET" (Sperry), Cullen still plays a vital part in the twentieth century conversation about race, often using formal lyric to present his cultural critique. Like Hughes, Cullen also wrote in response to the 1931 Scottsboro case—a poem dedicated to the American poets, entitled "Scottsboro, Too, Is Worth Its Song." Here, Cullen expresses his discontent with the pervasive silence among white poets, who sing "their sharp and pretty / Tunes for Sacco and Vanzetti" (lines 13–14), but "have raised no cry" (line 25) for the nine African American boys of Scottsboro and the history of mistreatment, where blacks were not afforded equal rights under the law. The poem thus directly confronts that silence, disenfranchising to an extent, as well as the one-sided propaganda where the miscarriage of justice was only worth an outcry for those of a certain colored skin. Nicholas Canaday, Jr., cites this work as significant, considering that "Cullen is the representative and symbolic figure of the Harlem Renaissance, and the Scottsboro tragedy of 1931 was the traumatic experience in the black community that ended this literary flowering" (119).

In a style similar to Brown, Cullen acknowledges the deeply rooted stereotypes of blacks that thrive in American society and serve as an underlying motivation to write. In his response to *The Crisis'* questionnaire about how the Negro should be best portrayed, Cullen noted that "[t]here can be no doubt that there is a fictional type of Negro, an ignorant, burly, bestial person, changing somewhat today though not for the better, to the sensual habitué of dives and loose living, who represents to the mass of white readers the by—all and end—all of what constitutes a Negro" ("The Negro" 193). Through this statement, Cullen advances a clear perception of the pitfalls of both white and black art, confronting the negative stereotype of the brute Negro, but also the thread of primitivism that many black authors advanced in their push to feed that insatiable hunger for the stories of black life. In response, Cullen suggests that the African American writer "must create types that are truly representative of us as a people" (193) and argues that "I [do not] feel that such a move is necessarily a genuflection away from true art" (193). Under this lens, poems such as "Scottsboro, Too, Is Worth Its Song" exemplify Cullen's literary and cultural aesthetics and thus are a valuable contribution to the larger Harlem Renaissance tradition.

Like Du Bois, White, and others who share his vision, Cullen strives for high culture in the high/low project of Negro art, using lyric forms to present an intellectual speaker free from the criticism and exoticism of the not-so-distant past. In its attempt to recast the Negro character and to reveal the true brute, after all, this work highlights the societal issues themselves, focusing its attention on the white poets whose "cries go thundering / Like blood and tears / Into the nation's ears" (Cullen lines 3–5) and through whose work "disease and death and all things fell" (line 8). Subtle yet blaring in his criticism, Cullen describes the Scottsboro case as "a cause divinely spun" (line 16) and as the epitome of "all disgrace / And epic wrong" (lines 19–20). Yet, despite the social ills, the case reveals and the power of poets to demand social change and be heard, the poets remain silent, never pleading en masse as they did for Sacco and Vanzetti. What Cullen thus highlights in these lines is an unwarranted optimism in these poets—a hope unfulfilled as "they have raised no cry" (line 25), leaving the speaker, absolutely dumbfounded, to "wonder why" (line 26). Were the cries of the Scottsboro nine not worthy of song? Was the mistreatment of blacks somehow less of a disgrace, less of an affront to the American founding ideals? Here, Cullen calls renewed attention to these issues, ending the poem with the implicit question, "Why?," rather than depicting the angry and violent black figure—that supposedly brutish and bestial figure long since stereotyped by white novels and movies past.

Ultimately, the value of Cullen rests in such portraits of the black experience, for "[w]hen the artist can . . . reveal the black experience in his art, he is thereby adding to our knowledge of the human experience" (Canaday 125) of which blacks were largely kept apart. In doing so, it is certainly possible that the "critics who assert that Cullen was not activist enough in orientation—and some are even harsher—would seem to have a narrow view of what a poet ought to be doing" (113)—a narrow view that Cullen attempts to address. Though a large number of his works are not as overt in their sociopolitical criticism as his Scottsboro text, issues of race pervade each text, at least informing the lens from which he sees the surrounding world, and thus, at a time of cultural awakening, bidding those newly awakened—as well as those still asleep—to finally sing. While he may have been on the outskirts of the Harlem Renaissance at the time he was writing, his works now hold a valuable place in the canon of New Negro texts, adding a new dimension to the era's artistic and intellectual work.

"America": Claude McKay and the Image of America's Sociopolitical Chaos

Like the authors before him, Claude McKay, too, was driven to write by the rise in interracial violence against black bodies that was exacerbated by the Red Summer of 1919. In an essay entitled, "A

Negro Poet," published in *Pearson's Magazine,* McKay describes the racial climate that so heavily shaped his impulse to write:

> In the South daily murders of a nature most hideous and revolting, in the North silent acquiescence, deep hate half-hidden under a puritan respectability, oft flaming up into an occasional lynching—this ugly raw sore in the body of a great nation. At first I was horrified, my spirit revolted against the ignoble cruelty and blindness of it all. (48)

And while this push to revolt is now celebrated with works such as "If We Must Die," anticipating the revolutionary spirit of the coming days, McKay was criticized by figures such as William S. Braithwaite for being a "violent and angry propagandist, using his natural poetic gifts to clothe . . . defiant thoughts" (208). Torn between his individual artistic-political vision and the older generation of Harlem Renaissance thinkers, who "often do not distinguish between the task of propaganda and the work of art" (McKay, "A Negro Writer" 133), McKay is then a vital figure in this central debate about the limitations and responsibilities of black art. His poetry, ardent in its social and cultural criticism, represents the modernist impulse to unveil what exists beneath long lost notions of respectability, while simultaneously using his work as a vehicle to catalogue the fluctuating "rhythm[s] of Africamerican life" (133).

In some of his more highly anthologized and criticized works, such as "America," McKay then uses traditional forms, in this case the Shakespearian sonnet, to express his perspectives on the state of race inequities and the complex relationship he has to "this cultured hell" (line 4). Here, McKay not only explicitly responds to the American racial hostility as "she feeds [him] bread of bitterness, / And sinks into [his] throat her tiger's tooth, / Stealing [his] breath of life" ("America" lines 1–3), he also uses form as a fundamental framework for his critique. Confined to just fourteen lines of iambic pentameter, McKay restrains his mounting frustration, challenging in content the image of the happy darky, content in his second-class state, while challenging in form the inferior position to which black poets (as primarily dialect poets in the past) were often relegated. Like Dunbar and Brown before him, McKay hence uses classical sixteenth-century form as a new rhetorical approach, framing his critiques in the Western literary tradition from which African American poetry is usually set apart. In doing so, McKay probes "the ideological contradiction manifest in the practice of joining tradition and dissent . . . to create a space in which to challenge white America's claim to cultural superiority" (Keller 448). Using the sonnet in this way, McKay is, therefore, able to express his growing discontentment with the racial discrimination throughout the United States, while at the same time, "gain[ing] a voice among those whose project of subjugation has been to efface the native cultural heritage of African-Americans and to silence the discourse of dissent" (Keller 448).

Still, McKay is often criticized for his decision to abandon the Jamaican dialect of his earlier works. In *Claude McKay: Rebel Sojourner in the Harlem Renaissance*, for example, Wayne F. Cooper attributes this later movement to the classical to Max Eastman's direction in the *Liberator*, in which McKay published forty-two poems throughout his literary career. He contends that "McKay essentially agreed that 'real' poetry adhered to Victorian poetic conventions" (Cooper 153) and thus turned from the dialect of *Songs of Jamaica* (1912) even though "his dialect verse had an originality of form, diction, rhythm, and subject matter absent in his sonnets and short lyrics" (151). This explanation, however, is too simplistic, negating the creative and intellectual project that McKay undertook in employing classical forms. Like his fellow poets of the Harlem Renaissance, particularly Langston Hughes and Countee Cullen, McKay never adopts a singular artistic endeavor. Polystylistic, his poetry employs a variety of literary and rhetorical forms in an effort to reflect the underrepresented voices of whom he describes as the serving class of Aframerican society. In shifting between dialect and classical forms, McKay employs the language of the disenfranchised and the language of power—"Quashie to Buccra" and "America," for instance, have similar criticisms, but different cultural contexts that, for McKay, necessitate that shift— but he also reflects the somewhat fragmentary project of the Harlem

Renaissance—the inability of black art to encapsulate African American expression into a singular, unified frame.

Critical of both the dominant white elite and the Negro intelligentsia (at times highly critical of McKay as well), his works thus interrogate those very concepts of what black art *should* be, transitioning in every novel and every poem to an alternative psychosocial site in hopes of uncovering (or perhaps discovering) what black art *could* be. In "A Negro Writer to His Critics," McKay brings that impulse center stage, claiming that his critics, "apparently under the delusion that an Africamerican literature and art may be created out of evasion and insincerity" (134), highlight a central stumbling block in the development of black art. For McKay, "[t]hey seem afraid of the bitterness in Negro life. But it may as well be owned, and frankly by those who know the inside and heart of Negro life, that the Negro, and especially the Aframerican, has bitterness in him in spite of his joyous exterior" (134). In this sense, black artistic expression could not focus solely on the joys of black life, celebrating the unique cultural values and experience of Harlem dancers and fast-paced cabarets. At the same time, black art could not only strive to put its best foot forward while "Negro critics [remained] apologetic" (134) of overtly revolutionary and radical texts. Ultimately, the Negro poet, like the black community at large, had been silenced for far too long; as his poems inherently reveal, the Harlem Renaissance was necessarily an opportunity for black poets and artists alike to let out those building screams.

The Poets' Lasting Song

Through each of these models presented by Hughes, Brown, Cullen, and McKay, we reach a deeper understanding of the ways in which the era's artists did, in fact, arrive "to mold and weld this mighty material about us" (Du Bois & Locke 503)—the rich and vibrant material of black cultural life. Celebrating and critiquing in concert, these authors exposed not only the beauty of a culture cast as inferior to that of whites, but also the deep-seated conflicts that contributed to the American racial wasteland. Through their poetic works, they offered readers of their time keen insight into a state of

---

affairs too often masked, each evoking the collective consciousness of the black community in an attempt to echo the songs of African American achievements as well as their distress and pain. From Hughes' "Christ in Alabama" to McKay's "America," these authors thus used their poetic works as alternative intellectual strategies for their socio-political critiques, essentially engaging the Negro intelligentsia as well as the Negro masses where others had faltered before. In doing so, they essentially recorded a much different perspective of history than memorialized in many newspapers and magazines. They combated that pervasive silence enforced by a Jim Crow culture and the constant threat of lynching. And they ignited that flame—that all too vital fire in the flint—that somehow kept burning as a reminder of the African American artistic-intellectual sensibility. "'Where are the young Negro artists to mold and weld this mighty material about us?,'" (Du Bois & Locke 503) asked Du Bois in a 1924 essay. As these poets reveal, "[E]ven as we ask, they come" (503).

Works Cited

Braithwaite, William S. "The Negro in Literature." *The Crisis* 28 (1924): 208.

Brown, Sterling. "He Was a Man." *The Collected Poems of Sterling A. Brown*. Ed. Michael S. Harper. Evanston, IL: Northwestern UP, 2000. 146–147.

_____. "Negro Character as Seen by White Authors." 1933. *Callaloo* 14/15 (1982): 55–89.

Canaday Jr., Nicholas. "Major Themes in the Poetry of Countee Cullen." *The Harlem Renaissance Remember*. Ed. Arna Bontemps. New York: Dodd, Mead, 1972. 103–125.

Cooper, Wayne F. *Claude McKay: Rebel Sojourner in the Harlem Renaissance*. 1987. Baton Rouge: Louisiana State UP, 1996.

_____, ed. *The Passion of Claude McKay: Selected Prose and Poetry, 1912–1948*. New York: Schocken, 1973.

Cullen, Countee. "Scottsboro, Too, Is Worth Its Song." *Countee Cullen: Collected Poems*. Ed. Major Jackson. New York: Library of America, 2013. 213–214.

Du Bois, W. E. B. & Alain Locke. "The Younger Literary Movement." *W. E. B. Du Bois: A Reader.* Ed. David Levering Lewis. New York: Henry Holt, 1995. 503–505.

Ford, Karen Jackson. "Making Poetry Pay: The Commodification of Langston Hughes." *Marketing Modernisms: Self-Promotion, Canonization, Rereading.* Ed. Kevin J. H. Dettmar & Stephen Watts. Ann Arbor: U of Michigan P, 1996. 275–296.

Graham, Maryemma. "The Practice of Social Art." *Langston Hughes: Critical Perspectives Past and Present.* Ed. Henry Louis Gates, Jr. & K.A. Appiah. New York: Amistad, 1993. 213–235.

Hughes, Langston. "Christ in Alabama." *The Collected Poems of Langston Hughes.* Eds. Arnold Rampersad & David Roessel. New York: Vintage, 1995. 143.

_____. "My Adventures as a Social Poet." *The Langston Hughes Review* 9–15.

_____. "The Negro Artist and the Racial Mountain." *The Langston Hughes Review* 1–4.

_____. "The Task of the Negro Writer as an Artist." *The Langston Hughes Review* 28.

Hutchinson, George. Introduction. *The Cambridge Companion to the Harlem Renaissance.* Ed. George Hutchinson. New York: Cambridge UP, 2007.

Keller, James R. "'A Chafing Savage, Down the Decent Street': The Politics of Compromise in Claude McKay's Protest Sonnets." *African American Review* 28.3 (1994): 447–456.

McKay, Claude. "America." *Selected Poems.* Ed. Joan R. Sherman. Mineola, NY: Dover, 1999. 30.

_____. "A Negro Poet." 1918. *The Passion of Claude McKay: Selected Prose and Poetry, 1912–1948.* New York: Schocken, 1973. 48–50.

_____. "A Negro Writer to His Critics." 1932. *The Passion of Claude McKay: Selected Prose and Poetry, 1912–1948.* New York: Schocken, 1973. 132–139.

Rowell, Charles H. "'Let Me Be with Ole Jazzbo': An Interview with Sterling A. Brown." *After Winter: The Art and Life of Sterling A. Brown.* Eds. John Edgar Tidwell & Steven C. Tracy. New York: Oxford UP, 2009. 287–309.

_____. "Sterling A. Brown and the Afro-American Folk Tradition." *Harlem Renaissance Re-Examined.* Eds. Victor A. Kramer & Robert A. Russ. Troy, NY: Whitston, 1997. 333–353.

Sanders, Mark A. *Afro-Modernist Aesthetics and the Poetry of Sterling A. Brown.* Athens, GA: U of Georgia P, 1999.

Sperry, Margaret. "Countee P. Cullen, Negro Boy Poet, Tells His Story." *Brooklyn Daily Eagle* 10 February 1924.

CRITICAL
CONTEXTS

Dawn in Harlem: Exploring the Origins of the Harlem Renaissance through Image and Text____

Carolyn Kyler

The Harlem Renaissance introduced a generation of artists who sought to re-imagine the "New Negro" as a powerful, creative, and inspiring figure for a new age. Emphasizing youth, new beginnings, and a bright future, this reimagining offered a complex, multifaceted figure who was both political and artistic, calm and revolutionary, an intellectual and a fighter. Three collections of creative work from this period showcase both the complexity and the potential of the New Negro. The Harlem issue of *Survey Graphic* (1925), *The New Negro: An Interpretation* (1925), and *Fire!!* (1926) represented a generational shift and a new way of thinking about central questions of cultural identity, political aspiration, and artistic innovation. Graphic works are a key element of this thinking, revealing the visual artists' connections with Western and African artistic traditions and amplifying the themes and motifs explored in the written works.

Visual artists made vital contributions to the Harlem Renaissance movement and to African American culture. The movement gave new opportunities to already established artists and encouraged the work of younger artists. Among the most prominent artists were photographer James Van Der Zee; sculptors Meta Vaux Warrick Fuller, Augusta Savage, and Richmond Barthé; and painters Aaron Douglas, Palmer Hayden, and William H. Johnson. These Harlem Renaissance artists were, according to art historian Mary Schmidt Campbell, the "first artists to develop a visual vocabulary for black Americans" (13). That visual vocabulary included several themes central to Harlem Renaissance literature: the centrality of Harlem culture and the urban landscape, the legendary figures and ordinary lives of African American folk culture, the significance of Africa as the cultural touchstone of the New Negro, and a vision of African American identity as young, new, and forward-looking.

Writers and artists of the Harlem Renaissance did not work in isolation from each other. Some artists, like Richard Bruce Nugent and Gwendolyn Bennett, were both writers and painters, and many important projects of the era—such as the Harlem issue of *Survey Graphic*, *The New Negro: An Interpretation*, and *Fire!!*—include both text and images. The images, by both black artists and by white artists, like Winold Reiss, illustrate and expand on the meanings of the texts, providing a concrete and multifaceted vision of Harlem Renaissance culture and the New Negro.

Dawn of the New Negro

Nowhere is the importance of the graphic image more powerfully expressed than in *Dawn in Harlem*, an illustration by the German-born artist Winold Reiss that appeared in the Harlem issue of *Survey Graphic*. Reiss' illustration depicts this new era using a series of intersections: between land and sky, between black and white, and between past and future—intersections that serve to frame much of the writing, art, and thinking of the Harlem Renaissance. *Dawn in Harlem* combines an urban landscape with natural elements of sun and sky. Both the urban and natural elements radiate, suggesting a movement that starts in Harlem, but will have effects well beyond it. Dawn never stands still—it cascades from one place to the next. Dawn is a moment poised between past and future, and Reiss invites us to consider what has come before, a past represented by the buildings of Harlem. But dawn always looks forward, suggesting that this landscape will be transformed and that the transformation will radiate out through space and time.

Fig. 1: Winold Reiss, *Dawn in Harlem, Survey Graphic* (Mar. 1925): 663.

The figure of the New Negro, which was to become a unifying concept of the Harlem Renaissance, was born long before the 1920s. As Henry Louis Gates, Jr., and Gene Andrew Jarrett note, "Almost as soon as blacks could write, it seems, they set out to redefine— against already received racist stereotypes—who and what a black person was, and how unlike the racist stereotype the black original could actually be" (3). By the early twentieth century, the term "New Negro" was being used by African Americans across the political spectrum to define their ideals and aspirations. Booker T. Washington, a leader whose values are sometimes considered antithetical to the later Renaissance, titled his 1900 collection of works extolling the accomplishments of African Americans, *A New Negro for a New Century*. In 1919, Marcus Garvey used the term as a rallying cry of the Pan-African movement, writing that "The New Negro has given up the idea of white leadership" (94). But in the 1920s, the "New Negro," which had become synonymous with a call for political change, became also a call for literary and artistic recognition. The Harlem Renaissance was the dawn of the idea that artistic accomplishment could further the goal of civic equality.

And, as exemplified by Reiss' *Dawn in Harlem*, the movement's leaders believed that changes originating in Harlem could radiate throughout the community, the country, and the world.

This idea of the "New Negro" and of a new dawn or new vision for African-American people can be traced through the poetry of the early twentieth century. James Weldon Johnson's turn-of-the-century poem "Lift Every Voice and Sing," which became known as the Negro national anthem, exhorts African Americans to march toward a bright future: "Facing the rising sun of our new day begun, / Let us march on till victory is won" (lines 9–10). The words of this poem, set to music by James Weldon Johnson's brother, John Rosamond Johnson, present an image of new people in a new day, informed and inspired by the past, but focused on the future. Johnson's remarkable career as an educator, lawyer, diplomat, activist, editor, and writer included both political and artistic success; fittingly, his vision of a new day included both political and artistic accomplishment.

In 1922, Harcourt Brace Jovanovich published *The Book of American Negro Poetry*, James Weldon Johnson's anthology celebrating the work of black writers; in the preface, Johnson presents a vision of art that anticipates and helps form the values of the Harlem Renaissance: "The final measure of the greatness of all peoples is the amount and standard of the literature and art they have produced. The world does not know that a people is great until that people produces great literature and art. No people that has produced great literature and art has ever been looked upon by the world as distinctly inferior" (9). Johnson defines art as the indispensable and crowning achievement of the New Negro, the accomplishment that cannot and will not be ignored. He asserts not only that artistic success is vital, but that artistic success will lead to political equality—a core theme of the era's vision.

Johnson's aim in his anthology was both to document the existing accomplishments of African Americans and to encourage and foretell greater work yet to come. He writes, "Much ground has been covered, but more will yet be covered. It is this side of prophecy to declare that the undeniable creative genius of the Negro is destined to make a distinctive and valuable contribution to

American poetry" (Johnson, *American Negro Poetry* 47). As with "Lift Every Voice and Sing," several of the pre-Renaissance early twentieth-century poems Johnson includes in his anthology sketch a vision of the New Negro in terms of a new day. Chicago-born poet Fenton Johnson wrote, "We are children of the sun, / Rising sun!" (lines 1–2). World War I veteran, teacher, and poet Lucian B. Watkins associated the sun of the new day with Africa and freedom—themes that Harlem Renaissance poets would also adopt—in his poem "Star of Ethiopia":

> Out in the Night thou art the sun
> Toward which thy soul-charmed children run,
> The faith-high height whereon they see
> The glory of their Day To Be—
> The peace at last when all is done. (lines 1–5)

And musician and poet Otto Leland Bohanan proclaimed in "The Dawn's Awake" that "The boon of light we craved, awaited long, / Has come, has come!" (lines 16–17). These poems proclaim a vision of a new day of progress, peace, and justice—a day that James Weldon Johnson believed could be hastened through poetry itself. In this formulation, night represents the discrimination, disenfranchisement, poverty, and violence of the Jim Crow era and dawn evokes the birth of equality, opportunity, and peace. But the image also works in more personal terms: darkness is a loss of identity, purpose, and recognition that the dawn will lift.

The link between politics and art can also be seen in illustrations of the time. One of the most striking images of the New Negro is the May 1923 cover of the educational issue of *The Messenger*, the influential labor-oriented African-American political magazine founded by A. Philip Randolph and Chandler Owen. The issue contains an essay on education and a range of reviews of books by or about African Americans. But the strongest message is conveyed by the cover, titled "The New Negro," which depicts a black man in the famous pose of August Rodin's sculpture "The Thinker." Both the subject of the work and its origin are significant. By adapting the work of a renowned French sculptor, this image portrays the New

Negro as an intellectual who transforms European traditions. And because this cover comes less than two decades after the first casting of the statue in 1904, the image connects the New Negro both to the classical philosophical traditions it evokes and to contemporary art. These connections illuminate two important themes of the Harlem Renaissance: first, the ideals of the Renaissance are born from both Western and African culture and, second, the Harlem Renaissance aimed to transform those cultures and make them new.

"Enter the New Negro"

The forerunner of Alain Locke's anthology *The New Negro* was a special edition of *Survey Graphic*, the social and political journal edited by Paul Kellogg. Kellogg got the idea for a special Harlem edition of the magazine after attending a dinner hosted by Charles S. Johnson in March 1924 honoring the publication of Jessie Redmon Fauset's novel *There Is Confusion*. The celebration "introduced the emerging black literary renaissance to New York's white literary establishment" (Wintz 81), including Kellogg, who asked Locke, a Howard University philosopher, to edit a special issue on Harlem. When Locke structured the Harlem edition of the *Survey Graphic* and when he wrote the introductory essay, "Enter the New Negro," he was drawing on an already-rich vocabulary and vision about a new day for African Americans.

In "Enter the New Negro," Locke exemplifies the "promise and warrant of a new leadership" by quoting Langston Hughes' poem, "Youth" (631):

> We have tomorrow
> Bright before us
> Like a flame.
>
> Yesterday, a night-gone thing
> A sun-down name.
>
> And dawn today
> Broad arch above the road we came.
> We march!

The exact purpose of the march is not specified. It could be a protest march, a call to fight against segregation, lynching, and other forms of violence and discrimination. Certainly it is a march that proclaims faith in the future and in individual and communal identity. Hughes' word choice echoes James Weldon Johnson's "Lift Every Voice and Sing": "Let us march on till victory is won" (10). Like poets of the previous generation, Hughes emphasizes the importance of the dawn—that moment of coming out of the darkness of the past and contemplating the possibilities of the future. But for Hughes, dawn is the present moment. Dawn is not simply a new beginning, but a unifying principle and call to action.

Vision is central to Alain Locke's approach in "Enter the New Negro," where he argues that the New Negro sees clearly what needs to be done—what lies ahead through that broad arch of dawn: "a common vision of the social tasks ahead" (632). He writes, "With this renewed self-respect and self-dependence, the life of the Negro community is bound to enter a new dynamic phase, the buoyancy from within compensating for whatever pressure there may be of conditions from without" (Locke, "Enter" 631). For Locke, the most crucial changes are in "the life-attitudes and self-expression of the Young Negro, in his poetry, his art, his education, and his new outlook" (631). And for Locke, a crucial strategy for presenting the Young Negro was through the use of images.

Beginning as an offshoot of the social work journal *The Survey*, *Survey Graphic* had a broader focus, was aimed at the general public, and emphasized visual elements. This emphasis on the visual was ideal for introducing the New Negro to a wide audience. As with the May 1923 *Messenger*, the cover of the *Survey Graphic*'s March 1925 issue depicts the New Negro with a single male image, this time the image of an artist, world-famous tenor Roland Hayes. By 1925, Hayes had performed to great acclaim in both the United States and Europe and just the previous year had been awarded the NAACP's Spingarn Medal for great accomplishment by an African American. The portrait of Hayes by Winold Reiss, who illustrated both this *Survey Graphic* issue and *The New Negro*, dominates the cover of the magazine. It includes only Hayes' face—a young man with a serious, determined expression. The viewer's attention is drawn to the gaze of the figure, eyes fixed resolutely on the future. The decoration of the cover, with bold geometrical lettering and designs, evokes both African tradition and the transformation of that tradition by modernism.

Featured within the March 1925 *Survey Graphic* issue are two series of portraits by Winold Reiss called "Harlem Types" and "Portraits of Negro Women" that continue to develop our mental portrait of the New Negro. Reiss selected these portraits from a series that he produced using both ordinary Harlem residents and well-known artists and leaders as his models; the cover portrait of Roland Hayes was one of this series. Many are distinguished by their youth and their devotion to education and books. In "Harlem Types," young men are represented by "A College Lad"—modeled on Harold Jackman, a friend and patron of Harlem artists—dressed seriously in a three-piece suit (Stewart 48). In "Four Portraits of Negro Women," young women take shape as "A Librarian"—dressed in hat, coat, and gloves and carrying a weighty book—and "Two Public School Teachers," whom we appear to have interrupted as they go over a book or report together. All these figures appear young, strong, and determined. All gaze steadfastly ahead, perhaps meeting the eye of the reader, perhaps looking toward the future.

The reaction to these portraits, especially "Two Public School Teachers," encapsulates one of the key debates of the Renaissance: how should black Americans be portrayed to a wider audience? While the teachers are clearly intelligent and accomplished—both wear Phi Beta Kappa keys—and dedicated to their work, some viewers saw them as confrontational or even frightening. Educator, writer, and activist Elise McDougald—whose portrait also appeared in the series and whose essay on black women appeared in the *Survey Graphic* Harlem issue and later in *The New Negro*—wrote to Alain Locke that one viewer of the portrait said that "[s]hould he meet those two school teachers in the street, he would be afraid of them" (qtd. in Stewart 50). And author Jessie Fauset, also represented in *The New Negro*, complained that the image was not "representative" (qtd. in Hutchinson 395). Aaron Douglas, whose work would later appear with his mentor Reiss' in *The New Negro*, attributed discomfort with Reiss' portraits to discomfort with ideals of beauty other than whiteness. He wrote in a letter to his wife, "I have seen Reiss' drawings for the New Negro. They are marvelous. Many colored people don't like Reiss' drawings. We are possessed, you know, with the idea that it is necessary to be white, to be beautiful" (qtd. in Kirschke 61). Still, questions of how to read Reiss' portraits have persisted. In 2005, critic Anne Carroll noted the tension between seeing the portraits as "exotic others" and realizing that "the subjects of these portraits do engage their viewers in a reciprocal gaze" (142). Ultimately, the portraits present a compelling vision of a strong, assertive, and diverse New Negro despite their initial negative reception.

Even the advertisements in the *Survey Graphic* Harlem issue contribute to our vision of the New Negro and to the emphasis on how that vision should be portrayed. The words in an advertisement for *The Crisis*—the magazine of the NAACP, edited by W. E. B. Du Bois—do not refer to "newness." They promise the facts and pique the reader's interest by claiming to be "the most hated, most popular, and most widely discussed magazine dealing with questions of race prejudice" (624). But in the advertisement, the viewer's eye is drawn to a photograph of a little girl, gazing hopefully forward, in a white dress with a large bow in her hair. This central image represents the newest of New Negroes, the coming generation. Two small silhouettes of young ballerinas at the bottom of the page further enhance the emphasis on youth, art, and vitality.

On the inside front cover of the magazine is a General Electric advertisement, seemingly unrelated to the content of the issue except for its emphasis on innovation—the importance to the future of what might seem like impractical research on topics like artificial lightning. The text even notes that "[m]any such experiments yield no immediate returns." Nonetheless, the advertisement's concept is relevant to the ideas of the New Negro in many ways. General Electric and the New Negro each have a vision of the future. The power and light of electricity can be connected to the sun images so common to the poetry of the Harlem Renaissance. The question of usefulness—what good is artificial lightning?—echoes one of the central questions of the Harlem Renaissance. How is art useful? Can the New Negro persevere even when not seeing immediate returns? And both the General Electric advertisement and the New Negro focus on issues of transmission—electrical and cultural, respectively.

While some of the visual elements in the *Survey Graphic* issue, like Reiss' portraits, are carefully crafted to develop a portrait of the New Negro, others, like the General Electric advertisement, may seem more serendipitous. But all contribute to the sense of newness and change evoked by *Dawn in Harlem*.

The New Negro: An Interpretation

Alain Locke quickly expanded the *Survey Graphic* issue into a book published by Boni Liveright as *The New Negro: An Interpretation* in 1925. The original dust jacket of *The New Negro* gives a sense of the multicultural aesthetic—African art blended with modernism—at play. The dedication page, "dedicated to the younger generation," announces the New Negro's emphasis on the future. Winold Reiss again did much of the artwork for the book and was credited in large type on the original title page. The original 1925 edition contains seventeen full-page illustrations by Reiss, most in color and on special paper inserted in the volume. The portraits include "The Librarian" and "The School Teachers," who had appeared in *Survey Graphic*, but also a range of more famous figures: writers Jean Toomer, Countee Cullen, Alain Locke, and James Weldon Johnson; singers Roland Hayes and Paul Robeson; educators Robert Russa Moton, Elise Johnson McDougald, and Mary McLeod Bethune; and influential leaders Charles S. Johnson and W. E. B. Du Bois. The portraits are placed to highlight the specific accomplishments of their subjects. For example, Cullen's portrait faces his poem "Fruit of the Flower," while Paul Robeson's is placed within Fauset's essay on theater, "The Gift of Laughter," an essay that highlights Robeson's performance in the revival of Eugene O'Neill's 1920 play, *The Emperor Jones*. Reiss' use of color emphasizes the individual identity of each subject; in several portraits, the face and hands are in color while the clothing is sketched in black and white. And some images—notably "The Brown Madonna," which opens the volume, and the portrait of Toomer—are outlined with a halo effect that positions the subjects as beacons and sources of inspiration.

The 1925 edition of *The New Negro* also includes six illustrations by Aaron Douglas, the young African American artist and student of Reiss who would become the leading visual artist of the Harlem Renaissance. Five more illustrations by Douglas were added by Locke to the 1927 edition. A native of Kansas and graduate of the University of Nebraska, Douglas had been drawn to Harlem when he saw the *Survey Graphic* Harlem issue; he was offered a scholarship by Winold Reiss and quickly found success working for *The Crisis* and *Opportunity* (Kirschke 13). His drawings amplify the meaning of the works they accompany, creating what art historian Caroline Goeser calls a "double-voiced narrative" (ix). One of Douglas' drawings in the 1925 *New Negro*, "The Sun God," accompanies James Weldon Johnson's poem, "The Creation: A Negro Sermon," a retelling of the Genesis creation story through the voice of a black preacher. Johnson's version, evoking both folk language and the rhythms of Walt Whitman, portrays a God who creates the world through speaking it:

> Then God smiled,
> And the light broke,
> And the darkness rolled up on one side,
> And the light stood shining on the other,
> And God said, *"That's good!"* (lines 9–13)

"The Creation," Johnson's one poem in *The New Negro* (he also contributed an essay, "Harlem; The Culture Capital") continues the tradition of implicitly comparing the Harlem Renaissance to a new dawn, in this case, the dawn of the world. Douglas' illustration captures the poem's focus on dawn, depicting a figure—presumably the "Sun God" of the title—striding ahead of a rising sun, arms reaching back perhaps to shape or carry the sun. Just as Johnson describes God as both male and female—"This Great God, / Like a mammy bending over her baby" (Johnson, "Creation" lines

84–85)—the "Sun God" has a masculine name and a feminine silhouette. The title also suggests an expansion of the meaning of the poem beyond the God of Genesis to include other gods and perhaps African traditions. The sun in the image expands in concentric circles that overlap the striding god. The concentric circle motif would become a hallmark of Aaron Douglas' work, appearing in many of his drawings and paintings. As Douglas scholar Amy Kirschke notes, the circles in Douglas' work may well have been influenced by the "concentric circles of energy" in Winold Reiss' *Dawn in Harlem* (29). Just as in *Dawn in Harlem*, the circular motif in "The Sun-God" suggests both newness and connection. The circles radiate out from the origin, the point of creation, thus carrying that newness into the world.

Another Douglas illustration, "The Poet," introduces the poetry section of *The New Negro*, and several of the poems develop the theme of the new generation and new vision as a new day. Arna Bontemps' "The Day-Breakers," which first appeared in the 1927 edition, gives voice to a generation that fights for change: "Yet would we die as some have done. / Beating the way for the rising sun" (lines 5–6). Langston Hughes incorporates sun images into several poems, including "Youth," the poem Locke quotes in his introductory essay. "Dream Variation" begins with the wish "to fling my arms wide / in some place of the sun" (lines 1–2) and "Our Land" with a vision of "a land of sun / Of gorgeous sun" (lines 1–2). The synthesis of words and images in *The New Negro* through examples like these presents the aspirations and accomplishments of a people rising with the sun of a new day.

Fire!!

The year after the publication of *The New Negro*, a group of young writers and artists started a magazine that attempted to define an even newer Negro, *Fire!! A Quarterly Devoted to the Younger Negro Artists*. In a statement written on the magazine's stationery, Aaron Douglas accentuated the project's youth, independence, and race pride:

We are all under thirty. . . . We are primarily and intensely devoted to art. We believe that the Negro is fundamentally, essentially different from their Nordic neighbors. We are proud of that difference. We believe these differences to be greater spiritual endowment, greater sensitivity, greater power for artistic expression and appreciation." (qtd. in Kirschke 87)

Wallace Thurman edited the issue in association with Langston Hughes, Gwendolyn Bennett, Richard Bruce Nugent, Zora Neale Hurston (who was not actually under thirty, but often claimed to be born in 1901), Aaron Douglas, and John Davis. With Hurston and Bennett among the inner circle, *Fire!!* presented the New Negro as both male and female. And the inclusion of both writers and visual artists—Douglas and Nugent—signaled the importance of images to this new enterprise.

Fig. 2: Aaron Douglas, cover of *Fire!!* Nov. 1926

The premiere issue of *Fire!!*—which turned out to be the only issue—featured a cover by Aaron Douglas, a stylized design inspired by Africa and by modernist aesthetics. The design shows the profile of a face in black with a sphinx and the title of the magazine set off in red. Many readers do not see the face right away; they see only the sphinx with a decorative border. On closer inspection, the sphinx appears to be part of a large earring worn by the person, who could be male or female. That gender ambiguity contrasts with the single male portraits who represented the New Negro in earlier publications and the predominance of men among the portraits in *The New Negro*. Here we have two gazing figures with the human—the new or newer Negro—harnessing the prophetic power of the Sphinx. Douglas' image parallels one of the most complete poetic visions of the New Negro, James Edward McCall's "The New Negro," published in the July 1927 issue of *Opportunity* and in Countee Cullen's collection *Caroling Dusk* (also illustrated by Aaron Douglas) the same year. McCall's sonnet concludes:

> Impassive as a Sphinx, he stares ahead—
> Foresees new empires rise and old ones fall;
> While caste-mad nations lust for blood to shed,
> He sees God's finger writing on the wall.
> With soul awakened, wise and strong he stands,
> Holding his destiny within his hands. (lines 9–14)

McCall's emphasis on vision—and challenges overcome—poignantly reflects his own life. According to the biographical note that he wrote for *Caroling Dusk*, McCall "was forced to abandon his medical career, following an attack of typhoid fever leading to total blindness. Undeterred by this misfortune, he at once set out to develop his literary talent" (34). Rather than physical vision, McCall establishes the vision of the New Negro as wisdom, strength, calm, and fearlessness.

The contents of *Fire!!* embody this same vision of fearlessness. *Fire!!* is an eclectic collection of poetry, fiction, drama, and visual images that transforms the motif of dawn into a consuming flame "weaving vivid hot designs upon an ebon bordered loom and satisfying pagan thirst for beauty unadorned" (1). The issue includes a story by Wallace Thurman about prostitution and one by Richard Bruce Nugent centering on a gay relationship. By their presence, these works make the statement that the writers are not afraid to confront any subject in spite of what either black or white readers might think. The new day created by the dawn of *Fire!!* is thus defined by freedom of expression and identity, including the ability to write freely about prostitution, drugs, and both heterosexual and homosexual relationships. The dawn of *Fire!!* breaks away not just from racism, Jim Crow, and old stereotypes, but from the political carefulness represented by Locke's *The New Negro* and Du Bois' *The Crisis*.

In addition to the cover, Aaron Douglas created a set of portraits for *Fire!!* titled "Three Drawings." Unlike his work in *The New Negro*, these portraits do not illustrate a literary text; as Martha Nadell notes, the drawings thus stand as independent works on their own terms (76). The first is of a preacher standing before a Bible on a pulpit, face turned upward while his eyes peer sideways toward the viewer. The second is a painter, absorbed in his work, eyes fixed on his canvas. The third is a woman with stylish haircut and hose, wearing an apron and carrying a tray, while she glances off to the side. As with Winold Reiss' "Harlem Types" in *Survey Graphic*, these line drawings provoke questions about different concepts of the New Negro and about how African Americans should be portrayed. Are the preacher and the artist opposing figures or two complementary roles? Why is the artist male and the server female? Could those roles be reversed? What will the future of the New Negro hold?

"Walkers with the Dawn"

Examining the beginnings of the Harlem Renaissance through both words and images illuminates some of these crucial questions about innovation, art, and culture that preoccupied Harlem Renaissance thinkers. What is innovative about the New Negro of the 1920s? While the idea of a New Negro predates the Harlem Renaissance, that ideal is defined in the 1920s by both the literature of the period and the images that portray the New Negro. Those words and images emphasize youth, strength, fearlessness, and vision. The images—often more than the words—present a diverse vision of the New Negro: both men and women, both adults and children, both artists and advocates, both famous leaders and ordinary people.

This diversity of images invites the viewer to consider the changes brought by the New Negro and New Woman and the future in store for the children of the Harlem Renaissance.

This intersection of words and images creates a framework for addressing central questions of the Harlem Renaissance: What is the purpose of art and how should African-Americans be portrayed? W. E. B. Du Bois declared that "all art is propaganda and ever must be" (49), while Langston Hughes proclaimed that "[w]e younger Negro artists who create now intend to express our individual dark-skinned selves without fear or shame" ("Negro Artist" 43–44). Alain Locke hailed the arts as "constructive channels" ("Enter" 633) while the editors of *Fire!!* called for a flame hot enough to "boil the sluggish blood" (1). But among this range of opinions, the defining documents of the Harlem Renaissance underline several key points. Producing art is important; art makes a difference to the world and to the position of African Americans, and so the unique talents of African Americans must be celebrated. Most importantly, despite disagreements about what art should look like, all agreed that art could advance equality. That vision is exemplified in the choice of the cover image for the Harlem issue of *Survey Graphic*—singer Roland Hayes—just as much as in Alain Locke's declaration within the issue that "the present generation will have added the motives of self-expression and spiritual development to the old and still unfinished task of making material headway and progress" ("Enter" 634).

The original readers of the *Survey Graphic* turned the page from *Dawn in Harlem* to find a page of seven Langston Hughes poems, including one simply titled "Poem":

> Being walkers with the dawn and morning
> Walkers with the sun and morning,
> We are not afraid of night
> Nor days of gloom,
> Nor darkness,
> Being walkers with the sun and morning. (664)

Together, Reiss' image and Hughes' words declare a new beginning, a new day, a day of fearlessness and celebration—themes that echo throughout the written and visual art of the Harlem Renaissance. Understanding the relationship between African and Western traditions, between aspiration and confrontation, and between past and future requires attention not to words or images alone, but to the horizon that joins them.

Works Cited

Bohanon, Otto Leland. "The Dawn's Awake." *The Book of American Negro Poetry*. 1922, 1931. Ed. James Weldon Johnson. New York: HBJ, 1969. 203.

Bontemps, Arna. "The Day-Breakers." *The New Negro*. 1925, 1927. Ed. Alain Locke. New York: Atheneum, 1992. 145.

Campbell, Mary Schmidt. Introduction. *Harlem Renaissance: Art of Black America*. 1987. New York: Abrams, 1994. 11–55.

Carroll, Anne Elizabeth. *Word, Image, and the New Negro: Representation and Identity in the Harlem Renaissance*. Bloomington: Indiana UP, 2005.

Cullen, Countee, ed. *Caroling Dusk*. 1927. New York: Citadel, 1993.

Du Bois, W. E. B. "Criteria of Negro Art." *The Crisis* (Oct. 1926). *Double-Take: A Revisionist Harlem Renaissance Anthology*. Eds. Venetria K. Patton & Maureen Honey. New Brunswick: Rutgers UP, 2001. 47–51.

Fire!! 1926. Metuchen, NJ: The Fire Press, 1982.

Garvey, Marcus. "The New Negro and the U.N.I.A." 1919. *The New Negro: Readings on Race, Representation, and African American Culture, 1892–1938*. Eds. Henry Louis Gates, Jr. & Gene Andrew Jarrett. Princeton: Princeton UP, 2007. 92–96.

Gates, Henry Louis, Jr. & Gene Andrew Jarrett. "Introduction." *The New Negro: Readings on Race, Representation, and African American Culture, 1892–1938*. Princeton: Princeton UP, 2007. 1–20.

Goeser, Caroline. *Picturing the New Negro: Harlem Renaissance Print Culture and Modern Black Identity*. Lawrence: UP of Kansas, 2007.

Hughes, Langston. "Dream Variation." *The New Negro*. 1925, 1927. Ed. Alain Locke. New York: Atheneum, 1992. 143.

_____. "The Negro Artist and the Racial Mountain." *The Nation* (June 1926). *Double-Take: A Revisionist Harlem Renaissance Anthology.* Eds. Venetria K. Patton & Maureen Honey. New Brunswick: Rutgers UP, 2001. 40–44.

_____. "Our Land." *The New Negro.* 1925, 1927. Ed. Alain Locke. New York: Atheneum, 1992. 144.

_____. "Poem." *Survey Graphic* (Mar. 1925): 664.

_____. "Youth." *Survey Graphic* (Mar. 1925): 664.

Hutchinson, George. *The Harlem Renaissance in Black and White.* Cambridge: Belknap, 1995.

Johnson, Fenton. "Children of the Sun." *The Book of American Negro Poetry.* 1922, 1931. Ed. James Weldon Johnson. New York: HBJ, 1969. 141–42.

Johnson, James Weldon. *The Book of American Negro Poetry.* 1922, 1931. New York: HBJ, 1969.

_____. "The Creation: A Negro Sermon." *The New Negro.* 1925, 1927. Ed. Alain Locke. New York: Atheneum, 1992. 138–141.

_____. "Lift Every Voice and Sing." *Norton Anthology of African-American Literature.* 2nd ed. Eds. Henry Louis Gates, Jr. & Nellie Y. McKay. New York: Norton, 2004. 794.

Kirschke, Amy Helene. *Aaron Douglas: Art, Race, & the Harlem Renaissance.* Jackson: UP of Mississippi, 1995.

Locke, Alain. "Enter the New Negro." *Survey Graphic* (Mar. 1925): 631–34.

_____. *The New Negro.* 1925, 1927. New York: Atheneum, 1992.

_____. *The New Negro: An Interpretation.* New York: Boni & Livewright, 1925.

McCall, James Edward. "The New Negro." *Caroling Dusk.* 1927. Ed. Countee Cullen. New York: Citadel, 1993. 34–35.

Nadell, Martha Jane. *Enter the New Negroes: Images of Race in American Culture.* Cambridge: Harvard UP, 2004.

Patton, Venetria K. & Maureen Honey. *Double-Take: A Revisionist Harlem Renaissance Anthology.* New Brunswick: Rutgers UP, 2001.

Stewart, Jeffrey C. *To Color America: Portraits by Winold Reiss.* Washington, DC: Smithsonian, 1989.

Watkins, Lucian. "Star of Ethiopia." *The Book of American Negro Poetry*. 1922, 1931. Ed. James Weldon Johnson. New York: HBJ, 1969. 211.

Wintz, Cary. *Black Culture and the Harlem Renaissance*. Houston: Rice UP, 1988.

Apathetic Critiques Revisited: Jean Toomer's *Cane* and Its Importance to the Harlem Renaissance_____

Gerardo Del Guercio

Writing in the 1920s, Jean Toomer patterned his most renowned work, *Cane*, around his life experiences in Hancock County, Georgia, after he departed Washington, DC, and worked temporarily as a substitute principal at a Negro industrial school in the Georgia town of Sparta. There, Toomer experienced an imaginative expression of poetry, drama, stories, and sketches that shaped *Cane*, a novel that starts in the pastoral South, turns to the urban North, and comes back to the South for its finale. Toomer set the southern portions of *Cane* in the town of Sempter—a metaphor on Sparta and the individuals and locales Toomer came across there during the fall of 1921.

Upon publication, *Cane* bewildered Toomer's contemporaries. They celebrated its poetic understanding of African American life as well as Toomer's brave staging of ethnic and sexual issues. As W. E. B. Du Bois stated, "Toomer's frank treatment of sex and sexuality, particularly how they were intimately interrelated to the formation of racial and class identity, set the tone for much of the work that considered this topic in the Harlem Renaissance" (171). As a result, artists of the Harlem Renaissance, the Black Arts Movement, and the later twentieth century, including Alice Walker, have continually alluded to *Cane*'s influence on their own writing. In *Cane*, it seems Toomer created a novel that demonstrated the uniqueness of African American life, especially during the 1920s, at the height of the Harlem Renaissance era.

Despite this positive reception, however, after its publication in 1923, several white American and African American audiences disregarded Jean Toomer's *Cane*. According to Langston Hughes, many black Americans did not praise Toomer's scrapbook of African American consciousness principally because they were frightened of it. As for white Americans, many simply ignored *Cane*. And even though most critical appraisals of *Cane* were positive, the general public remained apathetic. Despite this disinterest, *Cane*'s pioneering style and form rank it among some of the best African American writing in the canon. Drawing on commentaries both positive and apathetic from important publications of the 1920s, we can then gain a better understanding of *Cane*'s importance in addition to its influence on the Harlem Renaissance at large.

Early Criticisms of Toomer's *Cane*: Correspondence with Waldo Frank

Perhaps the strongest source of earlier criticism that Toomer received of *Cane* came from noted American novelist and literary critic, Waldo Frank, with whom Toomer began an intimate correspondence in August 1920. In a short letter from Frank, the former wrote to commend the piece "Kabnis," the final piece in *Cane*, as "big stuff" (Pfeiffer, *Brother* 102), noting that he did not "see its imperfections" (102). Frank continued his commentary on "Kabnis," stating that although Toomer would surely write stronger drama, the play was nevertheless "quite perfect as an expression of the man who wrote it" (102). Clearly, in Frank's opinion, a text of high-quality was one that reflected the spirit and intellect of the man, and Toomer was successful in this regard not only because he wrote about his people and more specifically about his personal life experiences, but because *Cane* was a bearing of his soul. And so *Cane* was thus a representation of a culture (a decidedly black culture) worth sharing with the surrounding world.

Frank's letter turned slightly toward negative commentaries on Toomer's writing, however, when he compared "Kabnis" to some of the shorter pieces in *Cane*. The letter commented that "[s]ome of the smaller sketches are no less powerful. Karintha, Avey, Becky, Esther, Calling Jesus, Rhobert, etc. The stories in which you attempted a more complex picture [such as] Bona + Paul, Box Seat are less perfect. There's a looseness here...and in much of the imagery a certain . . . amount of 'mere writing'" (Pfeiffer, *Brother* 102–103). Also, in response to his poems—works such as "Something is Melting Down in Washington" and "Prayers"—Frank described his work as "failures" and advised him "not [to] publish them in so beautiful a book." In doing so, he labelled Toomer a "poet in prose" who was "shackled + thwarted in the verse forms" (103). Still, the letter continued with Frank's overall praise of *Cane*, emphasizing improvement from an earlier version of "Kabnis." Simply put, Frank's recommendation was that Toomer tighten up pieces like "Box Seat" and "Bona and Paul" and to strengthen the weak verse so that the author make the text an accurate reflection of himself as the man Frank had come to know over the years.

Although Frank's negative commentaries on some of Toomer's writing were well argued, the lyrics serve as metaphors for the blues slaves would sing on the plantations and the lamentations that African Americans expressed while Toomer was composing *Cane*. Blues music is an important part of *Cane*, given that the oppression black Americans have endured throughout history was never properly eradicated. One of the main purposes of Toomer's novel, as well of the blues, is to express this cruelty. The opening lines from "November Cotton Flower" clarify this argument:

> Boll-weevil's coming, and the winter's cold,
> Made cotton-stalks look rusty, seasons old,
> And cotton, scarce as any southern snow,
> Was vanishing . . . (lines 1–4)

Undeniably, these lines convey that the American market economy and racial hierarchy stifled African Americans, like Karintha, into a subjugated existence. As Nellie McKay notes in *Jean Toomer: Artist—A Study of His Literary Life and Work, 1894–1936,* such "[i] mages of scarcity, drought, and death in the natural world of the poem parallel the oppression of race, sex, class, and economics that comprise the reality of Karintha" (93). His poem thus calls attention to an experience largely masked in many white-authored films and texts: oppression along race, gender, and class lines. The world he describes is the "dismal landscape" (McKay 93) in contrast to images of an internal blossoming within her (and inherently the black community)—"Brown eyes that loved without a trace of fear, / Beauty so sudden for that time of year" (Toomer, *Cane* lines

13–14)—"before exploitation eventually ruins her beauty, natural urges, zest for living, and innocence" (McKay 93).

Waldo Frank's correspondence with Jean Toomer continued with an undated letter expanding his critique. Frank wrote, "I have seen SO MANY THINGS WRONG, that I hasten to write you, in order that you may delay their making plates until you've had the time to make corrections" (Pfeiffer, *Brother* 143). In his letter, Frank noted seven errors that he spotted in *Cane*—most importantly that "Foreword by Waldo Frank" did not appear on the title page and that Toomer's name should be in larger font than his. Frank also noted that his should be more clearly stated and that the foreword contained several typographical errors. Lastly, Frank commented on an error in the typesetting of Toomer's poetry as well as an odd numbered blank page in the middle of the text, claiming that "[t]here should never be a blank odd numbered page in the middle of the book" (144). Though Frank's keen eye for proofreading certainly improved the quality of *Cane*, some of his comments may have overlooked a stylistic convention that Toomer tried to establish, whether knowingly or not. For instance, Toomer may have left a blank, odd-numbered page in his manuscript to convey a break from white established conventions. This is consistent with Toomer's larger project and goal as writer, given that prevailing structures of radicalized masculinity are at play in both *Cane* as well as in Toomer's larger critical reception. In doing so, Toomer may have intended to express himself in a manner that Frank was unable to recognize as an artistic convention, which perhaps signified a break in cultural identity caused by slavery or the once pervasive silence of the African American community.

Later in 1923, Toomer responded to Frank's critiques of *Cane* in a letter, wherein Toomer alluded to Sherwood Anderson. Toomer claimed that:

> when people—truly moved by *Cane* and valuing it . . . like it, I have smiled my appreciation of their responses, but have firmly shaken my head. When they, in all good faith have advised me, as Sherwood Anderson did, to keep close to the conditions which produced *Cane*, I have denied them. Never again in life do I want a repetition of those

conditions. And, of equal importance is the fact that *Cane* is a swan song. ("To Waldo" 156)

Clearly, as this passage demonstrates, Toomer wrote *Cane* to express his African American heritage and the sting his people endured throughout history, in addition to the painful events he never again wants his people to experience. *Cane* is a lasting contribution to American culture that retells the horrors of African Americans, and the short poem, "Portrait in Georgia," is an excellent example of this. Line two describes the unnamed woman's hair as "coiled like a lyncher's rope" to reveal the violence blacks have experienced throughout history, particularly in the early 1900s with a steady rising in black lynchings. Two lines later, Toomer depicts the "old scars, or the first red blisters" (line 4) to convey the many generations of blacks who have suffered. "Portrait in Georgia" then concludes with the image of "her slim body, white as the ash / of black flesh after flame" (lines 6–7). The contrast between the girl's pure "white" body and the "black flesh" that has been burnt "after flame" shows the pain many blacks endured post-slavery as "the image of a southern belle dissolves into a black man tortured and burned alive at the stake" (Callahan 78). Through this image, "the woman's features yield to the paraphernalia of lynching, until in a final chilling montage her white body becomes a smile for the black victim" (78). Indeed, *Cane* became a text that breaks the silence in African American culture so that future generations of oppressed individuals could articulate the tyranny their people have suffered.

During their relationship, Frank also composed a lengthy letter commenting on *Cane* as well as his play, "Natalie Mann." Part one of this five-section correspondence was Frank's harsh critique of the play, his main criticism that it was one filled "with deadness of texture" and that "life is not permeated into the whole thing" (Pfeiffer, *Brother* 34). Although Frank commended Toomer's use of "a vision…mothered and fathered of true temperament, passed on, intellectually," the letter continues with Frank's observation that the "texture drops out of your conception, becomes weak discussive talk" (35), making Toomer's piece slippery and one that required "rewriting rather than reconstructing" (34). By texture, Frank meant the lyric style deployed in "Natalie Mann," far different from the texture of "Kabnis," which Frank described as "superb" (35). This is interesting to note, given that Toomer's lyric style is usually considered his greatest strength (Pfeiffer, "Passing" 97). Undeniably, Frank's recommendation that Toomer continue to redraft "Natalie Mann" and other works points to shortcomings in early criticism, for it is Toomer's aesthetic choices, celebrated today, that have earned *Cane* recognition as a significant literary and modernist work akin to James Joyce's *Ulysses.*

Later, the letter continued with an analysis of Toomer's "Kabnis." In this second part of Frank's appraisal, he concluded that the play lacked structure—as "the reading mind does not catch on to a uniformly moving Life that conveys it whole to the end, but rather steps from piece to piece as if adventuring through the pieces of a still unorganized mosaic" (Pfeiffer, *Brother* 35–36). Frank's capitalization of "Life" implies how human existence should be the most structured part of an artistic work. Instead, in "Kabnis" the "bone-structure" (35) was imperfect, consequently eliminating it from being a finished work. According to Frank, "Natalie" was better thought out and, as a result, the superior work. Although Toomer's *Cane* does in fact demonstrate an incoherent narrative structure, its intention was two-fold: 1) to express an identity that racial injustice had fragmented and 2) to express a world gone mad—a purposefully modernist approach.

Beyond Frank: A New Set of Apathetic Critiques

Waldo Frank, however, was not Toomer's only outspoken critic. American poet and cofounder of The Double Dealer, John McClure, wrote to novelist and short story writer, Sherwood Anderson, on January 22, 1924, to condemn Toomer's use of dialect. In his letter, McClure declared that "[i]n my opinion [Toomer] cannot handle dialect" (161) and that "[h]e should mould his stories into lyrical rhapsodies rather than attempt to present them realistically" (161). A few lines later, McClure concluded that Toomer ought to rhapsodize if he wished to follow the "African urge" and become that "commanding and solitary figure" (161) many believed Toomer could in fact be. The "African urge" that McClure described here was rooted in expressing that fulsome, passionate, or overjoyed expression "he can accomplish, in his own fashion, better than probably nearly anyone" (161) he felt that Toomer's use of dialect did not accomplish.

In paragraph two of this letter, McClure continued his apathetic critique of Toomer's use of dialect. McClure argued that "I am sure that the stories in which you have written simply out of your own heart with your own natural intonation of speech are incomparably better than those in which you have constructed the language to fit the character. In other words, I am sure your genius is lyrical" (161–162). McClure's contention was that Toomer's dialect was inferior to his lyric form—a statement in line with the literary criticism from the 1920s that generally held a poor opinion of dialect. To illustrate his point further, McClure commented on the poor quality of prose in works of Anderson's like "I am a Fool" and "I Want to Know Why," concluding that, like Anderson, "[t]he moment [Toomer] attempts to make characters talk in the accents of life he falls from his highest level" (162). Argued here is that Toomer's work suffers where dialect is employed.

To evaluate McClure's position, a discussion of the connection to the larger tradition of criticism toward dialect in the Harlem Renaissance is necessary. James Weldon Johnson, for instance, started his writing career composing dialect verse. Along with his brother J. Rosamond Johnson, he set some of his dialect to music intended for the New York stage. Yet, James Weldon Johnson ultimately felt restricted by dialect and wrote in his preface to *The Book of American Negro Poetry* a statement that many of his contemporaries considered authoritative on dialect, particularly with regards to vernacular poetry. Despite praising Paul Laurence Dunbar for making faultless dialect poetry, Johnson nonetheless explored the limitations of the genre. Johnson stated that dialect includes "but two full stops, humor and pathos" (xl).[1] In an attempt to communicate a variety of emotions, writers would have to establish their own literary conventions and break from traditional forms. This new form would "express the racial spirits by symbols from within rather than by symbols from without, such as the mere mutilation of English spelling and pronunciation" (xli). Johnson is cautious to spell out that dialect itself is not intrinsically unpleasant. Instead, Johnson claims the reader has come to associate dialect with offensive stereotypes and images of blacks as either being impoverished or joyful and indolent. Also, because of the pessimistic associations that dialect garnered, a number of New Negro writers justifiably kept away from using it, since dialect echoed the scar of bondage and oppression carried over onto the minstrel stage.

The value in Toomer's approach that this criticism mistakenly overlooks is the reality it portrays of African-American life. In "Cotton Song," for example, Toomer presented a slave song that he believed accurately articulates the oppression black Americans experienced in the 1920s. By choosing to retain dialect words like "Nassur" (line 13) as well as "agwine" (line 16), Toomer successfully advocated that the suffering African Americans endured in the past remained felt during his time—an approach also adopted by Claude McKay and Sterling Brown in several of their earlier works. In sum, for Toomer, the dialect spoken in the past still accurately reflected the present condition of African Americans in the early to mid-twentieth century. Therefore, the culture he experienced and cataloged through *Cane* could only be expressed in African American vernacular forms.

Mixed criticisms also continued in the December 1923 issue of *Opportunity*, which included Montgomery Gregory's essay "Self-Expression in *Cane.*" In this article, Gregory credited Jean Toomer as the "native son who would avoid the pitfalls of propaganda and moralizing on the one hand and the snares of a false and hollow race pride on the other" (374). Certainly, Gregory was impressed with how Toomer's writing style reflected the soul and the collective vision of his people. Argued here is that Toomer successfully created a text whose intention was to express the place of African Americans in the early twentieth century, while at the same time expressing a universal dream blacks had of gaining racial equality—a direct contrast to other more propagandistic works of the era.

The essay soon turned less enthusiastic, though. Toward the end of the article, Gregory demonstrated how *Cane* had several important problems. One criticism Gregory had was in regard to the middle section of Toomer's book. In Gregory's opinion, the style in this segment of *Cane* "is more laboured and sometimes puzzling" (375). Gregory noted that "[o]ne feels at times as if the writer's emotions had run out of expression" (375), creating a dull text that was extremely difficult to read and understand. Certainly, the text slows the reader down with seemingly muddled and irrelevant passages. Gregory chose "Box Seat" to clarify this argument, celebrating how the story "reaches high points of excellence in the portraiture of 'Muriel', 'Dan', and 'Mrs. Pribby'," but condemning "its dramatic style, [which] limps at times with obscure writing" (375). Like criticism past, surely such views overlooked Toomer's attempts to signify the hard labor and pain African Americans have suffered throughout their history as well as the pain associated with retelling it.

Although the December 26, 1923, issue of the *New Republic* was generally a positive commentary on Jean Toomer, Robert Littell's remarks on Toomer's poetry and short sketches are also important. Littell convincingly advocated that even though the criticisms that Toomer's shorter texts were filled with obscure and oblique symbolism have disappeared, the pieces nevertheless remained flawed in his mind because of their "staccato beat" (126). Also, "[t]he sentences fall like small shot from a high tower" (126) that "pass from poetry into prose, and from here to Western Union" (126). To rephrase Littell's comments, Toomer's poetry and sketches were disconnected as well as uncoordinated and difficult to follow. A few lines later, Littell described "Kabnis" as a play with "no pattern in it, and very little effort at poetry" (126) and a glimpse into southern Negro life that left one puzzled. In Littell's point of view, "Kabnis" would have been a more effective piece had Toomer taken the time to develop it more and consequently better position the play in the context of its preceding arcs—the sections before "Kabnis" that Michael Krasny describes as "represent[ing] the neuroticized Black consciousness" (42). Still, as Krasny contends, this, too, is a purposeful approach, as "'Kabnis' thus incorporates . . . the artistic need for lyrical beauty and the discovery of terror of the first section; the stifled spirit and awakening consciousness of the second" (42).

Apathetic Criticisms Continued: Issues of Race and Intra-Racial Politics

Like several before, W. E. B. Du Bois, too, criticized Toomer's illustration of Georgia by contending that "[he] does not impress me as one who knows his Georgia" (171), given that Toomer had learned about the background he described from "the lips of others" (171) without crediting these people. Just as Du Bois complimented Toomer's fortuitous expressions found in "Karintha," he pointed out that Toomer's emotions were objective ones and that "one does not feel that he feels much and yet the fervor of his descriptions shows that he has felt or knows what he feeling is" (171). Similar to many of the aforementioned critics, Du Bois was disappointed with the supposedly muddled writing in pieces like "Box Seat" and "Kabnis," lamenting how these parts of *Cane* could have been clearer and, in the end, more enjoyable for Toomer's audience. Despite these negative comments on *Cane*, Du Bois ended his essay with the certainty that, with time, Toomer's art would flourish and ultimately reach its prime.

But perhaps the most startling critiques appear in Langston Hughes' canonical essay, "The Negro Artist and the Racial Mountain," which offers a negative assessment of a strictly "high class" segment of Negro culture. To Hughes, "high class" Negros were typically those whose parents were perhaps doctors, lawyers, school teachers, social workers, etc. who practiced white manners, arts, as well as religion, among other things. Hughes wrote this important critique to argue that black Americans should be proud of their customs and that they should move away from white practices as well as mannerisms so as to avoid negative white influence, while at the same time strengthen Negro culture. Likewise, Hughes' point was to denounce what he saw as a "high class" Negro desire to be white. According to Hughes, such a desire is detrimental to Negro heritage and lifestyle in general. In sum, Hughes contended that practicing white culture and ignoring Negro customs causes the Negro to stray from his cultural roots, creating a fragmented identity that has little understanding of its cultural self.

Hughes then continues with a discussion that might reveal the source of apathetic criticism surrounding Toomer's *Cane*. In this section Hughes asserts, "'Oh, be respectful, write about nice people, show how good we are,' say the Negros" (1270) to portray how some within the African American community were overly concerned with impressing whites in order to be accepted into the dominant white culture.[2] Hughes continues this section with the statement, "Be stereotyped, don't go too far, don't shatter our illusions about you, don't amuse us too serious. We will pay you,' say the whites" (1270). Argued here is that American whites wanted the African American people to remain submissive people who accept the "illusions" (1270) that Negros are below whites. Also, in repeating the contraction *don't* several times in this declaration, Hughes highlights the notion that whites are in a hierarchical position to give orders to blacks. By addressing the request that the Negro not amuse them too seriously, Hughes notes that Negros were often seen as simply entertainers, who do not have anything truly significant to express. In its attempt to transcend these demands and limitations in literature and art of the time, *Cane* paved its own path, earning the ire of several critics.

To continue, Hughes argues that both blacks and whites "would have told Jean Toomer not to write *Cane*" (1270). As a result, "the colored people did not praise it. The white people did not buy it. Most of the colored people who did read *Cane* hate it. They are afraid of it. Although the critics gave it goods reviews the public remained indifferent" (1270). Presented here are a few negative appraisals of *Cane*. To start, Hughes claims that black readers were afraid of Toomer's novel for the reason that it might have triggered antagonism among an African American community that was, in the minds of many, still subservient to the white. At the same time, the reviewers sometimes praised *Cane* for its style, but in general, the public (the white reading public) was apathetic, given that Toomer was writing a different side of black culture instead of reinforcing past stereotypes or feeding their hunger for literature of cabaret life.

As a final point, another rationale as to why Hughes' essay works well in relation to *Cane* is because of Toomer's conflicted racial identity. As Henry Louis Gates, Jr., and Rudolph P. Bryd contend, "Toomer was right to declare that he was of mixed ancestry, and that the opposition between 'white' and 'black' was too simplistic. But he was wrong to say that he had never lived as a Negro. He lived as a Negro while growing up. And then he decided to live as an ex-Negro almost as soon as the print was dry on *Cane" and that Toomer was, by today's standards,* "a Negro who decided to pass for white." Advocated in these passages is that Toomer was in fact a Negro for part of his life and that his refusal to accept his role as a *Negro* artist proved most problematic.[3] For Toomer, this racial conflict and disunity are a commentary on the Harlem Renaissance because of the overt pride in race that occurred in Harlem from about 1918 to the mid-1930s. Without doubt, Toomer chose to compose *Cane* in order to openly express his racial pride in addition to the conflicts he had with his own ethnicity,[4] even though he could rarely overcome his deviation from the dominant narrative of the time—a fact all the more evident in his later descent into obscurity.

Cane's Importance to the Harlem Renaissance and the Twenty-First Century

Clearly, Toomer's intention with *Cane* was to demonstrate a rebirth of African American culture—one that slavery had fragmented both in its heritage and identity. *Cane* was, for that reason, an important text to the Harlem Renaissance because of its renewed interest in African American traditions. At the same time, long paragraphs and the biblical tone-of-voice in segments of *Cane*, like "Fern," demonstrated not only the passion Toomer had at this point, but also a sociocultural critique. The following passage from "Fern" exemplifies this: "As you know, men are apt to idolize or fear that which they cannot understand" (16). Argued here is that one of Toomer's intentions in *Cane* was to demonstrate how humanity typically reveres or dreads that which it does not understand, particularly with regards to issues of culture and race. In turn, this creates a racist and xenophobic nation that oppresses groups like African Americans and rejects texts like *Cane*.

Jean Toomer's *Cane* therefore remains an important text in the twenty-first century, despite its criticisms, for its stylistic innovations and its argument that African Americans had a unique literary voice outside of stereotypes past. Toomer scholar Chezia Thompson-Cager has noted that:

> [a] double consciousness inherited from the previous century is what drives the twenty-first-century American reader of *Cane*. The dilemma of such celebrities as songstress Mariah Carey or golf genius Tiger Woods means that W.E.B. Du Bois' pronouncement of the color line as the greatest problem continues in the twenty-first century. (125)

Thompson-Crager reveals how race and individuality are still the most significant dilemmas facing the United States today—a core theme that present-day authors, including Toni Morrison; Henry Louis Gates, Jr.; and Valerie Smith, continue to express. In exploring the present as well as past social conditions of African Americans, Toomer thus composed one of the era's most important works.

In short, only through continued scholarship and discussion can we continue to demystify the importance *Cane* has had on the Western canon and its imprint on literary studies, moving beyond the several apathetic commentaries on Jean Toomer from the 1920s. Toomer's novel, after all, remains an important part of the Harlem Renaissance because of the innovative style and form he developed. In doing so, Toomer helped to revive interest in African American heritage and the African American literary tradition so that contemporary as well as future readers could appreciate the hardships, victories, and defeats African Americans have experienced throughout history. To end, present as well as future studies on African American literature like *Cane* can overcome the very limited viewpoints of past scholarship by demonstrating how such works were vital in the United States' development into a much more inclusive culture, accepting of the different racial backgrounds and cultures that authors like Toomer sought to explore.

Notes

1. Several key authors of the Harlem Renaissance faced similar criticisms for their use of dialect, which thinkers of the time heavily associated with the old Negro past. Zora Neale Hurston, for example, was widely criticized by Richard Wright for her use of vernacular expressions throughout *Their Eyes Were Watching God*—a thread of criticism that long overshadowed critical perceptions of her work. Recent scholarship, however, has sought to re-examine those widely-criticized texts.

2. Langton Hughes' reading fits into the larger framework of the Harlem Renaissance because it was during this period that black Americans began to be characterized for their intelligence as well as for their literature, fine art, and music. Because black Americans used these characteristics to defy the racism and to endorse their racial and social positions, if readers believed that a work advanced too heavily toward whiteness, they rejected it as diverting from the spirit of negritude that would captivate the twentieth century.

3. The same is noted later about poet Countee Cullen, whom Hughes directly addresses in "The Negro Artist and the Racial Mountain." Like Toomer, Cullen never wanted his art to be defined by race, though his work was heavily shaped and influenced by issues regarding race. For figures like Hughes, this created yet another divide within the younger generation of Harlem Renaissance writers.

4. This is illustrated, for instance, in the short story "Becky." The text opens and closes with the passage, "Becky as a white woman who had two Negro sons. She's dead; they've gone away" (7). Clearly, the cited passage expresses that miscegenation has always existed in the United States and that racial conflicts have traditionally destroyed equally families as well as the entire nation. Also, the same passage is repeated to close the story in order to reveal the cyclical nature of race mixing as well as racism in American culture.

Works Cited

Callahan, John. *The African-American Grain: The Pursuit of Voice in Twentieth-Century Black Fiction.* Urbana: U of Illinois P, 1988.

Du Bois, W. E. B. "Sexual Liberation in *Cane*." *Cane*. By Jean Toomer. Ed. Darwin Turner. New York: Norton, 1988. 170–171.

Gates, Henry Louis, Jr. & Rudolph P. Byrd. "Jean Toomer's Conflicted Racial Identity." *The Chronicle of Higher Education*. 6 Feb. 2011. Web. 22 June 2015.

Gregory, Montgomery. "Self-Expression in *Cane*." *Opportunity* 1 (December 1923): 374–375.

Hughes, Langston. "The New Negro Artist and the Racial Mountain." *The Norton Anthology of African American Literature*. Eds. Henry Louis Gates, Jr. & Nellie Y. McKay. New York: Norton, 1996. 1267–1271.

Johnson, James Weldon, ed. *The Book of American Negro Poetry*. San Diego: Harcourt, Brace, and Jovanovich, 1983.

Krasny, Michael. "The Aesthetic Structure of Jean Toomer's *Cane*." *Negro American Literature Forum* 4.2 (1975): 42.

Littell, Robert. "Cane." *New Republic* (1923): 126.

McClure, John. "John McClure to Sherwood Anderson (January 22, 1924)." *In a Minor Chord: Three Afro-American Writers and Their Identity*. Ed. Darwin Turner. Carbondale: Southern Illinois UP, 1971. 161–162.

McKay, Nellie. *Jean Toomer: Artist—A Study of His Literary Life and Work, 1894–1936*. Chapel Hill: U of North Carolina P, 1984.

Pfeiffer, Kathleen, ed. *Brother Mine: The Correspondence of Jean Toomer and Waldo Frank*. Urbana: U of Illinois P, 2010.

_____. "Passing and the 'Fast Yellowing Manuscripts.'" *Race Passing and American Individualism*. Amherst: U of Massachusetts P, 2010. 82–106.

Thompson-Cager, Chezia. "Epiphany: Toward a Unifying Theory." *Teaching Jean Toomer's 1923 Cane*. New York: Peter Lang, 2006. 123–130.

Toomer, Jean. *Cane*. Ed. Darwin Turner. New York: Norton, 1988.

_____. "To Waldo Frank (September 1923)." *In a Minor Chord: Three Afro-American Writers and Their Identity*. Ed. Darwin Turner. Carbondale: Southern Illinois UP, 1971. 156.

Turner, Darwin, ed. *In a Minor Chord: Three Afro-American Writers and Their Identity*. Carbondale: Southern Illinois UP, 1971.

Sugar *Cane* and Women's Identity in Selected Works of Zora Neale Hurston_____

Allyson Denise Marino

Women's bodies are described with allusions and direct references to sugar cane in much of the fiction work written by Zora Neale Hurston in the 1920s and 1930s. Two commonly studied short stories, "Sweat" (1926) and "The Gilded Six-Bits" (1933), as well as her most popular novel, *Their Eyes Were Watching God* (1937), figure both women's bodies and sugar cane as commodities to be owned, used, and discarded. Delia and Janie resist this identification, and, in doing so, reject the capitalist patriarchal system that has worked to shape their gendered identities. In "The Gilded Six-Bits," references to gender, sugar, and commodity systems are figured prominently as well; however, Missie May does little to resist her position. A reading of the works that highlights the role of sugar cane and its relationship to women's bodies acknowledges the specific material and historical conditions represented within the texts as well as within US and Caribbean history. The Caribbean is an important historical site, figuring directly or indirectly in the backdrop of much of Hurston's work due, in part, to her background as an anthropologist and her subsequent understanding of the African diaspora. The historical aspect of this reading is informed by another anthropologist, Sidney Mintz, and his significant work on sugar cane and colonial history. In much of African American and Caribbean literature, sugar cane is represented as a threatening menace in both foregrounds and backgrounds of these narratives. Its presence recalls a painful and violent colonial history, a history that has shaped women's gendered identities and the perception of their physical bodies.

As an anthropologist, Hurston traveled to Haiti for research, recorded in her book *Tell My Horse* (1938). She focused on Haitian folklore as part of her mission to catalog and study African folklore in the southern US and Caribbean, and she wrote *Their Eyes Were Watching God* during her time there (Jones 9). Critics such as Patricia

Stuelke, for example, have commented on the influence of Hurston's stay in Haiti on her work. Because of Hurston's knowledge of Haiti and the African diaspora, sugar cane, the most important shaping figure in new world colonial history, according to Sidney Mintz, figures within Hurston's fiction as a symbol of exploitation. Haiti's history is unique within the Caribbean because it was the site of first contact in the colonization of the New World as well as the first independent black nation and the second independent nation in the hemisphere. The early organization of labor in Haiti and the role sugar cane played within it was repeated throughout the Caribbean and modeled in the plantations of the southern US. By aligning the consumption of sugar cane with women's bodies and sexual identity, Hurston points to the gendered aspects of this exploitation. Through this lens, readings of both Hurston's anthologized short stories as well as her popular novel focus on the materiality of the body as a figure in colonial, imperialist, and transnational capitalist identity and the ways in which women's bodies are manipulated and shaped by the organization of labor as producers and consumers.

Common analyses of these works, influenced by the women's movement and black civil rights movement of the 1960s and 1970s and their frequent study by high school students or non-English majors at the college level, focus on an analyses of gender, especially those that look to the biblical references. These approaches, influenced by analyses by Alice Walker and Henry Louis Gates, Jr., among others, generally work well in classroom settings because of the accessibility of the allegorical and biblical symbols as well as the portrayal of heterosexual relationships and gender stereotypes. However, an approach that considers the economic basis for Caribbean and US slavery and the later capitalist economic systems presented in Hurston's narratives further illuminates the complexities of her work and allows a more nuanced examination of issues of gender, race, and class, thus highlighting her political awareness. Her contemporaries within the Harlem Renaissance movement, including Richard Wright and Alain Locke, offered negative reviews of her now most famous work, *Their Eyes Were Watching God*, which worked to push the novel into obscurity, citing the novel's lack of political awareness (Jones 9). However, later critics have situated her work as highly political. Barbara Smith argues that "one can only consider her apolitical if the political ramifications of relationships between the sexes are completely ignored" (27). Similarly, Sharon Lynette Jones explains that "Wright's and Locke's criticism that [*Their Eyes Were Watching God*] lacked depth stands in contrast to the later critical reaction to the novel as a complex analysis of race, class, and gender" (9). Both the politics of the time period and the material history that influenced it are inextricably a part of her narratives, a reading of which reveals complex systems of oppression.

Published in 1926, "Sweat" is set in Eatonville, Florida, a small town about six miles north of Orlando, established in 1887 as the nation's first black incorporated town. Hurston moved there with her family several years after its founding, and the town figures prominently in her work. Eatonville sits across the train tracks, as depicted in "Sweat," from the more economically advantaged Winter Park, a wealthier white town. Divided by racial lines, Eatonville has historically provided the support and workforce that bolstered Winter Park's economic development and wealth. In "Sweat," Delia works as a laundress for clients in Winter Park, a job that allows her to feel pride and some measure of self-satisfaction and independence. However, Sykes, her husband, is annoyed when she brings home the laundry of "white folks" (Hurston, "Sweat" 74). This is because Sykes is financially dependent on Delia. This important detail underscores the role of economics within the narrative as both the town and their marriage are shaped by an economic system based on race and gender.

In her article that considers the importance of economics within the text, "The Artist in the Kitchen: The Economic of Creativity in Hurston's 'Sweat,'" Kathryn Lee Seidel describes the narrative as the "unrelenting indictment of the economic and personal degradation of marriage in a racist and sexist society" and explains that it functions as "a documentary of the economic situation" of the town during this time (169). She further elaborates that "the economics of slavery" presented in 'Sweat'" present marriage as "an institution that perpetuates the possession of women as a form of profit" (172). Seidel points to the redemptive power of work for Delia as she has self-ownership and agency through her ability to work. However, Delia is essentially forced into this type of work, as it is the only source of work available to her.

In addition, the narrative suggests there is no employment for men because, at this point in Florida's history, domestic support—women's work—was needed more than agricultural and manual labor, jobs traditionally delegated to men, which is why Sykes is out of work and dependent on his wife. Therefore, Delia's access to the labor system within her marriage is not necessarily transcendent. She is still locked within a system of production and consumption, which, as she produces, consumes her body. Even the title of the story points to the primacy of the body and bodily experience within the text. Hurston thus describes the ways in which Delia is physically molded and shaped by work as her body is described as "thin" with "stooped shoulders" and a "sagging" posture ("Sweat" 74). Her limbs are "knotty" and her hands are worn and calloused (76). Hurston writes, "Her habitual meekness seemed to slip from her shoulders like a blown scarf" (75). Such images are also prevalent as Delia defends herself to Sykes as he threatens her with a whip in the opening images of the story. Describing her life to him, she says, "'Sweat, sweat, sweat! Work and sweat, cry and sweat, pray and sweat'" (75). The image of the whip and the description of an exhausted physical body recall the violent history of early capitalism in the US.

Sugar cane, an integral part of this early US history, figures in the background of "Sweat" as a symbol that points toward a reading of the historical context of the town. The men of the town chew sugarcane on the front porches on Saturdays (Hurston, "Sweat" 76). They say, gossiping about Delia and Sykes, that some men use women like sugarcane, "'wring[ing] every drop'" out of them until there is nothing left but a stalk to throw away (78). Here, women's bodies are compared to sugar cane, a crop with a violent history, and are, consequently, figured as natural resources, i.e., a consumable part of the land. In an economic system that separates consumers from producers, Delia's body *produces* for her own household, within her marriage, and is *consumed* by her husband. Likewise, her physical body is consumed as a resource as she labors for the wealthy women of Winter Park. In this way, she is part of a larger, historical world system that figures many racially and/or economically Othered women as producers of labor rather than consumers. Ultimately, their very bodies may be consumed as replaceable natural resources in this patriarchal and capitalist system of exploitation.

The ecofeminist frameworks offered by María Mies, Val Plumwood, and Vandana Shiva, among others, can be helpful in framing this type of reading. The patterns of the production and consumption of certain crops, particularly sugar cane, in both colonial and early US history have physically shaped geography and landscape as well as women's bodies. In her important study, *Patriarchy and Accumulation on a World Scale* (1989), Mies argues that capitalism's success has depended on the parallel exploitations of women, colonies, and natural resources. And in the text *Ecofeminism* (1993), Mies and environmental activist Vandana Shiva explain how patriarchy, subordination, and exploitation of the natural world have been linked. They write:

> Capitalist patriarchy or "modern" civilization is based on a cosmology and anthropology that structurally dichotomizes reality, and hierarchically opposes the two parts to each other: the one always considered superior, always thriving, and progressing at the expense of the other. Thus nature is subordinated to man; woman to man; consumption to production; and local to global. (5)

The importance of sugar cane as a food, dependent on changing tastes and the creation of "new needs," as Sidney Mintz refers to it, cannot be ignored here. In Deborah Barndt's *Women Working the NAFTA Food Chain: Women, Food, and Globalization* (1999, reprinted in 2004), Barndt explains that food is actually a code for a "deeper social process" which carries "stories behind stories" (14). She explains that food "shapes us—physically, personally, culturally," and she argues that:

Women are central to its production and consumption—from those who cultivate, pick and pack fresh produce in agribusinesses to those who work in assembly lines processing food into cans and bottles; from the cashiers who scan and weigh, price and package our purchases to the cooks and waitresses in restaurants who chop and cook and serve us meals. (14)

Although Delia does not produce food for wages in "Sweat," the historical trajectory of colonial development, including New World slavery, led to the development of the wage labor system, which has left her body physically transformed, an effect that was experienced by the original sugar cane harvesters in the Caribbean and US and that Hurston chooses to highlight within this work.

Sugar cane arrived in Haiti with Columbus in 1492. Already cultivated in parts of Europe, he carried it with him from the cane fields of Madeira, and the Spanish colonists immediately set to its planting and production (Japtok 478). Medical doctor and anthropologist Paul Farmer refers to the introduction of this crop as "an event that was to have enduring significance on this island, as elsewhere in the New World" (54). Twenty-seven years after Columbus' landing, the labor practices of the Spanish colonists in addition to the introduction of European diseases had wiped out an estimated 900,000 of the one million of the island's indigenous peoples (Bell 9). Needing to replace the loss of native labor to keep up with the increasing demand for sugar, Spanish colonists turned to Africa (Dash 3). By 1540, 30,000 Africans were enslaved on the island (Farmer 54).

The level of grueling labor required to produce sugar can be seen in the number of Africans brought to the island each year; by the 1780s, 30,000 Africans were brought to the island each *year*, producing three-quarters of the world's sugar supply with half of the world's sugar produced on the island (Farmer 56; Geggus 5). The average lifespan was about three years for a slave on a sugar plantation, and, often, for those who died during processing in the refinery, bodies were thrown into the vats of boiling syrup (Farmer 57). The entire population of a plantation was estimated to be replaced at least once in less than a decade's time. The overall population of slaves working on French sugar plantations made up half of all slaves held in the Caribbean. Under French control, Haiti became known as the "Pearl of the Antilles" and the "Eden of the Western World," producing more profit than any other Caribbean colony (Bell 9; Geggus 5). By the time of the first rebellions of the Haitian Revolution, more than three-quarters of a million slaves were producing what Mintz refers to as "the first commercially marketed soft drugs"—sugar (*Ancient* 9). As Mintz argues, the development of sugar cane and its industry was a shaping force in the development of the New World.

Similarly, the landscape of Florida has figured heavily in Hurston's narrative, including her own autobiography, *Dust Tracks on a Road* (1942). Robert E. Hemenway, Hurston's early biographer, writes that Hurston "had the map of Florida on her tongue" (9). After the state joined the Union in 1845, much of the previously unfertile land was manipulated by lowering the water table in order to grow sugar cane (Hollander 32). Its growth flourished well into the twenty-first century, and Florida is now the number one sugar producing state in the US ("Sugar"). Today, its production is a source of political and economic tension as well as the cause of environmental disasters due to the abuse of vital natural landscapes and ecosystems in attempts to accommodate the multi-billion dollar industry, and it continues to shape and influence the landscape of the state (Hollander 19). Historically-aware readings of Hurston's work demonstrate the role of the sugar industry in shaping Florida's economy and culture throughout the early twentieth century, as her characters are deeply affected by its impact.

Hurston continues her use of sugar and economics as literary symbols within the short story, "The Gilded Six-Bits." First, she emphasizes the important role of money in the narrative by its title, and critics have pointed to readings of marriage as economic transaction and to the influence of race. Hildegard Hoeller argues that for Hurston, "questions of money directly related to questions about her race" (1). In addition to the repetition of the themes of gender and race within Hurston's fiction, the alignment of women with sugar or sweetness continues as Joe, who works outside of the home at a fertilizer company, refers to his wife, Missie, who stays home and looks after domestic duties, as "sugar" and "honey," and he rewards her with "candy kisses," "chewing gum," and "sweet soap" upon his return from work each day (Hurston, "Gilded" 87). Along with the sweet treats, he also teases her with the money he has earned that day, playing a game of cat and mouse as he throws money at the house and Missie searches his body for the rewards.

Joe continues to reinforce the capitalist and gendered organization of labor by situating himself in the position of consumer and Missie May as the object or resource to be consumed. For example, as Missie reaches for more of the sweet potato cake she has prepared for dessert, Joe admonishes her: "'Ah don't want you to git no sweeter than whut you is already'" (Hurston, "Gilded" 89). He tells her, "'Sweetenin' is for us menfolks'" (89). Joe's work at a fertilizer factory underscores the historical conditions that led to the development of towns such as Eatonville, Florida, as an aftereffect of slavery, as the early history of slavery in the United States and Caribbean was based in large part on developing methods of agriculture, which was controlled by a ruling, mostly white, elite. Under this system of labor organization, Joe, mimicking the historical experience of economic slavery, is figured as a resource to produce labor. In turn, he replicates the organization within his own household. Hoeller explains that "while race defines Joe's economic dependence on white industry, gender defines Missie May's economic dependence on Joe" (768).

The antagonist, Otis D. Slemmons, foreshadowing Joe Starks in *Their Eyes Were Watching God*, is large in stature and compared to powerful white men in his physique and confidence. Joe, in "The Gilded Six-Bits," explains to Missie May that "'[a]ll rich mens is got some belly on 'em'" (89), which shows that powerful men consume because they do not have to produce within this system of labor, an important marker of power within the capitalist organization of labor. Also similar to Joe Starks, Slemmons flaunts his wealth by adorning his body with gold pieces, and even his mouth is "crammed full of gold teeths" (90). He, too, uses beautiful women as adornment to display his wealth and power. Observing this, Joe asks Missie May to dress up to go to the ice cream parlor to "parade" her in his own display of power (92). He beams when Slemmons acknowledges his wealth by referring to Missie May as "thirty-eight and two" (91), thus assigning her a monetary value. Joe may not have access to the monetary wealth of Slemmons, but he has another important commodity—a beautiful wife, again foreshadowing Joe Starks' display of Janie.

After Joe finds Slemmons and Missie May together, Joe taunts her with the gold pieces, which turn out to be artificial. As he leaves the pieces as reminders of her infidelity, he insinuates that she is a prostitute, selling her body for money. In this system of labor organization and division, women's bodies are, in fact, commodities, a point Joe has already made as he displays Missie May's beauty to show his own worth. His wife's body is the only commodity he has to show in this economic system. When the gold pieces are proven to be artificial, Hurston acknowledges the artificial nature of the entire system. What Joe interprets as a sign of Slemmons' access to the power held by powerful white men, something Joe wishes to access himself, turns out to be artificial, suggesting that there is no power to be had for the producers, black men, within the capitalist organization of labor during the time period of the narrative.

In the end, Joe forgives Missie and uses the gilded six-bits to purchase gifts for her in a store located outside of Eatonville, an act that is read as a symbol of redemption, or, according to Hoeller's argument, a symbol of rejection of the white economic system (Hurston, "Gilded" 774). However, Joe uses the money to buy sweets, suggesting that the system is too large to opt out. Sugar begins and ends the narrative, forever mediating Missie May and Joe's marriage and their gendered roles within it. The material facts of history are large, and the consequences reach far and wide. In this reading, the commodity system is inescapable and reinforced through Joe's purchase.

Their Eyes Were Watching God also displays the "economic politics" present in her early work with focus on the gendered aspect of these politics. References to sweetness begin early in the novel as Janie recounts her history to Phoeby after her return to Eatonville.

As Janie recalls the "pain remorseless sweet" as she is lying beneath the pear tree, the first reference to sweetness is in relation to her revelation on love and desire framed in the context of the natural world (Hurston, *Eyes* 11). Romantic and sexual relationships between men and women within the novel, and marriage, in particular, are represented in the context of sugar cane, or sweetness, in the background. Commenting on the role of sugar within the novel as a symbol of colonial exploitation in the Caribbean and US, Patricia Stuelke explains that "sugar becomes as a medium through which imperialist paternalism and violence diffuse into the text" (766). The history of sugar cane and its growth in the Caribbean and US influenced the development of black women's roles within the larger society and within communities such as Eatonville, developed as part of Reconstruction after the US Civil War, which Nanny references indirectly in her warnings to Janie about the gendered and racial organization of labor.

For example, immediately after Janie's revelation about the sweetness of her developing sexual awareness, she meets Johnny Taylor at her front gate and experiences her first kiss, witnessed by her worried grandmother, who watches from the confines of the house. Nanny's warning to Janie highlights the economic system that has shaped her gendered experience, including her bodily experiences, as they relate to the way she will experience her own sexuality and desire. Black women's experiences, according to Nanny's framework, are regulated by a capitalist and patriarchal system that links women's bodies and nature as natural resources to be commodified and used up as "mule[s]" and "spit cup[s]" (Hurston, *Eyes* 19). The thought of entering into marriage, essentially an economic transaction, at this point in the novel and according to Nanny's point of view, destroys the hope encapsulated by the image of the pear tree. Here, Janie realizes "that marriage did not make love" (24) as she begins to understand that economic necessity structures relationships.

After Janie marries Logan and settles unsuccessfully into the traditional domestic role of wife, Joe Starks appears in the road, an allusion to Johnny Taylor earlier in the narrative. Just as a discussion of sweetness preceded Janie's introduction to Johnny, her early dialogue with Joe also recalls images of sugar. Joe asks if Janie is married, explaining, "You ain't hardly old enough to be weaned. Ah betcha you still craves sugar-tits" (Hurston, *Eyes* 27). She responds, "Yeah, and Ah makes and sucks 'em when de notion strikes me. Drinks sweeten' water too" (27). She then takes him to the barn to drink "ribbon-cane syrup" (27), which they sip as Joe woos her with tales of his ambition and the future they could have together. He "wants to make a wife" (27) out of Janie, a prospect that is attractive to her at this point in the narrative. Until meeting Joe, Janie has experienced marriage as purely an economic transaction, influenced by Nanny's lectures. Marriage is discussed within the context of sugar cane in the background. Later, as Janie leaves Logan for Joe, she removes the "apron tied around her waist" (31), symbolically shedding the idea of marriage as a gendered economic transaction and the labor system that relegates her to the kitchen, so she believes at the time. However, she is eventually interpellated back into the economic system as Joe establishes a store in the "heart" of the town, and Janie finds herself to be another commodity on the shelf (38).

In Eatonville, the townspeople are impressed that Joe has the money and intelligence to buy up two hundred acres of land to own and develop. Speaking about Joe's access to wealth and power, the men in the town speak of Janie as a belonging of Joe's, similar to the land he has purchased: "You oughta know you can't take no 'oman lak dat from no man lak him. A man dat ups and buys two hundred acres uh land at one whack and pays cash for it" (Hurston, *Eyes* 36). Here, Hurston aligns land and women as property to be possessed or bought and sold. In fact, some of the land that Joe owns is used to grow sugar cane, which elicits more envy and ill will from the townspeople, especially when he banishes a man from the town for stealing some of it. The townspeople judge him for this action, explaining, "He had so much cane and everything else," implying, in part, his ownership of Janie (45). After discussing Joe's wealth and power, they find him "standing with legs wide apart" and "smoking a cigar" (37), an image of patriarchal power and prowess. According to this narrative configuration, the store is the center of town and land is the most important commodity. To own land is to access power. Thus, women are aligned with the land, as objects to be owned.

This idea is underscored as the narrative continues with the store opening. Joe tells Janie to dress up so she can stand on display in the store, along with the other commodities or resources available to be bought and sold. Tony Taylor makes a speech in praise and ends by stating, "Brother Starks, we welcomes you and all dat you have seen fit tuh bring amongst us—yo' belov-ed wife, yo' store, yo' land" (Hurston, *Eyes* 39), again aligning women and land together. Janie continues to embrace her own connection to land and the natural world, however, thus, not so much challenging this binary opposition, but perhaps reversing it, giving power to the primacy and importance of the natural world and women's position, whether biological or societal, within it. Janie finds the store pleasant enough when she can sit on the porch and talk with the townspeople, outside of the commodity system. She prefers the communal exchange of stories and gossip, creating friendships, rather than the culture of commodity exchange that Joe creates for her within the confines of the store. However, Joe blatantly aligns women with the natural world as he is scolding Janie—"Somebody got to think for women and chillun and chickens and cows," again, underscoring the connection of women with the land and natural resources (67).

Hurston continues to underscore the role of sugar in this economic framework as Janie performs her role as wife and shopkeeper in the store. Janie notices that "[t]he women got together the sweets and the men looked after the meats" as the town prepares a picnic (Hurston, *Eyes* 42). That evening Joe asks Janie's feelings on being "Mrs. Mayor," assuming she will deliver the same praise as the rest of the townspeople. She realizes he plans to "make a big woman" (43) out of her, thus shaping her identity according to his own conception of the gendered organization of labor and identity. Janie's own autonomous identity is not possible in this configuration of power that situates Joe as the master of land, goods, and wife.

Finally, after Joe's death, Janie finds the sweetness she was searching for, as far outside of the overarching system that has defined her up to this point as she can occupy, in Tea Cake, whose very name invokes sugar. He looks like "the love thoughts of women" (Hurston, *Eyes* 101) and makes Janie recall the blossoming sweetness of the pear tree, brought to ripeness again by his image. They share sugary Coca-Cola together, eat pound cake, and drink sweet lemonade. He tells her he is about to "turn into pure sugar thinking about her" (111). They play checkers, a game that Joe earlier forbids. Janie is thrilled that Tea Cake thinks that not only should she play, but that it is "natural" for her to play, a notion that stands outside of Joe's rigid definitions of men, women, and their subsequent allotted roles in life (94). Later, in the Everglades, she cooks him "navy beans with plenty of sugar" and prepares desserts for him when he returns from his day in the fields (126). Janie enjoys cooking for Tea Cake, a chore she resented during her marriage to Logan and a role that instigated a beating from Joe when she cooked a bad meal one evening.

Here, in a relationship within which she feels she has agency, she embraces this role. She tells her friend Pheoby, "'Tea Cake ain't draggin' me off nowhere Ah don't want tuh go'" (Hurston, *Eyes* 107). She continues, "'Dis ain't no business proposition, and no race after property and titles. Dis is uh love game'" (108). She recognizes that her grandmother's experience is not her own, and she tries to escape the patriarchal and capitalist system in her liminal position as a widow, which affords her a certain amount of freedom and power, and in her relationship with Tea Cake. After they are first married and Tea Cake takes her hidden money, she describes herself as a "horse grinding sugar cane," but refuses to accept it (113). Ultimately, although Janie resists the larger system, she is not able to escape it.

For a period of time, Janie and Tea Cake do resist the patriarchal and capitalist hierarchies present in Eatonville when they move to Belle Glade, Florida, "where dey raise all dat cane" (Hurston, *Eyes* 122). Today, Belle Glade, located on the southeastern side of Lake Okeechobee, is the home of the Sugar Cane Growers Cooperative of Florida. There, the remnants of the African diaspora in the Caribbean and US as well as the early twentieth-century immigration waves and subsequent development of a migrant workforce are on display, represented by the nightly mix of music and dance performed by the "Bahaman drummers" and blues musicians. Later, as they make preparations to leave for the hurricane, one man tells them, "'If Ah never see you no mo' on earth, Ah'll meet you in Africa'" (148). Here, too, the divisions between nature and civilization and male and female are ambiguous. Cane, cultivated and harvested in the Caribbean and US for three hundred years grows wild on the side of the road. Janie adds, "people wild too" and the "rich black earth" (125) covers their bodies. Men and women work side by side, and music and stories are exchanged rather than goods as community trumps systems of commodity, a sharp contrast to the position occupied by Joe's store in Eatonville. Despite this, Belle Glade is not a utopia. Mrs. Turner's presence and judgment serve as a reminder that the discourses of race and gender are firmly entrenched in the US during the novel's time period, represented by Tea Cake's disruption of the precarious harmony of the marriage through his physical abuse of Janie. In addition, although Janie and Tea Cake are working in the bean fields, the cane fields loom nearby as a menacing presence. It is here that Janie chases Tea Cake and another woman into the cane fields "one day when they were working near where the beans ended and the sugar cane began" (Hurston, *Eyes* 130). Although they physically remove themselves from Eatonville and the gendered capitalist system the town represents, the binary hierarchies are difficult to escape. The roles of both gender and economics as shaping forces in the lives of female characters is central to much of Hurston's work, underscoring her awareness of the deeply complicated colonial history of the Caribbean and US and its effect on women's lives.

Although Hurston wrote "Sweat" and "The Gilded Six-Bits" before she traveled to Haiti and began to incorporate more of the African diasporic experience into her writing, references to sugar in these short stories are still highly gendered. A reading of the role of sugar cane then reveals the alignment of women with this commodity, as a natural resource to be owned and consumed. The same alignment persists in the first half of *Their Eyes Were*

Watching God. While Janie, and women in general, are still defined within a gendered and hierarchal binary opposition, Janie reclaims the idea of sweetness as something apart from this patriarchal system. She identifies sweetness with the bees, outside of man-made manipulation and systems of exploitation and thus offers a model of resistance. Attention to this particular aspect of Hurston's writing reveals her complex understanding of the ways in which women's physical bodies and personal identities are influenced by the historical gendered and racial organization of labor.

Works Cited

Barndt, Deborah, ed. *Women Working the NAFTA Food Chain: Women, Food, and Globalization*. Toronto: Sumac P, 1999.

Bell, Beverly. *Walking on Fire: Haitian Women's Stories of Survival and Resistance*. Ithaca: Cornell UP, 2001.

Dash, J. Michael. *Culture and Customs of Haiti*. Westport, CT: Greenwood P, 2000.

Farmer, Paul. *The Uses of Haiti*. 3rd Edition. Monroe, ME: Common Courage P, 2006.

Geggus, David Patrick. *Haitian Revolutionary Studies*. Bloomington: Indiana UP, 2002.

Hemenway, Robert E. *Zora Neale Hurston: A Literary Biography*. Urbana: U of Illinois P, 1980.

Hoeller, Hildegard. "Racial Currency: Zora Neale Hurston's 'The Gilded Six-Bits' and the old-Standard Debate" *American Literature* 77.4 (December 2005): 761–785.

Hollander, Gail, M. *Raising Cane in the 'Glades: The Global Sugar Trade and the Transformation of Florida*. Chicago: U of Chicago, P, 2008.

Hurston, Zora Neale. "Sweat." *Zora Neale Hurston: The Complete Stories*. New York: HarperCollins, 1995.

_____. "The Gilded Six-Bits." *Zora Neale Hurston: The Complete Stories*. New York: HarperCollins, 1995.

_____. *Their Eyes Were Watching God*. 1937. New York: Perennial, 1990.

Japtok, Martin. "Sugarcane as History in Paule Marshall's *To Da-Duh, in Memoriam*." *African American Review* 34.3 (Autumn 2000): 475–82.

Jennings, La Vinia. *Zora Neale Hurston, Haiti, and Their Eyes Were Watching God*. Evanston, IL: Northwestern UP, 2013.

Jones, Sharon Lynette. *Critical Companion to Zora Neale Hurston: A Literary Reference to Her Life*. New York: Facts On File, 2008.

Mies, Maria. *Patriarchy and Accumulation on a World Scale: Women in the International Division of Labour*. 1986. London: Zed, 1998.

Mies, Maria & Vandana Shiva. *Ecofeminism*. London: Zed, 1993.

Mintz, Sidney. *Sweetness and Power: The Place of Sugar in Modern History*. 1985. New York: Penguin Books, 1986.

_____. *Three Ancient Colonies: Caribbean Themes and Variations*. Cambridge: Harvard UP, 2010.

Seidel, Kathryn Lee. "The Artist in the Kitchen: The Economics of Creativity in Hurston's 'Sweat.'" *Zora in Florida*. Eds. Steve Glassman & Kathryn Lee Seidel. Orlando: U Central Florida P, 1991. 110–120.

Smith, Barbara. "Sexual Politics and the Fiction of Zora Neale Hurston" *Radical Teacher* 8 (May 1978): 26–30. Web. 10 Mar. 2015.

Stuelke, Patricia. "Finding Haiti, Finding History in Zora Neale Hurston's *Their Eyes Were Watching God*" *Modernism/Modernity* 19.4 (2012): 755–774.

"Sugar and Sweeteners." *Economic Research Service*. United States Department of Agriculture, 14 Nov. 2014. Web. 2 Feb. 2015. <http://www.ers.usda.gov/topics/crops/sugar-sweeteners.aspx>.

Mobile Subjects in Faulkner, Larsen, and Thurman: Racial Parody and the White Northern Literary Field

Cheryl Lester

In an essay translated to English and published as "Flaubert's Point of View," Pierre Bourdieu offers a concise formulation of his methodological approach to cultural works, based on an analysis of "the specific social space in which the 'creative project' was formed" (541). As a "field" of cultural production, this space provides "an ensemble of real or possible positions" and a "universe of possible questions," and it functions as "a sort of common reference system that situates contemporaries, even when they do not consciously refer to each other, by virtue of their common situation within the same intellectual system" (541). A space of "homologous positions," the field is transformed by external factors like "economic crises, technological change, political revolutions, or simply the demand of a given group" (544). According to the position they occupy in the structure of the field, actors and institutions involved in cultural struggles adopt strategies aimed at preserving or transforming the established symbolic order and the institutions that reproduce it. Furthermore, they inherit the stakes, questions, and even theses of the struggle from "the state of the accepted problematic . . . inherited from preceding struggles, because this space orients the search for solutions and, hence, present and future production" (545).

Describing the structure of the field relevant to the literary production of Flaubert, Bourdieu discusses external factors pertinent to nineteenth-century Paris. Viewing the relevance of similar factors to the literary field in twentieth-century New York City, George Hutchinson draws on Bourdieu to situate the cultural production of both the Harlem Renaissance and American modernism within such a field. He argues in *The Harlem Renaissance in Black and White* that both Anglo-American and African American modernists took positions in an "intercultural matrix" of disputes—particularly regarding conceptualizations and representations of race, nation, and culture—aimed at preserving or transforming a white-dominated literary field (Hutchinson 7).

Typically classified and interpreted in the contexts of the Harlem Renaissance, black culture, and the urban north, Nella Larsen's *Quicksand* (1928) and Wallace Thurman's *The Blacker the Berry: A Novel of Negro Life* (1929) are not generally considered together with William Faulkner's *The Sound and the Fury* (1929), which is often viewed as a classic of the canonically white, agrarian Southern Renaissance. Following Hutchinson, however, we can situate these works and their interrogations of race, culture, and nation within the same space of possibilities, viewing them as homologous positions in the struggle to preserve or transform the literary field in which they were produced, distributed, and consumed.

Published in New York City in the late 1920s—*Quicksand* by A. Knopf, *The Blacker the Berry* by the Macaulay Company, and *The Sound and the Fury* by Jonathan Cape and Harrison Smith—these novels appeared during a peak in literary commerce and print culture that transformed the literary field and, as Hutchinson notes, may be related to external factors analogous to those that Bourdieu applies to transformations of the literary field of nineteenth-century Paris. For example, jobs produced by new institutions in publishing and other literary and cultural formations in the city opened the way to newcomers, often from far-flung regions, hoping to develop careers in literature and the arts. At the same time, as Bourdieu observes of nineteenth-century Paris, "enduring connections, founded on affinities of life-style and value . . . tied at least some kinds of writers to certain segments of high society" (546). Hutchinson makes use of observations relating to social and economic factors to make a compelling argument for viewing these novels within the same field. Following Bourdieu's analysis of the literary field as providing a way for young men and women of the "proletarian intelligentsia" (a term Bourdieu borrows from Max Weber) to make a living, in connection with others whose positions were obtained through informal ties to high society, Hutchinson's study of the agents, institutions, works, and audiences of the literary field offers suggestive directions for comparative readings like this.

The three novels emerge in the context of a literary field already transformed by shifts in the economy of the world system and the movement of masses of immigrants who came to New York City by ship and developed new literary institutions, agents, and audiences. Yet these novels participate in further refractions of the field produced by an array of intersecting external factors, particularly by the arrival in New York City and other cities in the north of masses of black migrants from the rural South. Through narratives about the struggles of newcomers to the urban North, these novels take positions in debates about conceptions and representations of race, nation, and culture. Aiming to transform subtle hierarchies that dominate the literary field, the novels engage in debates about racial ideals, imaginings of the nation along a North-South axis, and narrow conceptions of race-based propriety and aesthetic harmony or fit by examining their effects in everyday life.

Thurman's *The Blacker the Berry*, Faulkner's *The Sound and the Fury,* and Larsen's *Quicksand* do not aim at presenting the mobilization of blacks as national citizens of the labor force and World War I military operations, the mass migration of black laborers from the South, or the struggles of these migrant masses to survive racial management in their workplaces, domestic lives, or in the city streets. However, the narratives make no mistake about the significance of black mobility to the lives of their literate, educated protagonists or about the salience of the US North-South axis to the construction of racial and national imaginaries. The struggles for power, authority, and belonging represented in these novels participate in debates about racial, cultural, and national values and ideals whose impact on the literary field was intensified by mass black migration.

The cartography of racial debate in the field is evident in the mobile itineraries charted and explored within each narrative. Larsen's Helga Crane, apart from her trans-Atlantic crossings and two-year sojourn in Copenhagen and despite her return South at the end of the narrative, most nearly approximates an itinerary from the period of the Great Migration. Born in Chicago, Helga returns there briefly after she quits her teaching job at a black college in the South. By following her movements from Chicago to Harlem, Copenhagen, back to Harlem, and finally—in an abrupt reversal that concludes the novel—to rural Alabama, the novel signifies Larsen's engagement with external factors and debates about race pertinent to transformations in the structure of the literary field.

Although Thurman's Emma Lou Morgan initiates her journey in the West, in Boise, Idaho, i.e., from a region exorbitant to dominant narratives of the first peak of the Great Migration, the narrative nonetheless emphasizes her links to the South, southern migration, and reproduction throughout the nation of racial and cultural ideals believed to originate in the South. Her light-skinned maternal ancestors and their prejudice against dark-black skin are traced to the South, where they prospered sufficiently to join the earlier, far smaller black exodus that traveled to the West (Thurman, *Berry* 30). Although her three years in Los Angeles as a student at the University of Southern California distinguish her from the stream of black migrants whose movement north intensifies race consciousness across the nation, Emma Lou's flights and permanent relocation to Harlem, where the bulk of the narrative takes place, position Thurman and his novel in debates about conceptions of race that were aimed at attacking or defending structures in the literary field.

Finally, Faulkner's Quentin Compson travels between a small town in northern Mississippi, where most of the narrative of *The Sound and the Fury* is set, and Cambridge, Massachusetts, whose population, though vastly smaller, was as dense as that of New York City. Toward the end of his first year at Harvard, he spends a day traveling about incessantly as he makes preparations to drown himself in the Charles River. Quentin maps masculine identity and its intersections with race, nation, and culture onto North-South and trans-Atlantic axes, positioning Faulkner and his novel in the context of the author's efforts to enter and transform conceptions of the South within the literary field.

The access of the protagonists of these narratives to railroad and automobiles facilitates their transition to mobile lives.[1] Furthermore, the figuration of such travels, linked to the movement of masses of black southerners, places these texts in the context of debates within the literary field about race, culture, and belonging or fit, terms that figure in concepts of cultural nationalism or cultural racialism developed during the period. The particular struggles of these characters to secure membership in the elite social circles to which they hold tenuous and provisional claims correspond to hierarchies in the structures of the literary field that the authors of these novels seek to transform. Larsen challenges black elite injunctions against spontaneity and self-display and assumptions about their linkages with geographical and social location, Thurman satirizes black bourgeois prejudice against dark-black skin and those who deploy it against others and themselves, and Faulkner parodies the culture of white southern manhood and its dependence on those it pretends to master.

Helga Crane and the "Strenuous Rigidity of Conduct"

Placed in a double bind, Helga Crane's experience of racial, cultural, and national belonging is hindered by her placement at the crossroads of opposing imaginaries. One aligns with her undistinguished lineage, the other with the distinction she has provisionally earned among the black elite through her education and the value attributed to her bi-racial physical features. However, her membership among the racial elite is threatened when she refuses to conform to the strenuous regulation of her conduct, bodily expression, and self-display. In her view, these rigid codes of conduct suppress the unrestrained aesthetic practices that she not only views as ideals of the good life, but also associates with black folk. She attacks these codes as contradictions to the supposed "race pride" that dominates discourse among the black elites. Helga's repetitive confrontations with these contradictions inform the pattern of her travels; initially content in new surroundings and circles of friends, Helga grows dissatisfied with perceived hypocrisy and contradiction, feels powerless to produce change, resents the members of her elite circle, and abruptly takes flight.[2]

From the outset of the narrative, the two opposing imaginaries are depicted as a warring racial aesthetic. At one pole, the colors, fabrics, and lighting of her room, "furnished with rare and intensely personal taste" (Larsen 1), like her garments and slippers, face and hair, reflect her extravagant and "unrestrained" aesthetic taste (2). At the other pole, and in contrast to the satisfactions Helga finds in her own room with her own books, is the gossip of her fellow teachers, about violations of "the strenuous rigidity of conduct required" at Naxos (1). The pressure of this warring aesthetic receives further exposition with the "banal, the patronizing, and even the insulting remarks of one of the renowned white preachers of the state" (2). Like the gossip of the faculty, the preacher's lecture emphasizes the rigid codes that become a bone of contention for Helga and precipitate her departure from what he calls "the finest school for Negroes anywhere in the country, north or south" (3). The lecture expresses these codes of conduct in terms of aesthetics and describes good conduct and self-regulation as expressions of good taste:

> [I]f all Negroes would only take a leaf out of the book of Naxos and conduct themselves in the manner of the Naxos products, there would be no race problem, because Naxos Negroes knew what was expected of them. They had good sense and they had good taste. The knew enough to stay in their places, and that, said the preacher, showed good taste. (Larsen 3).

Having "never quite achieved the unmistakable Naxos mold" (Larsen 7), Helga has the bad sense and bad taste to reject the conduct expected of her. She breaks her engagement to a man from one of the first families and relinquishes a secure position in black high society, for example, by refusing to make herself "inconspicuous and conformable" (6) instead of remaining devoted to beauty, colorful self-display, and "nice things" (9).

Like a sewing factory, "ruthlessly cutting all to a pattern" (Larsen 4) or a military machine, producing automatons and marching them about in goose-step to the tune of "The Star Spangled

Banner" (12), Naxos figures largely in Larsen's critique of the narrow codes and routinization of what she identifies as the black elite code or aesthetic of conduct. As Helga prepares to leave Naxos and the South, her mind returns to clothing, color, and suitability or fit, focal points of her critique of hypocrisy in the discourse "of race, of race consciousness, of race pride" (17). As Helga argues, this profession of black pride is a pretense that suppresses "its most delightful manifestations, love of color, joy of rhythmic motion, naive, spontaneous laughter. Harmony, radiance, and simplicity, all the essentials of spiritual beauty in the race" (17). Yet Helga never develops a strategy for reversing what she experiences as the stifling hierarchy of elite aesthetic practice and sensibility.[3]

Helga reveals the fallacies in her imaginary map of aesthetic taste when she travels by train from Naxos to Chicago. In "the stuffy day coach" where she "sat with others of her race" (Larsen 20), i.e., with the people whose radiance and spontaneity she elsewhere aestheticizes and extols, Helga feels discomfort and disgust. She experiences "physical pain" from sitting amidst the "[l]aughing conversation," whining "bronze baby," audible crunch of the "black and tan pair" eating a cold fried chicken, sounds of a sleeping laborer and, finally, "a farmer carrying a basket containing live chickens" (23–24). At the end of the narrative, these confused intersections and imaginaries find prolonged and exaggerated expression in Helga's "mortification," "ridicule and self-loathing" (101). By implicating Helga in contradictions that intersect with those she criticizes, Larsen's narrative asserts its critical distance from its protagonist and strengthens the novel's position within debates about race consciousness, culture, and national belonging pertinent to the actors and institutions in the literary field.

Helga's self-mortification is figured as a desperate and spontaneous adventure in the streets of Harlem on a rainy night. She stumbles into a storefront church, finds a meeting in progress, and suddenly begins to weep in "great racking sobs," "to cry unrestrainedly," and to give "herself freely to soothing tears" (Larsen 104). Face to face with the singing, weeping, swaying, and clapping of a black ecstatic religious activity and aesthetic practice whose spontaneity and rhythmic motion would be frowned upon by her elite social circle, she views her surroundings as "an unknown world" whose "nameless people" fill her with disgust: "foul, vile, and terrible, with its mixture of breaths, its contacts of bodies, its concerted convulsions" (104–105). The adventure leads to Helga's sexual surrender and decision to marry the Reverend, the "rattish yellow man" from rural Alabama whom she does "not hate," not "him, the town, or the people. No not for a long time" (109). Refusing to conform as wife and member of the cultivated and respectable black bourgeoisie in Harlem or as wife and primitive exotic of an accomplished artist in the fashionable white society of Copenhagen, Helga settles in an illiterate black community in the South and the daily experience of misery, deprivation, and toil. Exaggerating Helga's mistaken mapping of a joyous black aesthetic with black peasant life in the agrarian South, Larsen challenges the structures of the literary field by attacking contradictions at the nexus of racial ideals, cultural practices, aesthetic codes of conduct, and national imaginings mapped on a North-South or trans-Atlantic axis.

Emma Lou Morgan and the "Right Sort of People"

By the time Emma Lou arrives in Harlem in *The Blacker the Berry*, she is well schooled in the disadvantages of dark-black skin. She leaves home in Boise, Idaho, where her mother and the blue-vein social set reject her because of her complexion. However, she finds the persistence of such discrimination when she tries to enter the society of the elite black students at the University of Southern California. After her first year, she returns to Boise for the summer and has a sexual relationship with Weldon, a medical student passing through Boise to find work so that he can return East with money to finance his education. When he accepts "the life of the road," a job as a Pullman porter and breaks off their relationship, Emma Lou is sure—although the narrator disputes her—that Weldon is governed by the prejudices of black bourgeois society (Thurman, *Berry* 36–37). The narrator disagrees and argues that Emma Lou's judgment is flawed, thus introducing critical distance and the element of satire to the presentation of what the narrator calls "the haunting chimera of intra-racial color prejudice" (38). While casting doubt on the veracity of a social disposition whose factual existence the narrative verifies time and again, the "haunting" effect of this chimera on Emma Lou is reported as a certainty that causes her to flee to an unknown town once again (38).

As with her first flight to Los Angeles, Emma Lou's journey to Harlem occurs without detailed exposition; Thurman provides no observations about how she travels, how long it takes, or what she observes or experiences along the way. Rather, as Alain Locke famously states of the abrupt relocation of migrant masses in the introduction to his special issue on Harlem in *Survey Graphic*, "A railroad ticket and a suitcase, like a Bagdad carpet, transport the Negro peasant from the cotton-field and farm to the heart of the most complex urban civilization" (630). Emma Lou's relocation is also accomplished with an aura of magic, in the space of a chapter break, after which several weeks have passed, and she awakens in bed, somewhat disheveled from "a night of stolen or forbidden pleasure" (Thurman, *Berry* 39). No longer victim of intra-racial prejudice, she also wields its wicked power, dismissing her new sexual partner as objectionably dark. Feeling the power of this reversal, she also believes that she has conquered time and space: "It did seem strange, this being in Harlem when only a few weeks before she had been over three thousand miles away. Time and distance—strange things, immutable, yet conquerable" (40). In fact, her virulent denigration of Hazel Morgan, whom she meets at USC, provides early evidence of Emma Lou's cruel tendency to react to humiliation by humiliating others. It may be such retributive violence in the literary field that Thurman means to criticize by introducing intra-racial color prejudice into debates about race and culture.[4]

Having moved to Los Angeles from Boise, Idaho, where she was the only black student at her high school, Emma Lou is overjoyed to meet "another colored girl" at USC, standing in line to pay fees (Thurman, *Berry* 14). Yet her pleasure turns to discomfort and disdain when the girl opens her mouth and announces in "a loud, harsh voice": "'My feet are sure some tired!' . . . 'Ain't this registration a mess?' . . . 'I've been standing' in line and clumbin' stairs and talkin' and a-singin' till I'm just 'bout done for.' . . . 'Is you a new student?'" (15). Her loud and strident voice and ungrammatical speech were only the first of Emma Lou's objections to associating with or being associated with Hazel Morgan.

On further observation, her disgust at Hazel's loud voice and inappropriate, ungrammatical speech is amplified by attitudes Emma Lou learned from the colored people back home. Drawing conclusions from Hazel's unseemly conduct, she wonders,

> Where on earth could she have gone to high school? Surely not in the North. Then she must be a southerner. That's what she was, a southerner—Emma Lou curled her lips a little—no wonder the colored people in Boise spoke as they did about southern Negroes and wished that they would stay South. (Thurman, *Berry* 15)

Thurman's voice is also loud and strident as he demonstrates how racial conduct, physical appearance, and aesthetic taste are mapped onto an imaginary North-South axis of the nation that circulates as far west as Boise.

Emma Lou is just beginning to amass the reasons why "she had no intentions of becoming friendly with this sort of person" and "would be ashamed even to be seen on the street" with her (Thurman, *Berry* 16). Hazel's red-striped sport suit, white hat, and white shoes and stockings suggest her lack of the good sense and good taste, vaunted by Larsen's white southern preacher at Naxos, "to know that black people had to be careful about the colors they affected" (16). Judging her as "flagrantly inferior," Emma Lou describes Hazel in a volley of hateful terms, even imagining Hazel's family as "ignorant and ugly" before deciding to make Hazel's black face the target of her exaggerated invective. Emma Lou denounces Hazel's features, stating that "[t]here was no sense in any one having a face as ugly as Hazel's," connects it to an undistinguished lineage, and maps the whole ensemble onto the South: "No wonder people were prejudiced against dark-skin people when they were so ugly, so haphazard in their dress, and so boisterously mannered as was this present specimen" (17). The narrator intrudes to explain that Hazel inherited her racial conceptions of color and conduct from her ancestors, "mulattoes or light brown in color," who "had segregated themselves from their darker skinned brethren" when they lived in the South and "continued this practice" when they migrated West and, later, North (30). The critical distance introduced by gaps between the knowledge of the narrator and the vague understanding of Emma Lou introduce parody and satire into Thurman's treatment of color prejudice.

Emma Lou's notions about the "the right sort of people" (Thurman, *Berry* 19) and "her vague idea that "those people on the campus who practically ignored her were the only people with whom she should associate" (30) suggest the cruel deployment of racial, cultural, and national imaginaries that Thurman argues against and hopes to transform among the actors (writers, agents, publishers, editors, etc.) and institutions (publishers, journal editors, societies, newspapers, reviews, etc.) of the literary field.

Quentin Compson and "God [who] is not only a gentleman and a sport; he is a Kentuckian too"

In *The Sound and The Fury*, a large section presents a significant day in the history of the Compson family. This is the day of Quentin Compson's suicide, eighteen years before the time period (three days in April 1928) in which the rest of the novel takes place. Without this section and its spatial location in a small, but densely populated city in the northeast, it might be harder to demonstrate persuasively that the novel positions itself within the literary field in which it was produced, distributed, and consumed. In any case, Quentin's brief and unsuccessful effort to amass prestige for himself and his family through education at an Ivy League university is intimately connected with the circumstances of his family in the South. By 1928, the plantation established by the Compsons before the Civil War is defunct, their house is dilapidated, and the household is running on scant resources, depending for its maintenance on the undercompensated labor and management of Dilsey Gibson, formerly the family slave, and the caretaking skills of her grandson Luster. Before Quentin's suicide, his sister Caddy also entered into a northern venture by accepting a financially advantageous proposal of marriage from a Harvard man from Indiana, but when her illegitimate pregnancy is revealed and the proposal withdrawn, she, too, disappoints the family's hopes of replenishing their depleted prestige and capital.

In the Quentin section, Mrs. Bland and her son Gerald can be seen as examples of the caricatured figures offered up in the narrative as parodies of the sort of people that Caroline Compson desires as fitting associates for her offspring. The incessant focus of Mrs. Bland on the production and reproduction of Gerald's social distinction provides an analog to Mrs. Compson's less energetic efforts to achieve the same end. Comparable to the exertions of Mrs. Bland, Mrs. Compson was responsible not only for the decision to sell a parcel of land so that Quentin could go to Harvard, but also to take her pregnant daughter to a summer resort in Indiana to find an advantageous marriage partner. Presented through exaggeration and parody, the narrative introduces critical distance into its figuration of the Blands and their place in Quentin's suicidal ideation. This distance strengthens the position of the novel in arguments about conceptions and presentations of white southern manhood in debates about racial, national, and cultural ideals.[5]

Quentin's thoughts turn to Gerald and his mother Mrs. Bland's ceaseless inflation of his presumed value as he stands on a bridge, gazes at the Charles River, and contemplates his shadow and suicide. He does not think at this point of what his biological mother might say about his suicide (and readers know, in fact, what she does say, eighteen years later, which is that Quentin left—in good taste—a note for the family). Knowing that his mother believes that his value needs shoring up, for example, by going to Harvard, Quentin thinks, by contrast, of Dilsey, whose racial location is associated with a set of values that is not subjected to parody: "What a sinful waste Dilsey would say" (Faulkner 90), drawing not only on the religious faith associated with her racial location, but also opposing the craven determination of value characterized by the management of social distinctions as practiced by Mrs. Compson, Mrs. Bland, and their like. Viewing himself as a mere shadow "leaning flat upon the water," Quentin contemplates Gerald as he rows along the river, engaged in an aesthetic practice that establishes and communicates his wealth, prestige, and refinement. Like Emma Lou Morgan at USC, Quentin displays an exaggerated consciousness of Gerald, from "his attitudes of princely boredom" to "his curly yellow hair and his violet eyes and his eyelashes" and "New York clothes" ("flannels, a gray jacket, and a stiff straw hat") (Faulkner 90, 91). Introducing critical distance, as Thurman does, Faulkner uses parody to highlight the linkages between Gerald's seemingly effortless demeanor as a participant in an exclusive cultural practice and the ceaseless exertions required of others (condensed in, but hardly confined to, the figure of the mother) to secure his elevated social status and valued racial features and clothing.

Shreve, Quentin's friend and roommate, offers ironic commentary on the role of the Bland family, especially of Mrs. Bland, in taking steps on Gerald's behalf that make it unnecessary for him to strive for racial, national, and cultural distinctions that he accepts as his natural endowments or entitlements. Shreve's commentary is all the more pointed because Mrs. Bland, who refers to him as "that fat Canadian" (Faulkner 106), views him as the *wrong* sort of person and tries *twice* to have him removed as Quentin's roommate.[6] He compares Mrs. Bland's efforts to manufacture her son's social distinction to the arduous labor of a "galley slave," on one hand, and to the profit-seeking enterprise of merchant, "sole owner and proprietor of the unchallenged peripatetic john of the late Confederacy," on the other (106). The parodic presentation of Gerald Bland and his mother contributes to debates about the incorporation of white southerners (white southern males, in particular) in the nation and national culture.

Through the figure of Mrs. Bland, a "remarkably preserved woman . . . grooming Gerald to seduce a duchess" (106), Faulkner enters debates about conceptions of race, male cultures of mastery, and the status of race in the nation. Like Emma Lou Morgan, Mrs. Bland is a parodic mouthpiece for the dissemination of distasteful tales about "Gerald's horses and Gerald's niggers and Gerald's women" (Faulkner 91), recidivist efforts to shore up Gerald's anachronistic white male mastery. She uses her wealth to rent apartments, his and hers, off campus, in Cambridge, and to hire cars that assure that their travels will be private and exclusive. From her careful selection and formal invitation of guests to her automobile ride on a parallel road as Gerald practices his rowing, Mrs. Bland is hyperbolically invested in the management of her southern son's prestige. As Quentin observes, if one believes the stories of Mrs. Bland, then one believes "that God is not only a gentleman and a sport; he is a Kentuckian too" (91). Faulkner's parodic treatment of white southern manhood and the investments required to preserve its value serve his interest in transforming the structures of a literary field located in the North and dominated by racial, cultural, and national ideals mapped onto northern imaginings.

Quentin maps Mrs. Bland's selection of the right sort of people as associates for her son along a vivid imaginary of the North-South axis and its pertinence to the nation. "She approved of Gerald associating with me," Quentin notes, "because I at least revealed a blundering sense of noblesse oblige by getting myself born below Mason and Dixon, and a few others whose Geography met the requirements (minimum)" (Faulkner 91). By a similar logic, mapped along the trans-Atlantic axis of Anglo-American modernism, he notes that Spoade also meets with the approval of Mrs. Bland, although "she had never been able to forgive him for having five names, including that of present English ducal house" (91–92). The northern setting of the Quentin section and its parodic presentation of post-Confederate white manhood situate Faulkner within debates about conceptions of race, culture, and nation and demonstrate his engagement with the literary field whose structures he wishes to transform to his advantage.

Conclusion

Following George Hutchinson, who argues persuasively that cultural production of the Harlem Renaissance and Anglo-American modernism should be considered within the same literary field, I examine three novels of the late 1920s in the context of debates about race, nation, and culture, aimed at transforming this literary field. The narratives of these novels can be viewed as complex story problems, whose imaginary resolutions are not reducible to the positions the novels take in the context of debates over structures of the literary field. Isolated and unhappy as wife and mother in rural Alabama, socially engaged as a teacher at a public school in Harlem, or disengaged altogether as a suicide, the concluding circumstances of these protagonists do not represent the authors' positions in relation to the field, but rather strategies for participating with more or less critical distance and, thus, more or less freedom in debates about structural change that might better serve their interests. Ultimately, the mobile subjects and imaginary North-South axis treated in these narratives serve to illustrate the way lineage, appearance, conduct, and speech are mapped onto conceptions and representations of race, culture, and nation.

Notes

1. For a timely view of the current conditions of mobile lives and their dependence on carbon-based mobility systems, see Elliott and Urry.

2. Pointing to an "astute reading" of *Quicksand* by Alain Locke, George Hutchinson notes that the novel "reveals the contradictions inherent in the binarism of American racial discourse" (204–205).

3. Deborah Katz, who effectively links the narrative's objectification of Helga Crane as an art object to "the racist logic that undergirds her uncomfortable, claustrophobic relationship to black bodies, including her own" (54n1). In the same volume, Trudier Harris views Helga Crane's dilemma as a psychological straightjacket; without considering her depiction in the context of broader debates, the cultural work of the narrative ends with the demonstration of a problem without a solution.

4. On Thurman's participation in debates about conceptions and representations of race in the literary field, see George Hutchinson's discussion of Thurman's "Negro Artists and the Negro" (241–243) and Thurman's 1927 essay in *The New Republic*.

5. Although she does not devote attention to Gerald or Mrs. Bland, Caroline S. Miles offers a useful investigation of how southern manhood is articulated through Quentin's encounters with racial Others.

6.   Simone Maria Puleo explores the "constellating 'fatness'" of Jason Compson, but overlooks its use in relation to Shreve.

Works Cited

Bourdieu, Pierre. "Flaubert's Point of View." Trans. Priscilla Pankhurst Ferguson. *Critical Inquiry* 14.3 (1988): 539–62.

Elliott, Anthony & John Urry. *Mobile Lives.* New York: Routledge, 2010.

Faulkner, William. *The Sound and the Fury.* New York: Vintage, 1990.

Harris, Trudier. "Afterword: The Complexities of Home." *Race and Displacement: Nation, Migration, and Identity in the Twenty-First Century.* Eds. Maha Marouan, Merinda Simmons, & Houston Baker. Tuscaloosa, Alabama: U of Alabama P, 2013. 211–220.

Hutchinson, George. *The Harlem Renaissance in Black and White.* Cambridge, MA: Harvard UP, 1995.

Katz, Deborah. "The Practice of Embodiment: Transatlantic Crossings and Black Female Sexuality in Nella Larsen's *Quicksand.*" *Race and Displacement: Nation, Migration, and Identity in the Twenty-First Century.* Eds. Maha Marouan, Merinda Simmons, & Houston Baker. Tuscaloosa: U of Alabama P, 2013. 43–56.

Larsen, Nella. 1928. *Quicksand.* Mineola, NY: Dover, 2006.

Locke, Alain. "Harlem." *Survey Graphic* 6.6 (1925): 629–30.

_____. "1928: A Retrospective Review." *Opportunity* 7 (1929): 8–11.

Miles, Caroline S. "Money and Masculinity: Economies of Fear in Faulkner's *The Sound and the Fury. Critical Insights: The Sound and the Fury.* Ed. Taylor Hagood. Amenia, NY: Grey House, 2014. 143–57.

Puleo, Simone Maria. "'Fat as You Is': Jason Compson's Bullied Body in *The Sound and the Fury. Critical Insights: The Sound and the Fury.* Ed. Taylor Hagood. Amenia, NY: Grey House, 2014. 212–26.

Thurman, Wallace. "Negro Artists and the Negro." *New Republic* 52 (August 1927): 37–39.

_____. *The Blacker the Berry.* 1929. Mineola, NY: Dover, 2008.

CRITICAL
READINGS

"Hectic Rhythms": Unseen and Unappreciated Knowledge in Harlem Renaissance Fiction_____

Jericho Williams

In *The Souls of Black Folk* (1903), W. E. B. Du Bois articulated an ambitious plan for expanding educational opportunities for a "Talented Tenth" of African Americans who would study to become intellectual, community, and social leaders. Du Bois felt that an insufficient number of African Americans had previously attended college between 1875 and 1900, which prompted his call for change (*Souls* 65). He worried that the stratification of society based on color and race did not bode well either for African Americans or for the prospect of an integrated, functionally dynamic America. Therefore, he theorized a "Talented Tenth" that would not "lightly lay aside their yearning" to learn and who would improve the prospects of their families and communities by attending universities in pursuit of a formal education based upon reading and interacting with a classical education curriculum (65). Du Bois argued that upon earning their degrees, this group of African Americans would occupy the privileged position of helping American society face a greater challenge. They would guide millions of African Americans, comprising the remaining ninety percent, away from focusing on the wrongs of the past and would help formulate the means for creating a better future. Du Bois' conception of a "Talented Tenth" would remain one of the central conceptual contributions of *The Souls of Black Folks* and a point of contention for a subsequent generation of Harlem Renaissance writers.

In response, two Harlem Renaissance writers, Claude McKay and Wallace Thurman, critiqued the Duboisian notion of the "Talented Tenth" in their novels *Home to Harlem* (1928) and *The Blacker the Berry* (1929). In these works, both McKay and Thurman detail how life in Harlem energized people, expanded their minds, and facilitated new or renewed possibilities for understanding their lives. Like Du Bois, each author considered the role of education in African American lives, although they both stopped short of accepting the notion that education should serve one talented group of individuals. For McKay and Thurman, everyday Harlem life proved that the educational process consisted of something more than traditional classrooms or lecture halls. In their delineations of the social interactions and of the transient movements coming both in and out of Harlem, each author posited a broader understanding of African American education. They imagined a process facilitated and directed in part by African Americans themselves through the expressions of art, conversations, observations about everyday life and the dissemination of knowledge accumulated from outside Harlem, sometimes from the margins of society, sometimes from university situations, and sometimes from overseas. McKay and Thurman depicted networks of African Americans who converged in Harlem from different places, crossing each other's paths. This vibrant network of people helped to define Harlem as an exchange point of knowledge, understandings, and culture that nurtured social understandings and the formation of new knowledge far different from traditional institutions of higher learning.

Though both Claude McKay's *Home to Harlem* and Wallace Thurman's *The Blacker the Berry* are well-known novels and feature unique lead characters looking for new directions in life, each novelist orchestrates his story differently. In *Home to Harlem*, McKay's "footloose and picaresque protagonist" Jake Brown lives a fast-paced lifestyle that engulfs readers in a string of adventures related to his yearning to return to Harlem, his temporary haven there, and then his hopeful exit at new stage in life (Washington 78). Likewise, Thurman's protagonist Emma Lou Morgan finds refuge in Harlem, but in contrast to Jake, she continually seeks to escape from perceptions of herself as an outsider due to her darker skin tone and a social climate of color prejudice. While Jake's real-life adventures wear down his body, Emma Lou's compounding internal struggle to find acceptance with the world outside of her takes a toll on her mind. As each character progresses, *Home to Harlem* develops as a novel more focused on exterior movements and events that propel Brown forward, while *The Blacker the Berry* spirals deeper into

Emma Lou's inner worries and insecurities as she reacts to an unjust social system that sorts people by their complexions. The separate and prominent emphases on external behavior and internal struggle encourage critical viewpoints that often suppose Jake as merely a primitive figure acting quickly and brashly in response to whatever happens around him and Emma Lou as a hypersensitive young woman excluded because of biases beyond her control. While both of these dominant perceptions of Jake and Emma Lou produce fruitful insights, they also overshadow other elements of each novel, particularly in relation to each author's criticism of a purely classical education as a means of improving the lives of African Americans. Authors McKay and Thurman warn that too heavy an emphasis on the division from their peers of a select group of formally educated African Americans has the potential to fail in its replication of an already exclusionary, stratified social system. Beyond the frame of Jake's exteriority and Emma Lou's interiority, both authors posit that, while a formal education may have its place in elevating the African American community, it must be supported by interaction and dialogue that will facilitate its use for helping others, rather than fostering greater class divisions.

What Lies Beneath a Primitive Façade?: Jake Brown's Education in *Home to Harlem*

Claude McKay's *Home to Harlem* recounts protagonist Jake Brown's return to Harlem after a stint overseas in the United States Army. Jake returns to the United States because he longs to live in Harlem, and when he arrives, he meets a woman named Felice, who seizes his attention and heart. She occupies his mind throughout the novel, and after a long and convoluted quest, they reunite and prepare to leave Harlem, presumably for a new beginning in Chicago. While the novel's conclusion suggests that Jake fulfills his longing for a kind, sensitive, and stable companion, much of its core documents his day-to-day life in Harlem. Jake frequents infamous locales and interacts with a large social circle of friends and acquaintances before leaving temporarily to work on a passenger train, where he meets an intellectual named Ray who becomes a close friend. Jake lives haphazardly at times, soaking in Harlem's around-the-clock liveliness, and he offers readers a tour of working-class Harlem life during the 1920s. Finally, Jake emerges a reenergized man, full of hope and possibility by the novel's end, when he and Felice prepare to make a move toward a better life, leaving readers hopeful for their future.

Contemporary critics place a strong emphasis on Jake as a primitive figure, an observation that derives from both the novel's publication date, the later scholarly attention to literary modernism, and commentary by W. E. B. Du Bois. Robert Worth notes that the great interest in the primitive elements of the novel resulted in part from the publication of Carl Van Vechten's *Nigger Heaven* (1926) a few years earlier. Composed by a white author, who intended to portray salacious aspects of Harlem life for an eager white audience, the novel ignited discussions because of its outsider perspective, while also facilitating genuine interest in works about Harlem lifestyles written by African Americans. Indeed, *Home to Harlem* was an immediate bestseller, selling eleven thousand copies during its first two weeks and fifty thousand within its first year of publication (Bronz 83). If the reception of Vechten's novel encouraged more demand for a grittier brand of everyday realism that characterizes and contributes to the success of *Home to Harlem*, it also inevitably embroils the latter book within discussions of a primitivist tradition that scholars claim diverges from the general sense of malaise central to discussions of literary modernism. Gary Holcombe, for example, describes Jake Brown's "lusty appetite for copious sexual activity" as the opposite of "modernist disintegration" (71). *Home to Harlem* offers something atypical from modernist works of the period in the way that Brown appears as reckless, celebratory, and unreflective. Its deviance from literary modernism in this major paradigmatic way unfortunately obscures or discourages further insight into Jake Brown. Despite what *Home to Harlem* has to say about education in African American lives, the novel's contextualization alongside Van Vechten's work and its oft-designated place as an anti-modernist, primitivist work by later critics continue impact the way modern scholars and students read and understand it.

To a greater degree than historians or modernist scholars though, W. E. B. Du Bois may be the person most responsible for the way scholars now consider McKay's novel as a primitivist text. He thought the novel depicted a warped portrait of African American life that a restrained white culture craved—one that glorified drunken behavior, sex, and violence. "In as bold and as bright colors as he [could]," Du Bois wrote, discontent with the way that McKay wrote about the criminal and immoral aspects of Harlem, before adding: "after the dirtier parts of its filth, I feel distinctly like taking a bath" (202). Du Bois' criticism inflamed McKay; skeptically, he questioned Du Bois' ability to assess how art reflected the real world, and he considered the review as evidence of the African American leader's inability to understand and empathize with the lives of some African Americans (McKay, *The Passion* 150). Though Du Bois later reconciled with McKay and even praised his second novel *Banjo* (1929), the initial contentious encounter continues to factor heavily into interpretations of *Home to Harlem*. William J. Maxwell notes, "[It] illuminate[s] a major fault-line in the history of the New Negro in New York, dividing Du Bois' 'Talented Tenth Renaissance' from 'the succeeding 'Negro Renaissance' built by its freethinking charges" (171). Consequently, *Home to Harlem*'s sharp commentary and exploration about the meaning(s) and value(s) of an education beyond book-study get subsumed by this towering theoretical divide, in addition to being stifled by problematic characterizations of the novel as a post-Van Vechten or anti-modernist text.

Throughout *Home to Harlem*, McKay challenges Du Bois' formulation of the pinnacle value of a classical education by showing that external forms of interaction far away from school settings also facilitate forms of learning. Even though *Home to Harlem* does not feature one school building or one formal educational experience, it begins with Jake thoughtfully reflecting about the knowledge he gained while serving in the United States Army. Readers learn that Jake deserted his assignment during World War I because his duties were limited to toting lumber to help build huts rather than fighting, what he imagined and hoped to do. Thinking about the disappointment with his World War I experience, Brown questions, "'Why did I ever enlist and come over here? . . . Why did I want to mix mahself up in a white folks' war?'" (McKay, *Home* 142). Here, McKay elaborates upon a common sequence in the novel—movement in pursuit of work or adventure—that provides some African Americans with life experience and knowledge not afforded to them by a university education. In the process, McKay shows that common experiences afforded to white culture, such as war and education, do not transfer equally to African Americans holding seemingly similar positions. Jake's post-Army experience in London, for example, exposes him to a different form of racial tension than what he knows from his experiences in Harlem.

Having experienced discrimination within the United States Army and witnessed racial clashes in London, Jake is also keenly perceptive of the systematic biases that oppress African Americans in Harlem, and his reactions extend far beyond merely primitive responses. He knows, for example, not to join a New York City union because of its exclusionary tactics. Soon after Jake finds a job unloading pineapples, a union representative encourages him to join alongside other workers. Jake refuses the offer based on an experience and racism: "But when I made New York I done finds out that they gived the colored mens the worser piers and hold the bes'n a' them foh the Irishmen. No, pardner, keep yo' card. I take the best I can k'n get as I goes mah way" (McKay, *Home* 160). Along with the obvious assaults on Harlem life, including unannounced police raids and brutality, Jake can identify the forms of oppression from social groups ostensibly employed to protect people from mistreatment and abuse. With the union rejection scenario, McKay shows that when racism dominates these organizations, the exclusive tactics do more than merely function as an apparatus of oppression. In time, they provoke a unified response by African Americans against hollow proclamations. In his criticism of unions, McKay suggests that with or without a formal education, African Americans in Harlem recognize inequity, talk about it, and react to it in a way that does not necessarily require a university education or understandings of the classical world. Pointedly, some of the better ideas in uniting against these sorts of inequities emerge from discussions in response to direct exposure to the realities of racism or everyday experiences that reveal something more immediate than classroom study.

Home to Harlem also suggests that the educational process encompasses spiritual growth, an aspect of the novel lost in discussions that stress the charms of Harlem's nightlife and Jake's nonchalant (or worse, ignorant) sense of festive ease. On the one hand, Jake parties excessively during multiple occasions and struggles to maintain his health. Yet on the other hand, from the novel's beginning, when Jake is away from Harlem, to his first escape aboard a train and then his final preparation to leave near the novel's conclusion, Jake clearly yearns for something greater than an ethos of perpetual disregard. In an instance that illuminates his spirit, McKay writes about "that strange, elusive something that he felt within himself, sometimes here, sometimes there roaming away from him, going back to London, to Brest, Le Havre, wandering to some unknown new port, caught a moment by some romantic rhythm, color, face, passing through cabarets, saloons, speakeasies, and returning to him" (McKay, *Home* 158). Here, Jake desires something more than the carefree life routinely noted by the book's critics. Even if he is not an ideal match for Du Bois' vision of a "Talented Tenth," the undercurrent of his spiritual yearning shows that he is fully capable of maturing in response to day-to-day educational experiences that help enlighten and enlarge his life. For instance, a significant moment detailing Jake's inner growth occurs when he realizes that the roles available to him within his social milieu are insufficient because they do not provide him deeper meaning. Jake realizes that he cannot live in the "usual sweet way," as a man of violence in pursuit of a life of ease, so he opts to join the railroad, where he undergoes a transformative experience through the relationship he forms with a co-worker named Ray (192).

When McKay introduces Ray, after Brown leaves Harlem and begins working for a railroad company, *Home to Harlem* again pushes beyond the boundaries of a Duboisian "Talented Tenth" paradigm in its increased exploration of the varieties of forms of education and their potential impact. Like Brown, Ray—originally from Haiti—travels to Harlem from afar. McKay's biographer Wayne F.

Cooper refers to Ray as a "wandering intellectual," who appears and disappears in *Home to Harlem* and who then resurfaces in McKay's subsequent novel *Banjo* (243). Cooper positions both Jake and Ray as vagabonds, with two differing personalities, in search of greater meaning in life. More often than not, Jake appears extroverted and to be living in the moment, while the more introverted Ray perpetually retreats into isolation, studying classic texts. In terms of perspective, McKay identifies a bit with both, although his ideal disposition is slightly closer to Jake's. Cooper writes, "[McKay's] main concern was with self-acceptance and the assertion of his race's positive existence in the immediate present. Whatever possibilities blacks had for advancement, as individuals or as a group, had to rest upon their present strengths" (263). To completely contrast Jake with Ray is to gloss over how the two types of wanderers interact and exchange thoughts and ideas. The shared interactions about their observations and beliefs help both of them (and Jake in particular) situate themselves among the vibrant, transient culture of Harlem. These exchanges are central to McKay's broader conception of what an education entails. In the midst of their conversations, both Jake and Ray inform one another and improve as human beings. Tossed together by circumstance, they learn through interactions in a way that eludes the limitations of preemptive categorization or separation into differing social or educational groupings.

Ray teaches Jake that a life of the mind can inform a life of action, which, in turn, impacts the way that Jake comprehends the world around him. When they first meet, Ray champions a literary life, for which Jake has no particular use. Jake discovers Ray reading Sappho, listens to Ray's reformulation of the story, and then questions the value of printed words. Ray responds by informing Jake about some of what he knows from reading, moving on from Sappho to the eye-opening details of the Haitian Revolution. Jake is resistant at first, but he begins to understand that what makes his friend unique and unpredictable stems from Ray's years of study. The explosive details of the Haitian Revolution help him to begin to change his perspective. Mesmerized, "[Jake] felt like he was passing through a dream, vivid in rich, varied colors. It was a revelation beautiful in his mind" (McKay, *Home* 201). While Ray's story does not fully convince Jake that a life of the mind is worth pursuing, it does convey the possibility that learning new information through print might help him understand himself and the others who surround him. Instead of a hierarchical dissemination of knowledge from expert to novice, to be memorized and privileged, McKay suggests that book knowledge best displays its value to an oppressed community when it helps with contextualization and insight rather than as a means of division or separation, which is a central critique of elitism in Du Bois' theory.

This latter point is what Brown communicates through his interactions with Ray, who struggles in dealing with how his education both empowers and isolates him. Among the railroad crew, Ray feels alone because he "possess[es] another language and literature that they knew not of" (McKay, *Home* 210). With the exception of his friendship with Jake, he disdains and distances himself from the other members of the railroad. During his lowest moment, he ingests drugs that leave him incapacitated for work the next day, which prompts criticism from his harshest critic, the railroad chef: "Better leave that theah nigger professor alone and come on'long to the dining-car with us. That theah nigger is dopey from them books o'hisn" (212). The chef positions Ray as a nonsensical man and abandons him, while Jake remains behind to help Ray get to a hospital. Later in the novel, the friends' roles change when Jake is ill because of his excessive drinking, and Ray counsels Jake to scale back on carousing so much. Jake replies that Ray's criticism reminds him of his Army days, when he received similar lectures designed "foh edjucated guys like you who lives in you' head" (235). In these two moments, McKay shows that while a person like Ray has a tougher time communicating with people resistant to education, any lifestyle that hinges on the overreliance of one thing—whether that be education or alcohol—can be unhealthy and unsustainable, regardless of class, race, or gender. In Jake's resistance to Ray's criticism of his lifestyle, McKay shows that what empowers or enlivens the African American community can also act as its antithesis at the most extreme lengths, when it becomes a façade of success or popularity.

Going beyond the assertion that Brown exists merely as a "crazy ram goat" primitive figure, *Home to Harlem* functions as a novel in which McKay privileges ideas of moderation, verbal interaction, and a willingness to be open to change from learning among a larger community, while pursuing one's own path of study or preferred form of self-expression (235). As Jake and Ray exit the novel, McKay leaves the semblance of hope for both characters. Before Ray seeks exile overseas, he verbalizes his change in thought after time spent with Jake. To James Grant, a college student working part-time who espouses a model akin to a Duboisian classical education, Ray imparts his revised idea of what it means to be truly educated: "No, modern education is planned to make you a sharp snouty, rooting hog. A negro getting it is an anachronism. We ought to get something new, we Negroes. But we get our education like—like our houses. When the whites move out, we move in and take possession of the old dead stuff. Dead stuff that this age has no use for" (McKay, *Home* 251). In other words, a modern education should not serve as a means to mirror white culture, nor should it blindly accept static values, assumptions, or understandings promulgated by its gatekeepers as truths. To support this theory, Ray shares a story that comprises the entire next chapter and that humanizes the lives of a pimp and his companion. In his account, Ray provides a far more complex telling about the pair instead of pronouncing a judgmental view that delimits both as morally reprehensible criminals. By way of this illustration, Ray acknowledges that old standards set by educational or cultural elites cannot take into account what their creators do not understand. The use of education must, therefore, manifest itself not through the ideal of an isolated, cloistered retreat (as Ray had once hoped for himself earlier in the novel), but through a combination of critical thinking and social engagement in the presence of a larger community.

Meanwhile, Jake hastily prepares to leave Harlem at the novel's end, convinced that moving to Chicago with Felice will provide a better life. Though he cherishes some aspects of Harlem life, Jake disdains the violence that continues to follow, confront, and haunt him. This realization becomes clear to him as he prepares himself to fight his former friend, Zeddy: "Yet here he was caught in the thing that he despised so thoroughly . . . Brest, London, America. Their vivid brutality tortured his imagination" (McKay, *Home* 290). With the violence he routinely encounters in mind, along with Ray's advice that a reckless, unexamined life would lead to a disappointing outcome and impact the possibility of a fulfilling relationship with Felice, Jake concludes that he must move on in order to pursue a healthier life. McKay suggests that if Jake's experience in Harlem is part of his formative evolution toward becoming a better man, there is also a point when he must follow Ray's path and venture elsewhere, as Jake's circle of acquaintances and his experiences in Harlem no longer offer him an opportunity to grow. Though they both come from different backgrounds, Ray and Jake move on to other places, having benefitted from learning from one another and the surrounding world.

Transcending Color's Divide: Emma Lou Morgan's Education in *The Blacker the Berry*

Wallace Thurman's *The Blacker the Berry* details the education of Emma Lou Morgan. Emma Lou is a very dark-skinned African American woman born in Boise, Idaho, within a social circle of family members who raise her to believe that a formal education is necessary to be considered a socially respectable person. The novel portrays her movement from Boise to the University of Southern California in Los Angeles, where she enrolls and drops out, and then to Harlem, where she finally earns a teaching degree. Thurman's central theme of the novel is how the effects of colorism, or the persecution of darker-skinned Others within racial or ethnic groups, can have a debilitating impact on the educational maturation of a young woman. As a part of this theme, he delineates how external color values influence inner perceptions of social inferiority that, in turn, can thwart the best-planned formal education. Ensconced in a doubly racist society, Emma Lou clings closer to an educational ideal as a means to escape the boundary of her skin. As this imagined avenue of escape becomes less promising and ultimately devoid of meaning, she feels disillusioned and bitter, though she continues to return to the idea that education and the company of well-educated people will solve all of her problems. Throughout this process, Thurman suggests that an ideal education for African Americans is not limited only to universities or teaching colleges, but also comprises coming to terms with oneself within one's social world and learning how to cope with internal anxieties and feelings of terror or hatred nourished by the realities of racism.

Thurman's heroine seeks a better life through education because it demands internal, mental work that allows her to separate herself from harsh judgments that appear during her childhood. As a dark-skinned daughter born into a family of light-skinned relatives, all living as part of a small minority of African Americans in Boise, Emma Lou experiences a variety of negative emotions from her closest relatives. Thurman writes, "It was her grandmother who did all of the regretting, her mother who did all of the bemoaning, and her Cousin Buddie and her playmates, both white and colored, who did the ridiculing" (696). Only one member of her family, her Uncle Joe, pays little attention to Emma Lou's skin color, and he urges her to escape Boise for a larger metropolis, where she might find acceptance as soon as possible. Here, at the beginning of the novel, Thurman provides a blistering critique of a separate and additional layer of racism within the African American community that condemns its darker members and that was especially arduous for women during the 1920s. In immediately focusing on the uncomfortable realities of color-designated hierarchies, Thurman asks not only in ways does a white society continue to exclude or oppress us, but also what do we gain or lose by nurturing exclusionary behaviors and categorizations on our own? Beginning in the first chapter, Thurman plunges readers into the fragile mind of a woman categorized as inferior to all others because of her external features. Detailing Emma Lou's lack of social support in her hometown enables Thurman a chance to challenge the notion that a solely formal educational experience can help African Americans overcome community dilemmas.

Emma Lou begins to seek a new opportunity in response to an alienating incident at her high school graduation. During a haunting scene, when she is the only person of color among her graduating class, Emma Lou walks to the stage to receive her diploma before returning to "her seat in that forboding [sic] white line, insolently returned once more to a splotch in its pale purity and to mock it with her dark, outlandish indifference" (Thurman 695). This situation briefly paralyzes Emma Lou, and she reflects upon it throughout the novel whenever she feels cast aside by other people. It is simultaneously a moment that makes clear the need for a potential rebirth and a memory punctuated by intense feelings of aloneness and exclusion. Attempting to take a step toward adulthood, she feels removed from her family and peers just before summoning the courage to move elsewhere and begin a life of her own. Her color severs her from relatives, whom she abandons for the remainder of the novel.

As a response to these ill feelings and with her Uncle Joe's blessing, Emma Lou seeks a better life through the pursuit of a college education because it entails mental work that will ostensibly allow her to distinguish herself in way that will help her triumph over the limitations of her skin color. She moves to Los Angeles to attend the University of Southern California and to seek acceptance from more diverse groups of people. Here, she experiences the ugly surprise that people of her own race hesitate to accept her because of the shade of her skin. As Catherine Rottenberg notes, Emma Lou is a "*too-black* girl . . . [amidst] black undergraduates . . . who have been interpellated into a world that constantly reinforces the desirability of whiteness" ("Wallace" 65). Yet, Emma Lou is not a passive receptacle of racism. She begins to internalize a systematic sorting of others similar to the process of her own exclusion, and this is part of what distinguishes Thurman's novel as an indictment of the limitations of university culture to liberate African Americans from societal racial and color prejudices. Emma Lou may be too dark to find acceptance from the social circle she wants, but she also harbors her own social hierarchies. She rejects Hazel Mason, a girl from Texas, because she is too loud and academically inferior and because she appears and speaks in a way that suggests her roots as a lower class African American from a southern state.

Thurman also suggests that Emma Lou mistakenly assumes that a college education will enable her to avoid ridicule. She thinks, "There was nothing romantic about going to college. . . . This getting an education was stern and serious, regulated and systematized, dull and unemotional" (716). For Thurman, these aims are hollow because, during the years designated for study, Emma Lou feels more emotionally isolated, as those around her assume she has no place in their company, and she assumes that those beneath her do not deserve her time or attention. She continually yearns to be accepted by the right kind of people—upwardly mobile, intellectual, and mostly light-skinned. Her isolation fuels feelings of insecurity tied to her complexion, and she abandons the university after another year of "drawing more and more within herself and becoming more and more bitter" (728). As Emma Lou leaves the university behind, Thurman ridicules college life if its primary purpose is to continue to uphold racial divides within both American and African American societies. Emma Lou learns that college is not a means to escape racial and complexion privileges, and Thurman suggests that there must be other means of social progress and acceptance.

From this point in the novel, Emma Lou moves to Harlem, which provides a much more thorough real-life education than the University of Southern California. Many commentaries about Emma Lou's experiences in Harlem contextualize it within the community's diversity in regards to race, gender, and sexuality. Daniel Scott III, for example, praises Thurman's depiction of a "nonessentialized, de-natured construction of the self," the author's attempt to portray a variety of people and their behaviors (and in particular, sexualities) as equally normal or acceptable (329). In describing Thurman's version of Harlem, Scott's criticism remains apt, yet Emma Lou's inner feelings and emotions are far more turbulent and conflicted within this purportedly more accepting place. If Harlem houses all forms of identities, it does not necessarily nurture them either equally or indefinitely, if at all. Emma Lou finds it difficult to locate both a reasonable job opportunity and a network of friends. She tours employment agencies, works as a personal assistant, and relocates often. Thurman portrays Emma Lou navigating a kaleidoscopic sequence of experiences and events only to repeatedly fall victim to her own insecurities and perceptions about her value based upon skin color.

Thurman may well be in accordance with those who envision Harlem as transformative for African Americans at the time, but he remains skeptical of the idea of an elite, formally educated social group. Scholar Amritjit Singh notes that Thurman maintained a "love-hate relationship" with Harlem—imagined as a place "staunch and revolutionary in its commitment to individuality and critical objectivity" (19). However, for individuality and critical objectivity to flourish, Harlem needs ways to foster livelihoods for African Americans as well as means to curtail apparatuses, policies, or behaviors that threaten to divide its inhabitants. He explores this notion in "Pyrrhic Victory," his title of the final part of *The Blacker the Berry*. In this section, Emma Lou finally faces her fears about education, returning in mind to the "searing psychological effect of that dreadful graduation night, and the lonely embittering three years, all of which had tended to make her color more and more a paramount issue and ill" (Thurman 808). She returns to school to take education courses and passes a teacher's examination in New York, which enables her to find a better job. Here, Thurman solidifies the contrast of Emma Lou's bitter experience desperately seeking acceptance among an upwardly mobile and judgmental peer group at the University of Southern California with her self-directed aspiration to become more knowledgeable in Harlem. Her new position empowers Emma Lou by providing her a better means of financial support within a venue that allows her to positively impact the lives of others.

If Emma Lou's approach to improving herself educationally is more productive in New York, Thurman insists that the process cannot be completely empowering until she accepts herself and outwardly reacts in response to her fears. Her Pyrrhic victory appears after she begins work as a teacher and tackles greater philosophical and personal issues. In the midst of a personal crisis, Emma Lou realizes that she must outwardly bear responsibility for her actions instead of cowering in response to her perceptions and chasing illusory ideals about the "right sort of people" (Thurman 817). Thurman writes, "What she needed to do now was to accept her black skin as being real and unchangeable, to realize that certain things were, had been, and would be, and with this in mind begin life anew, always fighting, not so much for acceptance by other people, but for acceptance of herself by herself" (828). Emma Lou's catharsis enables her to imagine that her education, her job, and her ability to decide whether or not to remain within a destructive relationship all function within the realm of her control. Acting upon this realization comes with heavy consequences, as Emma Lou must walk away from a man she loves and completely redefine her social life. In responding productively to her personal rebirth, Emma Lou must triumph over exclusionary circumstances, help foster community dialogue and interaction through sharing her experience, and decry social hierarchies based on prized skin tones or elite educations.

Beyond the Talented Tenth: A Call for a Greater African American Mission

Predictably, W. E. B. Du Bois initially criticized Thurman's *The Blacker the Berry*, just as he had Claude McKay's *Home to Harlem*, but a later essay indicates that he likely adapted his thinking due in part to the wisdom of both works. In a review of *The Blacker the Berry*, Du Bois argued that Thurman's work featured a loathing attitude toward blackness and a problematic racial outlook (250). Yet, a year later, he delivered a commencement speech at Howard University entitled "Education and Work" that suggests he had come to view the pursuit of a college education as hollow if not taken seriously with the betterment of all African Americans in mind. Du Bois noted,

> The ideals of colored college-bred men have not in the last thirty years been raised an iota. Rather in the main, they have been lowered. The average Negro undergraduate has swallowed hook, linc, and sinker, the dead bait of the white undergraduate, who, born into an industrial machine, does not have to think, and does not think. (92)

Like McKay and Thurman, Du Bois alludes to the idea that systematic oppression threatens to continue if college-educated African Americans follow their white counterpart's pursuits of cultural prestige and material gains. In calling on Howard undergraduates to avoid this fate, Du Bois identifies not only the need for a shift in thought regarding what a college degree meant to newly-graduated African Americans, but also the need for African American college graduates to think about, and work harder for, a means to help empower their larger communities. In this moment, Du Bois joins in tandem with McKay and Thurman to imply that a greater education encompasses many day-to-day African American experiences and that any form of social stratification based on schooling alone has the potential to replicate an elite white culture's exclusion of others.

Works Cited

Bronz, Stephen. *Roots of Negro Racial Consciousness*. New York: Libra, 1964.

Cooper, Wayne. *Claude McKay: Rebel Sojourner in the Harlem Renaissance: A Biography*. Baton Rouge, LA: Louisiana State UP, 1996.

Du Bois, W. E. B. "Education and Work." *The Education of Black People: Ten Critiques, 1906–1960*. Ed. Herbert Aptheker. New York: Monthly Review P, 2001.

_____. "Review of *The Blacker the Berry*, by Wallace Thurman." *Crisis* 36 (1929): 249–250. Microfilm. West Virginia University Library. 29 Dec. 2014.

_____. "Review of Nella Larsen's *Quicksand*, Claude McKay's *Home to Harlem*, and Melville Herskovits' *The American Negro*." *Crisis* 35 (1928): 202. Microfilm. West Virginia University Library. 29 Dec. 2014.

_____. *The Souls of Black Folks*. Mineola, New York: Dover, 1994.

Holcombe, Gary Edward. "The Sun Also Rises in Queer Black Harlem: Hemingway and McKay's Modernist Intertext." *Journal of Modern Literature* 30.4 (Summer 2007): 61–81.

Maxwell, William J. "Banjo Meets the Dark Princess: Claude McKay, W.E.B. Du Bois, and the Transnational Novel of the Harlem

Renaissance." *The Cambridge Companion to the Harlem Renaissance*. New York: Cambridge UP, 2007: 170–183.

McKay, Claude. *Home to Harlem*. New York: Library of America, 2011.

_____. *The Passion of Claude McKay: Selected Poetry and Prose, 1912–1948*. Ed. Wayne Cooper. New York: Knopf, 1973.

Rottenberg, Catherine. "Wallace Thurman's *The Blacker the Berry* and the Question of the Emancipatory City." *Mosaic: A Journal for the Interdisciplinary Study of Literature* 46.4 (December 2013): 59–74.

Scott, Daniel, III. "Harlem Shadows: Re-Evaluating Wallace Thurman's *The Blacker the Berry*." *MELUS* 29.3/4 (Autumn–Winter 2004): 323–339.

Singh, Amritjit. "Wallace Thurman and the Harlem Renaissance." *The Collected Writings of Wallace Thurman: A Harlem Renaissance Reader*. Ed. Amritjit Singh. New Brunswick, NJ: Rutgers UP, 2003: 1–28.

Thurman, Wallace. *The Blacker the Berry*. New York: Library of America, 2011.

Washington, Robert E. *The Ideologies of African American Literature: From the Harlem Renaissance to the Black Nationalist Revolt*. Washington, DC: Rowan & Littlefield, 2001.

Worth, Robert F. "*Nigger Heaven* and the Harlem Renaissance." *African American Review* 29.3 (1995): 461–473.

Toward a Theory of Art as Propaganda: Re-Evaluating the Political Novels of the Harlem Renaissance

Christopher Allen Varlack

In his 1926 seminal essay, "Criteria of Negro Art," William Edward Burghardt Du Bois—one of several key authors, also including Langston Hughes and Zora Neale Hurston, to examine the fundamental goals of African American art and the portrayal of the black community—argues that the essential component of a true black art is propaganda. This conception, in part, offered a direct response to the racial tension and discrimination of the time, while also reaffirming the vital characteristics of the New Negro that the progenitors of the Harlem Renaissance promised to usher in. In one of his more lasting ideological declarations, Du Bois thus offers the following consideration for his fellow artists and thinkers: "Suppose the only Negro who survived some centuries hence was the Negro painted by white Americans in the novels and essays they have written. What would people in a hundred years say of black Americans?" ("Criteria" 258). With the weight of such questions on Du Bois' mind, a 1926 issue of the *Crisis* sought to interrogate how the Negro ultimately should be portrayed in black art, asserting, "Most writers have said naturally that any portrayal of any kind of Negro was permissible so long as the work was pleasing and the artist sincere. But . . . the net result to American literature to date is to picture twelve million Americans as prostitutes, thieves and fools" ("The Negro" 190)—a glaring misrepresentation of a diverse and powerful black people still trapped largely under the stereotypes of the plantation myth.

Early twentieth-century American literature, after all, was severely marred by works such as the 1905 novel, *The Clansman: An Historical Romance of the Ku Klux Klan* by Thomas Dixon, Jr. The novel, for instance, heavily built upon racial caricature and minstrel myth, presented in one scene a cast of laughable and unintelligent black senators in the Reconstruction era South, running it amok and threatening the moral integrity of a once grand land by legalizing the controversial policy of miscegenation. Here, Dixon foregrounded the characters of Zip Coon—the perpetually unintelligent Negro unable to adjust to the intellectual standards of white society—and the Brute Negro—a savage and destructive black figure. In this startling over-generalization of the black community now growing since the days of the slave, Dixon presented not the educated New Negro, trying to advance a platform of social and economic uplift for the race, but rather the stereotypical "half child, half animal, the sport of impulse, whim, and conceit'" (292). In doing so, he reinforced what Charles H. Nichols, Jr. identified as the "Confederate romance" (201)—a term taken from Alfred Kazin to describe a tradition of post-Reconstruction literature lamenting the purportedly radical social and political shift of the postbellum world, inherently nostalgic for the "good old darkies" born into the world of slavery and the clear racial hierarchy that many believed ultimately suppressed the Negro's savage tendencies.

From Du Bois' standpoint, such works then left their readers with a heavily skewed and degraded image of black Americans—one that contributed to the steadily mounting racial tension of the early to mid-twentieth century (with the rise of the Klan and the Red Summer of 1919), while reinforcing the notion of Negro inferiority at the outskirts of a powerful white society. The same holds true of T. S. Stribling's 1921 novel, *Birthright*, which details the struggles of northern-educated Peter Siner, whose devotion to racial uplift and improving the already tense relationships between the area's Whitetown and Niggertown are disrupted by a strict racial order and impassioned love affair. Like *The Clansman*, the central plot of *Birthright* proves fundamentally problematic for the black writers of the Harlem Renaissance era concerned with the misrepresentation of black society and the hyper-vigilant focus on black primitivism among white authors, whom Zora Neale Hurston describes as Negrotarians. In these works, the Negro is seldom served by his education and thus "the implication of Stribling's novel is hard to miss" (Rhodes 192). As Chip Rhodes contends, the novel was a core part of the insatiable hunger among white audiences for literature of black life—one that offered a limited, yet highly popularized view of the African American condition, "passion that exceeds political calculation characteriz[ing] the real nature of blacks" (192). In this sense, the same old Negro persists—those "Uncle Toms, Topsies, good 'darkies' and clowns" (Rhodes 258) far removed from the educated black leaders, the intellectual vanguard Du Bois foresaw for the Talented Tenth.

Because of this glaring misrepresentation of black characters in fiction (and later in film), Du Bois sought the birth of a new movement in black art—art that could now "begin this great work of the creation of beauty" ("Criteria" 259), while correcting the pitfalls of American propaganda since "confined to one side while the other is stripped and silent" in the era's conversations of the post-slavery national identity and the shifting conceptions of race. Du Bois, however, was not alone in this creative and intellectual endeavor. In response to the *Crisis* survey, for instance, Walter White challenged the era's overwhelming interest in "the lower or lowest classes" ("The Negro" 193) and instead placed his emphasis on the lives of middle and upper class figures. "Life for any Negro in America has so many different aspects that there is unlimited material for the novelist or short story writer," he contended (193). "For the reasons I have already given, there is no lack of this material among upper-class Negroes if one only has the eye to see it." In contrast, in his widely anthologized essay, "The Negro-Art Hokum," George Schuyler questioned the ability of any black art (outside of Africa) to accurately reflect the racial experience of the diaspora, let alone the ideology that defined the spirit of the day. To him, "[T]o suggest the possibility of any such development among the ten million colored people in this republic is self-evident foolishness" ("The Negro-Art" 164), a fact he found all the more evident among those he referred to as "lampblacked Anglo-Saxon[s]." Both authors, engaging this conversation about how the Negro should be portrayed in art, are thus vital to considering the political novels of the Harlem Renaissance era, their works offering necessary critiques not just of American society at large, but also of the black community in an attempt to define and redefine this notion of the New Negro so vital to the twentieth century.

Deconstructing the "Confederate Romance": Transcending Zip Coonery in Walter White's *The Fire in the Flint*

Of the novels that best anticipated this call, the 1924 work, *The Fire in the Flint* by Walter White, proves one of the more significant, though generally under-read and under-appreciated in the larger body of Harlem Renaissance scholarship, considered less aesthetically powerful than other works of the time. In the novel, fundamentally opposing the popular stereotypes of Dixon and Stribling's works, White depicts a northern-educated black doctor named Kenneth Harper, who quickly discovers that "a life devoted to pure science is impossible and becomes involved more and more in the problems which his people face" (*A Man* 67).[1] Here, White foregrounds the movement toward social justice and presents valuable insight into the ways in which black authors of the era could effectively fulfill this expectation of propaganda and protest as part of a decidedly alternative intellectual strategy aimed directly at racial uplift and social change. Though the text has generally been overlooked in criticism present and past in favor of his more popular work, a 1926 passing novel entitled *Flight*, it transcends the stereotypical Zip Coon and Brute Negro figures (among others) that for too long had misshapen the American cultural imagination regarding race. In their places, he presents a much newer Negro whose "spirit of revolt against bigotry" (White, *A Man* 68) symbolized a necessary shift in direction for a black community far too long repressed.

White essentially begins his critique in his characterization of the novel's protagonist, Dr. Harper—a man desperate for increased opportunities denied him in a prejudicial South where the black community faced limited opportunities for social and economic mobility. In Central City, for instance, "he had always been made to feel that because he was a 'nigger' he was predestined to inferiority" (White, *The Fire* 15). White includes these details first to call attention to the very real presence of a social stigma surrounding blackness,

---

only afforded a second-class status within a society built upon ideals of equality and generally relegated to servile positions as bell boys and maids—the mules of an empowered white world. Under this lens, Harper's supposedly predestined inferiority is disenfranchising, lacking what Cheryl L. Harris describes as "property" (1714)—the historical advantages of white skin in terms of socioeconomic advancement. Harper's perceived inferiority, however, is certainly not static, for his time at Atlanta University and a medical school up north ultimately recast him to some degree as the quintessential New Negro that the Harlem Renaissance sought to promote. This characterization proves integral to the artistic and intellectual project undergirding White's significant, yet underappreciated work. According to Shadi Neimneh, in a 2014 article tracing the issue of interracial violence in literature of the Harlem Renaissance era, "White uses middle-class male protagonists as representative of the New Negro. They are educated, professionally successful, and refined, men after Du Bois' own heart. [The novel has] no prostitutes, cabarets, or vulgar talk/dialect to appeal to stereotypes about blacks" (174).

In constructing the novel this way, White then attempts to transcend the stereotypical vision of the past that invariably shaped societal perceptions of blacks—images not only of uneducated and inferior Negroes, but also images of the types of gin-loving, dice-rolling, hypersexualized black figures who crowd Harlem's buffet flats and cabarets. This, however, was only one part of a much more complex sociocultural critique at the heart of *The Fire in the Flint.* As the racial landscape of the 1910s and 20s grew increasingly violent, marked by a sharp incline in lynchings and Klan membership after the publication of *The Clansman* and its subsequent film adaptation, many in the black community demanded a counter-revolution of resistance in text, "including the freedom to depict revolutionary violence and harsh aspects about black life" (Neimneh 179). But with a cultural imagination still misdirected by past images of black violence, casting a black community as a consistent physical and sexual threat, White chose to avoid images of a violent protagonist, choosing an undying political activism instead as his platform to effect social change. As Neimneh contends, "Critics like Du Bois and White found in the depiction of blacks as violent men or as criminals a perpetuation of the stereotypes they fought against" (179), such as the stereotype of the brute and savage Negro. "Hence, they were careful to represent blacks more as victims of injustice than offenders or imitators of violence" (179) as part of an artistic and intellectual critique. Harper, for instance, opts to help organize the black sharecroppers of the region instead, hoping to further destabilize the already weakened socioeconomic hierarchy in place and, along with it, the notions of racial inferiority and/or superiority that were inextricably linked.

To accomplish this, White describes an intellectual transformation with Harper's character that parallels the shift in political mindset within the African American community at the time. Whereas he once believed that "Booker Washington was right. And the others who were always howling about rights were wrong" (White, *The Fire* 17), in time, his political passivity shifted as "he realized now that the burdens of his race had lain heavy upon him. He had suffered in their suffering, had felt almost as though he had been the victim when he read or heard of a lynching" (149). What White seems to describe in these pages is a clear shift away from the problematic accomodationism of Washington (a source of contention within the black community after his Atlanta Compromise address) as well as the accomodationism much closer to home: Harper's father was respected as the ideal Negro—one who knew to mind his own business—though that respect proved only temporary, since his family was later cheated of their inheritance by white business owners after his death. This shift, too, proves vital to the critique that extends far beyond the novel. From the plantation tradition, the notion of happy darkies and contented slaves was largely predicated upon their refusal to rebel, many crippled by an overwhelming fear of violent backlash or worsened conditions if they spoke out against their oppressive situations. Harper's willingness to act out reveals a far different Negro than the old Negro past. "He had changed," after all, "into a determined and purposeful and ardent worker towards the goal" (149) of racial uplift.

The final elements of White's critique emerge with the protagonist's death, when he is lynched at the end of the novel under the flawed belief that he had assaulted a prominent white woman. As David A. Davis notes, this scene is perhaps the most significant of White's entire work given "the idea of lynching [had] permeated the American racial imaginary, defining the nation's racial hierarchy . . . [and] dehumanizing the victim" (488). In choosing not to describe the grim details of Harper's lynching, simply offering an article published in Central City's local paper, the *Dispatch*, White, like "so many African American writers [sought] to veil the lynching as a means of humanizing the victims [in turn] dehumanizing [its] perpetrators" (Davis 488) previously glorified as the saviors of the South in Dixon's work. Society, in essence, had been operating under a startling misconception of lynching, just as it had long operated under a one-sided view of the American slave. As Du Bois contends in "Criteria of Negro Art," the responsibility of the Negro artist was to correct those critical mistakes by providing a much more accurate portrait of the nation's racial landscape. In the end, White does just that. Through the conclusion, he "subverts the lynchers' intended message [by] portraying the mob as beasts and implicitly questioning the values of a country that would fight for liberty abroad but condone brutality at home" (488). His text had thus become a mirror to the American face, calling attention to the complicity of white Americans in their own moral degradation and the ways in which some whites, very much savage themselves, had contributed to a "mongrelization" of sorts previously attributed only to blacks.

Because of its ideological considerations and its overarching protest against the increasing racial violence in the United States, *The Fire in the Flint* was a vital novel of the overall Harlem Renaissance tradition, even despite its arguable lack of aesthetic success. "Never before," claims Thomas Dyja, "without deference or pleading, had a book displayed the moral and intellectual degradation of white America through the eyes of an angry, disgusted black world" (75). In doing so, White relied on the forum of fiction and its historical implications for the black community—a tool of sociopolitical protest dating back perhaps to William Wells Brown's work *Clotel; or, the President's Daughter* and other works of antebellum fiction advancing the cause of abolition and increased freedoms for blacks. This work, to its core, is, therefore, an essential piece of artistic propaganda—a direct challenge to the existing racial hierarchy and the dominant racial narrative heavily constructed in the era's white-authored texts. And so, it too rings the message Du Bois later solidifies in his 1926 text: black authors of the time should "not care a damn for any art that is not used for propaganda" (259) as "all art is propaganda and ever must be, despite the wailing of the purists" who advocate the necessity of art for art's sake.

A Cross-Cultural Critique: Interrogating the Artificiality of Race in George Schuyler's Satirical *Black No More*

Produced toward the end of the Harlem Renaissance, George Schuyler's 1931 satirical text, *Black No More*, expanded White's central critique, challenging the rich history of Negro caricature and minstrel myth largely built upon a not-so-latent racism and pseudo-scientific belief of black inferiority. In this sense, the worlds of fiction and film served as the epicenter of a mounting racial debate as American citizens, black and white alike, attempted to understand the changing face of American society in the post-slavery and post-Reconstruction days. For authors such as George Schuyler, who would later use their creative works as alternative sites for a cultural and political critique, fiction became that much-needed forum to interrogate the artificiality of race as well as the notion of a national identity, "illuminat[ing] new market possibilities for the trade of racial property in commodity form" (Retman 1449) once restricted to a supposedly superior white elite. This trend is particularly apparent within *Black No More*—an important, yet also relatively under-appreciated work of the Harlem Renaissance era and noted for its engagement of racial conceptions, which heavily defined the racial wasteland that had become the United States. In the novel, Schuyler uses the invention of one Dr. Junius Crookman to upset the racial landscape of American society, offering the Negro masses far too long repressed an opportunity to literally turn white and, in turn, grasp for themselves the very real advantages historically denied them under that notion of whiteness as "property" (Harris 1714).

Desperately searching for increased legal rights, opportunities for social mobility, and any available avenues for economic advancement, the nation's black population flocks to Crookman's clinics—a scenario that Schuyler proposes as part of his overarching intellectual critique of the racial politics that governed the United States. Among them is Max Disher, the protagonist of the novel, one of the earliest candidates for the procedure that will give him white skin, and future leader in the Kings of Nordica (Schuyler's satirical reportraitizing of the Ku Klux Klan). Through Disher, Schuyler thus presents his critique of the racial mindset that had infiltrated all walks of the larger American society, declaring, "Sure, it was taking a chance, but think of getting white in three days! No more jim crow. No more insults. As a white man he could go anywhere, be anything he wanted to be, do almost anything he wanted to do, be a free man at last . . . and probably [even] be able to meet the girl from Atlanta" (*Black* 7). Under this construction, race becomes a reverse minstrel mask—a clear deviation from the dominant racial order that Fauset describes in her essay, "The Gift of Laughter," grease paint historically "used to darken but never to lighten" (164). Through this approach, Schuyler thus uses the forum of fiction—traditionally a tool of social commentary for the African American community engaging in issues of race—as an alternative site to probe the artificiality of race.

Because works such as *Black No More* move beyond the scientific misconceptions about racial inferiority and call into questions socially determined ideologies of race internal and external to the black community, as Charles Scruggs argues, they inherently characterize the different ways "various factors combine (such as color, class, and wealth) to create a society that is complicated in its codes of behavior" (187). The novel then illustrates Disher's attempts to negotiate that very complicated structure of codes no longer inhibited by what he perceives as the limiting forces of blackness—a color identity stigmatized in American society and stripped of the type of "property" only afforded whites. Here the narrator asserts, "He was through with coons, he resolved, from now on. . . . It thrilled him to feel that he was now indistinguishable from nine-tenths of the people of the United States; one of the great majority. Ah, it was good not to be a Negro any longer!" (Schuyler, *Black* 15). In this passage, Schuyler affirms that predominant critique of the Harlem Renaissance era—dissatisfaction with a pervasive hierarchy that impinges upon the opportunities and rights of minorities—a hierarchy largely built on existing notions of "race, which began as an anthropological fiction [and has since transformed into] a sociological fact" ("The Caucasian" 49).

Through such scenes, what Schuyler seems to offer is a startling review of the same flawed belief that Claude McKay, too, finds rampant in the American mindset—the notion "that the color line will be dissolved eventually by light-skinned Negroids 'passing white,' by miscegenation and final assimilation by the white group" (351). In the novel, this proves remarkably untrue. Life for many, after all, does not improve long-term, particularly for the Negro masses that undergo the treatment to obtain white skin, ostracized by the conclusion as the generation of now supra-white (where blackness was once condemned). At the same time, life does not return to the problematic order of the not so distant past, for the white leaders who attempted to preserve that racial divide were ultimately killed for the black ancestral blood coursing through their veins. As Jeffrey B. Ferguson posits in *The Sage of Sugar Hill: George S. Schuyler and the Harlem Renaissance,* his purpose, then, was to "extend the interracial community of laughter that he worked tirelessly to construct around the black/white racial divide" (212) and, "in opposing all attempts to mask the violent foundations of the American racial order . . . [he] undermines all comforting visions of a stable and orderly relationship between black and white" (213)— the type of relationship that texts such as Stribling's novel attempt to reinforce with the restoration of a socially and intellectually powerful white elite and a poor black community (even with its education) unable to advance from underneath.

Ultimately, for Schuyler, "the Aframerican is merely a lampblacked Anglo-Saxon" ("The Negro-Art" 164) and thus "it is sheer non-sense to talk about 'racial differences' . . . In the homes of the same cultural and economic level, one finds similar furniture, literature, and conversation" (165). In this sense, *Black No More* essentially serves the same political function as Schuyler's more traditional academic works, expressed in the wealth of newspaper articles and essays that he produced in the mid-1900s, also "advocat[ing] controversial political positions that contributed to his isolation and ostracism" (Leak ix) within both black and white intellectual circles. In his 1944 essay, "The Caucasian Problem," for instance, Schuyler criticized the overwhelming misuse of the "general terms 'Negro' and 'Caucasian,' 'black' and 'white' [as] convenient propaganda devices to emphasize the great gulf which we are taught to believe exists between these groups of people" (40) and to justify "the line of colonial subjugation and exploitation." Such essays work to collapse that gulf through a more critical and traditionally accepted scholarly lens while his novel, similar in critique and approach, offers readers much earlier a portrait of that new racialized landscape, albeit one fundamentally complicated by the problems that would undoubtedly emerge if the "psychological biracialism" (49), which preserves the divide, was not addressed.

For Ferguson, herein resides the strength of Schuyler's novel and the reasons it remains one of the more significant novels of the time—both part and critique of the larger Harlem Renaissance tradition. In a society turned on its proverbial head with leaders of the recast NAACP turned white and store shelves lined with skin bronzing creams, "the laughter resulting from this humor, in both its constructive and destructive guises, remains *Black No More's* strongest suggestion of a proper attitude toward the race question, even as it laughs at the whole idea of a proper attitude" (214). From Schuyler's point of view, if the Harlem Renaissance is then a failure, as many critics have since contended, it was not so because of its inability to advance the black freedom movement and affect clear socio-political change, as noted critic Harold Cruse asserts. Rather, it may very well be in the championing of race, just as problematic in preserving that "psychological biracialism" (Schuyler, "The Caucasian" 49) and the social significance of race. What is vital then about *Black No More* is that is promotes a portrait of American society in which black is finally no more, where the artifice of race is deconstructed (albeit temporarily), and where a pervasive race consciousness within and without the black community is targeted alongside those very same race mythologies that created this initial concern. For this reason, Du Bois describes *Black No More* as an "extremely significant [book] in Negro American literature" (523)— one that succeeds by "carr[ying] not only scathing criticism of Negro leaders, but of the mass of Negroes . . . [but also] slap[ping] the white people just as hard and unflinchingly straight in the face" (Rev. of *Black* 524).

The Political Aesthetics of the Harlem Renaissance: Socio-Political Engagement in Creative Text

Ultimately, as Jane Kuenz appropriately notes, creative works, such as *Black No More* are "especially valuable now not just for its comic and astute critique of the 'race hysteria' among white historians, anthropologists, and politicians, but for the way it links that hysteria with the parallel essentialist and primitivist rhetoric that emerged among Harlem Renaissance artists and intellectuals at the same time" (171). Color consciousness, after all, was a transplanted tradition, first explored in antebellum literature and the culture of slaves, where light skin offered newfound freedom (as well as fears), depending upon the author's vantage point. By engaging these existing traditions in the context of a new day and age (roughly 1919 to 1935 with the onset of the March riots), authors from Wallace Thurman to Nella Larsen all explored the continued implications of race in shaping the American and African American conditions, as well as the histories of these issues across time, gender, and geographic space. If the Harlem Renaissance was truly a period of cultural and ideological rebirth, as its progenitors promised it to be, the movement away from such traditional binaries of race was just as essential as uplifting the race, not the repetition of the same old conversations of race that had long since been issues of contention in black- and white-authored texts.

Together, *The Fire in the Flint* and *Black No More* thus offer a decidedly different critique than other novels of their time. Schuyler's text, an anti-passing novel in its underlying critique, seeks not to reinforce the tragic mulatto myth—a common criticism of other passing novels from White's *Flight* to Jessie Redmon Fauset's *Comedy: American Style*—but rather to steer the era in a new direction—one away from the racial divide to issues of class and economic power, hoping to reclassify "the categories of racial difference current in the Harlem Renaissance and white racist discourse into economic categories, where they are no longer signs of racial essences, but of whether [an individual was] conscripted into the service of US capitalism, where these same discourses work against the interests of the people they ostensibly protect" (Kuenz 188). White also works to refocus the narrative of the black-authored text, presenting an image of the New Negro as a highly intelligent figure, using his intellectual prowess to usher in a new dawn for a downtrodden black community. In doing so, these works essentially prefigured and fulfilled that Duboisian notion of art as propaganda respectively, using the imaginative forum of fiction as a space to propose new ways of being and new conceptions of American society at the same time as the era's greatest writers and thinkers used traditional academic forums (newspaper articles, essays, speeches, etc.) to set a political agenda for the time. As a result, though these works are sometimes criticized for their aesthetic success or simply forgotten over time, they play a valuable role in not only the Harlem Renaissance, but also the twentieth-century portrait (in flux at the time) of American life—a portrait in a multiplicity of colors and characters, no longer just stereotypes and no longer just black and white.

Note

1. The characterization that White offers of Kenneth Harper in *The Fire and the Flint* is particularly important in the scope of the Harlem Renaissance and its later criticism. Representing the black intellectual, Harper eventually overcomes the rampant isolation from the Negro masses that several writers and thinkers of the era

criticized, from Langston Hughes in *The Big Sea* to Claude McKay in *A Long Way from Home*. In presenting his protagonist in this way, White reveals his idea of the New Negro as an intellectual and part of the middle- to upper-class society, yet not disjointed from the larger black community his work should serve. This thus offers a startling contrast to the notion of crisis among the black intelligentsia that figures like Harold Cruse and Cornel West later cite in their works.

Works Cited

Davis, David A. "Not Only War is Hell: World War I and African American Lynching Narratives." *African American Review* 42.3/4 (2008): 477–491.

Dixon Jr., Thomas. *The Clansman: An Historical Romance of the Ku Klux Klan.* Lexington: U of Kentucky P, 1970.

Du Bois, W. E. B. "Criteria of Negro Art." 1926. *The New Negro: Readings on Race, Representation, and African American Culture, 1892–1938.* Eds. Henry Louis Gates, Jr. & Gene Andrew Jarrett. Princeton: Princeton UP, 2007. 257–260.

_____. Rev. of *Black No More: Being an Account of the Strange and Wonderful Workings of Science in the Land of the Free, A.D. 1933–1940.* 1931. *W. E. B. Du Bois: A Reader.* Ed. David Levering Lewis. New York: Henry Holt, 1995. 523–524.

Dyja, Thomas. *Walter White: The Dilemma of Black Identity in America.* Chicago: Ivan R. Dee, 2008.

Fauset, Jessie Redmon. "The Gift of Laughter." *The New Negro: Voices of the Harlem Renaissance.* 1925. Ed. Alain Locke. New York: Touchstone, 1997. 161–167.

Ferguson, Jeffrey B. *The Sage of Sugar Hill: George S. Schuyler and the Harlem Renaissance.* New Haven: Yale UP, 2005.

Gates, Henry Louis, Jr. & Gene Andrew Jarrett, eds. *The New Negro: Readings on Race, Representation, and African American Culture, 1892–1938.* Princeton: Princeton UP, 2007.

Harris, Cheryl I. "Whiteness as Property." *Harvard Law Review* 106.8 (1993): 1709–1791.

Kuenz, Jane. "American Racial Discourse, 1900–1930: Schuyler's *Black No More.*" *Novel: A Forum on Fiction* 30.2 (1997): 170–192.

Leak, Jeffrey B. Preface. *Rac[e]ing to the Right: Selected Essays of George S. Schuyler.* Ed. Jeffrey B. Leak. Knoxville: U of Tennessee P, 2001. ix–xii.

_____, ed. *Rac[e]ing to the Right: Selected Essays of George S. Schuyler.* Knoxville: U of Tennessee P, 2001.

McKay, Claude. *A Long Way from Home.* 1937. San Diego: Harvest, 1970.

"The Negro in Art: How Shall He Be Portrayed." 1926. *The New Negro: Readings on Race, Representation, and African American Culture, 1892–1938.* Eds. Henry Louis Gates, Jr. & Gene Andrew Jarrett. Princeton: Princeton UP, 2007. 190–204.

Neimneh, Shadi. "Thematics of Interracial Violence in Selected Harlem Renaissance Novels." *Papers on Language & Literature* 50.2 (2014): 152–181.

Nichols Jr., Charles H. "Slave Narratives and the Plantation Legend." *Phylon* 10.3 (1949): 201–210.

Retman, Sonnet H. *"Black No More:* George Schuyler and Racial Capitalism." *PMLA* 123.5 (2008): 1448–1464.

Rhodes, Chip. "'Writing up the New Negro': The Construction of Consumer Desire in the Twenties." *Journal of American Studies* 28.2 (1994): 191–207.

Schuyler, George S. *Black No More.* 1931. Mineola, NY: Dover, 2011.

_____. "The Caucasian Problem." 1944. *Rac[e]ing to the Right: Selected Essays of George S. Schuyler.* Ed. Jeffrey B. Leak. Knoxville: U of Tennessee P, 2001. 37–50.

_____. "The Negro-Art Hokum." *The Politics and Aesthetics of "New Negro" Literature.* New York: Garland, 1996. 164–165.

Scruggs, Charles. "Crab Antics and Jacob's Ladder: Aaron Douglas' Two Views of *Nigger Heaven." Harlem Renaissance Rex-examined: A Revised and Expanded Edition.* Eds. Victor A. Kramer and Robert A. Russ. Troy, NY: Whitston, 1997. 167–195.

White, Walter. *The Fire in the Flint.* Athens: Brown Thrasher, 1996.

_____. *A Man Called White: The Autobiography of Walter White.* Athens: Brown Thrasher, 1995.

"The Bitter River": Langston Hughes and the Violent South

Seretha D. Williams

The editors of the August 1921 edition of *The Crisis* published an English translation of a letter written by a Mexican national. The letter, published under the heading "Mexico Marvels," was submitted to *The Crisis* by Langston Hughes, "an American . . . living in Mexico" (171). Miguel de Zarraga, author of the letter, decries the re-emergence of the Ku Klux Klan and the rise of racial and religious hatred in the United States. He argues, "Lynch law was the product of this hate, and it is still practiced here with impunity" (171). Hughes, residing with his expatriate father James Hughes, submitted frequently to *The Crisis*, his formative poem "The Negro Speaks of Rivers" published two months earlier. The letter—with its focus on intolerance and tyranny—is consonant with Hughes' poetic vision, what Maryemma Graham describes as Hughes' social art (214). Hughes' submission of this letter is evidence that, from the beginning of his literary career, Hughes is socially and politically conscious and motivated to affect change. In 1921, Hughes was an aspiring student and writer who hoped to attend Columbia University in Harlem; he was not yet one of the leading voices of the social and political movement that would be described as a renaissance marking the birth of a new "Negro." Nevertheless, Hughes—the grandson of Mary whose first husband had been Charles Lewis Sheridan Leary, a participant in John Brown's Raid at Harper's Ferry, VA, and the grandnephew of the renowned lawyer, ambassador, and politician John Mercer Langston—was primed to use his art to denounce the pervasive and debilitating violence done to black bodies. America, post-slavery, continued to be a dangerous place for black people, and Hughes' canon reflects his preoccupation with the culture of violence that compelled Southern blacks to move en masse to other regions.

Ida B. Wells-Barnett's widely circulated pamphlet *Southern Horrors: Lynch Law in All Its Phase*; investigative lynching reports in African-American newspapers, such as Robert Abbott's the *Chicago Defender*; the prevalence of 1920s lynching dramas;[1] and the NAACP's campaign to implement anti-lynching legislation are a few examples of citizens' public efforts to eradicate American lynching culture. Hughes, too, makes public the "lawless killing of black men and women," acts Hughes proclaims are "old Southern custom going back to slavery days" (Mettress, *The Lynching* 125). Christopher Metress and W. Jason Miller, whose work builds upon the earlier scholarship of Trudier Harris and Sandra Gunning, have written extensively on lynching and Hughes' literary and journalistic responses to specific lynchings. Miller identifies four forms of lynching—spectacle, mob, legal, and domestic terrorism—in Hughes' canon (3–4). Furthermore, Miller proposes that the site of trauma, for Hughes, is specific and symbolic; his analysis draws upon the concepts of "topophobia" and "topophilia"[2] to explain Hughes' treatment of place and responses to lynchings. While Miller is interested in the recurrence of lynching as topic and trope in Hughes' poetry, Metress' study of Hughes concentrates more narrowly on Hughes' response to the Emmett Till lynching in 1955. By tracing the publication history of Hughes' poem "Mississippi—1955," Metress uncovers the poem's original context as a lynch poem. Miller's and Metress' analyses of Hughes' lynch poems, his treatment of place, and his overt (and covert) protests against American lynching culture are correct. Hughes historicizes the violence and oppression of blacks in America. He documents and reminds his readers of "the repeated suffering of the lynched black man" (Thurston). However, Hughes' poems about the violence of the American South perform and transcend the perfunctory tasks of documenting and decrying.

Richard Rankin Russell suggests, "Hughes' poems break the news of this tragedy through the power they draw from the blues" (153). Implicit in Russell's statement is the belief that bad news should be broken or carefully delivered. Hughes, then, in certain instances, serves as an itinerant mourner breaking the news of violent act after violent act. Violence in America, especially the South, he reveals, is persistent and pervasive. Approximately four thousand known lynchings of African Americans occurred in the South between the 1880s to the 1960s. Lynchings were only one form of violence African Americans endured. Hughes, a chronicler of black experiences, wrote extensively about the rape and exploitation of black women's bodies, the rampant domestic violence normalized in black heterosexual relationships, and the psychological trauma of oppression and economic disenfranchisement.[3] Hughes conveys this pervasiveness in his lynch poems by describing the violence as inherent to the natural landscape of the South. "Blue Bayou,[4]" "Song for a Dark Girl," "Christ in Alabama," "The Bitter River," "Mississippi—1955," and "Birmingham Sunday" are representative poems[5] that correlate violence and landscape, expanding upon core themes of the Harlem Renaissance introduced by other key poets, such as Claude McKay, Sterling A. Brown, and Countee Cullen.

"Blue Bayou" describes the tragic lynching of a man ensnared in an interracial "love" triangle. The speaker laments the loss of Lou to Old Greeley; the circumstances of this betrayal are unclear, but we do know that the speaker is black and Greeley is white. Hughes uses the environment of the bayou, a land feature unique to the lower Mississippi Valley region, to foreshadow the fated demise of the speaker. The bayou is blue with a blues that hovers over the land and the people who live there. The speaker has the blues because Greeley has taken his mate. As the speaker moves through the bayou, he grows agitated at his inability to stop Greeley or to protect Lou, who presumably is taken away against her will. Hughes uses the "setting sun," a standard blues motif, to indicate the action of the poem. The tension builds as the sun moves lower in the sky, and the climax of the poem occurs just as the sun sets. As the sun goes down, the protagonist dies. The sun, then, a part of the natural setting of the bayou, embodies the anger, hatred, and violence inherent in the racial landscape of the South. The slow pace of the poem replicates both the leisurely setting of the sun and the measured breaths of the speaker dying an agonizing death. His demise is accented by the repetition of the word *down*; the poem moves us downward until the sun and the speaker are no more. The ugliness of the lynching supplants the reader's image of the beauty of the bayou sunset. Hughes, through his description, gives poetic form to the physical and psychological violence rooted in southern culture and practice. Violence, he proposes, is inherent in the racial landscape of the South.[6]

Moreover, the italicized chant of the lynch mob is interspersed with the speaker's exhaustive account of his final moments. His voice remains calm, while the voice of the lynch mob is excited, as indicated by the command to *"Put him on a rope/ And pull him higher!"* (lines 20–21). The higher the speaker ascends, the lower the sun descends. The blue of the bayou diminishes, and by the final stanza, the bayou that was as red as fire (line 15) is now itself "[a] pool of fire" (line 23). What remains at the end of the poem is violence and blood. Although the imagery of the setting sun suggests the inevitability of the lynching, Hughes provides minimal description of the act itself. His restraint shifts attention away from the spectacle of the ritualized violence toward the human life in its final moments, and, in doing so, Hughes preserves a degree of dignity for the victim. The persona, now a disembodied voice, invokes a prayer in the last line: "Lawd I saw the sun go down!" (line 27). "Blue Bayou" suggests that "ultimately blacks are lynched because they are powerless, because they have none but God to protect them" (Jemie 144).

While "Blue Bayou" is told from the point of view of the lynching victim, "Song for a Dark Girl" describes a young woman's struggle to deal with the recurring image of her murdered lover. At the forefront of the poem is the girl's palpable grief. Here, the persona asks "the white Lord Jesus/What was the use of prayer" (lines 7–8). Though the question is not answered directly, indirectly the reader surmises the response. Hughes does not offer prayer. Rather, he raises poignant questions about African Americans' relationship to the religion of their oppressors and engages in a discourse with other texts within African American letters that ask similar questions about divine justice. Benjamin E. Mays' *The Negro's God, as Reflected in His Literature* calls attention to the rise of religious skepticism in the works of Harlem Renaissance writers, including Hughes and Countee Cullen. However, earlier texts, such as the slave narratives of Harriet Jacobs and Frederick Douglass, reflect similar tendencies by African American writers to question a God who seemingly does not answer the prayers of the black masses. In *"A God of Justice?": The Problem of Evil in Twentieth-Century Black Literature*, Quiana J. Whitted extends the theme of the abandoned masses forward to contemporary writers, such as Rachel Eliza Griffith, who write about post-Hurricane Katrina New Orleans.[7] Griffith, like Hughes, writes about tragedy and the seeming absence of God.

In the poem, expanding upon the earlier critique, the lover's black body, hanged on a crossroads tree, is positioned against the idea of the white Jesus. Through the figure of the crossroads tree, Hughes recalls the conventional use of this image in folk accounts of encounters with the devil and, in doing so, replicates the moral, racial, and religious intersections that complicate the culture of the South. Hughes evokes images of Christ's crucifixion, and by placing the black man on a "cross," he proposes that the man, like Christ, is persecuted by those who stand on the side of injustice and intolerance. The comparison equates black suffering with divine suffering; in this equation, whites, then, are on the side of evil. Moreover, the parallel placement of "my black young lover" (line 3) and "the white Lord Jesus" (line 7) in stanzas one and two ironically inverts the roles of the black lover and the white Jesus. Love, the mourning woman posits, is embodied in her lover, not in Christ; the lover, as a result, bears the burdens of the whites' sins. In the third stanza, competing images of Christian ideology and Christian practice fuse, and the speaker surmises: "Love is a naked shadow/On a gnarled and naked tree" (lines 11–12). The brutal practices of those who identify as Christian undermine the Christian doctrine of love.

The lover, now a figure of piety, does not transcend the physical, moving beyond the body into the divine; although the speaker describes his body as "a naked shadow" (line 11), the lover remains mortal. Hughes allows the image of the body hanging from the tree to speak for itself. He offers no direct commentary. Literally, the dark girl's love is hanged on the tree, and figuratively, the gnarled tree suggests the elusiveness of love in an environment so distorted and blatantly diseased. Certainly, whatever innocence the girl might have had has now been subsumed by the very grown-up reality of racial violence in the South. The ironic echoes of the Confederate anthem "Dixie" remind the reader that racial violence and intolerance are a part of the social fabric of the South. To illustrate this concept, the poem repeats the last line in the song; as such, "Way Down South in Dixie" serves as the unifying element or refrain for the poem. Hughes intentionally uses this song as a way of articulating complicated realities about the South. "Dixie" calls for Southerners to raise arms, to live or die for the ideals of the Confederacy. Unmistakably, Hughes avows southern culture is predicated upon its use of violence against black bodies. The light-hearted cadence of the poem underscores the absurdity of this tragedy; the female speaker mocks the South, using a voice dripping with sarcasm and contempt.

"Blue Bayou" and "Song for a Dark Girl," published in 1927, are indicative of Hughes' early responses to violence against blacks. The poems announce and decry the violence, but as Anthony Dawahare asserts, "Hughes' [Harlem Renaissance] subjects are politically incapacitated by a weariness of social oppression" (26). However, Hughes continued to develop his social art and began to write more overtly and boldly about injustice. The poem "Christ in Alabama," written in response to the March 25, 1931 arrest of nine young black youths on a Southern Railroad freight run, is a scathing indictment of the absence of justice in the Alabama legal system. The poem sparked heated debate because of its depiction of Christ as a lynched black man. "Christ in Alabama" and its accompanying satirical essay, "Southern Gentlemen, White Women, and Black Boys," were published in an unofficial local newspaper, *Contempo*, in North Carolina. Hughes explains in his second autobiography *I Wonder As I Wander*, "It was an ironic poem inspired by the thought of how Christ, with no human father, would be accepted were He born in the South of a Negro mother" (46). Linking the crucified black Christ, a recurrent metaphor in African American literary tradition, to the Scottsboro case proposes that the victims, although not physically killed, are lynched by the legal system and denied justice by humans and by God. As Whitted surmises, the displacement of Christ for the black man puts Southern white Christians in the role of crucifier (36). Certainly for Hughes, the Scottsboro Nine are emblematic of the violent lynching culture of the American South.

Hughes composes the stanzas in threes and, in doing so, evokes an alternate version of the holy family: the bastard son, the mammy/mother, the white master/father. In tercet one, Christ the son is "[b]eaten and black" (line 2); the image simultaneously recalls images of a crucified Christ, a whipped slave, and a lynched black man. Mouth bloodied, Christ by the fourth stanza is wholly human with no hope of emancipation from the "Cross of the South." His white father has forsaken him. The mulatto trope recurs as image and theme throughout Hughes' work; in this poem, the biracial Christ-figure attests to the hypocrisy of white Christian men who, on the one hand, impregnate black women and, on the other hand, treat black people as less than human. In tercet two, Mary the mother is "Mammy of the South" instead of a divine woman full of grace or the mother of God; furthermore, the victim of a rape or perhaps a coerced relationship, she is silenced, unable to decry the injustice enacted upon her body and her son's body. Finally, in tercet three, God the father is described as "White master above" (line 8), a phrase replete with biblical and historical meanings. The doubleness of the line reifies Hughes' underlying admonition: black suffering is without merit, and justice—legal and divine—is illusive.

In "Christ in Alabama", the characters seem as politically incapacitated as the personas in "Blue Bayou" and "Song for a Dark Girl." However, the tone of "Christ in Alabama" suggests an agency missing in the other two poems. Hughes' diction is intentionally confrontational; his imagery is sharp and specific. While the first two poems are impressionistic, "Christ in Alabama" is direct and sardonic. In "The Bitter River," Hughes is equally confrontational. First published in the Autumn 1942 issue of *Negro Quarterly*, "The Bitter River" documents and reacts to the lynching of Ernest Green and Charlie Lang on October 12, 1942. Green's and Lang's bodies were found beneath the Shubuta Bridge over the Chicasawhay

River in Mississippi. The bridge was known locally as the "Hanging Bridge," a suspension bridge where more than seven lynchings occurred (Miller 68). In the same year, Cleo Wright and Howard Walsh were lynched in Missouri and Mississippi, respectively. In "The Bitter River," the river functions on multiple levels. It is simultaneously the site of violence against black bodies and the symbol of the bitter racism that permeates the American South. The poem moves from the specifics of the lynching to a broader statement about African Americans' relationship to and encounter with the South. The imagery of the lines "the blood of the lynched boys . . . / Mixed with the hopes that are drowned there" (lines 11, 13) intimates that racial hatred has become a part of the natural topography or landscape. The poisoned river, then, is the source of strangled dreams (line 16), and the imagery of the bloodied river merges with the imagery of the red clay of the South to connote the pervasiveness of this tainting. The speaker's response to this contamination of American society is corporeal. He seems literally to taste the swill of oppression and exploitation, and he describes how "its gall coats the red of my tongue" (line 10).

Hughes moves from his abstraction of the oppression and exploitation of blacks to a more concrete delineation of the wrongs exacted upon this group. In stanza three, he draws upon the concluding image of stanza two, which posits that the river refracts light rather than reflects it, to discuss the absence of light—a metaphor for hope—in the lives of blacks. Some of these disenfranchised figures include sharecroppers, muggers, prostitutes, and labor leaders. Hughes calls by name the Scottsboro Boys and reminds his readers that not long ago:

> Behind closed doors liberal ministers and racist Governors debated the fate of black youngsters unjustly imprisoned. In 1937 the State of Alabama compromised, allowing four of the nine boys to go free. In return, the SDC promised that Communists would not agitate about Scottsboro. The Communists agreed, and such agitation, propaganda, and literature virtually disappeared. (Murray 85)

Hughes keeps alive the memory of the miscarriage of justice the Scottsboro Nine represent. Moreover, Hughes expands his definition of lynching to include victims of racism, classism, and sexism. Each named group exemplifies the downtrodden of American society for whom the American Dream has faded. Though their circumstances are different, these people are the victims of ideological hatred. He traces the source of oppression backwards to a slavery that left "grandfather's back with its ladder of scars" (line 35) and indicts the system of American injustice. The metonym of the steel bars imprisoning African Americans—physically and psychologically—takes over the imagery of darkness and sets up the stylistic shift in voice and tone in stanza four. The bars remind us of the steel of the bridge and that Hughes visited Kirby Prison where eight of the Scottsboro Boys were held.

In stanza four, Hughes disrupts the flow of parallelisms in earlier stanzas and interposes the persona of a "you" who seemingly represents the voices of whites who suggest, "Wait, be patient', you say/'Your folks will have a better day" (lines 38–39). The speaker and Hughes reject the call for patience. Instead, falling back on the image of the poisoned bitter river, Hughes implies that the level of deceit is so apparent that "[t]he swirl of the bitter river/Sweeps your lies away" (lines 48–49). Too much time has passed, and too little change has occurred. Fatigued, Hughes asserts, blacks are "tired of the bitter river! / Tired of the bars" (lines 88–89) and immune to the hatred they have been compelled to swallow without complaint for generations. Oppressive tactics have made them stronger not weaker. "The Bitter River" does not end as "Blue Bayou" and "Song for a Dark Girl" end, with a sense of resignation; instead, the poem and Hughes call for immediate action. Ritualized violence persists, despite grassroots and political efforts to enact legislation, and Hughes' language conveys the urgency of his plea.

The year 1955 would be just as urgent and dangerous. The brutal murder and lynching of Emmett Till, a fourteen-year-old boy from Chicago visiting family in Money, Mississippi, horrified most of the nation. Till was targeted because he allegedly flirted with a white woman. He was tortured and his body thrown into the river. Until

Christopher Metress' article, many scholars failed to connect Hughes' poem "Mississippi" to the Emmett Till lynching.[8] The original poem was untitled and appeared in Hughes' *Chicago Defender* column, "Here to Yonder," as an epigraph to the article "Langston Hughes Wonders Why No Lynching Probe." Hughes, then, granted permission to other news organizations to publish the poem with the title "Mississippi—1955." According to Metress, some publications misprinted the poem, and, later, Hughes revised the poem and changed the title to "Mississippi." The historical context and importance of the poem was lost as the specific markers to Till were edited out. Mettress' recovery work is vital. Reading "Mississippi" as a lament for Emmett Till enhances our understanding of the poem and of Hughes' intentions. Hughes not only announces the tragedy of Emmett Till, but he also invites readers to mourn. The poem, an epigraph to the column, breaks the news. It prepares readers for the bad news of the article—the news that, again, nothing is done to stop the violence. It situates Till alongside Lang and Green, other fourteen year olds who were lynched. In the article, Hughes asks whether nothing will be done to stop the murder of children. The mutilated body of Till is not on display. Instead, Hughes focuses on the grief, the loss of life. In the moment of 1955, a year after the Supreme Court decision *Brown v. Board of Education*, Hughes understands the nation needs to mourn this life, these lives. Indeed, Hughes denounces this pervasive violence and insists something be done, but he also grieves Till, Ernest, and Green.

News articles and photographs do not facilitate this contemplation and grieving in the same ways as poetry. When Hughes writes about lynching in other media, his purpose is different. The poem opens with a contest of sorrow, pity, and pain. The lines are exclamatory statements. The speaker is traumatized, but not surprised. The original draft of the poem, according to Metress' research, ends with the lines:

THAT TEARS AND BLOOD
SHOULD MIX LIKE RAIN/ IN MISSISSIPPI—
AND TERROR, FETID HOT,
YET CLAMMY COLD,
REMAIN. (lines 18–23)[9]

Till's lynched body haunts the poem. Terror remains. Hughes' subsequent revisions of the poem assert that terror not only comes again to Mississippi, but also remains. Actually, it never left. Russell asserts that the poem asks us to engage in a deep imaginative identification with that tortured body and soul" (157), although the body itself is not present or described. According to Myisha Priest's close reading of the poem and column, "Hughes calls for the named and unnamed dead to stand forth in the body of his column, addressing the political utility of the lynched body" (62). Priest and other scholars cite the Till murder as a galvanizing event for the development of the American Civil Rights Movement.

Eight years later, another horrific act of violence would shock America, and Hughes would be called upon to name the dead and to eulogize murdered black children. "Birmingham Sunday," an elegy, announces and denounces the murder of four African American girls killed by a bomb in an Alabama church in 1963. The racially motivated attack on the Sixteenth Street Church outraged the nation and marked a turning point in the struggle for civil rights. The deaths of the four girls—Cynthia Wesley, Denise McNair, Addie Collins, and Carole Robertson—framed a larger debate over racial integration. Police Commissioner Eugene "Bull" Connor and other city officials incensed the community by blaming the bombing on the 1954 Supreme Court decision *Brown v. Board of Education*. Hughes' poem calls for an appropriate and immediate response to this violence, but of equal importance, it focuses on the bloodshed and the lives lost. Hughes' authorial pose in "Birmingham Sunday" is consistent with his earlier poetic responses to violence; he situates the primary tragedy—the deaths of four little girls—squarely at the center of his denunciation.

In stanza one, the speaker positions the serenity of Sunday school next to the violent explosion of dynamite that blew out the walls and windows of the church and displaces the innocence of the children's prayers with the chaos and inexplicability of bloodied walls. Hughes' language is graphic: "With spattered flesh / And bloodied Sunday dresses / Torn to shreds by dynamite" (lines 6–8). He recounts the specificity of the horrific scene and then blurs the imagery of red by conflating the red blood of the girls with the Red (or Communism) of China. He raises images of two Chinas—an ancient China that invented dynamite and a Red China, a contrast that somehow links the bloodiness of this Birmingham event to the Chinese Communist Revolution. The underlying meaning or subtext of the stanza suggests that the United States is hypocritical in its criticism of undemocratic civilizations. Here in America, little girls are blown up in sacred spaces, while politicians are preoccupied with defending the nation from a perceived threat by a "godless" Communism. Moreover, Hughes' reference to the Chinese invention of explosives locates the violence in Birmingham in a broader historical context. War and hatred span centuries and millennia. These martyred girls and the Civil Rights Movement are a part of a larger historical struggle against intolerance.

In the second stanza, Hughes revisits this idea of the dynamite. This time, the dynamite refers to a different type of explosion, a collective response to this act of hatred. Hughes again invokes China, asserting that the difference between a Chinese response and African American response is that Christian influence teaches African Americans to do unto others as they would have them do unto them. He points again to hypocrisy. This time, he singles out self-proclaimed southern Christians, who would attack a church in the name of racism. The ideology and practice of non-violence, upon which the Civil Rights Movement was predicated, the speaker suggests, might be ineffective in bringing about change among people who do not subscribe to their own religious teachings. The poem tells us that "Four tiny girls" (line 1) await action; their deaths must be avenged, but, first, they must be mourned.

Certainly, in the final stanza of the poem, the speaker calls for new songs "among magnolia trees (line 27)," a symbol of the South. President John F. Kennedy, assassinated in November 1963, only two months after the Birmingham bombing, had called for legislation on civil rights in the summer of 1963. President Lyndon Johnson signed the Civil Rights Act of 1964 the following summer. Hughes' call for change was answered, only to a degree. The deaths of these four girls served as one impetus for social upheaval in the 1960s, but violence persists in the South. On June 17, 2015, nine African Americans were and killed during Bible study at Emmanuel A.M.E. Church in Charleston, SC. The shooter is white. The continued violence against black bodies thus speaks to the relevance of Hughes' poems even today, as Hughes' response to violence evolved over his career. During the Harlem Renaissance, his poetry described and documented black suffering, but increasingly, his poetry made direct appeals for action. Moreover, Hughes, recognized the African American community's need to mourn. He bestowed dignity upon the victims of violence and created opportunities within his poems for readers to mourn the dead.

Notes

1. Judith L. Stephens' article, "Racial Violence and Representation: Performance Strategies in Lynching Dramas of the 1920s," provides a detailed summary of the development of the lynching drama genre. Stephens posits, "lynching dramas function as a dynamic cultural text by both conserving the memory of this particular form of racial violence and continuing to evolve as a theatrical genre on the American stage" (656).

2. Miller's proposed "topophilia" captures the affection a person connects to a place. He uses "topophobia" to describe the fears and anxieties a person associates with a place (9).

3. "Mammy of the South," "Mulatto," and "Cross," for instance, address the exploitation and rape of black women's bodies by white men. The allegation of raping a white woman generally was enough justification for lynch mobs to lynch black men and for juries to sentence them to death. Hughes challenges the supposition that black men were sexual threats and suggests, instead, that white men posed a greater threat to black women. Hughes offers the existence of fatherless "mulatto" children as evidence. Hughes, in addition, addresses the violence done to black women by black men. Poems such as "Bad Man," "Beale Street," and "Evil Woman" attest to the danger of being black and female. Joyce Ann Joyce and Donna Akiba Sullivan Harper discuss Hughes' depiction of black women and his treatment of black women's issues including rape and domestic violence. See Joyce's "Race Culture, and Gender in Langston Hughes' *The Ways of White Folks*" in *Langston Hughes: The Man,*

His Art, and His Continuing Influence and Harper's *Not So Simple The "Simple" Stories by Langston Hughes* for further discussion of gendered violence in Hughes' short stories.

4. The versions of Hughes' poems referenced are those included in *The Collected Poems of Langston Hughes* edited by Arnold Rampersad and David Roessel. However, I refer to Hughes' original draft of "Mississippi," which is also known as "Mississippi—1955" and as an untitled work.

5. In "Red Clay Blues," for example, Hughes addresses the African American migrant experience. The poem contrasts the hard concrete of the city with the red clay of rural Georgia. The red clay is a metonym for the culture of the South. In "Georgia Dusk," the landscape and sky betray the truths that belie the beauty of the South. For Hughes, Georgia spaces are transformed by the racism and violence; the sky and wind, contaminated by the ugliness of hate, bleed and cry. Blood is "in the Georgia dusk." The wind "scatters hate like seed." The first two lines of "The South" establish Hughes' dualistic reading of the American South. In line one, the personified South is "lazy, laughing," but Hughes immediately juxtaposes this initial image with one of the South as a carnivore "With blood on its mouth" (line 2). Hughes continues to develop this juxtaposition of the South as a site of great beauty and tradition and a site of brutality and intolerance. Simultaneously, the South is "sunny-faced" (line 3), "idiot-brained" (line 5), "child-minded" (line 6), and "magnolia-scented" (line 12).

6. James de Jongh describes Hughes' use of place as a "spatial signing" or application of "spiritual geography" inherited from figurative practices of earlier black writers. Other critics, too, parse Hughes' treatment of place. Hughes, in fact, constructs extended metaphors or conceits using nature as his trope. These Hughesian conceits draw on a particular set of images—land, water, sun, and trees—and express what for Hughes is almost inexpressible.

7. Whitted analyzes Griffith's poem "Hymn to a Hurricane" included in *Callaloo*'s special issue "American Tragedy: New Orleans under Water" (183).

8. Hughes also wrote the lyrics to "Money, Mississippi Blues," a song about Emmett Till. Metress was instrumental in the recovery of that text as well. See Metress' *The Lynching of Emmett Till: A Documentary Narrative* for further discussion of the song.

9.   Hughes ends the version of "Mississippi" in *The Collected Poems of Langston Hughes* with the lines, "That tears and blood/ Still mix like rain/ In Mississippi!" (lines 18–20).

Works Cited

Dawahare, Anthony. "Langston Hughes' Radical Poetry and the "End of Race." *MELUS* 23.3 (Autumn 1998): 21–41.

de Jongh, James. "The Poet Speaks of Places: A Close Reading of Langston Hughes Literary Use of Place." *A Historical Guide to Langston Hughes*. Oxford: Oxford UP, 2004. 65–84.

de Zarraga, Miguel. "Mexico Marvels." *The Crisis* 21–22 (1921): 171.

Gates Jr., Henry Louis, and K. A. Appiah, eds. *Langston Hughes: Critical Perspectives Past and Present*. New York: Amistad, 1993.

Graham, Maryemma. "The Practice of a Social Art." *Langston Hughes: Critical Perspectives Past and Present*. Eds. Henry Louis Gates, Jr. & K. A. Appiah. New York: Amistad, 1993. 213–235.

Harper, Donna Akiba Sullivan. *Not So Simple: The "Simple" Stories by Langston Hughes*. Columbia: U of Missouri P, 1996.

Jemie, Onwuchekwa. "Or Does It Explode?" *Langston Hughes: Critical Perspectives Past and Present*. Eds. Henry Louis Gates, Jr. & K. A. Appiah. New York: Amistad, 1993. 135–171.

Joyce, Joyce A. "Race, Culture, and Gender in Langston Hughes' *The Ways of White Folks*." *Langston Hughes: The Man, His Art, and His Continuing Influence*. Ed. James C. Trotman. New York: Garland, 1995.

Metress, Christopher. "Langston Hughes' 'Mississippi—1955': A Note on Revisions and an Appeal for Reconsideration." *African American Review* 37.1 (Spring 2003): 139–148.

_____. *The Lynching of Emmett Till: A Documentary Narrative*. Charlottesville: U of Virginia P, 2002.

Miller, W. Jason. *Langston Hughes and American Lynching Culture*. Gainesville, FL: U of Florida P, 2011.

Priest, Myisha. "Flesh that Needs to Be Loved: Langston Hughes Writing the Body of Emmett Till." *Emmett Till in Literary Memory and Imagination*. Eds. Harriet Pollack & Christopher Metress. Baton Rouge, LA: LSU Press, 2008. 53–74.

Rampersad, Arnold & David Roessel. *The Collected Poems of Langston Hughes*. New York: Vintage, 1995.

Russell, Richard Rankin. "Down in the Delta: Tallahatchie County, Mississippi, and Langston Hughes' Blues Poetry about Emmett Till." *Five Points*. 16.2 (Winter 2015): 147–163.

Stephens, Judith L. "Racial Violence and Representation: Performance Strategies in Lynching Dramas of the 1920s." *African American Review*. 33.4 (Winter 1999): 655–671.

Thurston, Michael. "Black Christ, Red Flag: Langston Hughes on Scottsboro." *College Literature* 22.3 (Oct 1995). *Academic Search Complete*. Web. 6 Jul. 2015.

Whitted, Quiana. *"A God of Justice?": The Problem of Evil in Twentieth-Century Black Literature*. Charlottesville: U of Virginia P, 2009.

Racial Connections in "Time Space": A Chronotopic Approach to Johnson's *The Autobiography of an Ex-Colored Man*

Holly Simpson Fling

Though the enslavement of Africans occurred in various parts of the world, in the United States, the institution of slavery was primarily a southern phenomenon because, in contrast to the industrialized North, with crops such as cotton, rice, and sugarcane, the South was more agrarian. If enslavement is a vocalization of the South, then each racial issue following emancipation is an echo of that cry, a gouging of an unhealed wound. These reverberations are not uniform, though; they string together various points in an asymmetrical web that constrains African Americans. Those who are able to pass for white, however, are often able to avoid racial constraints. This unjust national history resounds in James Weldon Johnson's text, *The Autobiography of an Ex-Colored Man*, as the economic and political underpinnings of racism drive much of the plot, propelling the passing body through time-space intersections, points where space meets with time to disrupt traditional power structures and allow for social change.

Juda Bennett explains in *The Passing Figure: Racial Confusion in Modern American Literature* that while tens of thousands of blacks are estimated to have passed for white, especially between 1880 and 1925, the necessity of secrecy *then* makes it difficult to document passing *now* (2). Obviously, passing happened during other periods (Bennett 3), particularly before emancipation, but for such a large number of passers to have been narrowed down to this specific time period between 1880 and 1925 suggests that blacks were passing simply to be treated as humans—to avoid sitting in the Jim Crow car or to make their way to the ballot box without being harassed. The passing body, then, can be thought of as a metonym for the dehumanizing problems and hazards blacks experienced from enslavement into the twentieth century, from lynching and Jim

Crow to complications due to economic competition between races and disenfranchisement.

The significance of time-space intersections in *The Autobiography of an Ex-Colored Man* can be understood through an interpretation of M. M. Bakhtin's concept of the chronotope. In *The Dialogic Imagination*, Bakhtin defines the chronotope as four-dimensional, inseparable "time space" (84), and he perceives "[t]he image of man [as] always intrinsically chronotopic" (85). In Johnson's novel, for example, the ex-colored man himself is an embodiment of time and space. As he ages and matures through the years and over the course of the text, his body both *is* a space and *takes up* space; it is both an ever-changing inner-space due to his shifting thoughts and ideas, and it transforms the space through which he moves. For Bakhtin, "[i]n the literary artistic chronotope, spatial and temporal indicators are fused into one carefully thought-out, concrete whole" (84); thus, the three-dimensional space of the ex-colored man's body and the one-dimensional time of his life—that is, the fragments of his life that he offers in his narrative—come together at a specific point to create a single four-dimensional entity, his character. Approaching *The Autobiography of an Ex-Colored Man* through Bakhtin's chronotope, then, reveals how the act of racial passing, a metonym for seemingly disparate nineteenth-century racial issues—enslavement, lynching, Jim Crow, economic competition between blacks and whites, and disenfranchisement—mobilizes race as a means of propelling African American literature into the twentieth century.

As a child growing up during the second half of the nineteenth century, the ex-colored man assumes that he is white; he only recognizes his racially mixed background after the schoolteacher excludes him from a group of "white scholars" (Johnson 11). This realization unsettles the protagonist, as, after observing the way African American children are treated by white children, he has "a very strong aversion to being classed with them" (15). Once he is marked as "colored" (11), however, he ineluctably "pass[es] into another world" (14), a "time space" in which he finds that an African American "is forced to take his outlook on all things, not from the viewpoint of a citizen, or a man, or even a human being, but from the viewpoint of a *colored* man" (14). For the protagonist, this loss of white privilege is disconcerting to the point that he becomes "reserved" and "suspicious" (15).

These feelings appear to stem in part from the unknown, the taboo subject of race, as when he later reads Harriet Beecher Stowe's *Uncle Tom's Cabin*, the text provides the protagonist with enough understanding that he is finally able to communicate openly about race with his mother. He recalls, "What she told me interested and even fascinated me; and, what may seem strange, kindled in me a strong desire to see the South" (Johnson 30). During the nineteenth century, the South contrasts sharply with the North, where he has lived for most of his life, but, because the protagonist does not experience the full effects of dehumanizing racism in the North, he appears to believe that he cannot be touched by these forces in the South either. He becomes further encouraged after becoming immersed in his friend Shiny's graduation performance of Wendell Phillips' "Toussant L'Ouverture," an abolition speech about heroism. The ex-colored man explains, "I felt leap within me pride that I was colored; and I began to form wild dreams of bringing glory and honor to the Negro race" (Johnson 32). The speech triggers a realization that he is part of a larger group, and in that moment, he imagines himself the hero of his newly claimed race; however, this vision is only possible due to his position in the North.

Once the ex-colored man actually experiences the oppression of the South, he forgets his aspirations, only recalling them years later when he is in Berlin and hears a man develop the ragtime music he had just played into a classical piece. Amazed, he realizes,

> I had been turning classic music into ragtime, a comparatively easy task; and this man had taken ragtime and made it classic. The thought came across me like a flash—It can be done, why can't I do it? From that moment my mind was made up. I clearly saw the way of carrying out the ambition I had formed when a boy. (Johnson 103–4)

The protagonist, caught up in the act of survival in the years after his mother's death, needs to step outside of the space of the United States to regain focus. Traveling through Europe, then, enables a clearer analysis of the United States culture from the outside looking in, and this examination affects him in a manner similar to the inspiration he feels during Shiny's speech. He explains, "The desire to begin work grew stronger each day. I could think of nothing else. I made up my mind to go back into the very heart of the South, to live among the people, and drink in my inspiration first-hand" (Johnson 104). Though Farah Jasmine Griffin claims the South is "a site of terror and exploitation" (5), she also acknowledges that it is the "site of the ancestor" (5). While black roots clearly reach much farther than the South, memories of this location as an ancestral site are fresher than those of Africa because, at this point, formerly enslaved men and women are still living, still sharing stories, and still singing songs from the past. "Time space" as an inseparable entity is important to the ex-colored man's decision to leave his benefactor and travel to the South because he knows he must return to this specific location if he is to collect these songs before those who knew them firsthand, those who sang them alongside others as they worked in the fields, are gone.

Bakhtin discusses literary development as "unfold[ing] not so much in a straight line as spasmodically, a line with 'knots' in it" (113). In Johnson's text, these knots can be seen as points where racial events take place. The songs with which the ex-colored man plans to work are not only a vital part of African American culture, but also a tool with which to prevent future knotting because they offer a new perspective, a different way of thinking about race. He recalls, "I gloated over the immense amount of material I had to work with, not only modern ragtime, but also the old slave songs— material which no one had yet touched" (Johnson 104). While the South itself is not the original ancestral site, these "old slave songs" are a link between the culture of the enslaved Africans' homelands and the new culture they built in the United States as well as a bridge to an improved future. From the distance of Europe, the ex-colored man recognizes the songs for what they are: a connection between the past, present, and future as well as a means of asserting the value of an oppressed race. Bringing their value to the surface, then, is a way to push past traditional boundaries and propel the African American culture into the twentieth century.

According to Griffin, as African Americans migrate, some migrants alter their new environment while others are altered by the new space (51–52). In the ex-colored man's case, his life is affected by the "time space" through which he passes. Recently back from Europe, the experience of stepping outside of his culture makes him more sensitive to the injustices to which some Americans seem have become numbed. In fact, when a white mob lynches a black man, while the protagonist remains "fixed to the spot where [he] stood, powerless to take [his] eyes from what [he] did not want to see," others in "the crowd yelled and cheered" (Johnson 136). The protagonist does see, though, and he believes himself to be safe, as he is "sure [his] identity as a colored man had not yet become known in the town" (136). Though he may be physically safe, his emotions turn out to be quite vulnerable while he watches the flames that "leaped up as high as their victim's head" and hears the victims "cries and groans" until they are "choked off by the fire and smoke" (136). "It was over before [he] realized that time had elapsed" (136), but the horror of this event elicits the ex-colored man's life-changing decision to leave behind his dreams of bringing honor to the African American race and to instead head for New York. He explains,

> I argued that to forsake one's race to better one's condition was no less worthy an action than to forsake one's country for the same purpose. I finally made up my mind that I would neither disclaim the black race nor claim the white race; but that I would change my name, raise a mustache, and let the world take me for what it would (Johnson 139).

When the ex-colored man declares he will not claim a race, he means he will not *explicitly* claim a race, but by allowing society to bestow white privileges upon him, he does in fact claim a race; he claims whiteness, as his acceptance is an implicit claim.

It may seem that the ex-colored man takes the cowardly way out by refusing to label himself black or white, but his stand is actually courageous on two levels: personal and social. He acknowledges a personal risk when he begins his narrative by claiming, "I feel that I am led by the same impulse which forces the unfound-out criminal to take somebody into his confidence, although he knows that the act is liable, even almost certain, to lead to his undoing. *I know that I am playing with fire* [emphasis added]" (Johnson 1). "Playing with fire" is a common expression, but the ex-colored man's use of it here is even more generic because he has yet to establish a "time space" context. This fire imagery does resonate in a much later scene, however, when he, passing as a white man in the South near the turn of the twentieth century, watches in horror as a group of white men lynch a black man. As the ex-colored man hears the cry, "'Burn him!'" (136), the full implication of his confession becomes clear: he has taken advantage of privileges reserved for white men, which puts him, too, at risk for lynching, for being burnt at the stake.

Though certainly passing is a form of self-preservation, the ex-colored man also aspires to reveal the value of an oppressed culture. Most people are confined to one side of the color line or the other, and how people are divided depends upon the perspective of the time;[1] however, the passing body experiences both sides of the color line, revealing color as a continuum and proving that the world is never simply black and white. For the protagonist to be able to pass, then, puts him in a unique position of power, as he has access to spaces that he would have otherwise been denied admittance to at the time. Passing as white means that he also has access to spaces that are reserved for whites as well as access to the conversations that are usually contained within those spaces. For example, while traveling from Nashville to Atlanta by train, he enters the smoking section, where he becomes privy to a conversation of various perspectives that "turned upon the Negro question" (Johnson 116), the primary debate of the time. This scene is significant because there is a chronotopic layering. The interior spaces of the railroad cars are racially divided during this time due to Jim Crow laws, but the laws are only enforced in specific states. Additionally, the cars themselves are traveling through "time space" as they transport people, which Bakhtin argues, are chronotopic (85). This "time space" layering in the novel is parallel to Bakhtin's description of chronotopes. As he puts it, "Chronotopes are mutually inclusive, they coexist, they may be interwoven with, replace or oppose one another, contradict one another or find themselves in ever more complex interrelationships" (Bakhtin 252). Chronotopes, then, are volatile, which means that the "time space" layering in Johnson's text is significant in that it mirrors the layers of confusion and questions of which the Negro question is comprised.

One of the men the protagonist encounters in the smoking section of the car is careful in his approach to the Negro question because, as a Jewish man, he knows "that to sanction Negro oppression would be to sanction Jewish oppression" (Johnson 116). By including the Jewish man in his narrative, the ex-colored man emphasizes the power of social constructionism; those who are in power label others, and because Jewish people were already stereotyped as ambitious and successful during the latter half of the nineteenth century, they could easily be regarded as a threat to white economic power. Indeed, according to James S. Allen, "The factors which have created the Negro question are basically economic, and serve as the foundation for the social and ideological system which excludes the Negro from the body politic" (7). Another passenger, the Texan, argues that education and the ballot are essentially wasted on blacks. From his argument, it seems clear that these are merely part of his problem. He contends that "anything . . . is better than having niggers over you" (Johnson 117). It can be presumed he means anything is better than blacks being *economically* over whites, as with so much social upheaval at the time, whites feared losing their dream, specifically the *American* Dream.

Andrew Vogel examines how, after emancipation, whites supported the color line as a means of maintaining the American Dream as a white dream (148). While the American Dream is largely concerned with economics, Vogel emphasizes that it cannot be separated from "family, home, security, prosperity, dignity, and freedom" (148), which closely aligns it with racial issues. Certainly, whites perceived blacks as a threat to the home and family; in Johnson's novel, even the old Union soldier, "who stood firmly on the ground of equal rights and opportunity to all men" (116), agrees, he "wouldn't consent to [his] daughter's marrying a nigger" (119). Such hypocrisy is likely in part what W. E. B. Du Bois means when he claims, "The problem of the Twentieth Century is the problem of the color-line" (35), but the passing body disrupts this line of thought.

Before the men depart the smoking section, "[e]verybody except the professor partook of the generous Texan's flask" (Johnson 120). *Everybody* implies that the ex-colored man, too, drinks from the flask, that he places his mouth on the opening, an indirect kiss for these men who insist they will never allow their daughters to marry a black man. In performing the act of placing his mouth on a racist white man's flask and then recounting it in his narrative at a time when anxieties are already running high over the Negro question, the ex-colored man fractures the "safe" white space of the smoking section. In *Passing: Identity and Interpretation in Sexuality, Race, and Religion*, María Carla Sánchez and Linda Schlossberg describe passing as "a highly charged site for anxieties regarding visibility, invisibility, classification, and social demarcation" (1), an interesting way to think about it since it positions passing—something usually considered to be a performance—as a space. Thinking of passing as a space, then, not only positions the passer in what Sánchez and Schlossberg refer to as an "unmarked . . . position of privilege" (5) but also, if, as Bakhtin affirms, the image of man is chronotopic (85), as the ex-colored man travels through "time space" into the future, he will arrive in the twentieth century still carrying this privileged position, and in a new era, the space of privilege takes on new meaning.

While the act of passing can certainly offer the passer a privileged position, this position is not always as "unmarked" as Sánchez and Schlossberg describe. For example, the rich white gentleman, the protagonist's benefactor, is possibly passing as well, but his privilege is *overtly* marked. When he first arrives at the club, the narrator describes him with details that do not actually allow us to put together an image of his appearance: "clean-cut, slender, athletic," young-looking, despite a bit of gray at the temples, "clean-shaven . . . [with] regular features," and bearing a "stamp of culture" (Johnson 84). Once the benefactor and the protagonist leave for Europe, the protagonist is treated more like a friend than an employee. The protagonist explains, "He bought me the same kind of clothes which he himself wore, and that was the best; and he treated me in every way as he dressed me, as an equal, not as a servant" (95). The benefactor's conduct suggests that he perceives the protagonist to be on the same level or a similar one to his own. Not only does the protagonist find the benefactor "entirely free from prejudice," but he also learns that the benefactor "[has] given more study to the race question in the United States than you may suppose" (106). For a man who does not appear to work, as he spends at least a year traveling abroad, it seems odd that he would spend so much effort on the race question if it did not affect him personally. As Sánchez and Schlossberg point out, whites are always passing since they do not have to think about race, except for when it becomes visible (5). If the benefactor were white, then, it would be unlikely that he would be so concerned with the race question, and if he is, in fact, free from prejudice, it seems unlikely that he perceives a threat to race, all of which implies that he is not white, but rather passing like the protagonist.

If the benefactor is indeed passing, the protagonist either does not know, or, more likely, he does not wish to subject his benefactor to the same risks he takes upon himself, for as Sánchez and Schlossberg claim, passing can be a matter of life or death (4). As the ex-colored man travels toward the South, he passes so that he can ride in the Pullman "because through [his] experience with [his] millionaire a certain amount of comfort and luxury had become a necessity" (Johnson 115). On his way back to the North after witnessing the lynching, however, he passes out of "[s]hame at being identified with a people that could with impunity be treated worse than animals" (139). As Jacqueline Denise Goldsby points out, "[L]ynching's cultural logic changes over time" (42), but it seems that this logic can change over space as well, and the ex-colored man recognizes that the space of the South is not safe, a recognition that necessitates his passing.

One of the primary reasons the South is not safe for blacks is that whites see them as a threat. Prior to the lynching scene, the ex-colored man notes how the white men are "comparatively silent" concerning "some terrible crime [that] had been committed" (Johnson 135). This silence suggests that no crime has actually occurred; in fact, the lack of an explicit claim by the white men implies an implicit warning toward blacks. As Trudier Harris discusses, lynching is a means of depowering, if not completely getting rid of African Americans. She writes, "Lynchings were carefully designed to convey to black persons in this country that they had no power and nothing else whites were obligated to respect" (Harris x). Harris' description makes lynching sound like a mind game, which is true; however, power is not only generated through intimidation and oppression, but also through access to money, authority, and knowledge. Indeed, though lynchings occurred throughout the United States after emancipation, they became "knotted" up with the South due to whites' fear of losing control over physical and metaphorical spaces, such as property, women, wealth, education, and political influence. This fear was the primary catalyst for violent acts, such as lynching.

In Ida B. Wells' 1895 pamphlet, *A Red Record*, she explores the "three distinct eras of Southern barbarism" that Frederick Douglass had noted in a previous article (76). According to Wells, the first excuse whites gave for lynching blacks was "the necessity of the white man to repress and stamp out 'race riots,'" but, since no black person was ever found guilty, whites were forced to come up with a new excuse (Wells 76). Next, because Southern white men resented blacks' new right to vote, they argued, "This is a white man's government" (77). Wells explains that this mindset led to the cry, "No Negro domination," under which groups such as the Ku Klux Klan, the Regulators, and other "lawless mobs" murdered blacks "whose only crime was the attempt to exercise their right to vote" (77). Despite the risk, Wells describes how, due to the black man's belief that "in that small white ballot there was a subtle something which stood for manhood as well as citizenship," he "clung to his right of franchise with a heroism which would have wrung admiration from the hearts of savages" (77). By creating a set

---

of socioeconomic roadblocks, such as poll taxes and literacy tests, southern whites were able to strip blacks of their political voice (Medvic 29). Of course, successfully disenfranchising blacks also meant that southern whites no longer had an excuse for lynching; without political power, "Negro domination" was impossible (Wells 77). A third excuse then became necessary. At this point, white men justified killing blacks because, as they claimed, they needed to protect white women from assaults, but as Wells points out:

> During all the years of slavery, no such charge was ever made, not even during the dark days of rebellion, when the white man, following the fortunes of war went to do battle for the maintenance of slavery. While the master was away fighting to forge the fetters upon the slave, he left his wife and children with no protectors, save the Negroes themselves. And yet during those years of trust and peril, no Negro proved recreant to his trust and no white man returned to a home that had been despoiled. (79)

As Wells shows, this last excuse was illogical. White men were not afraid for the safety of white women; white men were afraid of losing control of white women, just as they were afraid of losing social and political control. For whites to explicitly express this fear would have been to admit that they did not actually have the power they asserted, yet the violence they exhibited toward blacks, especially in the South during this time, hints at the desperation they felt at the prospect of losing control over multiple facets of their lives.

When whites lost their authority over blacks during emancipation, their position at the top of the social hierarchy was destabilized. Reconstruction saw white Southerners' attempt to regain that authority by revoking African American civil rights. President Andrew Johnson allowed the enforcement of oppressive "black codes," but Northerners challenged President Johnson's support ("Black Codes"). During post-Reconstruction, the period during which James Weldon Johnson's novel is set, Southerners again imposed restrictions on African Americans, this time in the form of Jim Crow laws. Despite Frederick Douglass' argument that Jim Crow was a "virtual re-enslavement of African Americans"

("The Frederick Douglass Papers"), the federal government failed to protect African American constitutional rights. Jim Crow existed within a specific "time space," the post-Reconstruction South, and the only way the ex-colored man can escape this expression of deep racism—which has its roots in slavery, is nourished by economic competition, and results in horrors such as Jim Crow, the loss of civil rights,[2] and lynching—is by passing as a white man.

As a man ahead of turn-of-the-century America's "time space," the protagonist does not perceive race and color to be important to a person's identity; thus, passing only becomes an issue when he confesses his love to his future wife, as he struggles with "whether to ask her to marry [him] under false colors or to tell her the whole truth" (Johnson 134). He finally decides, "[T]he more [he] knew this girl, the less [he] could find it in [his] heart to deceive her" (135). While this indication of guilt and his ultimate decision to reveal the facts of his birth make the statement that race and color do matter, his actions do not appear to be so black and white when analyzed alongside Sánchez and Schlossberg's argument that passing creates an "alternative set of narratives" (4). The protagonist is driven by shame to create a persona that will allow others to assume he is a white man. In this case, he merely tells a story about his white heritage, and it is a true story, if not a complete one; however, he does recognize that his narrative is likely to conflict with that by which white people live, his future wife included.

When the protagonist writes to his future wife, arguing for the power of love in overcoming racial differences, he is implicitly working toward a mixed society with *mixed* meaning, both unsegregated and a population that includes biologically mixed people. After developing what Du Bois calls "double-consciousness" (8), Johnson's protagonist comes to perceive himself through his wife's eyes, or, at least, how he presumes his wife might eventually come to see him. The ex-colored man explains, "I was in constant fear that she would discover in me some shortcoming which she would unconsciously attribute to my blood rather than to a failing of human nature" (Johnson 153). Though his fear is driven by socially constructed misperceptions about race, after his wife's death, this double-consciousness solidifies his disillusionment in the belief that society can improve. Thus, because the protagonist's children, like himself, are products of a racially mixed relationship, he elects to pass them off as white. That is, instead of offering his children the best of *both* cultures—his own and his wife's—he renounces his birthright, along with his dreams and talent, to "keep the brand from being placed upon [his children]" (153). As Vogel argues, "[P]assing reinforces the color line even as it transgresses it" (165), and this is especially true here at the end of the book. Though it is easy to be angry with the narrator for walking away from the work of bringing pride to the African American race, it is important to remember that just by telling his story, he undermines the color line to some degree, slowly pushing it forward into the "time space" of the twentieth century and weakening racism's dehumanizing effects.

While it may be an imagined mark between races, the color line has real consequences, but, similar to how a musician experiences the full range of notes, occasionally breaking the mold to create a new piece or genre, people with blood from more than one race running through their veins challenge socially constructed notions and labels. Johnson seems to believe that the way to dissolve the color line's power is through a racially hybrid society, as, like mixing classical and African music into ragtime, creating a culture that combines blacks and whites can lead to a space in which racism no longer exists. If this is true, though, why does he back off at the end of the book, allowing the ex-colored man to completely assimilate into white society? It seems that Johnson's indecisiveness may be intended to mirror the confusion that passing brings to the color line. In Johnson's novel, the passer undergoes a transition that mirrors the cultural change between the nineteenth and twentieth centuries. As Giulia M. Fabi argues, Johnson "presents passing for white as the result, rather than the cause, of cultural alienation and divided racial loyalties" (92–93). The protagonist emerges, then, as a chronotopic representation of time—the transition to modernity—and space—a world traveler whose experience in the Southern United States substantially impacts the rest of his life.

Notes

1. At different points in time, groups that are now considered white were labeled as non-white in the United States, such as Italian, Greek, and Irish immigrants.

2. While the loss of civil rights has much to do with racism, it should be acknowledged that whites were not wholly responsible. In *The Souls of Black Folk,* Du Bois disputes Booker T. Washington's argument for being so compliant with whites, claiming it would only lead to further oppression of blacks. Washington asks blacks to give up political power, civil rights, and higher education in exchange for economic power, and for these allowances, they have been disenfranchised, been legally labeled inferior, and lost institutional training aid (Du Bois 42–43).

Works Cited

Allen, James S. Introduction. *The Negro Question in the United States.* New York: International, 1936. 7–12.

Bakhtin, M. M. *The Dialogic Imagination: Four Essays.* Ed. Michael Holquist. Trans. Caryl Emerson & Michael Holquist. Austin: U of Texas P, 1981.

Bennett, Juda. Introduction. *The Passing Figure: Racial Confusion in Modern American Literature.* New York: Peter Lang, 1996.1–8.

"Black Codes." *History.* A&E Networks, 2014. Web. 1 Dec. 2014.

Du Bois, W. E. B. *The Souls of Black Folk.* New York: Library of America, 2009.

Fabi, M. Giulia. *Passing and the Rise of the African American Novel.* Urbana: U of Illinois P, 2001.

"The Frederick Douglass Papers at the Library of Congress." *Library of Congress.* Library of Congress, n.d. Web. 1 Dec. 2014. < http://www.loc.gov/collection/frederick-douglass-papers/about-this-collection/>.

Goldsby, Jacqueline Denise. "A Sign of the Times: Lynching and Its Cultural Logic." *A Spectacular Secret: Lynching in American Life and Literature.* Chicago: U of Chicago P, 2006.

Griffin, Farah Jasmine. *"Who Set You Flowin'?": The African-American Migration Narrative.* New York: Oxford UP, 1995.

Harris, Trudier. Preface. *Exorcising Blackness: Historical and Literary Lynching and Burning Rituals*. Bloomington: Indiana UP, 1984. ix–xiii.

Johnson, James Weldon. *The Autobiography of an Ex-Colored Man*. Ed. William L. Andrews. New York: Penguin, 1990.

Medvic, Stephen K. *Campaigns and Elections: Players and Processes*. New York: Routledge, 2014. *Google Books*. Web. 15 June 2015.

Sánchez, María Carla & Linda Schlossberg, eds. Introduction. *Passing: Identity and Interpretation in Sexuality, Race, and Religion*. New York: NYU P, 2001. 1–12.

Vogel, Andrew. "Blurring the Color Line: Race and the American Dream in *The Autobiography of an Ex-Colored Man*, *Passing*, and *Cane*." *The American Dream*. Ed. Keith Newlin. Ipswich, MA: Salem, 2013. 146–167.

Wells, Ida B. *A Red Record. Southern Horrors and Other Writings: The Anti-Lynching Campaign of Ida B. Wells, 1892–1900*. Ed. Jacqueline Jones Royster. Boston: Bedford, 1997.

Framing Racial Identity and Class: Magnifying Themes of Assimilation and Passing in the Works of Johnson and Hughes_____

Charlotte Teague

The Harlem Renaissance was a time that scholars regard as the foremost cultural explosion for people of color in America's history. In fact, at no other time in history was there a greater collective effort where African Americans boldly sought to define art, music, and literature as it related to their own lives than during this brief span of time. Of course, one of the most interesting characteristics of this age was that artists felt free to tell what they considered to be the truth about the Negro or black experience and, at the heart of this experience, were issues of racial identity and class. In his 2008 critical text, *The Harlem Renaissance: A Brief History with Documents*, author and critic Jeffrey B. Ferguson discusses general questions of racial identity. He asserts that "writers and thinkers of the Harlem Renaissance focused intensely on matters of heritage, black culture, black consciousness, and many other issues related to the general questions 'Who am I?' 'Who are we?' and 'Where do we find ourselves?'" (Ferguson 17).

In the scope of the Harlem Renaissance, these questions are central to the discussion of identity and class because the questions are rooted in the African American consciousness. Many authors raised their voices to advance the effort to educate society about this dichotomy and, by doing so, began a discussion that continues to this day. Prominent authors of the period, James Weldon Johnson and Langston Hughes were at the forefront of this conversation. Through their works, they give readers a varying spectrum of the issues that surrounded this sacred topic, though they are very different in their approaches. Certainly, while there are others, such as Nella Larsen, whose writings illuminate these issues, Johnson and Hughes are considered pioneers, whose literary expressions and transformational works cannot be disregarded. Their literature, in particular, is polysemous, seamless, and polarizing. It thereby establishes a historic frame for racial identity and class that encompasses assimilation and passing in the African American or black community.

Passing and *assimilation* are both terms that are heavily referenced in connection to the Harlem Renaissance. Passing in the 1900s is typically referred to as living life as a white person, while actually being considered legally black based on ethnicity and the social standards of racial identity. Cheryl I. Harris refers to this person's action to "pass" in her acclaimed article, "Whiteness as Property," as "transgressing boundaries, crossing borders, spinning on margins, and traveling between dualities of Manichean space, rigidly bifurcated into light/dark, good/bad, white/Black" (1711). Similarly, others have defined it as wearing a mask in order to assimilate or "fit in" with the mainstream or majority race. In essence, the person who is "passing" is "carrying a false passport" and "not merely passing, but trespassing" (1711). In this instance, trespassing is used to denote a black person's faulty or illegal pronouncement of place and existence, which constitutes belonging, and belonging is a vital component of racial identity. Johnson's and Hughes' treatment of racial identity is complex and unique because they frame "assimilation" and "passing" respectively through the use of class structures that are, at times, both conscious and subconscious. In fact, their literature shows that "ethnic identity is achieved through an active process of decision making and self-evaluation" (Phinney 502). Ultimately, these two very different authors are successful at framing racial identity and class through the themes of assimilation and "passing" by using experimentation and expanded characterization in their novels, The *Autobiography of an Ex-Colored Man* (1912) and *Not Without Laughter* (1930).

Magnifying Themes of Passing in Johnson's *The Autobiography of an Ex-Colored Man*

To begin, many consider James Weldon Johnson to be one of the most prominent figures of the Harlem Renaissance, although his major fiction work is considered a precursor to the period. Since it was largely "ignored by the literary world when it was first published in 1912," its reappearance later, during the Harlem Renaissance period, was very noteworthy (Fleming 106). In fact, according to noted scholar Robert Fleming, *The Autobiography of an Ex-Colored Man* "came to be one of the most influential books of the period upon its republication in 1927," and so, "not only writers of the 1920s but novelists of the 1950s and later must acknowledge a debt to Johnson" for his monumental literary contributions (106). In addition to his fiction, he is also well known for his poetry. His famed, *The Book of American Negro Poetry* (1922) is an important work of the period that is distinguished by creativity and depth, and acclaimed scholar Eugene Redmond called *God's Trombones* (1926) Johnson's masterpiece and one of the best books of Afro-American poetry ever written (Fleming 110). Moreover, his writings as a civil rights worker are sharp and poignant. He is noted to have fought for the passage of the Dyer Anti-Lynching Bill[1] through his social and political writing. Without doubt, his contributions are widespread and all encompassing, for he was not only a brilliant fiction and nonfiction writer, but also has a lasting legacy as a poet and civil rights icon of the era.

James Weldon Johnson was clearly a man of deep thought, and at the core of his legacy is his agenda to expose racism and share his comprehensive consciousness about racial identity and class. This prominent theme embodies much of his writings, and it is at the heart of his defining work, *The Autobiography of an Ex-Colored Man*. In this work, Johnson crafts his protagonist as a man struggling with the double-consciousness that W. E. B. Du Bois discusses in his influential book, *The Souls of Black Folk* (1903). Readers are introduced to the main character and immediately perceive that he does not know that he is even black. He recounts, "I went home and told my mother how one of the 'niggers' had struck a boy with a slate. I shall never forget how she turned on me. 'Don't you ever use that word again,' she said, 'and don't you ever bother the colored children at school. You ought to be ashamed of yourself" (Johnson 7). This selection gives readers critical insight that his mother has not told him about his racial background, nor does she intend to tell him that he, too, is colored. In fact, he believes that he is a part of the dominant race and, therefore, identifies with the colored children as "niggers." It is not until his race is identified to him and for him in front of his entire class by his teacher that his racial consciousness is awakened. According to the text, one day at school the principal asked for all the white scholars to stand, and the protagonist stood with them; then it happened. The unnamed narrator recalls, "The teacher looked at me, and calling me by name said, 'You sit down for the present, and rise with the others'" (7).

It should be noted that the use of the word *other* is not just a marker of difference but also a term, often linked to racial identity and class, that is characterized by negativity and racism. The term is connected to the power maintained by the majority population to execute dominance over the minority population, in this case, blacks. Dominance can be connected to gender, sexuality, class, religion, etc., but in Johnson's presentation of Otherness in the referenced novel, the usage is directly connected to race. The teacher uses it as a means of subjugation to "put the protagonist in his place," and herein lies the origins of the usage of the term *Other*. It is historically given as a negative designation, and Johnson's employment of this expression shows his keen awareness of this ideology. By referring to the black children as "the others," the teacher consciously relegates the child protagonist to a lesser race and class, though the protagonist is very much unaware of the complexity of this placement at the time.

Still in shock, the young boy hurried home fast to confirm or affirm these emotional findings that would haunt his life forever. At this point in the novel, he is perplexed by his identity, and as he looks in the mirror at home, he "notice[s] the ivory whiteness of [his] skin" (Johnson 8). Perhaps for the first time, he is bewildered. He had witnessed his teacher's actions that placed him formally in the black category, and he had heard the black children say, "'We knew he was colored'" (7). He is indeed confused, and of course, this confusion is a part of Johnson's literary crafting of his character. Not only is it symptomatic of the struggle connected to racial identity, this confusion forms the foundation for readers to understand the duality of his protagonist's character. The term *duality*, after all, is

Critical Insights

intertwined with the double-consciousness that Du Bois employs and made famous during the period. Du Bois' description of "two souls, two thoughts, two unreconciled strivings; two warring ideals in one dark body, whose dogged strength alone keeps it from being torn asunder" (2) is central to the racial identity and class discussion and to the narrator's emerging sense of self.

According to Richard Schaefer in the *Encyclopedia of Race, Ethnicity, and Society,* "Double consciousness prompts one to reflect on the twoness of being a U.S. citizen as well as Black" (2). The consciousness that is displayed by the unnamed narrator is dual or "double" because he has had to learn what it means to be a black man in a white world, and he tries to understand what it takes to navigate in the world with this information. Johnson's exploration of double-consciousness in the novel is also monumental because the novel is written in a confessional tone, and according to Eugene Levy, "in writing his work as he had actually lived it, he made it part of the most expressive literary tradition of the race—the first person narrative" (129). Through these efforts, Johnson attempts to "allow his character to attain self-conscious manhood, to merge his double self into a better and truer self" (Du Bois 2) that will become capable of making a positive contribution to the race. According to Du Bois, "[I]n this merging he wishes neither of the older selves to be lost" (3), so then the ultimate goal is for this duality to be managed in a positive way; however, Johnson's unnamed protagonist struggles to balance double-consciousness as he fights an internal battle with racial identity and class issues.

In addition to the racial identity and class issues presented through the protagonist's character, readers are also shown the intricate part that his mother plays in constructing and deconstructing a man who wrestles with his true black identity and class placement. When the unnamed narrator finally asks his mother, "'Mother, mother, tell me, am I a nigger?'" (Johnson 8), she does not readily respond. Arguably, she knew that this day would come. Was she secretly hoping that it would not? Did she believe that her son would not have to face his blackness? The narrator then tells his readers, "There were tears in her eyes, and I could see that she was suffering for me" (8). Johnson masterfully shows that the mother is keenly aware of the struggle that is before her son because of this newfound identity and, as a result, tells him, "'No, my darling, you are not a nigger'" (8). The novel, however, lets readers know the innermost feelings of the protagonist, as he states, "The more she talked the less was I reassured" (8). He is in a state of limbo at the point of this conversation, and he wants his white identity confirmed. He finally asks her, "'Well, Mother, am I white?'" (8). It is not a surprise that the mother never answers this question. She leaves it open for deliberation, but Johnson makes it mostly clear that his narrator knows the truth of the matter at this juncture. He has been wounded deeply, and this wound forms a foundation for his very fragmented life. Eugenia Collier proclaims that, at this point in the novel, "The die is cast. In this moment of crisis his mother has denied his blackness but not his whiteness. The psychological journey is well under way" (367).

At this point, the work moves into the most profound part of the book: the narrator's quest to deal with his blackness. He starts by recounting that "fateful" day in school. It cannot be misconstrued that the use of the word *fateful* is very much full of purpose. Johnson wants readers to understand that a person's fate is indeed tied to his or her racial identity and that identity could have disastrous consequences and implications. In fact, the fate of the black man, as the narrator discovers, was tied to violence, racism, discrimination, and even death, with a stark increase in lynchings during the early to mid-twentieth century. With this newfound awareness, the narrator admits, "There did come a radical change, and, young as I was, I felt fully conscious of it, though I did not fully comprehend it" (Johnson 9). Johnson shows readers the transition that his narrator makes into a new world. Readers do not hear the happiness that was present in the tone of the narrator before his discovery. His tone is now solemn and horrid, and that horrid sense is characterized by a shift in the "self," for his eyes had been opened, and he had gotten his "bearing" (19).

He has become racialized and a member of a marginalized class overnight. As a result, he is forced to assimilate. By learning the status of other black children, the protagonist affirms "that theirs was mine" (Johnson 10), indicating his recognition that he, too, has the status of a black man. At the same time, he laments, "I now think that this change which came into my life was at first more subjective than objective" (10). Because he is very descriptive in his feelings, readers are able to understand the layers of black identity, and this was precisely Johnson's major point for crafting the novel as an autobiography with an unnamed narrator; the focus is on racial identity rather than on the man himself. In Johnson's view, the protagonist represents a larger sector of black society, and thus, he becomes a mirror for the entire African American race.

His discussion about the ramifications of his newfound identity is strategic. He says, "I grew reserved, I might say, suspicious. I grew constantly more and more afraid of laying myself open to some injury to my feelings or my pride" (Johnson 10). Certainly, this was a result of viewing the world now with "colored eyes." He elaborates, "I looked out through other eyes, my thoughts were colored, my words dictated, my actions limited by one dominating, all pervading idea which constantly increased in force and weight until I finally realized in it a great tangible fact" (9). It is through these words that Johnson builds a frame for racial identity and class. This framework dominates the novel and establishes what it meant to be black in America at that time, and it also provides some reasoning why many who could "choose" not to be black by "passing" into white society chose to do so, as does the unnamed narrator in the novel.

Toward the end of the work, he states, "I finally made up my mind that I would neither disclaim the black race nor claim the white race; but that I would change my name, raise a mustache, and let the world take me for what it would" (Johnson 90). Because a person's identity forms the foundation of who he or she is, a person is only able to embrace and project to the world what lives within, and he or she must make a conscious effort to do so. The racial identity of Johnson's protagonist is unclear or scrambled; by the conclusion of the novel, he does not make that conscious effort. As a result, as Donald Goellnicht points out, "The Narrator chooses to pass for white and thus deny his black racial and cultural heritage; his act of repression [is] a movement from the subordinate to the dominant culture performed in order to be finally and socially successful by the standards of white bourgeois society" (28). Collier, too, puts this phenomenon into perspective by giving Johnson praise for his articulation of a major issue of the black race. Because the unnamed narrator is neither, he is unable to embrace oneself over the other self; therefore, "Johnson has given us insight into the whole problem of dual heritage. Afro-Americans are neither African nor American, and yet are both. We are torn, as is the Narrator, between two cultures with conflicting views" (Collier 373).

Johnson writes, "And this is the dwarfing influence which operates upon each colored man in the United States. He is forced to take his outlook on all things, not from the viewpoint of a citizen, or a man, nor even a human being, but from the viewpoint of a colored man" (9). The narrator refers to this phenomenon as a "funnel" of sorts with a "narrow neck." The influence of this identity pattern is obvious. According to the text, the colored man's "thoughts are often influenced by considerations so delicate and subtle that it would be impossible for him to confess or explain them to one of the opposite race" (9). Johnson further argues that "this gives to every colored man, in proportion to his intellectuality, a sort of dual personality" (31). Consequently, he belongs fully to neither world. This duality is complex, and Johnson's purpose for presenting this complex subject is still important today. Race still is an intricate part of a person's identity, and it cannot be fully erased. Johnson wants readers to understand this point. While a person's sense of self is not only defined by race, typically for people of color, race is the defining characteristic for how the world views them. The funnel is Johnson's tool to clarify that being black is a part of the everyday humanness of a black person, and this humanness is how identity is shaped and projected.

So then, how does one cope with this duality that Johnson presents? A very direct answer, seemingly dictated by society, is that one must assimilate or pass into this new world, and Johnson's work takes readers on a journey to show what it means to do both at different places in life. Based on this journey, Collier presents a rather raw indictment that has merit:

> There is, I think, psychological truth here. A great many black people, light skinned or not, accept white values; within them lurks the desire to be white. Johnson has lain bare his desire in this symbolic person of the Narrator. And this revelation lies perhaps the greatest value of the book. (373)

Perhaps Johnson does project this desire through his protagonist. After all, he does create a protagonist whose racial identity is severely fragmented. At different times, he indeed desires to be white. He begins as a black boy who believes that he is white. He then grows into a black man who wants to be a credit to his race; he wants to embrace his black heritage and assimilates into the culture of blackness. As he ages and after living virtually as a white man while abroad, the unnamed narrator decides that being black in America is not safe and not in his best interest, so he makes the final decision to *pass* for a white man the remainder of his life with some minor regrets. The fragmentation engulfs his life. He assimilates, and then he passes. Through this depiction, Johnson highlights how the narrator is transgressing between the two spaces, unable to find a home that soothes his soul. Because the protagonist spends his life fluctuating between the two, the themes of assimilation and passing are magnified in the work.

Magnifying Themes of Assimilation in Hughes' *Not Without Laughter*

In his definitive critical work, *Harlem Renaissance* (1971), acclaimed author and professor, Nathaniel Irvin Huggins wrote, "Langston Hughes belonged to Harlem even before he came" (24). This statement, while puzzling, is a perfect way to describe Hughes' relationship with the time and place. Even today, he is typically regarded as the most well-known and prominent figure of the Harlem Renaissance. Melvin Dixon reinforces this fact when he writes, "When Langston Hughes died in 1967 at the age of 65, he had achieved the status of being the most popular, prolific, and most versatile black writer in the United States" (120). This achievement is not a surprise, considering that he published more than fifty works, including his most famous and heavily anthologized poems, "The Negro Speaks of Rivers" (1921), "A Dream Deferred" (1951), "Mother to Son"(1922), and "I, Too, Sing America" (1926). These works, along with his other publications, establish him as an American literary icon.

Although his magic is most naturally presented in his poetry, Langston Hughes also wrote works of drama, nonfiction, and fiction. Included in this body of work is the novel, *Not Without Laughter*. This classic, while less widely read, is a coming-of-age account of a young boy, Sandy, and his family. The significance of the work lies in the author's portrayal of the black American experience, which necessarily includes issues of racial identity and class. Unlike Johnson's novel, Hughes' novel is not solely about one man's life as it relates to the profound themes; *Not Without Laughter* intersects the lives of four women and its male protagonist to magnify themes of assimilation and passing through experimentation and expanded characterization. This idea is certainly embodied in *Not Without Laughter*. Hughes' central character, Sandy, is referred to as James, his legitimate name, by his aunt Tempy as a constant reminder of class and social constructs. He is a character who grows in his world rather than one who oscillates between two worlds. In addition, Hughes' character is steady in his physical, mental, and social growth pattern. The *intricacies* of the novel are being told through his eyes, although he is arguably scarcely old enough to comprehend the racial undertones of the initial situation. Sandy seems to be keenly aware of his place in society before the age of ten.

Elizabeth Shultz, in her noteworthy article, "Natural and Unnatural Circumstances in Langston Hughes' *Not Without Laughter*," references the work of M. M. Bahktin and addresses Hughes' work as a "double-directed discourse" (1178). She argues that "Hughes constructs a dominant narrative in *Not Without Laughter* that relies upon natural imagery to appeal to its mainstream readers . . . and also significantly slips a subversive subtext into the narrative under this conventional and non-controversial guise"

(Shultz 1178). She asserts that Hughes' attention to racism, poverty, and the richness of the African American culture is the "subversion subtext" of the work. This appraisal seems to ignore the possibility that Hughes intentionally uses nature as a decoy or backdrop in the work in order to interweave racism, poverty, and African American culture into the landscape of the novel, as these issues relate to racial identity and class. The aforementioned issues, though skillfully presented, are not muted for readers. Hughes does not give into what Pulitzer Prize–winning novelist Toni Morrison calls "the white gaze."[2] On the contrary, he clearly and boldly articulates his vision through the expanded characterization of the women.

Sandy's Aunt Harriet is the youngest of the three children born to Aunt Hager in the novel. Her character is central to the development of the themes of racial identity and class because she refuses the lifestyle, religion, and social demands that are seeking to entrap her. Instead, she struggles to live the life of her dreams, even though prostitution is a consequence of her choice. Through Harriet's character, Hughes gives readers the music of the African American culture. She sings and dances to the sounds of jazz and blues, and no matter how much her mother persists, she will not abandon the music because it is a part of who she is. In essence, it is her racial identity. Mary Jo Moran in a review published in the *English Journal* writes that "Harriet brimming with rebellion, turns to prostitution, for a time, in an effort to retain her pride in herself and her blackness" (58). It is not a surprise that, at the end of the novel, Harriet is successful in becoming a jazz singer, and she has not had to "sell her soul for a mess of pottage" (Johnson 100), unlike the narrator in Johnson's text.

In contrast, Aunt Hagar's identity is wrapped up in religion, and Sandy's mother, Angee's identity is wrapped up in a man, and so neither of them are able to move from the poverty that defines their minds and their class. In fact, their characters represent valuable lessons for Sandy because he sees the negative outcomes of their respective actions. Hager dies a poor, old, and sick washwoman; Angee remains alone, even though she has turned her life upside down and abandoned her son to be with Jimboy, her wandering husband, who still leaves her for the final time to enlist in the army. Moreover, Angee is the most disillusioned of all the characters because she does not want her son to finish his education. She remarks, "He ought to be wanting to help me, anyway. Instead of that, he's determined to go back to school" (Hughes 216). Indeed Sandy understands as a young adult that the only way to advance as a Negro and to feel good about oneself is through proper understanding and self-reflection. At the height of maturity, he says, "I'm more like Aunt Harriet—not wanting to be a servant at the mercies of white people forever . . . I want to do something for myself, by myself . . . Free" (210). At this juncture, the reader sees that Sandy has a healthy sense of self and, thereby, racial identity. Angee serves as the catalyst for his understanding of this plight because it is so obvious that she does not understand her own. The people in the marginalized class she represents are unaware that they are living in what Hughes maintains is the "basement of life, with the door to the light locked and barred—and the white folks live upstairs" (189).

Tempy, Aunt Hagar's oldest child and Sandy's aunt, is perhaps the most controversial character in the novel. As Moran writes, "She has broken with her family and her people, in an attempt to be accepted by the town's middle class white society" (58). Tempy's quest for acceptance and disavowal of her own race certainly magnifies the themes of assimilation and passing in *Not Without Laughter*. Hughes is very strategic as he presents this character in the novel. Shultz contends, for example, "By alienating her from nature, Hughes underscores her desires not only to identify with the color and the material prosperity of Stanton's upper-class whites, but also to distance herself from the rich African-American culture embraced by the other members of her family" (1185). She successfully assimilates into the white culture, but she is unable to fully pass because her skin is too dark to do so; however, she pushes the boundaries of what it means to "pass" because she makes it clear that she wants no part of being a Negro or "nigger."

As Hughes expresses, Tempy believes, "Colored people certainly needed to come up in the world. . . . Up to the level of white people—dress like white people, talk like white people, think like white people—and then they would no longer be called 'niggers'" (171). She does everything that she possible can to deny her racial identity. She even changes from the Baptist church to the Episcopalian church and remarks to her mother, "'There's never anything niggerish about them—so you know, mother, they suit me'" (Hughes 110). When she departs her mother's home after this conversation, the text denotes, "When she had gone, everybody felt relieved—as though a white person had left the house" (110). There are so many references to Tempy's anti-blackness that it is clear that Hughes is making a strong point. This character serves as the antithesis of Harriet, who is proud of her racial identity. In addition, as John Shields argues in his article, "Reconstructing Langston Hughes' *Not Without Laughter*," "It is through Tempy that Hughes develops the notion that class is as powerful as race in dividing the town" (606). Tempy, who is black herself, shows the greatest amount of disdain for poor black people in the narrative.

Not Without Laughter's amazing strength lies in character development rather than in plot. From the protagonist's perspective, Hughes crafts a novel that is multidimensional in its presentation of racial identity and class. Because Sandy is a young child when the novel starts, his character's maturation is an obvious vehicle for Hughes' exploration of Sandy's psyche. Part of the maturation process is an examination of class and racial identity and these were filtered through the racism and prejudice pervasive in the setting. For instance, Sandy pays special attention to the world around him, particularly when it snows; he sees "the whiteness covered everything" (Hughes 104). Hughes uses the snow covering the city as a symbol for racism and white power, and Shultz asserts that he, "not only retains the symbolic association between snow and white racism, but also associates Sandy with blackness and darkness, indicating that he has matured not only enough to assume his own racial identity but also to protest against both racism and the snow" (1181). Obviously, the snow is symbolic of the coldness and hardness of the white world, and Sandy learns early what his parameters in that world will be.

He has a friend, however, who does not have these same parameters purely because he was born with skin light enough to "pass" into white society, and he vows to do so. In fact, his friend, Buster, boldly states his intentions: "I'll be in some big town passing for white, making money, and getting along swell. And I won't need to be smart either—I'll be ofay! So if you see me some time in St. Louis or Chi with a little blond on my arm—don't recognize me, hear! I want my kids to be so yellow headed they won't have to think about a color line" (Hughes 186). Intertwined with this magnification of the issue of passing in the novel constantly looms class. Being white is associated with getting a good job, and getting a good job is connected to being white. Sandy even questions going to school at one point in the work. He laments, "Maybe school don't matter . . . To get a good job you had to be smart—and white, too. That was the trouble, you had to be white" (188). Sandy processes this truth by reflecting on the lives of the other characters in the narrative. In doing so, he resolves, "There's no advancement for colored fellows" (189). He concludes, life is "always back doors" for the Negro, and this reality is even true for Tempy (189).

Notwithstanding, the strength of Sandy's character is that he is able to move beyond these thoughts through his maturity. He sees through the lives of W. E. B. Du Bois and Booker T. Washington that he *can*, in fact, overcome obstacles and achieve the wishes of his grandmother, Aunt Hager. In the face of adversity, it is indeed possible for him, like all black men, to become a "great man." By embracing his racial identity and moving forward with his dreams, he will be able to "help the whole race" (217) and live life on his own terms rather than those dictated by the dominant white society.

Framing Racial Identity and Class: The Lasting Legacies of Johnson and Hughes in the Harlem Renaissance Era

While the contemporary discussion about racial identity and class has become much more complex, scholars generally agree that both are social constructs, which are an intricate part of the African American experience. These social constructs are often discussed because African Americans are living in a world characterized by an oppression in which they are considered minorities in a majority culture. These considerations complicate black life, since there is a history of racism, discrimination, and marginalization that is present and pervasive based on the color of one's skin. While many authors have sought to define and characterize these notions, no other Harlem Renaissance writers were more successful than James Weldon Johnson and Langston Hughes. These literary giants framed racial identity and class by magnifying themes of assimilation and passing in their noteworthy novels that were often overlooked when scholars first began discussing distinctive works of the Harlem Renaissance that relate to those prominent themes.

Inherently, *The Autobiography of an Ex-Colored Man* and *Not Without Laughter* are different in their approach, but they are quite similar in their intentions. They both use experimentation and expanded characterization to present the psychological impact of the racial identity and class issues on their main characters. Johnson's novel chronicles the troubled life of one man who moves back and forth like a pendulum between the white world and the black world because he has the ability and the choice to pass or assimilate into white society. On the other hand, Hughes gives readers one male and four female characters who do not have the capability to truly pass into white society, although one of them would like to do so. Hughes is quite forthright in painting this as a flaw of Tempy's character; however, Johnson demonstrates more sensitivity for his unnamed narrator, who feels that he has made the best decision for his future by choosing to live his life as a white man, though he feels remorseful at the end of the novel for doing so. Even though these characters were fictional, they were based on the truths revealed by the Harlem Renaissance. Thus, the characters in these novels have the potential to inform our understanding of the African American condition and to shape future discussions about the meaning of being black in the United States.

Notes

1. The topic of lynching is especially connected to the Johnson's novel because an actual lynching is presented as a turning point in the

narrative. After the protagonist witnesses a black man being lynched by an angry mob of white people, he is deeply horrified and he resolves, at that moment, to live his life "passing" as a white man. For Johnson, lynching was a terrible act of terrorism that is a part of the history of America. It was a phenomenon that was used to maintain white supremacy and dominance after slavery, resulting in the lynching of thousands of African Americans in the South from the late 1800s until around the 1940s. While these acts of violence were primarily perpetrated in the South, the acts were accepted by the entire country because lynching was never outlawed officially. Even though the Dyer Anti-Lynching Bill was a bill proposed in 1922 by the United States Congress to make it a crime to lynch black people in America, it never became law in the country. The bill was passed by the House of Representatives, but it was never passed by the Senate.

2. It is widely known that Hughes was in a precarious position during much of his career. He was being supported by Charlotte Mason, who was known as his white "Godmother" and patron, and she is known to have raised some objections and suggested changes to some of his writings. In fact, Shields discusses the objections as censorship (612), and this is certainly connected to Morrison's usage of the term "the white gaze." While there are many definitions for "the white gaze," scholars typically agree that the term references the idea of looking at the world from a white perspective or through the lens of white expectations and experience. The argument is that history and the very existence of black people have become "white-washed." In an interview with Bill Moyers, Morrison characterizes "the white gaze" as the state in which African American authors are expected to address issues from a white perspective in their writings. Morrison further argues that readers can feel "the white gaze" because the narrator is explaining elements that an African American audience would already know.

Works Cited

Collier, Eugenia. "The Endless Journey of an Ex-Coloured Man." *Phylon* 32.4 (1971): 365–373.

Dixon, Melvin. "Beneath the Crystal Stair: Langston Hughes Art and Personality." *Callaloo* 21 (1984): 120–123.

Du Bois, W. E. B. *The Souls of Black Folk*. 1903. New York: Dover, 1994.

Ferguson, Jeffrey B. *The Harlem Renaissance: A Brief History with Documents*. Boston: Bedford/St. Martin's, 2008.

Fleming, Robert. *James Weldon Johnson*. Boston: Twayne, 1997.

Goellnicht, Donald. "Passing as Autobiography: James Weldon Johnson's *The Autobiography of an Ex-Colored Man*." *African American Review* 30.1 (1996): 17–33.

Harris, Cheryl I. "Whiteness as Property." *Harvard Law Review* 106.8 (1993): 1707–1791.

Huggins, Nathaniel Irvin. *Harlem Renaissance*. New York: Oxford, 1971.

Hughes, Langston. *Not Without Laughter*. New York: Dover, 2008.

Johnson, James Weldon. *The Autobiography of an Ex-Colored Man*. New York: Dover, 1995.

Kostenlanetz. Richard. "The Politics of Passing: The Fiction of James Weldon Johnson." *Negro American Literature Forum* 3.1 (1969): 22–24, 29.

Levy, Eugene. *James Weldon Johnson: Black Leader Black Voice*. Chicago: U Chicago P, 1973.

Moran, Mary Jo. "*Not Without Laughter*." *The English Journal* 663 (1977): 58.

Phinney, Jean. "Ethnic identity in adolescents and adults: Review of Research." *Psychological Bulletin* 108.3 (1990): 499–514.

Schaefer, Richard. "Double Consciousness." *Encyclopedia of Race, Ethnicity, and Society*. Thousand Oaks, CA: SAGE, 2008. 412–414.

Shields, John P. "Never Cross the Divide: Reconstructing Langston Hughes' *Not Without Laughter*." *African American Review* 28 (1994): 601–613.

Shultz, Elizabeth. "Natural and Unnatural Circumstances in Langston's *Not Without Laughter*." *Callaloo* 25.4 (2002): 1176–1187.

"Why Hadn't She Spoken That Day?": The Destructive Power of Racial Silence in Nella Larsen's *Passing*

Holly T. Baker

For African Americans, the act of "passing" as white is a practice situated in a philosophy of contradictions. Passing is both liberating and imprisoning in its purpose of assimilating oneself into a dominant white culture, while at the same time instilling fear of discovery and self-revelation in its practitioners. For two centuries, black American poets and novelists have addressed the troubling nature of passing in both white and black contexts. In the short story "The Wife of His Youth," for example, Charles W. Chesnutt, the son of two mixed-race freemen born in the postwar South, tells the story of a biracial man, Mr. Ryder. Mr. Ryder is a prominent member of the Blue Vein Society, an organization of mixed-race individuals who are "more white than black" and which promotes the practice of intermarriages with a goal to "lighten" the race, that is, to become more white. Justifying himself and this controversial position, Mr. Ryder states, "Our fate lies between absorption by the white race and extinction in the black. The one doesn't want us yet, but may take us in time. The other would welcome us, but it would be for us a backward step" (Chesnutt).

The tension between assimilation and self-assertion exhibited in Mr. Ryder's statement, though written more than a hundred years ago, highlights the instability of the position experienced by one of mixed race in America, then and now. And in the unspoken spaces of Mr. Ryder's bold claims of selfhood is a secret that, when revealed, exposes the reality of his own fears of self-revelation and an identity and past he does not wish to claim. Mr. Ryder is a pseudonym, his origin is slavery, and the wife of his youth, whom he has not seen in twenty-five years, is a black woman. Initially, Mr. Ryder is compelled to silence her to hide the truth that he was not born a freeman, a past and identity he regards as shameful. In the end, however, after verifying others' collective opinion that it is good for a man to acknowledge his wife, he confesses that the black woman in their midst is his estranged wife. Although his breaking of the racial silence is written as an act of bravery and less of duty, his confession is not brave at all, in that it is delivered only at the allowance and verified approval of the guests in attendance, all who are aligned with the ideology of the superiority of whiteness. Whether through silence or speaking, these actions are dictated by and measured against the opinion of the white majority. This hegemonic force is the same imperative that influences the silent spaces in Nella Larsen's *Passing*, written approximately thirty years after Charles W. Chesnutt's 1899 short story, a novel still concerned with the black race's entrapment between absorption and extinction.

In *Yearning: Race, Gender, and Cultural Politics*, bell hooks expresses a fear that has accompanied black Americans for centuries, that of being "out of our place—not conforming to social norms, especially those set by the white supremacy, which would lead to destruction, even death" (1). Blackness is, in itself, a marker of difference, easily spotted and swiftly condemned to status as a second-class citizen, both institutionally (as with Southern segregation laws) and in social reality (as with unlawful discrimination). hooks' fears are not unfounded, as in American history as well as in the modern day, white racism against black people is seemingly justified when people of color engage in any aberrant behavior or when their actions do not conform to acceptable behaviors established and accepted by white rule.[1] In Nella Larsen's 1929 short novel *Passing*, however, it is the *un*sanctioned *conforming* to social norms that leads to death and destruction, suggesting the impossibility of black reconciliation with a white world.

Irene Redfield, a woman of both African and European ancestry, embodies the liminal tension of being able to "pass" as white, aided by a mask of silence, while simultaneously embracing and defending her black heritage, leaving her perpetually "out of our place" (*Yearning* 1) as hooks describes it, and so in constant danger of exposure and destruction. Irene is set at odds with Clare Kendry, a childhood acquaintance who has been passing as white for years, seemingly without guilt or regret. Irene disapproves of Clare's undetected assimilation into white society; nevertheless, throughout the novel, she joins Clare in silent solidarity during moments of possible self-revelation. By performing silence, Irene denies her own identity and thereby falls victim to white hegemony that would see her, a black woman, remain both silent and oppressed, despite superficially (that is to say, on the surface) seeming to be part of that dominating force that encroaches on black spaces, even when no white people are physically present; by performing silence, she is therefore unwittingly complicit in the suppression of black voices and speeds the destruction of those who would choose to pass without consequence. The dangers of vocalized self-assertion—and consequently, self-actualization—are realized in both physical and metaphorical destructions of selfhood that occur when that silence is broken in both public and private spaces.

While both Irene and Clare perform silence, readers are given access only to Irene's internalized struggle and the tension between what she thinks and what she vocalizes. Equally important, it is through *Irene* that the racial silence of the novel is first encountered, which highlights the oppressions already enacted upon her race. At the beginning of the novel, the power of vocalized language emerges as a theme when Irene, sitting alone in a restaurant surrounded by white people and being invisible among them as a black woman who can "pass," first becomes discomfited when she notices another woman staring at her. Incredulous, but fearful that she has been identified as non-white, she raises her emotional defenses: "Irene felt . . . anger, scorn, and fear slide over her. It wasn't that she was ashamed of being a Negro, or even of having it declared. It was the idea of being ejected from any place . . . that disturbed her" (Larsen 150). Although she asserts to herself that she is not ashamed of her race, it is evident that she fears the consequences of the declaration itself and the influence of language to convict her as an intruder in the all-white space. Already, owing to the whiteness of the space she finds herself in, Irene is nervous of the white gaze and is on her guard, and she is primed to notice others' wariness and potential hostility in return: "by some sixth sense she was acutely aware that someone was watching her" (149). But the white gaze alone does not have power to condemn her as an intruder. It is the *declaration* of being named *Negro* that scares her. Here, Larsen clearly establishes the societal power of the spoken word. Given that language has the power to damn a woman like Irene, it is no wonder, then, why she would find greater security in silence.

The woman who has spotted her and identified her as black is Clare Kendry, a childhood acquaintance who left the black community and has been successfully passing as white ever since. Without ever revealing her past or black identity, Clare joined white society, married a white man, and had a daughter whom she was relieved to discover was light-skinned, like herself, lest the child's, and her own, true heritage be exposed. Because there are no obvious physical markers, Clare's assimilation is possible only because she does not *speak* of her origins, and so with the act of passing comes an inherently enforced silence, lest she reveal herself. Thus, Clare's true identity is doubly shielded—she wears a mask of whiteness and a mask of silence. bell hooks, writing of the masks black people wear in white spaces historically and now, gives voice to the internal and, therefore hidden, anxieties existing under the mask: "As in the old days of racial segregation where black folks learned to 'wear the mask,' many of us pretend to be comfortable in the face of whiteness only to turn our backs and give expression to intense levels of discomfort" (hooks, *Black Looks* 169).

On the surface, Clare does not seem bothered by her lifestyle or anxious about her secret. But as Irene observes, "Appearances . . . had a way sometimes of not fitting facts" (Larsen 156). She suspects that what Irene thinks of as Clare's "ivory mask" (157) is disguising the truth of how she feels about passing at all. That is, feeling out of place, removed from black spaces, but not fully integrated into white, and furthermore, unable to return. Her liminal position irritates Irene, as Cherene Sherrard-Johnson notes in "'A Plea for Color': Nella Larsen's Iconography of the Mulatta," because "[Clare] is a woman without regard for the boundaries of either white or black society whose presence reflects the hypocrisy and desires of both groups" (854). Clare has done what Irene *could* do—disregard the racial boundaries and pass as white—but what Irene has chosen not to do in favor of aligning herself with the black race; what Clare does, she views as a betrayal.

Nevertheless, the notion of passing intrigues Irene and inspires her with questions; and although Irene desires to interrogate Clare's passing at this meeting, she cannot broach the subject. Larsen writes,

> She wished to find out about this hazardous business of "passing," this breaking away from all that was familiar and friendly to take one's chances in another environment, not entirely strange, perhaps, but certainly not friendly. What, for example, one did about background, how one accounted for oneself. And how one felt when one came into contact with other Negroes. But she couldn't. (157)

Irene's compulsion to keep silent on the subject stems from a number of influences. For one, as emphasized earlier, their meeting takes place in a white space, that is, a space of oppression due to the white people whose mere presence enforces a mask of silence. This oppression, hinted at even before the reader becomes aware that Irene herself is not in fact white, is manifest in her discomfort of the gaze of others and her own shyness of holding another's eyes too long: "She tried to treat the woman and her watching with indifference, but she couldn't. All her efforts to ignore her, *it* [emphasis added], were futile" (Larsen 150). White space here might just as easily be equated with *public* space or any space existing beyond the security of the known and relatively safer black home, neighborhood, or community. In this sense, public space is most certainly defined by the majority and, therefore, the white hegemony.

A less obvious reason for Irene's silence (i.e., her resistance to questioning Clare's decision to pass as white) is that she is uncomfortable with the very concept of passing, despite the fact that she herself is, in that very moment, taking advantage of her light skin color, which is serving to mask her own blackness, allowing her to sit in a white space without consequence; her discomfort usurps any curiosity and perpetuates her mode of silence. After relating to Clare the facts of her own life over the past twelve years of separation, Irene tries to excuse herself to leave without asking after any of the details of Clare's life. She finds herself uneasy as she realizes she has a "very definite unwillingness to do so" (that is, discover the truth of Clare's situation and family in the white world) and that she is "quite well aware of the reason for that reluctance" (Larsen 155). Those reasons are embedded in disapproval, a position which becomes more apparent as the novel progresses, but which, in this moment of uncertainty, she is unable to articulate in her unwillingness to interrogate either Clare or her own feelings of ambivalence toward passing.

Catherine Rottenberg, in her essay "Passing: Race, Identification, and Desire," explores this position of ambivalence, both in Irene and Nella Larsen. She writes,

> Many analyses have attempted to determine whether or not Larsen's use of passing can be seen as a subversive strategy, that is, whether the narrative serves to reinforce hegemonic norms of race or whether it ultimately posits passing as a viable survival strategy, which has the potential to disrupt "the enclosures of a unitary identity." (Rottenberg 435)

Irene can certainly be read as one who "represent[s] the subject who appropriates and internalizes hegemonic norms of race" (Rottenberg 436), and it is her recognition, however resentful, of her subjectivity within a racial hierarchy that both establishes and reinforces her silence on the matter of passing, a position that has no power tending toward resistance. To speak (that is, to break the silence that has been enforced upon her) and articulate her disapproval or even a defense of her own race would be an act of defiance, and to perform this kind of defiance in a white space would invite the consequences deemed appropriate, not by Clare, but by the white majority already there (e.g., she might have to suffer the humiliation of being asked to leave), thereby stripping her of her own white mask, her dignity, and even her autonomy as the controlling power reinforces its authority and reestablishes her silence—this time as an absence. It is this threat of absolute silencing—absenting and destruction—that black Americans fear (hooks, *Yearning* 1).

The hegemonic norms that Rottenberg names have power that extends beyond the boundaries of white spaces and penetrates what might otherwise be considered black sanctuaries. In Irene's own home and with her own family, further silences persist, arising from tensions that also center on race. Although Irene is light enough of skin to be able to pass as white, Brian, her husband, cannot pass, nor can their children. And though Irene identifies as black and holds strong allegiance to her race, insofar as she condemns others for abandoning it, she and Brian are not aligned in all aspects of what it means to defend the race. Where Irene stops herself from giving voice to her non-majority-compliant thoughts, Brian is much bolder and outspoken; he is also more political and openly critical of white oppression. Irene, on the other hand, though exhibiting some passion on the subject of passing, shies away from openly debating him, especially when she feels her own position is less defensible or insufficiently supported. Attempting to articulate her ambivalence about her encounter with Clare to her husband and about her failure to speak in defense of the race when confronted with Clare's husband, John Bellew, for fear of exposing herself, Clare, and others as black, Irene tells Brian, "'It's a funny thing about 'passing.' We disapprove of it and at the same time condone it. It excites our contempt and yet we rather admire it. We shy away from it with an odd kind of revulsion, but we protect it'" (Larsen 185–86). Through Irene, Larsen expresses the complexity of paradoxical emotions black people wrestle with as oppressed subjects. Her words are contemplative, reflective, and interrogating, not only of her own attitude toward passing, but of that of her people.

Brian's response cuts through the contradictory philosophies and straight to a behavioral, Darwinian understanding of passing: "'Instinct,'" he says, "'of the race to survive and expand'" (Larsen 186). This attitude, while perhaps less refined and more animalistic in nature, recalls Mr. Ryder's own sentiments in Chesnutt's "The Wife of His Youth": "'Our fate lies between absorption by the white race and extinction in the black.'" This dismissive explanation can be read almost as a logical, or at least a biological, acceptance of miscegenation (Joo), ignoring the complex of history and culture;

and though engaging in the dialogue, Brian's answer is abrupt, almost curt in its assertion, leaving Irene little ground for argument. And in fact, she poses none. After giving a quick example of how whites engage in the same self-preservative and self-perpetuating behavior as blacks through colonizing territories across the globe and procreating with the native inhabitants (Larsen 186), Brian repeats his first conviction about survival, and Irene, despite her disagreement with his claims, falls silent. Larsen writes of her silence with respect to her husband: "Many arguments in the past had taught her the futility of attempting to combat Brian on ground where he was more nearly at home than she. Ignoring his unqualified assertion, she slid away from the subject entirely" (186).

A feminist or gendered reading of this conversation certainly seems to imply a clear division of masculine and feminine domains in which Brian, as man and husband, is more assertive in his speech and claims the final word on the matter, and Irene, as woman and wife, performs submissiveness and ultimately silence within the marriage. Though a valid reading, the argument being made here is that this conversation becomes uncomfortable for Irene, not because she is a woman—there are many other instances in the novel where she clearly asserts her own will within the family—but because of the broader despotic, hegemonic influences that have encroached on the home of a black family, thus disrupting the harmony in the home. The bigotries and concerns Irene and Brian contend with outside the home cannot be divorced from the lives they live within it and become the greatest sources of contention within their marriage. To escape American prejudice against people of color, Brian wants to leave New York and move to Brazil where there is acceptance of color and intermarriages. Fearing a departure from the familiar, however racially prejudiced, Irene firmly opposes him, which almost leads to the dissolution of their union. Instead, Brian relents, as Larsen writes, and "there had been, in all the years that they had lived together since then, no other talk of it" (187). Silence on the subject persists, and yet behind it, Irene fears that Brian, resentful of her, his job, and his country, would one day leave.

Irene prefers not to think about the prejudices and injustices that exist beyond the walls of her home, however, and insists on shielding their two children, Ted and Junior, from the harsh realities distinct to their race, that they might have a happy and innocent childhood. Contrarily, Brian chooses to speak freely to them of matters such as racial hatred and violence. The ideological disagreement comes to a head one day when, at the dinner table, Ted asks his father why only colored people were ever lynched. This critical moment recalls the severity of racial hatred and justified fear in the communal black consciousness, one to which the boys have not yet been exposed and which the novel does not treat directly. Though Brian tries to answer his son's question, Irene chastises her husband for discussing such a thing and terminates the conversation. Later, when they are alone, she mandates, "'You're not to talk to them about the race problem. I won't have it'" (Larsen 232). But Brian fights back, calls her stupid, accuses her of harming the children in their preparation for life as black Americans, and refuses to stop teaching them. Larsen then writes, "Under the lash of his words she was silent" (232). The termination of this argument does not resolve it in either triumph or concession; rather, it is a breaking of dialogue, forestalling an honest exchange of ideas and progress toward a positive resolution.

In *Yearning*, bell hooks is critical of this mode of silence—not just the silencing of black voices *inter*racially but more significantly the power of white hegemony to silence black voices *within* the race, one to another, as between Irene and Brian, or even, in other contexts, between Irene and Clare. Hooks explains the mentality that influences many black people not to engage in internal conflicts, suggesting that they "feared that disagreement among themselves might disrupt feelings of racial bonding and solidarity" (hooks, *Yearning* 6), a fear especially pertinent when solidarity is so important for mere survival, let alone Brian's "expansion of the race." However, hooks argues that such disagreements are actually productive, even necessary, for enacting any political change. She writes,

> As we educate one another to acquire critical consciousness, we
> have the chance to see how important airing diverse perspectives

Critical Insights

can be for any progressive political struggle that is serious about transformation. Engaging in intellectual exchange where people hear a diversity of viewpoints enables them to witness firsthand solidarity that grows strong in a context of productive critical exchange and confrontation. (hooks, *Yearning* 6)

On a local level, this disruption plays out within the Redfield household. Irene's insistence on silencing unpleasant discussions or educating their young children in hooks' "critical [social] consciousness" (hooks, *Yearning* 6) about race prohibits possible progress toward a more equitable society. Not only does she keep herself from understanding or sympathizing with Brian's position, but she also prohibits herself from exploring the question she herself posed, thereby retarding her exercise in self-reflection and disabling her from either understanding or clearly articulating a diverse opinion. Irene's attempt to shield her children is a sympathetic one, but rather than nullifying the children's deep-rooted fears (those existing within the collective black consciousness), she dismisses them, downplaying the reality of racial prejudice at best, disregarding it as inconsequential or imaginary at worst. By creating a mode of silence in the Redfield household on matters as important as racial injustice in the interest of keeping the peace, Larsen shows how easy it is to keep a marginalized group oppressed: condition them to perpetuate their own oppression. If vocalizing objections, however warranted, leads to discomfort and encourages silence, then the possibility of revolution is greatly diminished and leads only to a furthering of the oppression and destruction of the race.

This act of perpetuating silence within the race is seen in more startling execution when Irene visits Clare and Gertrude (another woman who can pass and who married a white man, although, unlike with Clare's marriage, there is no secrecy as to her race). Although all three of them share in the ability to pass and the conversation leans naturally toward its discussion, it is not long before the subject causes discomfort for each of them in their circumstances, not least of all because their opinions are not aligned. Before long, their discomfort is manifest in polite "smiles of mutual reservation" (Larsen 169). What might have evolved into an honest discussion on the merits and drawbacks of passing cannot be performed for two reasons. First, they are in a white space (the Kendry home) enacting white traditions (they are sitting for tea) and having white conversation; the absence of any white people does not change the whiteness of the space. And second, they have internalized hegemonic rule that labels discussion about race and passing as taboo in that black people themselves are taboo. Thus, Irene does not feel able to speak freely, and the conversation soon turns away from the subject altogether. Though *speech* continues, it is hollow, as it is void of real content in the interest of politeness. Larsen writes how "Clare began to talk, steering carefully away from anything that might lead towards race or other thorny subjects" (169–70).

Silence, here, is not the absence of sound, but the absence of significance, an open exchange of ideas, either conflicting or unified, which leads to this important, though disturbing, moment of Irene's acceptance: "For a while the *illusion of general conversation* [emphasis added] was nearly perfect. Irene felt her resentment changing gradually to a silent, somewhat grudging admiration" (Larsen 170). Larsen's use of the word *illusion* is significant in the context of silence. Silence can easily be misread as acquiescence, placidity, and contentment, when in fact placidity and contentment are an illusion, another type of mask shielding the more profound discontentment and anger that broils underneath the unmarked surface. But worse, as in Irene's case, the long-practiced mode of silence may actually, over time, begin to deceive its practitioner into believing in his or her own state of contentment. For Irene, this is a state of "grudging admiration," which, given enough time, may transform into "admiration" and a loss of the displeasure that arises in her when she fails to speak out and defend her race. In its capacity to negatively or counter-productively alter attitudes, silence smothers autonomous selfhood and transforms black people into the very kind of people the whites would design them to be: absent.

Perhaps the most critical moment in the novel, where the tension accompanying fear of revelation is at its peak, occurs when Irene meets John Bellew, Clare's white husband. Because Bellew is ignorant of his wife's race, Irene is forced into a position where she must keep silent to protect not only Clare's identity but her own, especially as it becomes starkly apparent that Bellew holds unequivocally racist views. He calls his wife "Nig," a pet name commenting on how the color of her skin has seemed to darken over the years of their marriage; and when questioned as to whether he dislikes Negroes, he responds strongly and unambiguously, "'I don't dislike them, I hate them. . . . They give me the creeps. The black scrimy devils'" (Larsen 172). At his words, Irene's ire flares. Larsen writes, "There was a brief silence, during which she feared that her self-control was about to prove too frail a bridge to support her mounting anger and indignation. . . . [But] the impulse passed, obliterated by her consciousness and the danger in which such rashness would involve Clare" (172). Her anger is dually silenced, first by the outside threat of danger and second by her own self-censorship. Although this might be read as either self-mastery over her emotions (unlikely) or even as Brian's notion of survival and therefore self-preservation, it is more likely that, given the context of the first reason, she does not speak (fear of outside, cultural forces), and what may seem to be self-control is really evidence of hegemonic forces intruding upon and usurping *inner*-spaces, private spaces, or selfhood itself.

This moment of silence plagues Irene for weeks to come with the question: "Why hadn't she spoken that day? . . . Why had she failed to take up the defense of the race to which she belonged?" (Larsen 182). The answer, a social reality, is not a surprising one. As bell hooks articulates, "All black people in the United States, irrespective of class status or politics, live with the possibility that they will be terrorized by whiteness" (*Black Looks* 175). The danger here is not imagined, but grounded in historical precedent and the reality of both physical and psychological harm. Larsen alludes to those psychological and physical harms both in the abstract (when Irene's children ask about lynching) and the specific (when Irene considers the disturbing *Rhinelander v. Rhinelander*[2] case as precedence when she wonders what might happen to Clare if Bellew were to discover her blackness). Once again, it is fear of white hegemony that silences Irene from speaking and defending her race.

But although her silence here is a matter of self-preservation and even the preservation of the other "passing" black women in the room, most notably Clare, that same silence has the potential to prove, ultimately, destructive.

Although Irene's silence has potential consequences for herself and her race, the destructive power of her silence is realized most dramatically in Clare in two significant ways. First, silence can be described not only as that which is left unspoken, but more significantly as the *absence* of language—the signifier to the signified. As Benjamin Whorf, an American linguist and contemporary of Nella Larsen, suggested, it is language that shapes experiential reality (Halliday 48–55). Therefore, in the absence of a signifier, the signified suffers. Not only does the signified lack verbal assertion, it also lacks actualization in a communal reality, thereby lessening, on a metaphorical level, its authenticity, transforming the signified into an absence itself.

In the last third of the novel, Irene's silence with respect to Clare as a meaningful person begins to break her down as Clare hurtles toward a permanent absenting: her inevitable death. Although Clare is now a more *tangible* presence in Irene's life, Irene's ambivalence toward her, her waffling between "joy and vexation" (Larsen 208) at her comings, refuses to manifest itself in language. Larsen writes, "Irene, while secretly resenting these visits . . . , for some obscure reason which she *shied away for putting into words* [emphasis added], never requested that Clare make an end of them" (209). Irene is not alone in her ambivalence, which is repeated in her husband: "It couldn't be said that [Clare's] presence seemed to please him. It didn't annoy or disturb him. . . . That was all" (209). Neither Irene nor her husband is especially fond of Clare, but they do not reject her. This failure to *articulate* places Clare in a precarious place, as far as linguistic reality is concerned within the narrative. Just as she is neither black nor white in a cultural existence, she is also liminal in her identity of definition, and the erasure of the expression of a thing results in the erasure of the thing itself. If she does not exist in language, she does not exist anywhere, turning her liminality into *nothingness*, existing neither in language nor in language-making reality. As Nell Sullivan suggests, the novel's title and primary concern, passing, can also be read as "the subject's disappearance in the narrative" (373). Disappearance, or absenting, is a sure form of both permanent silence and destruction.

Within the narrative's own reality, Clare's destruction is made certain in Irene's silence. When Irene next encounters Bellew, he sees her in the presence of another black person, placing her and, consequently, Clare at risk of exposure once again. Irene knows this, but she deliberately remains silent and fails to inform Clare of this encounter, which would serve as a warning and prepare for a confrontation with her husband. As it happens, when Bellew learns the truth and confronts Clare in his wrath, Clare falls out of a window to her death. This moment in the narrative is left intentionally ambiguous, suggesting that either Bellew or Irene may have pushed her or that Clare committed suicide. The uncertainty of her cause of death is significant, in that Irene, the witness closest to the scene, *cannot,* for years to come, remember what truly happened. Her silence had inspired a guilt-ridden conscience and fear of outcome—an effect of white terrorization—which augmented in time to a kind of paranoia and madness (Carr). Not only does Irene secretly wish Clare dead so as to be rid of the burden of her and of the consequences of passing she represents, but her failure to remember what really happened to cause Clare's death is itself a kind of destruction—an erasure of truth and so of a history that would rewrite black oppression as blameless. In this way, Irene's silence and inaction, which is caused by white hegemonic forces, arguably leads to Clare's death, suggesting perhaps that racial silence—and more important, racial *silencing*—has the devastating power to destroy the whole race.

Notes

1. Examples of de jure and de facto racism run rampant throughout American history. Particularly in our own day are numerous instances of blacks being characterized as threatening and dangerous—from police shootings of unarmed black men, to police brutality against peaceful black protestors, to mischaracterizations of black children

as more disobedient, more dishonest, and more prone to criminal behavior than white children (Rich).

2. See Thaggert, Madigan, and Carlson. The infamous *Rhinelander v. Rhinelander* case of 1925 highlights how passing, for African American women in particular, may have serious consequences on an institutional level. In 1924, Leonard Rhinelander, a white man from a prominent and wealthy family, married Alice Jones, of English descent, including one parent of mixed ethnicity. Leonard's father, Philip Rhinelander, responding to claims in the press that his son had married a "Negress" (Carlson 138), convinced his son to sue for annulment of the marriage on the charge that Alice had lied about her race. What makes this case particularly notable is the decisive evidence the defense used to prove that Leonard Rhinelander could not possibly have been ignorant about his wife's race. Baring her to the waist before the eyes of the jury, lawyers, and Leonard Rhinelander himself, the defense exposed the "truth" of her color, which could not be mistaken for white and which Leonard had witnessed himself before entering into the marriage. Through this humiliating tactic, the defense convincingly argued its case, and the jury agreed that Rhinelander had entered into the marriage with full knowledge of Alice Jones' racial background. In the end, Jones received monetary settlements, but the humiliation of exposing her body in a court of law could not be repaired so easily.

Works Cited

Carlson, A. Cheree. *The Crimes of Womanhood: Defining Femininity in a Court of Law*. Chicago: U of Chicago P, 2009.

Carr, Brian. "Paranoid Interpretation, Desire's Nonobject, and Nella Larsen's *Passing*." *PMLA* 119.2 (2004): 282–295.

Chesnutt, Charles W. "The Wife of His Youth." *The Charles Chesnutt Digital Archive*, Stephanie P. Browner, ed. Web. 6 Nov. 2013.

Halliday, M. A. K. "Systemic Background." *Systemic Perspectives on Discourse. The Collected Works of M. A. K.* London: Continuum, 1985.

hooks, bell. *Black Looks: Race and Representation*. Cambridge, MA: South End P, 1992.

_____. *Yearning: Race, Gender, and Cultural Politics*. Cambridge, MA: South End P, 1999.

Joo, Hee-Jung Serenity. "Miscegenation, Assimilation, and Consumption: Racial Passing in George Schuyler's *Black No More* and Eric Liu's *The Accidental Asian*." *MELUS* 33.3 (2008): 169–90.

Larsen, Nella. *Quicksand & Passing*. 14th edition. Ed. Deborah E. McDowell. 2004. New Brunswick, NJ: Rutgers U P. American Women Writers Ser.

Madigan, Mark J. "Miscegenation and 'The Dicta of Race and Class': The Rhinelander Case and Nella Larsen's *Passing*." *Modern Fiction Studies* 36.4 (1990): 523–529.

Rottenberg, Catherine. "Passing: Race, Identification, and Desire." *Criticism* 45.4 (2003): 435–452.

Rich, Motoko. "School Data Finds Pattern of Inequality along Racial Lines." *New York Times*. The New York Times Company, 21 Mar. 2014. Web. 19 June 2015.

Sherrard-Johnson, Cherene. "'A Plea for Color': Nella Larsen's Iconography of the Mulatta." *American Literature* 76.4 (2004): 833–869.

Sullivan, Nell. "Nella Larsen's *Passing* and the Fading Subject." *African American Review* 32.3 (1998): 373–386.

Thaggert, Miriam. "Racial Etiquette: Nella Larsen's *Passing* and the Rhinelander Case." *Meridians: Feminism, Race, Transnationalism* 5.2 (2005): 1–29.

Just Passing Through: The Harlem Renaissance Woman on the Move_____

Joshua M. Murray

The Harlem Renaissance was a period of flux and transition. Writers and visionaries called for a fresh and modern identity for peoples of the black diaspora, and in the monumental volume *The New Negro: An Interpretation* (1925), Alain Locke emphasized the need for artists, musicians, and writers who could inject a black modernism into works of the twentieth century. The resultant literature examined the daily life of the New Negro, incorporating themes of race, class, social status, and transition, mirroring the principal issues of the day. Though there were nearly as many critics as there were advocates of the movement, it nonetheless made a lasting impression on American literature and culture.

Within three novels of the Harlem Renaissance, Walter White's *Flight* (1926), Jessie Redmon Fauset's *Plum Bun: A Novel Without a Moral* (1928), and Nella Larsen's *Quicksand* (1928), the protagonists' liminal states involve the problematic and indefinite blurring of racial and gender categories, which allows us to trace the subsequent dichotomous trends toward transition and stagnation. The concept of liminality is complex and nuanced, yet Victor Turner conveys its defining characteristic succinctly: "betwixt and between" (95). In realizing their liminal status—in essence, an irreconcilable feeling of instability and incompleteness—the characters of these novels view Harlem and other cities at times as idealized, therapeutic places. In these stories, travel and transition occupy a thematic role. Each protagonist becomes dissatisfied with some aspect of life and, therefore, chooses mobility as a hopeful remedy.

Simultaneously, the unique position of the African American race during the Harlem Renaissance creates a liminal space. The majority of the minor characters in these novels successfully avoid this state of transition and marginality by joining certain prescribed communities, either in Harlem or elsewhere. The protagonists who fail to conform, however, find themselves forced into a period of restlessness and transition. Thus, the degree of liminality is twofold: first, the characters are marginalized within their personal communities due to their race, gender, or both, and second, their choice of transition as an attempt to resolve their issues creates a geographical flux, existing between cities. Their inability to locate an appropriate community following their transitions leaves them in suspension, thereby remaining liminal until they concede to an alteration in their personal lifestyles and/or identities.

The first two novels, White's *Flight* and Fauset's *Plum Bun*, portray protagonists who employ passing in conjunction with their travels. Both Mimi Daquin and Angela Murray decide to pass as white following a move, a choice that briefly elicits a desired happiness. In the end, both women decide to follow their convictions and identify as black, though the conclusions are not without problems of their own. Larsen's *Quicksand* deviates from the first two works in that protagonist Helga Crane does not pass for white in the novel, though she does travel frequently and finds herself torn between racial identities. Helga's transnational quest for selfhood falls flat in the end when she relegates herself to a life she had previously disdained: marrying a Southern minister and mothering five children. In each case, the protagonists find themselves dissatisfied, and they therefore turn to geographical transition as an attempt to escape feelings of inadequacy and inferiority. Despite this valiant impetus for mobility, the leading women find true freedom elusive. Each novel presents an inevitably and unavoidably problematic "resolution," though two of the three presumably maintain that an adequate outcome has been achieved.

Racial and Social Mobility in White's *Flight*

Of the three authors considered here, Walter White has traditionally received the least scholarly attention. He stands out within this essay as the only male writer, though others not examined here, such as Wallace Thurman, have utilized female protagonists in their novels. Nonetheless, White creates a compelling tale in which protagonist Mimi Daquin employs various devices including passing and travel to outwardly express her introspection on matters of race, religion, and war. While Mimi's apparent freedom at the conclusion of White's book has been called "uncomplicated" (Belluscio 214) in comparison to her formative journey and the experiences of other Harlem Renaissance protagonists, she still leaves room for us to question whether she truly achieves her sought-after resolution in the end.

Foregrounding *Flight* on the notion of transition, White introduces Mimi to the reader in the Atlanta train station, a quintessential house of transportation at the turn of the twentieth century. The reader only learns of the Daquins' origins in New Orleans through an extended flashback. Once White has established Atlanta as the primary setting through the first chapter, he utilizes the second chapter to explain the Daquins' love of New Orleans and subsequent reluctance to move to Atlanta. The reader also learns here of the Daquin family's history, namely that Mimi's mother Margot died when the daughter was only nine years old, and Mimi's father Jean remarried two years later to Mary Robertson. The new Mrs. Daquin therefore creates the tension that ultimately leads to the family's relocation to Atlanta, as she searches "for the progressiveness and bustle and eager hurrying" she had left behind in her native Chicago (White 31). In this familial iteration, we first see the Daquins arrive in the station on the first page of the novel.

While the plot would remain relatively unchanged were these two initial chapters inverted, the seemingly innocuous narrative choice prefigures what will become Mimi's modus operandi throughout the latter half of the novel. In fact, the novel halves itself nearly perfectly with the Atlanta setting occupying the initial twelve chapters and Mimi's travels to Philadelphia, New York, and Paris permeating the final twelve. While the first half maintains a physical stagnancy, Mimi's experiences in matters of love and race lay the psychological foundation for the forthcoming disillusionment that urges her forward and outward. For instance, soon after the Daquins' move, Mimi discovers the extent to which race plays a role in delineating Atlanta's social boundaries. New Orleans, especially for Mimi and her father, had been a place of racial ambiguity, or at least one of racial insignificance. One of Mimi's foundational moments then occurs when, in Atlanta, she realizes the distinct societal bounds enacted based on race:

> "Her own people." The phrase interested her. In New Orleans she had thought all people were hers—that only individuals mattered. But here there were sharp, unchanging lines which seemed to matter with extraordinary power. This one was white—that one black. Even though the 'white' one was swarthy while the 'black' one might be as fair as the whitest of the white. (White 54)

In moments such as this, not to mention the horrific race riot she witnesses firsthand, Mimi becomes acutely aware of the place she occupies within American society, one in which her racial identity obviates her more personal characteristics.

Though these experiences jointly work to create inner turmoil, they ultimately have little to do with her departure from the southern metropolis. Instead, Mimi's status as woman plays a larger role in her exodus. When Mimi spends a passionate night with Carl Hunter, son of Mrs. Daquin's best friend, she becomes pregnant. Initially joyful of her and Carl's tangible creation of love, she becomes disheartened when Carl, the Hunters, and Mrs. Daquin all greet the news less than enthusiastically. Faced with the options of abortion or forced marriage in order to "give the kid a clean name" (White 150), Mimi chooses a third alternative. She could not accept the option of marriage, for she would constantly feel "that she had done something disgraceful and by that means had married into their family" (153). Even the diction here indicates the sexist manner in which society views Mimi as the sole guilty party and in which marriage would be a gift granted by Carl. Prior to her discovery of the pregnancy, Mimi realized rather presciently her dismal fate:

> Here I am, she mused, a woman, a Negro. Life for me if I were white would be hard enough, but it's going to be doubly so when I have race problems added to my own difficulties as a woman. She toyed idly with the notion as to what her lot would have been if she had been born white . . . . The idea was not attractive. (White 125–26)

Nonetheless, Mimi soon opts for an intranational move to escape the innate sexism of the South, more so than the racism. Because her father had died soon before the realization of the pregnancy, Mimi chooses easily to move to Philadelphia and maintain her uncompromised physical and ideological independence.

As Mimi soon realizes, a simple shift in setting cannot eliminate the issues she faced in Atlanta. While in Philadelphia, poverty and motherhood present Mimi with obstacles that keep her barely afloat. She eventually determines that she cannot continue down this path, so she places her son *Petit* Jean in an orphanage. When her past "crimes" catch up with her and her social circles begin to deteriorate through gossip and speculation, Mimi decides with finality to transition once more, this time from black to white. As Amanda M. Page aptly describes, "In a twist on the standard plot, White creates a heroine who passes as much to avoid bourgeois African-American constructions of female respectability as to avoid white racism" (107).

During this period, which lasts a decade, Mimi achieves success never previously available to her. Professionally, Mimi ascends to the rank of second-in-command at Francine's, a posh boutique in Manhattan. In conjunction with this new job, Mimi gains access to upper class social circles, and she also begins spending a quarter of each year in Paris. Personally, Mimi marries an eligible white bachelor, Jimmie Forrester, whereby she appears to truly find happiness and love, two objectives she had previously thought lost causes. Despite these achievements, when Mimi attends the theater with a friend, she experiences a "sudden rekindling of the race-consciousness which had lain dormant for nearly ten years" (White 293). A simultaneous rekindling of dissatisfaction occurs, and she resolves soon thereafter to leave her white husband and procrastinate obtaining freedom no longer.

In the end, Mimi contends that she has found the solution that had heretofore remained undetected. For the first time since much earlier in her life, Mimi feels a satisfaction she had sought through her various moves and transitions. She acts upon this newly realized emotion by deciding to leave Jimmie without so much as a word. Following an exuberant emergence into the world without hindrance, we see the famous and oft-cited final paragraph of Mimi's story. Here, she provides the reader with her thoughts on how she has finally achieved freedom: "'Free! Free! Free!' she whispered exultantly as with firm tread she went down the steps. '*Petit* Jean—my own people—and happiness!' was the song in her heart as she happily strode through the dawn, the rays of the morning sun dancing lightly upon the more brilliant gold of her hair" (White 300). In light of Mimi's final experience, Page contends, "Though suspicious of racial purity, White nonetheless concludes *Flight* with the heroine reaffirming her commitment to black identity. With this commitment comes a corresponding allegiance to the fight against white racism on behalf of the international community of color" (95). Through this statement, she takes White at his word when he details Mimi's transcendent awakening.

Despite Page's insistence, this conclusion remains problematic. At this point in the novel, Mimi has become entrenched within an identity quite opposite of what she proclaims. She has lived in Manhattan passing as white for nearly a decade. She has lived apart from her son, the *Petit* Jean to whom she apostrophizes her declaration for upwards of twelve years; he has presumably found happiness "in the kindly French family with whom he lived" (White 239) after Mimi removed him from the Baltimore orphanage. She also plans to leave Jimmie abruptly. Though his prejudice shines through frequent racist comments, Mimi admits to him candidly, "'I do love you—love you as I've never loved before—love you as I know I'll never love again'" (259). With these facts in mind, we must question the truth behind Mimi's words. Surely she has the intentions of following through with these sentiments, yet we cannot underestimate the difficulty by which her proposed actions can be accomplished.

By examining these inconsistencies within Mimi's final pronouncement, we can understand the degree to which a reentrance into her old life—a return to motherhood and her discarded race—would be obstacle-laden at best. Instead of following this line of reasoning in an attempt to attack Mimi personally, however, this reading of *Flight* enables us to see how pervasive and restricting ideologies of racism and sexism were at the time. In addition to encouraging Mimi's multiple escapes, they also create a possible inability for her movement in the opposite direction.

The Transnational Savior in Fauset's *Plum Bun*

Plum Bun: A Novel Without a Moral, Fauset's second novel, addresses several controversial issues of the early twentieth century, such as passing, miscegenation, and racial identity. This last item provides the central conflict of the novel, as Angela Murray struggles with her self-identity and the choice of whether or not she should use her light-skinned complexion to pass as white. This decision does not come easily for Angela, who attempts to work and live in her hometown of Philadelphia before finally deciding to start afresh in New York following several incidents of racial prejudice. She concludes that her only chance at equality is through a physical and transracial move. Therefore, Angela undergoes a series of geographic transitions, first to New York and then ultimately to Paris, following a trajectory similar to that of Mimi Daquin. During this process, she effectively changes her name and her ethnic identity through the act of passing. Angela and other characters in the novel use elements such as geographical community and skin color as part of a purposeful identity construction; however, despite these conscious efforts to avoid racism and achieve happiness and success in New York, the realization of these objectives is only possible through the necessarily transnational act of moving to Paris.

Brent Hayes Edwards has vocalized this recurring trope specifically in relation to the Paris setting in Harlem Renaissance fiction:

> It is as though certain moves, certain arguments and epiphanies, can only be staged beyond the confines of the United States, and even sometimes in languages other than English. In other words, why does James Weldon Johnson's *The Autobiography of an Ex-Colored Man* . . . place in Berlin the narrator's realization about using folk materials in classical composition? Why does Jessie Fauset's *Plum Bun* need that Paris ending . . . ? (4–5)

In a similar vein, Tyler Stovall examines the significance (and irony) of Paris to African American intellectuals: "More so than in the United States, even New York, African-Americans found that in Paris the abstract ideal of worldwide black unity and culture became a tangible reality. . . . French colonialism and primitivism thus paradoxically combined to foster a vision of pan-African unity" (90). Using these discussions as a foundation, the objective here is to demonstrate why Angela does, in fact, require a Paris relocation to conclude her search.

In order to understand completely Angela's need and desire for Paris, we must first realize the interconnectedness of her identity construction with her initial decision to move from Philadelphia to New York. During her adolescence in Philadelphia, several factors contributed to her personal conception of race within society. Immediately, in the first chapter of *Plum Bun*, the reader is confronted with Angela's formative ideas on race. Very early in her life, she concludes that skin color is a defining feature of a person: "Color or rather the lack of it seemed to the child the one absolute prerequisite to the life of which she was always dreaming. One might break loose from a too hampering sense of duty; poverty could be overcome; physicians conquered weakness; but color, the mere possession of a black or white skin, that was clearly one of those fortuitous endowments of the gods" (Fauset 13–14). Lending to this thought process, Angela's mother unknowingly instills in her daughter the emphasis on color, as they regularly spend their Saturdays strolling from "Fifteenth to Ninth Street on Chestnut" (16), passing as white. As Fauset delineates in the novel, these excursions with her mother reinforce the young Angela's infatuation with light skin. Her mother's model of passing, coupled with personal experiences with color prejudice, lead to Angela's decision that a life in Philadelphia surrounded by familiar people and situations holds no future for her. Thus, her decision to choose a new location is simultaneously a decision to embody a new identity. In moving to New York, Angela discovers a new life characterized by distance from family, home, and race.

Initially, she discovers that she can pass as white just as easily as she did in Philadelphia without calling any unwanted attention to herself. For instance, soon after arriving in New York, she enrolls in an art class in Cooper Union, where she soon begins to make friends in high social circles. Through these connections, she also quickly catches the eye of several white suitors. Therefore, as part of Angela's continued transition from Philadelphia to New York, she completes her identity transformation from black to white by pursuing a relationship with Roger Fielding, a rich and eligible white bachelor. Despite Angela's hope that this geographical and racial move will grant her the satisfaction she desires, her time with Roger proves to confound her attempt at identity construction as she unsuccessfully endeavors to understand her own attraction to a racist man. She clearly still feels a strong connection to her African American lineage; this emotion becomes evident when Roger forces a group of black guests out of a restaurant, making Angela's "heart sick" (Fauset 134). As a result, however, we begin to see the perpetual tension at play within the novel, as Angela fails to distance herself immediately from Roger and the white life he represents, despite her resolution to do so following the event. Her immediate trajectory takes her in the opposite direction, ultimately placing her as mistress to Roger. During this time, he takes care of her financially, but she has no power in the relationship. When it begins to deteriorate, she finally leaves Roger and decides that she wants happiness most of all at this point in life, even if it means that she must "come out" as black.

It might go without saying, then, that despite her vast new experiences in New York, Angela never truly obtains happiness, as she discovers that heartache is a universal quality, especially following her relationship with Roger. The closest she comes to achieving true happiness occurs when she begins to see Anthony Cross for who he is, a potential love interest. She also discovers that he too was merely passing as white; unfortunately, during Angela's time with Roger, Anthony has become engaged to her sister Jinny. While in New York, she also forges somewhat of a friendship with Rachel Powell, an African American who earns a scholarship to

Paris, but then loses it due to her racial identity. This relationship ultimately encourages Angela to reveal that she herself is also African American, which leads to her final attempt at self-discovery by moving to Paris.

Entrenched within this search for identity, even before Angela seriously considers a relocation to Paris, is an underlying transnationalism that provides hints toward the international conclusion. For instance, while still in Philadelphia, Angela gains the attention of her academy art instructor, Mr. Shields, and his wife. When visiting with them one night, she confesses that:

> she was restlessly conscious of a desire for broader horizons . . . . "Perfectly natural," they agreed. "There's no telling where your tastes and talents will lead you,—to Europe perhaps and surely to the formation of new and interesting friendships. You'll find artistic folk the broadest, most liberal people in the world." (Fauset 64–65)

Despite the fact that the Shieldses soon contradict their own words when they realize that Angela is black, this idealized report of Europe nevertheless stays with Angela as she progresses through life post-Philadelphia.

When she begins to flourish in her artistic circles in New York, under the new alias Angéle Mory, she acquaints herself with fellow intellectuals who have traveled Europe extensively and who tout its cosmopolitan atmosphere. Again, unbeknownst to her friends, Angela latches onto the idea of moving to a more liberal locale not from the perspective of her artistic interests, but because of her search for racial acceptance. While this yearning for a saving transnational experience remains implicit for much of the novel, it appears more overtly as her expectant trip approaches in the final section of the novel:

> As for Angela she asked for nothing better than to put all the problems of color and their attendant difficulties behind her. She could not meet those problems in their present form in Europe; literally in every sense she would begin life all over. In France or Italy she would speak of her strain of Negro blood and abide by whatever consequences such

exposition would entail. But the consequences could not engender the pain and difficulties attendant upon them here. (Fauset 340)

In this way, Fauset utilizes the voice of Angela to explicate the racial differences between America and Europe. Essentially, a true freedom to live as herself, to fulfill the self-definition for which she searches, can only be achieved outside the confines of the United States. In this way, Angela's desire for Paris is necessary. When she finally arrives in Paris, things do not immediately improve, however, as she feels a sense of loneliness and homesickness. Nevertheless, she attends school and finds work as an artist. But, at the very end of the novel on Christmas Day, Anthony Cross arrives for Angela with the news that their love can finally be consummated. Free of the constraints of American society, Paris becomes "an idealized space that, due to its different social context, presents the possibility of future transmutations and negotiations of modern black female identity" (Rottenberg 282). In this way, *Plum Bun* becomes as much a critique of American society as it is a critique of joint racism and sexism.

The presumed moral of the story (despite the novel's subtitle *A Novel Without a Moral*) is that regardless of her decision to pass as white for the majority of the novel, Angela realizes the importance of her racial heritage and ultimately embraces it. Yet this all occurs while Angela is in New York, prior to her departure for France. In fact, though the entire book builds up to and anticipates the Paris resolution, only the last of the novel's twenty-seven chapters occurs in Paris. Thus, despite the positive ending with Anthony's arrival, the transnational elements and specifically Angela's realized desire to venture to Paris, while downplayed throughout much of the novel, create the only possible reconciliation of Angela's ethnic identity with a sense of success or happiness. Just as Angela's identity lies outside and between the neat lines of race, so too must her final self-realization occur following a transnational move outside and between national borders. This trope places *Plum Bun* firmly within an established category of Harlem Renaissance texts, as the transitory emphasis acts as a metaphor for the liminal societal state

African Americans experienced at the time. The final scene provides the most significant statement on social and inter-ethnic identities, then, as Angela and Anthony, two African Americans who passed as white while in the United States, finally unite and reclaim their identities in Paris as a result of a transatlantic remove.

Elusive Freedom in Larsen's *Quicksand*

Larsen's *Quicksand* takes a similar route in that, like White's and Fauset's novels, it features a female protagonist who finds herself in a subjugated state and chooses to mobilize in an attempt to locate an accepting community. Whereas both Mimi and Angela utilize their light skin to pass, Helga remains concretely identified as biracial, never feeling complete belonging with either racial group. This liminal state of a racial in-between becomes the impetus for all of the conflictual issues, as Helga's inability to locate a racial home pushes her from one location to the next, one hopeful savior to the next. In fact, if we can emphasize the significance of passing for white in the previous two novels, we must stress as emphatically Helga's attempt to pass for black during much of this novel. Just as Mimi and Angela feel the need to conceal their black heritage, Helga attempts to obscure her white lineage when within her African American social circles. Ironically, during her years in Copenhagen with her white family, Helga never feels the urge to pass or withhold her racial identity. This state of being between races leads to a lengthy journey from one city to another before ultimately ending in the same place it began. More than Mimi and Angela, Helga constantly finds herself in motion. Over the course of the novel, Helga moves from Naxos (a southern school modeled on Tuskegee) to Chicago to Harlem to Copenhagen, then back to Harlem and finally to Alabama. As Michel de Certeau proposes, "Every story is a travel story—a spatial practice" (115). Clearly, Helga's story functions as a travel story, in which she finds herself constantly in transition, both physically and figuratively.

More accurately an inward than an outward quest, Helga attempts to find satisfaction and selfhood through physical and geographical relocation, yet each new stop on her journey fails to achieve her desired outcome, a liminal resolution. As Cheryl A. Wall demonstrates,

> Intelligent, idealistic, and attractive, Helga Crane, Larsen's memorable protagonist, embarks on a journey toward self-discovery that seems destined to succeed. When it ends with Helga mired in poverty and hopelessness, the victim seems willing to accept the blame. Throughout the novel, Helga has pondered her "difference," which she perceives as a personal flaw that makes her unable to take advantage of the opportunities she is offered. In truth, the flaw is Helga's accurate perception that to succeed on the terms she is given, she must play herself false. While Helga, alone among Larsen's major characters, never considers passing for white, she is keenly aware that the image she projects is fraudulent. (96)

Wall astutely notes the sense of "in-between," in which Helga feels trapped. In this way, examining writings about and by women of color relies much more heavily on the theory of liminality as opposed to hybridity, as there is more of an omission of identity rather than a duality of identity. Helga fails at code-switching in her various locations, and she encounters a feeling of perpetual marginalization. Despite the friction she encounters, Helga resolutely resists compromising her search for truth and satisfaction, at least until the perplexing conclusion.

In each location, her dissatisfaction becomes progressively exacerbated, leading to her withdrawal from each localized society and relocation to the next. Helga depends upon the promise of each new destination until the bizarre twist in the end, when she marries a reverend and returns to Alabama. The fact that she finds herself in six different locations throughout her story (in both Harlem and the South twice) conveys important aspects of her life. Each new space creates the possibility for her desires to be quenched and her liminality resolved. Michael Keith and Steve Pile understand the importance of these spaces in which Helga finds herself as they posit, "Spatiality should simultaneously express people's experiences of . . . displacement (a feeling of being out of place), dislocation (relating to alienation) and fragmentation (the jarring multiple identities). Spatialities represent both the spaces between multiple identities and the contradictions within identities" (225). These qualifications exactly parallel Helga's various geographical experiences. For instance, the feelings of displacement and dislocation occur throughout the novel, especially at Naxos due to her lack of "noble" ancestry and in Chicago as a result of her dismissal by her uncle's wife. Her prime instance of fragmentation occurs during her time in Copenhagen: she arrives due to her relation with her white aunt, yet she feels her conspicuously dark skin constantly receives unwanted attention as exotic. At each metropolitan juncture, one of these qualities appears, thus reinforcing Helga's continued seeking.

For Helga to achieve ultimate freedom, she must successfully eliminate her dissatisfaction. She comes close to this at times, such as when she becomes reacquainted with Dr. Robert Anderson from Naxos. Clearly she has feelings for Dr. Anderson, even if she keeps this veiled from herself. She has several other relationships in the novel, yet no matter what her feelings, she finds herself trapped and attached to her despair and discontent; in each instance, her only response is escape. Through her continuous searching, Helga admits the inability to locate the elusive satisfaction she seeks: "Why couldn't she be happy, content, somewhere?" (Larsen 83). Her problematic interactions with romance cause her ultimate conclusion to appear that much more confusing. After turning down three possible suitors, Helga surprisingly and abruptly marries Rev. Pleasant Green, whom she barely knows at all. After unsuccessfully attempting to find satisfaction through her constant transitioning from one place to another, Helga feels that marriage becomes the only way she can conclusively terminate her mobility. Her resolution does succeed in a way, as it eliminates her frequent relocation; consequently, she falls into a more dissatisfied state than when she began her journey. Her defining identity leaves her, as she becomes the wife of a traditional, southern preacher. No longer someone who looks forward to expressing herself through clothing choices and dances, Helga resigns herself to a life of passivity, subjugation, and motherhood. Following the birth of her fourth child, she experiences a sickness that almost kills her. She then decides to leave her husband and escape her oppression, yet the novel ends "when she began to have her fifth child" (136). Thus she has been removed from her liminality for so long that she cannot successfully become mobile again, even though to remain in her present state means more depression and discontent. Helga's story therefore conveys the most damaging result of a removal from liminality.

In the end, while Victor Turner's initial theories on liminality anticipate a positive outcome, following the forward movement of a rite of passage, liminal spaces created at the crossroads of race and gender can create much more destructive products. Though conventional racism obviously factors into these situations, the presence of intraracial prejudice and sexism in these three novels is what encourages a transitory existence for the female protagonists. Approaching these novels through a liminal framework exhibits the many communal and societal "in-betweens" available for individuals to become subjugated and invisible. Though *Flight* and *Plum Bun* conclude with ostensibly optimistic resolutions unlike *Quicksand*, all three highlight the presence of transition and mobility during the Harlem Renaissance, by nature a movement striving for change. As these novels demonstrate, women of color received a "double dose" of discrimination. In each of these cases, the only real goal for these protagonists is to find a place in which they can feel the freedom to define themselves and live without compromise. In examining the common trajectory of these novels, then, we can move toward a more complete and nuanced understanding of life in the United States as a woman of color. Simultaneously, in realizing the recurring themes of space, liminality, and transition, we can perhaps create a new framework by which to read and comprehend the many unexplored avenues latent within African American fiction.

Works Cited

Belluscio, Steven J. *To Be Suddenly White: Literary Realism and Racial Passing*. Columbia: U of Missouri P, 2006.

de Certeau, Michel. *The Practice of Everyday Life*. Trans. Steven Rendall. Berkeley: U of California P, 1984.

Edwards, Brent Hayes. *The Practice of Diaspora: Literature, Translation, and the Rise of Black Internationalism.* Cambridge: Harvard UP, 2003.

Fauset, Jessie Redmon. *Plum Bun: A Novel Without a Moral.* 1928. Boston: Beacon P, 1990.

Keith, Michael & Steve Pile, eds. "Conclusion: Towards New Radical Geographies." *Place and the Politics of Identity.* London: Routledge, 1993. 220–226.

Larsen, Nella. *Quicksand.* 1928. New York: Penguin, 2002.

Locke, Alain, ed. *The New Negro: An Interpretation.* 1925. New York: Albert and Charles Boni, 1927.

Page, Amanda M. "Consolidated Colors: Racial Passing and Figurations of the Chinese in Walter White's *Flight* and Darryl Zanuck's *Old San Francisco.*" *MELUS* 37.4 (2012): 93–117.

Rottenberg, Catherine. "Jessie Fauset's *Plum Bun* and the City's Transformative Potential." *Legacy* 30.2 (2013): 265–86.

Stovall, Tyler. *Paris Noir: African Americans in the City of Light.* Boston: Houghton Mifflin, 1996.

Turner, Victor. *The Ritual Process: Structure and Anti-Structure.* Chicago: Aldine Publishing, 1969.

Wall, Cheryl A. *Women of the Harlem Renaissance.* Bloomington: Indiana UP, 1995.

White, Walter. *Flight.* New York: Alfred A. Knopf, 1926.

Grimké's Sentimentalism in *Rachel:* Subversion as an Act of Feminism_____

Lisa Elwood-Farber

Rachel (1916) was chosen by the National Association for the Advancement of Colored People's Drama Committee as a production to counter the anti-Negro propaganda used by the film, *Birth of a Nation* (1915). Grimké's play was going to stage a pro-Negro message to show "the lamentable condition" (Hull 117). While her productions were few in number, her literary influence is worth exploring, particularly as a precursor to the Harlem Renaissance. While there were many in favor of the play, critics claimed that *Rachel* promoted race suicide, since the lead character, Rachel, refuses marriage that would bring "more black babies" to a racist world. The play, however, does not start off so lamentable, with Grimké's Victorian setting and female protagonist who talks and behaves like a sentimental woman from a British novel. Yet, as a black woman in this sentimental setting, complications arise. Through *Rachel,* Angelina Weld Grimké subverts a well-known genre to expose a racist world to audiences. We begin to see evidence of Jane Tompkins' argument that American sentimentalist literature "attempts to redefine social order" (xi). In the play *Rachel*, Grimké uses the sentimental genre to present a female protagonist who is forced to resist a racist, patriarchal world by refusing her God-ordained right as a woman in 1915. Grimké uses the major tenets of sentimental literature to critique the dominant ideology, but then subverts those parameters to address race consciousness in white America. Rachel's refusal to get married and have children is not only a protest to protect her unborn children, but also a call to social change for the black mother.

Sentimentalism is class-based. Samuel Richardson, an eighteenth-century British writer, is argued to have "branded" the sentimental tradition with his novels, *Clarissa* (1748) and *Pamela* (1740). According to Nancy Armstrong, "He systematically rewrote the sexual practices and domestic lives of English people" (1). Later, there developed an actual social ideology called the true womanhood ideal. The ideology, sometimes found in sentimental literature, defined women's sexuality and domestic life using religion, motherhood, home, and family. For example, in *Pamela*, a mere servant girl and dutiful daughter writes letters to her parents expressing her fear of becoming unchaste when she is kidnapped by her master and held prisoner for many months. This novel explores Pamela's ability to withstand the true test of her religious devotion to a higher being. Once published, Richardson was an instant sensation in both illustrating proper behavior for young women and for questioning the conventions that require that behavior. As Americans began writing, they appropriated the sentimental tradition in their captivity narratives, their religious monologues, and their own fiction. These novels were used to teach women and girls proper social etiquette for a lady. For instance, Susanna Rowson, a British American writer, revealed to women what happens when the true womanhood ideology is not a woman's priority in her popular novel, *Charlotte Temple* (1791). Poor, parentless Charlotte succumbs to the charms of a stranger and is abandoned in a hovel to lament her condition after her baby dies.

While some women certainly wrote to adhere to the social expectations, many other women writers used the genre to illustrate social injustices towards their gender. In the 1980's, Jane Tompkins argues that "their bid for power [was] by posting the kingdom of heaven on earth as a world over which women exercise ultimate control" (qtd. in N. Armstrong 5). Using the genre, many women writers critiqued these cultural trends in their fictional characters. Nancy Armstrong argues that Harriet Beecher Stowe was one of the first as she portrays the seduction fable with a young child, thereby altering the tradition to fit her racial framework within her work. There are a few women writers who have also exposed the racist underpinnings of such an ideology. For example, in Harriet Jacobs' *Incidents in the Life of a Slave Girl* (1861), she exposes herself as an example of how the ideology is not within reach of the slave sister. Throughout her slave narrative, Jacobs continues to remind her white readers that the life of a slave girl does not offer the same opportunities bestowed upon white girls regarding a proper marriage, a family, nor a home where she can keep her children safe. Similar to her sentimental sisters in writing, Grimké promotes her agenda within the tale she weaves where Rachel's every decision in life was led by heart-felt emotions. Most women of lower or lower-middle class did not have access to the luxuries of living the sentimental life, only reading about it. While many strived for those ideals, it was a goal most never attained due to economic, social, and cultural oppression. Characters like Rachel and Ma Dear in Grimké's play are shown through the sentimental lens, but only to prove the point and illustrate how race prohibits a black woman from the life of a sentimental woman.

Grimké, in 1916, finds her own rhetorical needs fulfilled within this very framework. With the guise of the sentimental, Grimké points out complications regarding gender and race within the patriarchal and racist world her character is facing. In Claudia Täte's *Domestic Allegories of Political Desire*, she argues that "black writers apparently appropriated many sentimental conventions to give expression to their social concerns and to demonstrate their intellectual competence in terms that the dominant culture respected" (64–64). Using the rhetoric of sentimentality assists them in creating what Susan K. Harris calls "the overplot," where writers get to subvert "the lessons encoded in these novels" (qtd in Täte 65). Täte also argues those sentimental fictional novels would have been the cheapest form of literature most people had access to at the turn of the twentieth century; outdated literature meant cheap literature. She purports that many African American women writers would have been reading those outdated versions of popular fiction. Grimké, therefore, uses the familiar techniques of sentimentalism, within the framework of the true womanhood ideology, to write a play about a middle-class black girl. While sentimentalism is a good place to express the specific, gendered experiences of female characters in a female-centered plot, it is important to note that those same techniques can also be useful in exposing racism. Knowing her audience, Grimké shows her sophistication as a writer by using this particular genre to advocate for social change, helping to usher in a similar drive within the Harlem Renaissance. She uses the major techniques of sentimentalism to critique an earlier predominant ideology, but then subverts those parameters to address race consciousness in white America.

Victorian Setting

One place where Grimké subverts the genre is in the opening scene of the play, where audiences glimpse Victorian sentimentalism in the setting. The Loving family struggles but, despite that struggle, still maintain a partial view of the domestic ideology. First, there arc Jean-Francois Millet's *The Reapers* and Edward Burne-Jones' *The Golden Stairs*, both paintings simply framed but present in the scene. This is indicative of a Victorian setting, regal and serene as a home with a family that appreciates art. Next, there is a bookcase filled with books, which is another characteristic of Victorian literary high art. Education through the means of reading and discussing literature is considered elitist for the upper-classes. Education for blacks was a core value for the burgeoning Harlem Renaissance. Because of her personal history of being the niece of Angelina Emily Grimké Weld, the famous white abolitionist, and raised in a mixed family, she was most likely surrounded by white students throughout her education as the only black student. Nevertheless, she was educated, which is an experience the aspiring black community of literary hopefuls, Alain Locke and W. E. B. Du Bois, wanted to promote in black art. Finally, Grimké finishes the scene with a cozy chair and a lamp with which to sit and read comfortably. The room is decorated simply, yet with the utmost sophistication as the fireplace mantel holds a clock and vase ornaments, the windows are dressed with "white sash curtains," and there is a "table covered with green cloth" (Grimké, *Rachel: A Play* 124). Over the dining room table is "a chandelier with four gas jets enclosed by glass globes" (125), which allows them to see each other during dinner, but, even further than that, they are enlightened. While middle class, the Loving family setting resembles an educated, book-reading, culturally familiar group of people. The paintings on the wall are a delicate aesthetic, which expresses the Loving family value of culture and art. The books on the shelf show an appreciation for education and leisure reading as a source of domestic tranquility. Finally, they have electricity, which is still considered a luxury in the 1916 black family home. These are the qualities that the proponents for changing perceptions of race were looking to promote in the black race, which is why this play may have been chosen by the National Association for the Advancement of Colored People's Drama Committee as a production to counter the anti-Negro propaganda.

Writing for both white and black theater-goers, Grimké worked hard to portray both inspirational characters who were also dynamic in their questioning of the social system. The Loving family appreciates art, reads good literature, and exudes good taste in decorations. Using this setting, Grimké knew her audience's tastes and played to them with her opening scene. Perhaps if theater-goers and readers alike could see this family like their own, her use of the sentimental could be convincing in exposing racism. At the same time, she uses other descriptive words to remind her audience of the fine line between the highs and lows. For example, the very first sentence includes "scrupulously neat and clean and plainly furnished" and, later on, "a simply framed, inexpensive copy" for the artwork (Grimké, *Rachel: A Play* 124). She may have hoped to reach her audience with the commonality of artwork and literature, but gently reminds them of the "lamentable conditions" of the black family. Because the plot of this play revolves around a story within a story, it is important to map out the framework. When Mrs. Loving finally tells her children about their father and older brother, the sharp contrast between this sentimental setting and Grimké's position as a black dramatist presenting the condition of the black family becomes very clear. Mr. Loving was a newspaper columnist who wrote an article demanding an end to the lynching of black Americans. He was told to retract the statement, and when he refused, white men showed up at his house and dragged him and his oldest son to be lynched. Mrs. Loving said she could hear the "rustling of the trees" that night, symbolizing theirs and many more black men and women dying at the hands of lynch mobs. Here Grimké highlights this low point in the play with her notions of sentimental appeasement for her white theater-goers.

Virtuous Women

Grimké follows the sentimental pattern in her play when she uses Mrs. Loving and Rachel as virtuous women. Mrs. Loving, the mother of both Tom and Rachel, has been a widow for the last ten years; hence, she is a woman who has renegotiated the notion of virtue. Mrs. Loving sits in her neatly decorated parlor with her needle and thread, while her children run errands for her. She is what most would consider a true woman. She sits by the light of the window and does her needlepoint, an art form for white women. They even went to the academies to learn how to do this kind of work. It was considered a necessity, but, for the most part, it was a way for white women to express themselves. However, in contrast, Mrs. Loving must sew in order to feed her children; she uses it as a means of survival. She mends clothes for other people and makes a meager living. She sews so much that her fingers ache and her eyes are strained. On many levels, there is major propaganda here. W. E. B. Du Bois supported this play due to how Grimké anticipates notions of art as propaganda as she slowly unfolds the life and past life of Mrs. Loving. Mrs. Loving looks the part of the true woman, but upon further investigation, readers learn that she is black and poor. Sewing is a livelihood for her, not a decorative version of art. But, did Grimké's white audience make those connections to their own world? Would they have been able to draw the kinds of conclusions Grimké may have been aiming for?

Her play, after all, was going to stage a pro-Negro message. The playbill for its premiere production contained the following message: 'This is the first attempt to use the stage for race propaganda in order to enlighten the American people relative to the lamentable condition of the ten million of colored citizens in this free Republic" (Hull 117). To Grimké, *Rachel* was to be used to put out a message of a "lamentable condition." Therefore, it was produced on March 3 and 4 of 1916 at the Myrtilla Miner Normal School in Washington, DC, and again the following year in lower Manhattan in New York

City; finally, it was presented in Cambridge the following month at St. Bartholomew's Church (Miller 87). After that, it was self-published, which Gloria T. Hull believed was required "to make it to the consciousness-raising instrument that Grimké wished it to be" (120). For the most part, the audiences responded in favor of the play: "Of the fifty reviews and notices published as of April 21 were favorable" (Miller 122), and while her productions were few in number, her influence on the Harlem Renaissance is worth exploring. *Rachel* is "believed to be the first extant twentieth-century black, full-length straight drama produced in the United States" (Hatch qtd. in Miller 75) and, to this day, it remains the "center of twentieth-century black dramatic theory" (Miller 75).

Not only is *Rachel* a good representation of the true womanhood ideal by way of the aesthetics of the home and Mrs. Loving's talent at sewing, but with the main character's talent for singing and playing the piano. Rachel is an artist, which is something Du Bois would have appreciated, since he believed in using art as propaganda. At the same time, she is reminded by her mother to "be ladylike" (Grimké 4). She knows how to play the piano and sing. She celebrates that musical talent by playing and singing for her mother, while she sits by and watches, remembering what happened ten years ago that night when her husband and her son were dragged from her home to be lynched by a white mob. The dualism created by the music and the voice of her young, innocent daughter singing, juxtaposed with Mrs. Loving's recollection of what happened to her loved ones so long ago, is remarkable. Grimké exposes the racist ideals of the white liberal reader who watches the heartbreak of a mother, Mrs. Loving, while enjoying the entertainment of the music. This parallels the current scene of audience goers enjoying a play about a black family in the North, while many black family homes across the country are being invaded by white mobs, who lynch husbands and sons. In the preceding years of 1914 and 1915, an average of fifty black Americans were lynched per year leading up to the production of *Rachel* in Washington, DC. The year after the play's premiere in July 1917, thousands of people with the NAACP marched down Fifth Avenue to protest lynching and other forms of discrimination. The time in which this play was written, produced, and directed is pivotal in historicizing the plot development and the propaganda agenda. In his essay, "Can the Negro Serve the Drama?," W. E. B. Du Bois argues that Negroes as "actors and dramatic writers have a wonderfully rich field to exploit in their own terrible history of experience," which speaks to the beginnings of the Harlem Renaissance (12). The breadth of experiences black writers had access to is overwhelming and should not be limited. Grimké begins this much-anticipated exploitation in a way that should be used by modern critics as the foreground for the Harlem Renaissance movement.

Sentimental Motherhood

Grimké's main character and central theme focus on motherhood and all the passion and emotion that goes into being a mother. In the beginning of the play, she "can't resist any child" because she loves "little black and brown babes best of all," and she feels she needs to "protect them" (*Rachel: A Play* 135). Grimké's plight of motherhood as God-ordained is her central theme in this play, which is a direct tactic of the sentimental framework within which Grimké is writing. Using religion to express emotional connection to motherhood is one way Grimké plays on the dominant ideology of women and children. In fact, Rachel claims that "God spoke to me through some one, and I believe . . . I know now why I just can't resist any child. I have to love it—it calls me—it—draws me" (12). She wants to reach the sympathies of white women who know the true desire and fulfillment of motherhood as something only God can bring. In fact, Grimké's own letters imply her desire in making that connection with her audience:

> If anything can make all women sisters underneath their skins it is motherhood. If, then, all the white women of this country could see, feel, understand just what effect their prejudice and the prejudice of their fathers, brothers, husbands, sons were having on the souls of colored mothers everywhere, and upon the mothers that are to be, a great power to affect public opinion would be set free and the battle would be half won. ("*Rachel.* The Play" 414)

Motherhood is a universal commonality for women across race and class borders, and for many literary texts, the appeal to motherhood is an attempt on the author's ability to reach the sentimentalities of her readers. As Rachel purports in Act I, "The loveliest thing of all the lovely things in this world is just being a mother!" (*Rachel: A Play* 12). This is a place where the act of motherhood is common, but the outward experience of how mothering is negotiated is vastly different. She is trying to connect with that "common," so she can expose differences and, hopefully, make change. In her personal reflection of the play, Grimké writes, "The appeal is not primarily to the colored people, but to the whites" ("*Rachel.* The Play of the Month" 413). Her attempt at reaching out to white women was to find a "vulnerable point in their armor" that they might even become "friendly" (414). Grimké uses a tactic many other writers used before: the female bond. She forges ahead with a woman's initiative of finding a point of commonality with other women.

She stated that this "vulnerable point" could be the notion of motherhood, and she takes that idea and stages a family of love that evokes heartfelt sympathies for others by taking in orphaned children, doting on an ailing mother, and expressing all the anxiety and hope for the future of God's children. Rachel's obsession from the beginning of the play is motherhood. She wants to have lots of brown babies to "protect them." There is something about them that "clutches at [her] . . . heart" and "because" she "love[s] them best," she "pray[s to] God every night" to give her "little black and brown babies—to protect and guard" (*Rachel: A Play* 13). Her entire world is babies. Protecting the future of her unborn children becomes Rachel's battle cry. With lynchings all around her, job discrimination, and childhood trauma due to race provocations in school, Rachel sees no other way to protect them than to not have them in the first place. Looking around at their world in 1916, audience participants must acknowledge the problem when Rachel and John begin to think about the future. As potential black parents, what horror would it be to bring more black babies into the world only to have them mistreated, discriminated against, or worse, lynched?

Subversion of Sentimental Motherhood

After telling the story about how her husband and her son were murdered in the South by lynching, Mrs. Loving connects the face of Jimmy (little neighbor) with George (her son). This sense of nostalgia for the past happens in the beginning of Act II, when Mrs. Loving recalls her first born son, George, and how much little Jimmy looks like him. Part of the ideal sentimental woman was the privilege of motherhood. Most white women, who had access to those ideals, did not have to look at little boys who remind them of their dead children from years past. Many writers from the Harlem Renaissance era make substantial connections with their racial heritage, specifically in telling their story, by looking at the fundamental privileges awarded to the white race and denied to others. When Rachel then asks her mother if Jimmy had lived in the South, her question of whether or not he, too, would be threatened with lynching becomes equally troublesome. What has changed since the slave mother who watched her sons being whipped, sold, or even murdered right in front of them to the early 1900s black mother who must watch a white mob drag her son out of her home to be lynched? Rachel quickly understands what life will be like each day she sends her "little black and brown babies" out into the world. She begins to question her destiny: "Is life so terrible? How can life be terrible, when the world is full of little children" (Grimké, *Rachel: A Play* 13).

Grimké ends this act with the connection to religion and our racist nation[1]: "And so this nation—this white Christian nation—has deliberately set its curse upon the most beautiful—the most holy thing in life— motherhood!" (Grimké, *Rachel: A Play* 28). When Rachel states these words, thereby questioning her future dream and wish to become a mother, Grimké forces her audience to recognize the inner turmoil of the black mother. By expressing her doubts about how society will treat her "brown babies," *Rachel* is thought to become a battle cry for women to deny themselves and save all the future brown babies from this horrible and tragic end. This battle cry was a source of contention for the NAACP decision to use *Rachel* as the counter-argument for the film, *Birth of a Nation*.

Alain LeRoy Locke did not support the play. In fact, he did not want to give the award to Grimké because he believed the play promoted race suicide, which was the opposite of what he envisioned for black art; he wanted to move away from protest writing (Miller 83). The act ends when Rachel faints as all sentimental heroines must do at some point in the novel, usually when she realizes she is in greatest danger of losing her most precious gem: her virtue. However, Rachel faints when she realizes she cannot save her future babies, like Mrs. Loving could not save her own son and husband from the lynch mob. This parallelism is abundantly clear: white women worries and black women worries are significantly different.[2]

Sentimental Marriage

One of the main characteristics in the current ideology and sometimes in sentimental literature is for the woman to "obey" and concede to the man's wishes. This act of submission was part of the ideals of what Victorian society considered true womanhood. She had to be submissive to man: her father, her brother, and, finally, her husband. Rachel shows some of these characteristics, but it does not last. In this sense, Rachel is not considered a Victorian woman due to class-status and her race. In the beginning of the play, she is very nervous, as illustrated in her reaction at being left alone in the presence of a man outside her familial circle as she is "attempting, however, to be the polite hostess" (Grimké, *Rachel: A Play* 129). Rachel understands her place as a woman in the early 1900's. She knows that she is supposed to behave with elegance, virtue, and piety. Because a man is in her presence, maintaining this space is important to the domestic ideals of the sentimental true woman. Rachel expresses her interest and her true hopes and desires for her future: "It's lucky for me that I love to keep house, and cook, and sew. I'll never get anything else" (169). In the world of sentimentality, that is an open invitation for John to ask Rachel to marry him. She is the perfect nineteenth-century true woman fictionally living in the twentieth century. This conversation is set up for audiences to understand how love, courtships, and marriage proposals work for the sentimental woman. First, it is established that she is a woman, old enough for marriage; next, that she is domesticated and can take care of a household; and, finally, that she is in love, too. Grimké offers a strong illustration of how this notion of sentimentalism works within the framework of her play about a black family. Using John and Rachel as examples of the ideal representations of love and marriage becomes useful in juxtaposing their wants and desires. John wants to bring a wife to his new home and start a family. At first, Rachel seems to want the same future; however, once she hears stories from her own mother and Mrs. Lane, she begins to question her children's future. This is the lamentable condition of the middle-class black family, according to Grimké. Thinking about their own future together and being in love is the easy part; the lamentable part becomes the thought of their future generations.

Subversion of the Sentimental Marriage

Most important to this storyline is that Rachel and John are black, which means there are other factors. Tom, Rachel's brother, brings this up a bit earlier: "'Each year, the problem just to live, gets more difficult to solve. How about these children if we're fools enough to have any?'" (Grimké, *Rachel: A Play* 168). When Tom brings up the notion of children, he is setting up Grimké's main point. Rachel is slowly becoming aware of the repercussions of having "little brown babies" and her own desire to fulfill her God-given destiny is weaning. According to the ideals of sentimentalism, a woman's most important role in life is her ability to have children and continue the family lineage in the father's name and bloodline. This is reinforced later on in the play when another character, Mrs. Lane, tells Rachel not to marry, which implies that she wants Rachel to avoid her mistake of having a child whose physical features are less than desirable and that white people hate even more. Rachel begins to really think about her future now. She falls into a four-day depression, during which she stares blankly and does not respond to others. The realization that she cannot have the life of a true woman because she is black begins to weigh on the audience. The roses that John sends as a sign of his affection are torn and shredded as Rachel comes to this realization. Readers hear this lament as she compares the roses to the babies that will never be born: "No, little rosebuds, I may not touch you. Dear, little, baby rosebuds, I am accursed" (63).

Rachel's rejection of motherhood is a major turn of events. Throughout most of this play, Rachel embraces her womanly obligation to become a wife and mother. As soon as readers are comfortable with the notions of sensibility that Grimké brings into the plot, Rachel tears them to shreds and stomps them out of her life forever. This is a symbolic "tearing to shreds" of the ideals of true womanhood that Grimké is slowly doing in these climatic moments. As Rachel tears the rose petals, Grimké lifts the veil of white privilege and racial tension. It is no longer difficult to understand her message. Rachel's frustrations are clearly portrayed in her heartfelt moment of realized racial discrimination. Finally, Grimké exposes the truth that black mothers live every day in America. Grimké is tearing and shredding the nostalgic and sympathetic reading we have been enjoying up to this point of the play. This is Grimké's way of subverting the tradition. All along, we are charmed by the aesthetics of sentimentalism: the name "Loving," the beautiful environment, the intimate relationship between John and Rachel, Mrs. Loving and Rachel, even all the children who follow Rachel around each day, all relating to her love and desire to become a mother. We buy into the sentimentalist frame. We are convinced Rachel can have it all. When Rachel realizes she cannot have it, we are left to wonder how this happened. When she rejects marriage to John Strong, it is the equivalent of Grimké rejecting the confines of the sentimentalist genre. When John tells Rachel that he has a place of his own with nice furniture and artwork on the walls, and all it needs is a good woman but she refuses, it is the same as Grimké refusing to adhere to the sentimental racist agenda. While Rachel may love John and want to marry him, she will never give the white race another brown baby to torment, torture, and lynch like her father and brother. While Grimké uses the sentimental fictional genre, as a black woman writer, she shows how her story does not fit the aesthetic.

Subversion as an Act of Feminism

When Grimké challenges the ideology of the sentimental fictional woman, simultaneously she adheres to a feminist agenda. Because Rachel is middle-class woman, she does not spend her days working in the field or being employed by white people. Instead, she continues to go to school. In the first scene, Rachel walks in carrying a pile of books that she sets down on the table. She has just returned from school. Not only is Grimké celebrating the middle class by having her characters living in the North in a quaint apartment with artwork on the walls, but she presents Rachel, an educated woman. In other plays during that time period, educating the female was always a struggle in the text. For the mother of black children, however, an education takes on a more complex meaning: hope, survival, and future. Mary Burrill's 1919 play, *They That Sit in Darkness*, for example, was the first extant black drama on the problem of birth control. It is about a young black woman whose mother's death causes her to give up her education. Lindy realizes that her mother is very sick, but continues to pack her bags. She is supposed to leave for Tuskegee the next day. When the nurse comes out of the room, Lindy knows it is bad news and rushes in to be by her mother's side as she passes away. The mother's death is the result of bearing too many children. Her mother's death and the lack of healthcare for impoverished women is the cause of young women like Lindy missing out on education.

In Grimké's rejection of motherhood, she plays on feminist notions of womanhood. If women have multiple children, they face health problems and perhaps even death. In other texts, when women choose motherhood over education, they perpetuate the cycle of poverty in their young lives. This feminist stance upon Grimké's part is astonishing at such an early stage in second-wave feminism. Motherhood has always been seen as a woman's duty to country, in order to produce heirs. Her role in the domestic sphere was to add to the American ideal of large families that can spread notions of patriotic discourse and the American Dream. By rejecting motherhood, Grimké purports an argument about ideal womanhood. Is marriage and family the ideal? For a black woman, this ideal is distorted when it coexists with fear of violence and possible lynching. Instead, Grimké presents her readers with an educated young woman who seriously contemplates her future with the man she loves and the children she may one day bring into this world. Compared to these other plays, Grimké seems to be asking readers to question this destiny and think seriously about life as a black mother in 1916 America.

A Tie to Historical Change

Ultimately, Rachel was at the foundation of the Harlem Renaissance beginnings. Grimké begins many discussions: motherhood, race in the North, and lynching. This play was one of the first theatrical performances that discussed lynching in America. Putting that heavy reality in her sentimental play about a mother figure like Ma Rachel is paramount in her construction of race relations in early America. While many wealthy white people go about their everyday lives of privilege, many others, who are just as educated and worthy, suffer in the depths of the institution of race. It is eye-opening right at the time the Harlem Renaissance began really taking hold of literary, musical, and social spaces. Previous black dramatic productions emphasized comedy with "black-faced minstrels done by white men and Negroes" because "Americans expected Negroes on the stage to make them laugh, but they expected nothing else and allowed no effort for a long time toward serious drama" (Du Bois 12). Grimké brought serious drama to the stage with her sentimental story of a black woman in crisis. She started the conversation on protest writing in the guise and in conjunction with notions of art and so, her play works twofold toward the burgeoning Harlem Renaissance.

It is, therefore, important for us to know women like Grimké, who must not become one of the many "forgotten" black women writers who, as Henry Louis Gates, Jr., claims, "in general have remained buried in obscurity, accessible only in research libraries in overpriced and poorly edited reprints" (xxii). Since Grimké's personal history contains so much richness with her parental connections, it is important to see how that plays out in her writing and not to forget how integrated we truly are as a nation. Grimké herself is from an integrated family; her father, Archibald Grimké, was the son of a black slave woman, Nancy Weston Grimké, and her white master, Henry Grimké. The family name was made famous by Henry's two sisters, Angelina and Sarah, through their work with abolition and women's rights. The ties this one African American female playwright has to our American historical roots are numerous. This is important when mapping out the framework of her writing style and the performance of her play because her life experiences add depth to this seemingly pleasant and sentimental play. Since Grimké's personal history contains so much richness with her parental connections, it is important to see how that plays out in her writing. This personal history of women and civil rights' activism in her lineage reflects in her "act of subversion" with her use of sentimentalism in the play, *Rachel*, which illustrates the racist undertones to the entire social structure in the early 1900's, setting the stage for the Harlem Renaissance to come.

Notes

1. In African American literature, this theme dates back to the slave narratives past, such as Douglass' *Narrative of the Life of Frederick Douglass, An American Slave*. Religion was used as a tool to deconstruct the racial construction of slaves and critique the presumptions of whiteness on the part of the slave master.

2. bell hooks argues that feminism was built on the notion of a universal struggle against patriarchy, but in organizing its criticism that way, it excludes black women, who have unique struggles based upon race. In her book, *Feminism is for Everybody*, hooks argues that "[u]topian visions of sisterhood based solely on the awareness of the reality that all women were in some way victimized by male domination were disrupted by discussions of class and race" (3). Therefore, Grimké is one of the many who brings up the question of race when discussing women's lives and feminism.

Works Cited

Armstrong, Nancy. "Why Daughter's Die: The Racial Logic of American Sentimentalism." *The Yale Journal of Criticism* 7.2 (1994): 1–24.

Armstrong, Julie Buckner. "'The People took Exceptions to her Remarks...': Meta Warrick Fuller, Angelina Weld Grimké, and the Lynching of Mary Turner." *Mississippi Quarterly* 61.1–2 (2008): 113.

Case, Sue-Ellen. *Feminism and Theater*. New York: Methuen, 1988.

Delap, Lucy, Louise Ryan, & Teresa Zackodnik. "Self-determination, race, and empire: Feminist Nationalists in Britain, Ireland and the United States, 1830s to World War One." *Women's Studies International Forum* 29 (2006): 241–254.

Du Bois, W. E. B. "Can the Negro Serve the Drama?" *Theatre Magazine* 38.268 (July 1923): 12, 68.

Dickerson, Glenda. "The Cult of True Womanhood: Toward a Womanist Attitude in African-American Theatre." *Performing Feminisms: Feminist Critical Theory and Theatre*. Ed. Sue-Ellen Case. Baltimore: Johns Hopkins UP, 1990.

Gates, Henry Louis, Jr. "Introduction." *Selected Works of Angelina Grimké*. Ed. Carolivia Herron. New York: Oxford UP, 1991. 413–416.

Grimké, Angelina Emily Weld. "*Rachel*. The Play of the Month: The Reason and Synopsis by the Author." *Selected Works of Angelina Grimké*. Ed. Carolivia Herron. New York: Oxford UP, 1991. 413–416.

_____. *Rachel: A Play in Three Acts*. Boston: Cornhill, 1920.

Gourdine, Angelina. "The Drama of Lynching in Two Black Women's Drama, or Relating Grimké's *Rachel* with Hansberry's *A Raisin in the Sun*." *Modern Drama* 41.4 (1998): 533–545.

Herron, Carolivia, ed. *Selected Works of Angelina Grimké*. New York: Oxford UP, 1991.

hooks, bell. *Feminism Is for Everybody: Passion Politics*. Cambridge, MA: South End P, 2000.

Hull, Gloria T. *Color, Sex, and Poetry: Three Women Writers of the Harlem Renaissance*. Bloomington: Indiana UP, 1987.

Lee, Josephine. "Teaching *a Doll House, Rachel*, and *Marisol*: Domestic Ideals, Possessive Individuals, and Modern Drama." *Modern Drama* 50.4 (2007): 620–637.

Miller, Henry. *Art or Propaganda: A Historical and Critical Analysis of African-American Approaches to Dramatic Theory, 1900–1965*. Dissertation, CUNY, 2003.

Perkins, Kathy A., ed. *Black Female Playwrights: An Anthology of Plays Before 1950*. Bloomington: Indiana UP, 1989.

Täte, Claudia. *Domestic Allegories of Political Desire: The Black Heroine's Text at the Turn of the Century*. New York: Oxford UP, 1992.

Tompkins, Jane. *Sensational Designs: The Cultural Work of American Fiction 1790–1860*. New York: Oxford UP, 1985.

"Where is that "Ark uv Safty"? Tracing the Role of the Black Woman as Protector in Georgia Douglas Johnson's Plays_____

Brandon L. A. Hutchinson

Many African American women playwrights of the early 1900s, such as May Miller, Mary P. Burrill, and Georgia Douglas Johnson, joined in the crusade against lynching by writing and staging one of America's greatest horrors. While the overall number of victims of lynching had declined by the beginning of the twentieth century, the number of African American deaths increased. Where in the late nineteenth century African American victims did not far exceed those of their white counterparts, 90 percent of the victims were African American at the dawn of the new century (Perkins & Stephens 8). In their artistic endeavors, African American women playwrights not only sought to protest lynching as a racially motivated hate crime, but to illuminate the specific impact of lynching on families, most specifically on women and mothers who sought to protect their loved ones. An example of this is Angelina Grimké's *Rachel* (1916), which is cited as being "the first non-musical written, produced, and publically performed by African-Americans" (Perkins & Stephens 24) that brought to the stage both the physical and psychological horror of lynching, while paying special attention to the impact of racism and sexism on the African American woman. An examination of lynching dramas will bring to the forefront the nature of lynching and the widespread ramifications for black families, and in this case, black mothers who sought ways to protect their male children. Georgia Douglas Johnson, a prolific and frequently published writer of the Harlem Renaissance uses her lynching dramas to portray the black mother's experience during the early 1900s in *A Sunday Morning in the South* (1925), *Blue-Eyed Black Boy* (1930), and *Safe* (1929) as one with many bitter contingencies as she tries to protect her family from lynching.

A lynching drama is defined in *Strange Fruit: Plays on Lynching by American Women* as "a play in which the threat or occurrence of a lynching past or present, has major impact on the dramatic action" (Perkins & Stephens 3). According to Judith Stephens, there are three characteristics that are commonly found in women's anti-lynching dramas. First, the action generally takes place in the home, immediately creating a women's domestic sphere. The setting is either the kitchen, living room, or dining room and the play usually opens with the woman cooking, cleaning, praying, or sewing. The function of the domestic sphere, in particular the significant relationship between the black woman's home and resistance, empowerment, and the affirmation of humanity during especially oppressive political climates, continues to be studied. For example, bell hooks asserts in *Yearning: Race, Gender and Cultural Politics* that the sphere black women were often pushed into—or expected to stay in—became a place of activism. This "homeplace," as hooks terms it, is what Jacqueline Jones considers to be a place of "domestic nurture" (Jones 323) or an environment where the family is protected from white society. While Johnson seeks to recreate the homeplace on stage, her intention is also to show how quickly this atmosphere becomes muddied with tension, hostility, and fear. In one minute, black women may be caretaking or reminding their sons or grandchildren of their worth, but in the very next, the home can be entered and the son dragged away and lynched. This results in a "theatre of jarring contrasts and incongruity" (Stephens 9) for those who consider the American home to be affiliated with protection. The short time in which the home can change from a place of resistance to one of terror is illuminated in these anti-lynching plays.

Emerging from this woman's sphere is the second characteristic, the black woman's voice. Stephens points out that there are generally two primary black women speakers. One of the female speakers is the neighbor or a friend of the family who brings the news of a recent incident that will most likely end in a lynching. The second and most important speaker is the mother or grandmother who is overtaken with fear once knowing that her son or grandchild may not only be considered a suspect, but also lynched. The exchange of the news strengthens our notion of the woman's sphere as we wait to see how the women will work together to protect and attempt to save the black male. The third characteristic then becomes what Stephens calls an "alternative medium" (10). It is manifested through music, poetry, or prayer and can take the shape of background church music, spirituals, or verses/prayers incorporated in the dialogue. The inclusion of Christianity via prayer, songs, or revival meetings creates a juxtaposition that exposes the hypocrisy in white Christian communities and highlights the unyielding faith in black communities. The inclusion of the religious component simultaneously aids the playwright in creating a socially accurate representation of religious southern community members as women's church groups were often dedicated supporters of anti-lynching organizations, like the Association of Southern Women for the Prevention of Lynching (ASWPL). Through the incorporation of the "alternative medium," playwrights often revealed the variance in beliefs of the Christian populace as some believers used religion as a coping mechanism to increase their faith, while others used it as a basis to oppress others.

While Georgia Douglas Johnson uses all of the aforementioned elements in her plays to convey the black mother's struggles to protect her sons or grandsons from lynching, the difference in their conclusions shows that, while black mothers were intricately linked by shared circumstance, the ways they approached their realities were far from monolithic. In the first play, *A Sunday Morning in the South* (1925), Johnson tells the story of a grandmother who cannot prevent her grandson, Tom, from being lynched. Sue Jones, a seventy-year-old grandmother whose lifetime spans from slavery to freedom, is first seen in her home preparing breakfast. She sings verses from a spiritual as she waits for her grandsons, Tom and Bossie, to awaken. The hymns from the nearby church can be heard in the home and Sue's singing solidifies our perception that she is a Christian woman. When the play opens, Sue is found singing this verse: "Jes look at the morning star . . . We'll all git home bye and bye" (Johnson, *Sunday* 31–32).

Through the use of the alternative medium, Johnson shows the transformative effect of the spiritual. Sue Jones is shown, even if only momentarily, being taken out of her earthly experience. For many blacks, the understanding that God's protection will come "bye and bye" served as a reminder that legal oppression in the form of Jim Crow laws and lynching practices did not necessarily indicate spiritual oppression (Levine 80). Sue's singing of the "morning star" referenced in Revelation 22:16 serves as a steady reminder of her faith in God and His promise to her that regardless of her earthly experience, she will be welcomed into heaven. While the significance of the afterlife cannot be denied in our interpretation of the verse, it is important to note that the "bye and bye" also encompasses the daily happenings of a people. While she knows inherently that she will attain a better life after death, her courageous acts of resistance show her rooted in the present; her efforts to change the world she lives in for herself and grandsons becomes the emphasis of the play's action and direction.

Sue Jones' home is to be seen just like any other. It is warm, cozy, and filled with people who believe in God and who care about the world they live in. Sue is shown preparing breakfast while singing along to the church hymn she hears from next door. When the boys awaken, the family eats, neighbor Liza joins them, and what follows is a discussion about the community's news. Johnson's portrait of the Jones' family as law-abiding and just is immediately apparent as they discuss the case of a white woman who was attacked the night before. Although this small community is aware of the frequency with which black men are blamed for crimes that they did not commit (particularly rape), Johnson illuminates their steadfast support of the law and belief in justice. For example, Sue believes that the guilty should be punished by the law and that it should be an "ark uv safty to pertect the weak and not some little old flimsy shack that a puff of wind can blow down" (Johnson, *Sunday* 33). In their discussion of the law's shortcomings and its distinct impact on the lives of black males, Johnson brings to the forefront the known practices of lynchers—like whites blackening their faces so as to frame and kill blacks—to further underscore the fact that there is no protection under the law for blacks. In the juxtaposition of Sue, Liza, and Tom with supposed law-abiding citizens, Johnson not only questions the integrity of whites who commit these crimes, but she also illuminates their false sense of justice. Tom, knowing the inequities that exist within the legal system, believes that education can help and protect his community. Tom's belief in education as a transformative force mirrors the ideas of African American intellectuals like Alain Locke who saw its connection to social and cultural recognition (Locke 50).

Tom Jones is more radical than his literary predecessor, Uncle Tom who is described by Richard Wright in the epigraph of *Uncle Tom's Children* (1936) as the "cringing type who knew his place before white folk." Similarly, Harriet Beecher Stowe's Tom learned to be content in whatever station he found himself. Tom Jones, on the other hand, feels an impulse to change the law, to "make em strong" (Johnson, *Sunday* 33) and is hopeful that with education he can make a difference. Sue, too, is confident that despite the other deaths of innocent black men, her grandsons will be safe in the violent world in which they live. Sue's confidence in her ability to protect her grandson, coupled with Tom's dreams for a better legal system, serve as a bitter backdrop for the play's action. Not only is Tom unable to step into his desired role as an agent of change, but Sue Jones is shown trampled by the power of white male authority: her homeplace is permanently altered when the police barge in and she is unable to carry out her role of protector.

The officers' penetration of Sue's sphere of protection is strikingly similar to rape; their unwanted entry is both a psychological and physical violation that leaves behind only an illusion of protection, since she cannot really offer it. Once the officers barge in without consent, Sue's inability to protect is further underscored by the men who have predetermined Tom's fate without adequate investigation. The officers bring with them the victim, whom Tom allegedly raped. She is uncertain that Tom is the rapist, but the white men force her to accuse him, changing Tom's life forever. The woman's "I-I'm not sure" means to the officers that "he fits your description perfect" (Johnson, *Sunday* 34). In this example, Johnson indicates not only how the hierarchical position of white men impacts blacks in their everyday lives, but gender relationships as well.

The subordinate position of all women is not to be missed, as Johnson portrays both the victim and Sue Jones silenced by white male authority. Although the victim is allowed to utter some words, she is cut off by the officers, who impose a viewpoint that supports their ulterior motive. Similarly, Sue is shown to be equally ineffectual in that she cannot prevent the men from entering her home with the use of her words nor can she interject without being told, "Shut up, your word's nothing" (Johnson, *Sunday* 34). Although Sue is silenced in this instance, Johnson is not. Sue's silencing is an opportunity for Johnson to portray the power relations that virtually stripped from the black woman the right to defend herself and family against white male authority. The fact that she is able to make this argument shows her ability, in her own life, to transcend sexist ideology that worked to keep black women voiceless in their daily lives.

While Johnson could attack lynching through the written word, mothers unfortunately could do little to prevent it. Johnson uses this fact to heighten the emotional intensity of the play as Tom is being taken from his home, which has suddenly been converted from a comforting sanctuary to an atmosphere of terror and helplessness. As Johnson stages Sue (and Liza) in the homeplace, where she is left to think about how she can save Tom, we have a chance to study the ironies that are a part of her role as a former mammy. After Liza suggests that Sue rely on the "good white folks" (Johnson, *Sunday* 35) she has worked for, Sue decides to ask Miss Vilet, a white woman whom she nursed as a baby, to help. In her mind, Vilet, the daughter of a judge, is the potential lifeline that could save Tom. However, the foreshadowing that Johnson provided through the silencing of the white woman tells the reader that Sue's hopes will be dashed. Vilet, as a woman, would not be able to stand up to a man, even if it is her father. Also, we are given little reason to believe that women working across racial lines to end lynching would be a probable solution. In fact, Johnson does not even stage a conversation between Vilet and Matilda, a neighbor who was sent to bring word about Tom's dire circumstances, indicating both the racial and gender politics of the time. It is made clear that Sue's role as mammy has no significant bearing when it comes down to protection. Where Johnson points out that black and white women alike do not have the power to prevent lynching, it still remains ironic that Sue, who was once required to nourish and raise white children through her role as mammy and/or wet nurse, is still denied the very right to protect her own.

In *A Sunday Morning in the South,* Johnson thus captures the black woman who served in roles that required her to care for and protect white children, while simultaneously forfeiting the opportunity to do the same for her own. Johnson's *Blue-Eyed Black Boy* (1930), like *A Sunday Morning in the South*, addresses the issue of protection, while paying close attention to the turmoil the protagonists find themselves in due to their race, gender, and roles as mothers. Although the mother in *Blue-Eyed Black Boy* is able to save her child, Johnson does not stray from portraying the reality of the angst-filled black mother struggling to protect her children. In this way, *Blue-Eyed Black Boy* and *A Sunday Morning in the South* begin similarly in that the characters are immediately shown to exhibit the characteristics Americans prided themselves on having. Both Mrs. Waters and Rebecca, like Sue Jones, are family- and community-oriented, religious, moral, and caretakers of their homes. In this play, Johnson broadens her portrait of black women's moral sensibilities to include more than following the rules of the law; in *Blue-Eyed Black Boy,* Johnson explores the impact that race and gender have on the choices black women can or must make regarding their sexual freedom. This is best conveyed when Mrs. Waters says, "I ain't carried myself straight all these years for nothing" (Johnson, *Blue-Eyed* 47) to which her daughter Rebecca responds, "Well, I sure have tried to walk straight all my life" (47). Johnson emphasizes time with the inclusion of phrases like "all these years" and "all my life" to underscore the daily and lifelong struggle black women endure to "walk straight."

The conversation that Johnson stages between mother and daughter picks up on the unfortunate difficulties black women have had in maintaining their virtue due to precarious situations they found themselves in as a result of their race and status in American society. Johnson's literary predecessor, Harriet Jacobs, foregrounds the power dynamics that often prevented slave women from being autonomous sexual agents in her narrative, *Incidents in the Life of a Slave Girl* (1861). By detailing the constant threat she was under due to Dr. Flint's (a white married man forty years her senior) consistent efforts to dominate her mentally and sexually, she corrects the stereotype of the licentious slave woman who was only made "prematurely knowing" (Jacobs 28) due to her slave master's ability to manifest his control and sexual desire. In her illumination of Dr. Flint's behavior, she forces the audience to shift any criticism of black slave women as immoral to the true criminals, the white masters. For both Jacobs and Johnson, the struggles specific to the black woman and her sexual identity are thus undoubtedly shaped by the intersection of race and gender. Each writer forges a conversation that speaks to a pride and honor in being able to "walk straight," while also displaying the uneasiness that comes as a result of having to make choices that seem to discount its very meaning. For example, in the slave narrative, Jacobs shows this by making the case that her choice to have sex out of wedlock with an unmarried white man, Mr. Sands, in efforts to win her freedom and ultimately end the onslaught of sexual stalking from Dr. Flint, did not dirty her moral character. Her choice—while freeing her from adultery, but distancing her from purity—details the difficulty slave women had in manifesting the concept of walking straight in their everyday lives.

In *Blue-Eyed Black Boy,* Johnson continues to make visible the controversial choices black women make in the protection of themselves and their families. The specific nature of Mrs. Waters' struggle to walk straight is not made apparent until her son, Jack, is arrested for attacking a white woman. While the audience is to understand that interracial sex was somehow linked to the Waters' family past given Jack's eye color, there is a major silencing of the subject within the family. Even as the two adult women prepare for Rebecca's wedding, there is no conversation specific to Mrs. Waters' sexual history other than her pride in and commitment to walking straight. In fact, Rebecca is so bound by the family's culture of silence that she is completely ignorant of how Jack got his eye color. However, once Jack is arrested, his pending fate flings Mrs. Waters into the role of protector, which not only reveals the reason for Jack's blue eyes, but most importantly highlights a discomforting post-slavery reality—walking straight had not gotten any easier for black women.

The unraveling begins when Hester enters the Waters' home and tells the family that Jack, who was beaten and dragged to the jail by the police, is due to be lynched as a result of attacking a white woman. Rebecca's fiancé, Dr. Grey, offers to drive over to get the judge, immediately displaying his ignorance of the law and its bias towards blacks. The combination of his strategy, along with the name he is given by Johnson, separates him from the women who are set up by the playwright to be the characters who make the smartest decisions in this situation. The name "grey," which means in between black and white, or indeterminate, is used to show a type of wrongful ignorance that shapes his opinion of the law. The women, however, are very clear on how the law works and do not have allegiance to or faith in America's judicial system.

As in *A Sunday Morning in the South*, the solution to save the family from a lynching rests in the lap of the mother. First, Mrs. Waters sends Rebecca to the room to locate a little tin box hidden on the left side of her trunk. Once Rebecca retrieves the box and Mrs. Waters sorts through it and finds a small ring, Dr. Tom Grey is sent to the governor's house with these instructions: "Fly over to Governor Tinkhem's house and don't let nobody—nobody stop you. Just give him the ring and say, Pauline sent this, she says they going to lynch her son born 21 years ago, mind you say twenty one years ago—then say—listen close—look in his eyes—and you'll save him" (Johnson, *Blue-Eyed* 50). Although Dr. Grey, Hester, and Rebecca are unsure of how the ring can prevent a lynching, since Mrs. Waters does not disclose the particulars of her relationship to the governor, Mrs. Waters is confident that Jack's life will be spared. The confidence that Mrs. Waters displays speaks volumes on the power white men have in society. This is made even clearer when

Mrs. Waters not only expresses her faith in God, but in the governor as well. Even as she sees white men, rifles drawn, riding on their horses to the jail where Jack is housed she proclaims, "Trust in God, daughter—I've got faith in him, faith in—in the Governor—he won't fail" (50). Johnson equates the power of the governor with the power of God to imply that, in the 1900s, white men were like God; they controlled all things. While the governor can intervene and protect, black husbands and fathers, by contrast, are often powerless when trying to protect their own families from lynching. It is not to be lost on the reader that Dr. Grey and Rebecca will not be so lucky in their roles as protectors once they become parents.

In order to sustain the mysterious significance of the ring and how it can save Jack, Johnson has Mrs. Waters disclose just a little more of her past through prayer. Praying aloud this time, Mrs. Waters exclaims, "Lord Jesus, I know I've sinned against your holy law, but you did forgive me and let me hold up my head again. Help me again dear Jesus—help me to save my innocent child . . . Let his father" (Johnson, *Blue-Eyed* 51). After a momentary pause, she continues cautiously with "you understand all, I mean sweet Jesus—come down and rise with this wild mob tonight—pour your love into their wicked hearts" (51). Johnson's use of the ring complicates the ambiguous relationship between Mrs. Waters and Governor Tinkhem. Could the ring symbolize a love relationship of some kind? Perhaps it was a token of affection given to her after she birthed Jack. Since interracial marriages were forbidden, the governor could not marry Mrs. Waters, so the ring, instead of the man, stood as his stand-in and as a kind of payment or symbol of the hypocrisy of the separation of races.

While the nature of the relationship remains ambiguous, what is seen to be absolute truth is the governor's ability to alter the course of Jack's life. Where the outcome of this play differs from *A Sunday Morning in the South,* Johnson is unflinching in her portrait of the sociopolitical climate that rendered black mothers unable to be the sole protectors of their children. She shows that faith nor hard work alone, both tenets advanced by Harlem Renaissance writers as meaningful tools for social progression, were proven ineffective in producing the tangible outcome black mothers desired. In *Blue-Eyed Black Boy*, what Mrs. Waters had—the ring—was not enough on its own to save Jack, just as it was not enough for Sue Jones to rely solely on Vilet or even God. In the social world that Johnson creates, the position of the white male with sovereign power is portrayed with accuracy, as ultimately both Mrs. Waters and Sue Jones needed the power of a living white man to make the difference in the lives of the men they aimed to spare.

Likewise, Johnson also shows the lengths black mothers will go to in efforts to protect their children in her play *Safe* (1929). As in the two previous plays, the action occurs in the home with the black woman speaker as the main character. The alternative medium, prayer, is not used as explicitly as it is in *A Sunday Morning in the South* or *Blue-Eyed Black Boy,* but belief in God is evident. The dramatic action in this play differs from the other two in that it features a mother trying to protect a newborn versus a grown son. *Safe* opens with Liza Pettigrew shown in her home with her mother and husband. While she is finishing up some last-minute sewing for her due-any-minute-now baby, John, Liza's husband, is reading the paper and Mandy Grimes, her mother, is resting. While John reads, he discovers that Sam Hosea has been caught, arrested, and jailed for a crime unlike Tom's or Jack's. He is not accused of attacking a white woman, but of self-defense, or to use Liza's terminology, "trying to be a man and stan[ding] up for hissef" (Johnson, *Safe* 29). Sam defends himself after being slapped by his boss in a dispute over wages. Mandy, aware of the danger that comes from this type of retaliation says, "That's mighty unhealthy sounding business for this part of the country. Hittin' a white man, he better hadder made tracks far away from here I'm er thinking" (27). Sam, however, is lynched before he ever has a chance to escape.

Johnson's staging of the lynching of Sam Hosea is a deliberate reference to Sam Hose, who was lynched April 23, 1899. He was not only accused of killing his landlord, Mr. Crawford, in a dispute over crops, but he was also charged with raping Mrs. Crawford. Sam Hose, like the staged Sam, was taken from jail, tortured, and lynched. In *Safe,* Liza therefore becomes the vehicle for Johnson to explore and imagine the impact of the lynching on the mother. As in *A Sunday Morning* and *Blue-Eyed Black Boy,* the news of the impending lynching is brought by a black woman. Once John leaves after hearing the news from Hannah about the lynching, the Pettigrew home is transformed into a woman's space similar to Sue Jones' and Mrs. Waters'. Liza, Mandy, and Hannah are left alone to discuss the impact of lynching and to figure out how Sam can be saved.

In John's absence, Liza's distress about Sam's lynching heightens. Mandy and Hannah question whether she can withstand the emotional devastation with the baby's impending arrival. As the noise increases and the horses and footsteps draw nearer, the impact of what can happen to Sam becomes more real to Liza. While pacing the floor, she asks the other women whether or not they think Sam will be hanged. Mandy encourages Liza to move away from the window, but the distance does not shelter Liza from what she hears next. Sam is heard offstage shouting, "Don't hang me, don't hang me! I don't want to die! Mother! Mother!" (Johnson, *Safe* 29). Unlike Tom or Jack, Sam is not just referred to once; he has been taken from the home, but he is instead directly brought into the action of the play when his voice is heard on stage. Sam's urgent pleas do not only heighten the horror of what will happen to him, but they showcase the shared fate of mother and son as they are equally unable to make substantial changes in their circumstances. Sam is unable to defend himself with just recourse nor is his mother able to protect him. It is this reality that shapes how Liza feels about being a parent of a male child. In fact, when she speaks of Negro boys, she shows how adamant she is about not having any. She says, "What's little nigger boys born for anyhow? I sho hopes mine will be a girl. I don't want no boy baby to be hounded down and kicked 'round'" (28). Through the portrayal of Liza's feelings, Johnson underscores the intersection of race and gender, making it very clear that Negro mothers were left to grapple with the troubling truth that their sons' fates were often sealed by their genetic make-up.

Liza's desire to birth a daughter becomes even more significant to her as she is forced to step into the role of Sam's symbolic mother, who is kept from protecting him. When she hears the boy scream for his mother, Liza is forced to momentarily experience what she believes will be her inevitable reality if she births a son. This feeling of despair and anxiety brings forth her own birth pains. While she is waiting for the doctor, Sam's death weighs heavily on her mind. Unable to forget him, she asks her mother, "Did you hear him cry for his mother? Did you?" (Johnson, *Safe* 30). Her mother encourages her to forget Sam and to concentrate on birthing a healthy baby. Before she enters her room, she repeats her mother's instructions: "Born him safe!. . .Safe" (30). In this moment, it is as if Liza understands how questionable the idea of "safety" is for black families, and it foreshadows her choice to protect her own child through an act of infanticide. After the doctor delivers him and his back is turned, she strangles the baby she says repeatedly, "Now he's safe—safe from the lynchers!" (32).

What Liza does to protect her child parallels the real life incident of fugitive Margaret Garner, who in the latter part of January 1856 killed her baby daughter to prevent her from enslavement. Liza's staunch resolve to protect her son echoes Garner's preference for death to slavery. After Garner killed her child, she pleaded for death and to be tried for murder. In fact, she saw death as the only option and was prepared to "go singing to the gallows rather than be returned to slavery" (Aptheker 12). Johnson's act of historical retelling marks the connection between slavery and "post slavery" experiences in regards to brutal forms of oppression and mother-love. While the demise of slavery did not stop the mental, physical, or psychological abuse of black people, nor did it stunt a mother's desire to exhaust all costs to protect her child. In this play, the non-traditional act of killing becomes equated with protection. It is the only answer that Liza has that will save them both—him from what she feels will be a predictable and agonizing death and herself from the terrible angst of not being able to protect.

Johnson's *A Sunday Morning in the South, Blue-Eyed Black Boy,* and *Safe* each visit the issue of lynching from the perspective of black mothers, who all desperately sought to protect their children in very controversial ways. Sue Jones risks her life and speaks directly to aggressive and racist policemen on behalf of her grandson. And when that fails, she tries to save Tom by relying on her good white people. Unfortunately, she is unable to save him from his death. If not for the ring and help from the governor, Pauline Waters, too, would have suffered the same emotional turmoil as Sue. However, she is able to save her son by using her previously hidden interracial sexual relationship with Governor Tinkhem as her leverage to protect. In contrast, Liza Pettigrew in *Safe*, intervenes by killing her newborn son, protecting him before a lynching could even be a possibility. Within each of the three plays, Johnson's blatant plea against lynching is made evident through her detailed portrayal of the exhausting mental toll taken on the black mother, who strove to protect her children by any means—a testament to the racial climate of the twentieth century.

Works Cited

Aptheker, Herbert. "The Negro Woman." *Masses and Mainstream* 11 (February 1948): 12.

Brown-Guillory, Elizabeth. *Their Place on the Stage: Black Women Playwrights in America.* New York: Praeger, 1988.

Davis, Angela Y. *Women, Race, and Class.* New York: Random House, 1981.

Harris, Will. "Early Black Women Playwrights and the Dual Liberation Motif." *African American Review* 28 (1994): 205–221.

hooks, bell. *Yearning: race, gender, and cultural politics.* Boston: South End P, 1990.

Jacobs, Harriet. *Incidents in the Life of a Slave Girl.* New York: Signet, 2000.

Johnson, Georgia Douglas. *"A Sunday Morning in the South." Black Female Playwrights: An Anthology of Plays before 1950.* Ed. Kathy Perkins. Indiana: Indiana UP, 1991. 31–37.

_____. *"Blue-Eyed Black Boy." Black Female Playwrights: An Anthology of Plays before 1950.* Ed. Kathy Perkins. Indiana: Indiana UP, 1991. 47–51.

_____. "Safe." *Wines in the Wilderness: Plays by African American Women from the Harlem Renaissance to the Present*. Ed. Elizabeth Brown-Guillory. NY: Praeger, 1990. 26–32.

Jones, Jacqueline. *Labor of Love, Labor of Sorrow: Black Women, Work, and the Family, from Slavery to the Present*. New York: Vintage, 1995.

Levine, Lawrence W. *Black Culture and Consciousness: Afro-American Folk Thought from Slavery to Freedom*. New York: Oxford UP, 1977.

Locke, Alain. "The New Negro." *The Portable Harlem Renaissance Reader*. Ed. David Levering Lewis. New York: Penguin, 1994.

Perkins, Kathy, ed. *Black Female Playwrights: An Anthology of Plays before 1950*. Indiana: Indiana UP, 1991. 31–37.

_____ & Judith Stephens, eds. *Strange Fruit: Plays on Lynching by American Women*. Bloomington: Indiana UP, 1998.

Wilkerson, Margaret, ed. *9 Plays by Black Women*. New York: Mentor, 1990.

Wright, Richard. *Uncle Tom's Children*. New York: Harper Perennial 1936.

"Don't knock at my door, little child": The Mantled Poetics of Georgia Douglas Johnson's Motherhood Poetry_____

Michelle J. Pinkard

"One of the Least of These, My Little One"

The infant eyes look out amazed upon the frowning earth,
A stranger, in a land now strange, child of the mantled-birth;

Waxing, he wonders more and more; the scowling grows apace;
A world, behind its barring doors, reviles his ebon face:

Yet from this maelstrom issues forth a God-like entity,
That loves a world all loveless, and smiles on Calvary! (Johnson 120)

Georgia Douglas Johnson's brief poem is one of the featured motherhood poems published in her 1922 collection *Bronze: A Book of Verse.* Contained in these dense couplets are the gender and race motives, ideologies and relationships that arguably reflect the driving force behind the Harlem Renaissance. Many characteristics of Renaissance writing are included: a version of spirituality that honors the virtues of the oppressed, vivid depictions of the imprisoning forces of marginalization, and the push toward something better, to be something better. But, beyond fulfilling most of the content criteria for Renaissance poetry, this poem includes another cultural trope that is often overlooked as a component of the movement by critics both within and beyond the era: motherhood and, specifically, the experience of mothering within an oppressed reality. While the mother in this poem is not explicitly present in the lines of Johnson's work, it is she who is capable of viewing the world through both the weariness of the oppressed and the innocence of an infant. Her only source of solace to a child burdened by a "mantled" birthright is a daunting comparison to the crucified Christ. Johnson's poem is indicative of the work Harlem Renaissance women poets were doing to articulate their individualized disillusionment with their respective marginalization and to define, for themselves, their unique gendered role in the burgeoning racial movement of uplift. A close reading of her poetry will show that the conceptualization of black motherhood is at the center of this poem and the progression of the Harlem Renaissance Movement.

Johnson's contribution to the literary movement is an impressive feat. She is the most productive female poet of the Harlem Renaissance, publishing three volumes of poems—*The Heart of a Woman* (1918), *Bronze* (1922), *and An Autumn Love Cycle* (1928)—between 1918 and 1938 at a time where few women published even one volume. While Johnson also wrote short stories, one-act plays, and songs, her reputation rests on poetry, as she was the most anthologized woman poet in the New Negro movement. Claudia Tate sheds light on the poet's placement in the Harlem Renaissance:

> Neither a subscriber to Victorian ideology nor a fully modern woman, Johnson stood between those of the generation who understood sex as the husband's conjugal right, race as fixed and poetry as sedate, speculative wonder on one extreme, and those of the next generation who assumed sexual liberty, fluid racial identities and poetic sensibility of social activism on the other. (xix)

Much of Johnson's motherhood poetry presents a speaker confounded in her role to raise a "mantled" child. The word *mantled*, meaning "cloaked in darkness," is a central motif in *Bronze*. What distinguishes Johnson's motherhood poetry from other women poets of the era is her focus on the intra-cultural pressure to silence gendered concerns. In this context, writing poems that break the silence becomes a radical pursuit.

Though the construction of black motherhood has long been a pressing concern in cultural studies, few have considered the issue in the context of the Harlem Renaissance. Scholars like Maureen Honey, Cheryl Wall, Claudia Tate, and Gloria Hull have made significant strides in rescuing New Negro women's poetries from obscurity by securing the placement of women writers in the Harlem Renaissance canon. However, examining New Negro Women poets and their work through the analytical framework of *intersectionality*—which considers the lived experience of those who embody multiple layers of marginalization—illuminates the gendered aspects of this race movement and the women writers' responses to it. Intersectionality, in turn, offers scholars the necessary tools to approach New Negro women's poetry as a contribution to a legacy of resistance via strategic measures in representation. Revisiting poets like Johnson, writers who were analyzing and theorizing their own Intersectionality before Kimberlé Crenshaw coined the term in 1989, provides insight into this historically significant moment.

"The Damnation of Women:" Renaissance Leaders Discuss Motherhood

The construct of Black motherhood is especially intersectional, as it is both gendered and raced. Motherhood would become a central focus of the Harlem Renaissance movement, at one time serving as its primary symbol in its ability to personify uplift, strength, and renewal. The men of the era were acutely aware of the symbolic power of mothering in Black communities and often evoked the concept to fight negative cultural imaging. While gender has too often been removed from race discussion, what has become clear is that the New Negro woman's primary gift, sacrifice, and obligation to the racial uplift movement was motherhood. Kevin Gains depicts this cultural atmosphere of the movement in *Uplifting the Race,* explaining that "amidst the violent racism prevalent at the turn of the twentieth century, African-American cultural elites struggling to articulate a positive black identity developed the middle-class ideology of racial uplift" (4). Ultimately, the belief that one could escape social and political injustice by indoctrinating middle-class values gained momentum within the Renaissance and beyond. Notably, these values, which lauded education and a version of sexual morality rooted in class, became the very premise of racial uplift.

Intersectionality argues that it is reckless to review middle-class ideology without peeling through its race and gender implications.

A Du Bois essay, poignantly titled "The Damnation of Women," illuminates most sharply black women's obligatory contribution and sacrifice to the movement via motherhood:

> The world wants healthy babies and intelligent workers. Today we refuse to allow the combination and force thousands of intelligent workers to go childless at a horrible expenditure of moral force, or we damn them if they break our idiotic conventions. Only at the sacrifice of intelligence and the chance to do their best work can the majority of modern women bear children. This is the damnation of women. All womanhood is hampered today because the world on which it is emerging is a world that tries to worship both virgins and mothers and in the end despises motherhood and despoils virgins. (164)

As empathetic as Du Bois' review may be, the essay ends with the familiar lauding of an idealized strong black woman and her ability to endure her predestined, "damned" role of Negro mother. He writes: "Today the dreams of the mothers are coming true. We have still our poverty and degradation, our lewdness and our cruel toil; but we have, too, a vast group of women of Negro blood who for strength of character, cleanness of soul, and unselfish devotion of purpose, is today easily the peer of any group of women in the civilized world" (Du Bois 186). Though seemingly complimentary, within Du Bois' description are gender expectations tantamount to sacrifice and submission in the name of racial progress. The cost of this imaging would be that black women were socialized into sacrificing their sexuality and individuality for the race movement.

Yet, while many black women, informed and inspired by uplift, would use motherhood/mothering as a site for resistance to raise empowered children who reject racial stereotypes, they hardly conformed to the patriarchal dicta that demanded they accept maternal suffering in silence. Nor did they consider themselves relegated solely to the domestic sphere. Even women like Johnson, who arguably subscribed to tenants of Black Victorian respectability and gentility, would become "race women" in their community activism, educational aptitude, and professional success.

For many women who struggled with negotiating the public sphere of race and the domestic sphere of gender, poetry would become an accessible outlet to express their disillusionment with being asked to mother like the culturally idolized, middle-class white mother, but without the access to white privilege—a salient concern in working, middle, and "leisure" classes (McDougald). In the face of crippling racist imaging, Black male leaders wanted to prove that the New Negro woman was the epitome of femininity; she would be celebrated with the crown of "strength" for her ability to fulfill gender roles under the shared umbrella of race. A comparison of poetry by Langston Hughes and Johnson will help to illustrate this gender-specific approach to racial uplift.

Consider Hughes' famed poem "Mother to Son." Encased in domesticity, as both the setting and metaphor of the poem is a staircase, the mother's sole purpose is to encourage her male child toward progression by modeling her strength of character, her determination, and her courage. In reference to her socially worn, "splintered" condition, the mother asserts the following:

> I'se been a-climbin' on,
> And reachin' landin's,
> And turnin' corners,
> And sometimes goin' in the dark
> Where there ain't been no light (Hughes lines 9–20)

Hughes' mother reflects the archetypal black mother who frequently appears in black male-authored literature. She is elevated through an inner strength. Her modesty is larger than life. She survives by putting her head down and burrowing forward. And, not as apparent, but certainly understood, she is asexual. Her lack of reference to a mate with the singular "I" equally depicts this women's struggle toward ascension as singular.

The poem is thus participating in the aforementioned racial uplift response of confronting extremely negative race imaging with extremely positive race imaging. Anne Stavney explains, "Defending their women against these primarily white, racist assertions, black males produced an idealized image of black womanhood in the form of the 'moral mother.' From civic leader to politician to writer to artist, black men of the 1920s and 30s promoted an ideology of glorified black motherhood" (534). What Hughes is depicting, if not arguably endorsing, in "Mother to Son" is the raced woman's intersecting role to nurture, sustain, and prepare her children for life in a racist society. His speaker has mastered this technique as she is unflinching in both the lived response to oppression and in her instructions to the son as she demands:

> So boy, don't you turn back.
> Don't you set down on the steps
> 'Cause you finds it's kinder hard.
> Don't you fall now— (Hughes lines 14–17)

Hughes' mother speaker not only overcomes her oppression in her ability to continue to endure it; as noted in her closing remarks, "I'se *still* climbin' [emphasis added]" (line 19), she does so without complaint. Her instruction, while inspirational on its face, is not so much about change as it is about endurance. And, her gendered example of endurance would appear to be her most significant contribution to the movement.

By contrast, Johnson's motherhood poems reveal a more conflicted and vulnerable woman. Her construction of the New Negro mother is not as absolute as Renaissance leaders often presented. Johnson's mother persona is fluid, contemplative, and responsive. In lieu of crafting a stoic mother who personifies the willing representation of racial uplift, Johnson's motherhood poems primarily present a woman who is arrested in doubt. This layering of race and gender is evident in "Shall I say, 'My Son, You're Branded?'" The poem explores the reality of having to make children aware of their own oppressed existence. Unlike Hughes' determined speaker, Johnson's mother-speaker experiences a doubt-ridden paralysis in her inability to negotiate the gendered call to nurture with the racial uplift mandate to educate. Consider the following lines of the poem:

> Shall I say, "My son, you're branded in this country's pageantry,
> By strange subtleties you're tethered, and no forum sets you free?"

Shall I mark the young lights fading through your soul-enchannelled eye,
As the dusky pall of shadows screen the highways of your sky?

Or shall I, with love prophetic, bid you dauntlessly arise,
Spurn the handicap that clogs you, taking what the world denies,
Bid you storm the sullen fortress wrought by prejudice and wrong
With a faith that shall not falter, in your heart and on your tongue!
(Johnson 121)

The gendered expectation to nurture and protect the male child is disrupted by racial norms and conditioning. The mother's tumult is in conversation with the very principles of racial uplift. With this work, Johnson questions the prioritization of race from both a mother's perspective and from a lived experience. This duality, again, fractures the mother-identity from the individual identity, all of which shows the multidimensionality of the speaker's experiences. She is not solely a mother; implied in her indecision is an experience with the world that pushes beyond the maternal sphere. That experience has inspired a series of questions that not only trouble her mothering, but speak to the core of a marginalized identity. To what degree does awareness of this "branded" condition help the oppressed? To what degree does the awareness hinder? The question is not resolved in this poem, but a point is made in the asking. While the speaker does not come to a resolution, the mother's frustration is understood with the emphatic exclamation point that concludes the work. Johnson's intersectional analysis of New Negro motherhood offers a more comprehensive review of gendered elements of racial formation.

Yet, despite efforts like those of Johnson, it was the image of the strong, racial champion New Negro mother that prevailed during the era. This subsuming mother became a symbol of the entire movement as evidenced in the 1925 publication of *The New Negro*. Notably, at this Renaissance moment, the movement had found its footing and was diving into the American conscience with a surge of artistic creativity unparalleled by any black cultural movement that preceded it. Artists strategically used literature, music, and art to fight social ills, to give voice to silenced communities, and to testify to their own humanness. Renaissance leader Alain Locke edited and released *The New Negro* in a celebrated effort to document the movement's progression. The collection's frontispiece, titled *The Brown Madonna*, which depicts a young Negro mother and her infant child, exemplifies women's role in uplift, while symbolizing the spirit of rebirth that mobilized the movement.

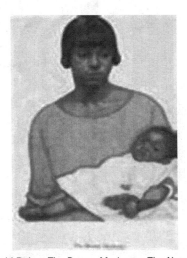

Fig. 1. Winold Reiss, *The Brown Madonna. The New Negro* (1925)

Locke's decision to use *The Brown Madonna* is particularly telling when we consider the purpose-driven nature of the collection. While proclaiming the objective for racial renewal and redefinition, the portrait also promotes a non-sexualized, domesticated version of black womanhood. Emily Orlando points out that the image, created by Austrian painter Winold Riess, exemplifies the ironically virginal black mother role heralded by men of the era:

> So here again the image of the Madonna is revisionist in that she is Africanized—as a gesture of race pride—yet it serves to send a message to black women that the role of self-sacrificing attendant is one of the few available to her. Further, the reference to the Immaculate Conception recalls Christianity's emphasis on the Madonna's reliance upon a male savior for redemption. She is not so very empowered after all. (65)

Perhaps, then, the religious underpinning of the work explains Riess' choice to avert the women's eyes and to press her lips shut. Her joy, or lack thereof, is irrelevant. She is silenced. She humbly accepts her obligation without the confrontation that direct eye contact implies. The New Negro woman's identity development was in a precarious position within the race movement. Exploring gender topics that considered sex-based subjugation and conflict was frowned upon if they hindered the prioritized race-driven center of the movement. Consequently, much of the Renaissance motherhood poetry was disregarded as distracting, if not irrelevant, musings, despite the works' multilayered analysis of matters of resistance, identity, race, and gender relations.

Read anew, however, Harlem Renaissance women's poetry offers authoritative and viable contributions to the continuing debates circling mothering in an oppressed reality. Several concerns frequently emerge in Johnson's poetry: 1) the legacy of slavery and its intrinsic link to black mothering, 2) the contradicting and hypocritical racist and sexist expectations of motherhood that work to silence women, and 3) methods of resistance and empowerment in motherhood. In presenting speakers who are mothers, or speakers who are daughters, or poems that perform acts of mothering on the reader, Johnson clearly understood motherhood as a multifaceted political site of protest.

"The mother soothes her mantled child"

Johnson certainly understood the communal, yet complex, value of mothering as evidenced in the lines of her poems. Her poetry boldly presents the vulnerability and internal struggle of mothering within racist society. Doing so not only satisfies Renaissance dicta that demands art be used as a means to fight against racism and subjugation, but it also calls into question many of the beliefs that permeated early twentieth-century black culture. Kevin Quashie contends that because of the intersectional race and gender implications of mothering, black women have inherited a naturally political relationship with motherhood—whether they choose to participate in the institution or not. He explains how black mothering can, in many ways, be an impossibility: "if being a good mother is to secure the best for one's child, the Black mother cannot be a good mother and can hardly be a mother at all" (Quashie 66). Johnson's poem titled "The Mother," which launches the motherhood series in *Bronze,* best captures this experience. The work is composed of three stanzas and surveys the relationship of a mother to her "mantled child." The child is male, another recurring theme in Johnson's motherhood poems. Admittedly, her choice in the child's sex may reflect her own experience, as her children were male. However, her constant revisiting of the child's sex throughout these poems becomes a tool to explore gendered relationships.

Gender meets race most explicitly in the following as the speaker explores the eroding presence of slave history:

> The mother soothes her mantled child
> With incantation sad and wild;
> A deep compassion brims her eye
> And stills upon her lips, the sigh.
>
> Her thoughts are leaping down the years,
> O'er branding bars, through seething tears,
> Her heart is sandaling his feet
> Adown the world's corroding street. (Johnson lines 1–8)

The vulnerability of the black mother is explicated in ways that vividly contrast with racial uplift imaging. The ability to protect, to love, to mother is inhibited by the world's corrosion. The poem makes a brief, but poignant, reference to slavery ("O'er branding bars") in its attempt to show the constricted condition of the marginalized mother. All she has to offer the child is love, but in an unjust world she knows that will not be sufficient.

What is fascinating about this work is its layering: though the poem's mother places the mantled male child's suffering at the forefront of the discussion, the poem itself positions her silent struggle as a necessary point of inquiry. Consider the final lines of the poem: "And Only God will ever know/ The wordless measure of her woe" (Johnson lines 11–12). Readers must approach these revelatory lines through an intersectional framework to investigate the conflicting, racialized, and gendered experience of silencing oneself and being silenced by others. Johnson uses the literary medium, one of the few available to women of the era, to break through such confines by providing the words for "the wordless measure of her woe" (line 12).

As Johnson's poem succeeds in highlighting, the constant defense of racial identity coupled with the fight for gender visibility must have posed an immeasurable challenge for New Negro women. While she clearly worked to fulfill this responsibility, her writing, her lyrical verse—complete in ballad stanzas and heptameter couplets—reflect a connection to Victorian ideologies that still vexes critics who temper the poet's success by dismissing her work as predictable and trite. One needs only to consider Hull's assertions. She summarizes reader impressions of Johnson's poetry in the following: "A modern reader does not usually find her efforts very impressive—mainly because of the sameness of her themes and manner, and her conventional style. She writes either melancholy love lyrics or muted, attenuated poems of racial protest" (Hull, "Black Women Poets" 93). Johnson received many accolades for her significant contribution to the Renaissance, but her harshest critics found fault with her seemingly indirect approach to race concerns.

Comparatively, Tate salvages Johnson's work with a comprehensive review. Tate argues that the poet's position as a traditionalist did not equate to an abandonment of race matters. Instead, Tate affirms that Johnson's poetic style and anachronistic verse was part of the poet's strategy to veil opinions fostered by social oppression. She asserts, "this perspective offered her the means to describe freedom, beauty and especially her renegade sexuality without the censure of her peers" (Tate xviii). To consider Johnson's dilemma would be to imagine devoting one's creative energies only to a fragment of identity at the expense of all other aspects. Alternatively, Johnson's strategically intersectional response challenges both racial and gendered norms.

In response to critics who accused her of not being concerned with race matters, Johnson penned *Bronze*. In musing over the inspiration of *Bronze*, Johnson confessed the following to Arna Bontemps in 1941: "My first book was *The Heart of a Woman*. It was not at all race conscious. Then someone said—she has no feeling for the race. So I wrote *Bronze*—it was entirely racial" (160). She prefaces the text with an explicit declaration that she will be the voice of the oppressed: "This book is the child of a bitter earth-wound. I sit on the earth and sing—sing out, and of my sorrow" (Hull 161). Interestingly, the preface is grounded in maternal symbolism. The text is explicitly designed to serve as representation for silenced communities—a sustaining premise of the Renaissance. Despite the dismissive reviews, much of the work survives because of its representations of the lived experience of women and mothers of color.

One of Johnson's most sustaining and troubling poems is included in the motherhood section of *Bronze*. Simply titled "Black Woman," the work skews the conception of mother. Indeed, it is unabashedly universal in its labeling. Peppered with exclamation, it tells the story of a woman who rejects motherhood under the cloud of racism. Consider the lines of the second and final stanza of the poem:

> Don't knock at my door, little child,
> I cannot let you in,
> You know not what a world this is
> Of cruelty and sin.
> . . . .
> You do not know the monster men
> Inhabiting the earth,
> Be still, be still, my precious child,
> I must not give you birth! (Johnson lines 1–4, 13–16)

Johnson's highly anthologized poem was originally titled "Motherhood" when it was published in a 1922 edition of *The Crisis*. In later publications, the poem would appear newly minted as "Black Woman," as it is in *Bronze*. Orlando is astute in noting that the "dual classification underscores the inextricable link between motherhood and black women and the problematic assumptions therein" (91). More to the point, the title change signifies a cultural norm that flourished in black middle-class circles of the Renaissance elite, who often made no distinction between woman and mother identities. As both identities—woman and mother—are innately gendered, it becomes increasingly necessary to read beyond the male voices of the era. Johnson's title changes, for example, evidence her keen awareness of the complexity and ironies of this dual classification as she presents a speaker who defies both race and gender expectations by rejecting motherhood.

In voicing the concerns of the "Black Woman," Johnson is operating on many levels. First, one must return to her use of punctuation in the work. She is emphatic about her decision not to give birth. The repeated use of the exclamation ushers away notions of an apologetic tone, giving the speaker visibility and determination. The tone is one of outrage, which builds in momentum as readers approach the second stanza. While the speaker explains her logic for not wanting to give birth, the child's repeated plea, a knock that comes "time and time again" is met with a destabilizing abruptness. Johnson's technique is striking here: the conversation is crafted between a would-be mother and her unborn child, but the writer's message is probingly directed toward the "monster of men" and disrupting the silence of her confliction. The question soon becomes, who are these monster men who are denying black women their most intimate, heart-felt desire?

In the context of the New Negro movement, the most obvious answer regarding the source of poem's tension would be the growing population of racial supremacists. After all, artists of the era were looking for innovative ways to combat rampant lynching and the ever-growing juggernaut that would become Jim Crow. Such a targeted attack would certainly satisfy Renaissance elite, as she articulated was part of the goal in penning *Bronze*. However, informed by Tate and Stavney's argument of double-coding in New Negro women's poetry, the reading of this poem offers new insights. Considering the poem's title suggests the audience for whom the work is written, and one wonders if the work is not gesturing toward men of her own race as well. To give credence to this interpretation, consider the historically-rooted dynamics of the black male-female relationship.

As Patricia Collins explains, it is extremely difficult for black women to publicly criticize their male contemporaries in a reality where the concern of racism overshadows sexist practices. She writes:

> The controlling image of the superstrong Black mother' praises Black women's resiliency in society that routinely paints us as bad mothers. Yet, in order to remain on their pedestal, these same superstrong Black mothers must continue to place their needs behind those of everyone else, especially their sons. (Collins 188)

In this vain, Johnson's "Black Woman" speaker builds her own agency in asserting that she will not simply acquiesce to this demand without seeing some transformation in men. Accordingly, the speaker asserts that, despite all of the discussion of the New Negro woman's obligation to racial uplift, ultimately the decision to give birth is hers and hers alone. In doing so, the poem presents both resistance to an oversimplified heteronormative ideology and an unexpected illumination of gender empowerment.

Notably, not all of the maternal poems in Johnson's *Bronze* explore models of resistance. One of the most revered gifts of motherhood is the physical and symbolic creation of a new generation and all the hope that this act entails. Johnson depicts this conception in her short poem, "Utopia":

> God grant you wider vision, clearer skies, my son,
> With morning's rosy kisses on your brow;
> May your wild yearnings know repose,
> And storm-clouds break to smiles
> As you sweep on with spreading wings
> Unto a waiting sunset! (125)

Again, the poem considers the relationship between a mother and son. However, much can be garnered from its gendered implications if the poem is read within the racialized context of the era. The power dynamic in the mother-son relationship is shifted to the female entity. Still, this speaker appears to be passing the symbolic torch to the male child as it is he who is equipped with "spreading wings" that will help him make it to the "waiting sunset." In this regard, implicit in the speaker's prayers for the young male child is commentary about the movement's momentum of the current. Inherent in this prayer is a hope for "wider" vision and for restraint.

The work also reflects the gendered culture of sacrifice as this *every*mother begrudgingly accepts the current tumultuous "storm cloud" conditioning of her life under the promise of a beautiful tomorrow. In its compelling use of imagery, the writer uses beauty to confront and reject hate. Ultimately, explorations of a black gendered aesthetic in Renaissance poetry provide fertile ground for more inclusive discussions of black literature. Nearly a century later, readers now have an opportunity to explore shadowed, female Harlem Renaissance poets like Johnson with wider, more amplified lenses. An intersectional analysis of the Renaissance woman's representational contribution of motherhood not only gives voice to a silenced aspect of movement, but it also offers insights into the ongoing challenge of defining the role of motherhood in black culture.

Works Cited

Collins, Patricia Hill. *Black Feminist Thought.* 2nd ed. New York: Routledge Taylor & Francis Group, 2009.

Crenshaw, Kimberlé. "Demarginalizing the Intersection of Race and Sex: A Black Feminist Critique of Antidiscrimination Doctrine and Antiracist Politics." *University of Chicago Legal Forum* 140 (1989): 139–167. Web.

Du Bois, W. E. B. *Dark Waters: Voices from within the Veil.* New York, NY: Harcourt, Brace & Howe, 1920.

Gaines, Kevin K. *Uplifting the Race: Black Leadership, Politics and Culture in the Twentieth Century.* Chapel Hill: The U of North Carolina P, 1996.

Hughes, Langston. "Mother to Son." *The Norton Anthology of African American Literature.* 2nd Edition. Eds. Henry Louis Gates & Nellie McKay. New York: W. W. Norton & Company, 2004.

Hull, Gloria T. *Color, Sex, and Poetry: Three Women Writers of the Harlem Renaissance.* Bloomington: Indiana UP, 1987.

_____. "Black Women Poets from Wheatley to Walker." *Negro American Literature Forum*. 9.3 (1975): 91–96.

Johnson, Georgia Douglas. *Selected Works of Georgia Douglas Johnson*. Ed. Henry Louis Gates, Jr. New York: G.K. Hall & Co., 1997.

Locke, Alain, ed. *The New Negro: An Interpretation*. New York: Alheneum, 1968.

McDougald, Elise Johnson. "The Task of Negro Womanhood." Ed. Alain Locke. *The New Negro: An Interpretation*. New York: Alheneum, 1968.

Orlando, Emily. "'Feminine Calibans' and 'Dark Madonnas of the Grave': The Imaging of Black Women in the New Negro Renaissance." *New Voices on the Harlem Renaissance: Essays on Race, Gender, and Literary Discourse*. Eds. Australia Tarver & Paula Barnes. Madison: Fairleigh Dickinson UP, 2006.

Quashie, Kevin Everod. *Black Women, Identity, and Cultural Theory: (Un)Becoming the Subject*. New Jersey: Rutgers UP, 2004.

Schwarz, A.B. Christa. *Gay Voices of the Harlem Renaissance*. Bloomington: Indiana UP, 2003.

Stavney, Anne. "'Mothers of Tomorrow': The New Negro Renaissance and the Politics of Maternal Representation." *African American Review*. 32.4. (1998): 533–561.

Tate, Claudia. Introduction. *Selected Works of Georgia Douglas Johnson*. Ed. Henry Louis Gates, Jr. New York: G.K. Hall and Company, 1997.

Wall, Cheryl A. *Women of the Harlem Renaissance*. Indianapolis: Indiana UP, 1995.

Writing Across the Color Line: Carl Van Vechten's *Nigger Heaven* and the Insatiable Hunger for Literature of Black American Life____

Christopher Allen Varlack

In her 1925 essay examining the state of the black theatre, "The Gift of Laughter," Jessie Redmon Fauset acknowledges that in the early to mid-twentieth century, heavily characterized by its Jim Crow culture and the blackface minstrel tradition, "there is an unwritten law in America that though white may imitate black, black, even when superlatively capable, must never imitate white. In other words, grease-paint may be used to darken but never to lighten" (517). Published in the groundbreaking anthology, *The New Negro: An Interpretation*, edited by Alain Locke, these words speak to a pervasive racial hierarchy that had infiltrated even the depths of the American cultural imagination, inevitably shaping not only the direction of American and African American art, but also the dominant image preserved of black life—caricatures of Zip Coon and Sambo that received wild acclaim both at home and abroad. At the same time, these words reveal a startling dynamic made all the more important with the publication of two of the era's most significant, yet still grossly under-examined texts: the 1926 novel *Nigger Heaven* by white author and "undisputed downtown authority on uptown night life" (Huggins 100), Carl Van Vechten, and its counterpart, Zora Neale Hurston's 1948 *Seraph on the Suwanee*.[1] While both novels breached the color line so rooted in the nation's culture and politics, the former received a greater degree of critical attention as one of the era's most controversial and widely criticized novels, ultimately published amidst an increasing demand for literature on the fast-paced, jazz-induced subculture of Harlem's dance halls and cabarets.

While both of these novels endeavored to "start Harlem thinking" ("Novel About Harlem" 2), inherently interrogating that very notion that Fauset gave voice to years before, only the former seemed to call forth (at least on a national stage) issues of representation and cross-racial voicing so vital to the era's production of literature, film, and art on the lives of blacks and whites alike. Because of this, through *Nigger Heaven*, Van Vechten's "name became synonymous with white exploitation of black culture" and the cult of primitivism—"an association [that] still holds today—that is, when he is remembered in connection with the Harlem Renaissance at all" (Bernard, Introduction xv). Such texts, after all, historically sought to reinscribe the existing stereotypes of the brute Negro or the exotic primitive in the tradition of Thomas Dixon, Jr.'s *The Clansman: An Historical Romance of the Ku Klux Klan* and T. S. Stribling's *Birthright*, both of which ultimately contributed to what Sterling Brown identified as the "hardening [of] racial character into fixed moulds" (84). Through caricaturizing their black characters in these ways, they depicted the black community as fundamentally Other, their perceived inferiority at the time considered a biological and sociological fact. Novels in this tradition thus denied the New Negro that the Harlem Renaissance sought to present, and, as a result, these works, Hurston later remarks, demonstrate a clear "lack of curiosity about the internal lives and emotions of the Negroes" (117).

For many critics and thinkers of the time, however, Van Vechten's work represents a much different stereotyping and exploitation of the Negro—one often hyper-focused on the era's night life and cabaret culture at the exclusion of other aspects of a culture much more diverse and unique. W. E. B. Du Bois, for instance, condemns *Nigger Heaven* in his 1926 review as participating in this problematic history of racial caricaturizing, describing it as "an affront to the hospitality of black folk and to the intelligence of white" (81). For Du Bois, a prominent activist and avid critic of Harlem Renaissance era texts, "I read 'Nigger Heaven' and read it through because I had to. But I advise others who are impelled by a sense of duty or curiosity to drop the book gently in the grate and try the Police Gazette" ("Rev. of" 82). Similarly, Hugh M. Gloster describes the novel as exploring "the alleged animalism and exoticism of Harlem folk" (310) and thus suffers from "t[aking] particular delight in emphasizing—even in exaggerating and distorting—the primitive aspects of his milieu" (311). Together these remarks represent just a sampling of a widespread body of early criticism that challenged what they perceived as Van Vechten's disconcerting portrayal of blacks as savage and atavistic beings—a stereotype in and of itself that the New Negro was eventually, at least in theory, intended to correct.

This, however, is only one aspect of a much more complex project than current scholarship on the novel seems to present.[2] Unlike other works that later attempted to feed the insatiable hunger for black American life by depicting the hyper-sexualization of Harlem or foregrounding that jazz and cabaret culture that heavily attracted droves of whites, in *Nigger Heaven*, Van Vechten does at times attempt to offer that "clear moral or intellectual perspective" that Nathan Irvin Huggins claims is missing from the novel, but necessary in order "to engage the reader in the dramatic issues of Negro life" (107). In these moments, Van Vechten focuses on the plight of the black intellectual, not "Negroes in the South or white contacts or lynchings" (Kellner 80), essentially moving beyond the speakeasies of Harlem to the psychological turmoil that unfolds among the "rich and poor, fast and slow, intellectual and ignorant" (80) outside of the cabaret. By presenting the internal struggles of Mary, an educated librarian attempting to harmonize her ethnic and intellectual sides—too often isolated in literature and discourse of the time—and Byron, an aspiring author who feels the tension of the ever-present color line, he is able to present to the American cultural imagination new insight into a very real, very complex figure previously denied—that of the New Negro. His goal here is not to reinscribe old myths like white-authored texts past. Rather, his goal is to help "start Harlem thinking" ("Novel About Harlem" 2)—and the larger United States as well—about the dynamics of race and the shifting African American identity of the post-Reconstruction age. Therefore, by probing Carl Van Vechten's *Nigger Heaven* and its crossing of racial boundaries, we can trace the early development of the black intellectual figure in text and the ways in which such cross-racial voicing may, in fact, have been used to elevate (or celebrate) contrary to Fauset's initial critique.

Beyond "Savagery:" Van Vechten's Problematic Primitivism Revisited

In the scope of criticism surrounding the novel, one of the core concerns, as Robert Worth notes in his 1995 article, "*Nigger Heaven* and the Harlem Renaissance," is that it essentially offers an unflattering portrait of the burgeoning black intellectual—one that "presents black intellectual life as a pathetic, almost futile endeavor" (464) that results in the protagonist's eventual decent back into Negro savagery. Though this critique is certainly fair, few, if any, novels of the Harlem Renaissance ever fully describe the black intellectual's unhampered journey to the life of the mind. In his second novel, *Banjo* (1929), for example, Claude McKay depicts a somewhat deracinated Ray, who returns to the arguably less encumbered life of the Negro folk, in this case the vagabond life on the beaches of Marseilles, after becoming discontent with the limitations of the life of the mind in a society where blacks are left perpetually disadvantaged by a pervasive color line. In *Black No More* (1931), George Schuyler depicts the demise of the "black" intellectual, as members of a satirized NAACP (perhaps including even Du Bois himself) rush to Dr. Junius Crookman's sanitariums in hopes of overcoming the burdens of blackness and finally taking advantage of the privilege associated with white skin. Similarly, in Nella Larsen's *Quicksand* (1928), Helga Crane finds little peace at Naxos or among the intellectual black elite in New York, eventually entering into what proves a crippling descent (into motherhood and marriage) with the Southern preacher, Reverend Pleasant Green. In this light, the character of Mary, a librarian, and her conflict between models of bourgeois respectability and ethnic ties integral to *Nigger Heaven* are not too different—a fact that inspires the sage of Sugar Hill, Schuyler himself, to write that "Negroes, like other folk, don't like the truth. . . . If it is a filthy book, then one must reply that it could be nothing else, considering his subject" (14).

As Schuyler then suggests, *Nigger Heaven* is more than just a filthy book, an overwhelming amount of criticism far too limited in its disdain for the novel, based largely on its use of potentially racially charged epithets, such as *nigger* and *savage*, in describing the Negro race. For instance, in one of the novel's more controversial passages, Van Vechten writes, "How many times she had watched her friends listening listlessly or with forced affection to alien music, which said little to the Negro soul, by Schubert or Schumann, immediately after losing themselves in a burst of jazz or the glory of an evangelical Spiritual . . . Savages! Savages at heart!" (89). Though Gloster has interpreted this passage as a clear indication that Mary "is convinced that her people are essentially savage" (311), this interpretation is limited at best. Instead, Van Vechten calls attention to an often present divide between the black intellectual and the masses to reveal the psycho-social turmoil all too common among the intellectual elite. These intellectuals, at least according to Hughes, aspire to whiteness, abandon the core customs and values of the black community, and thus face a self-imposed isolation from their culture, both present and past. This, however, does not describe Mary, who seems critical in this passage of those who ascribe to standards of whiteness as superior to the art and culture of blacks. Rather, these words ultimately seem to praise the unique and vibrant black culture of the African American people in a way not at all dissimilar to Hughes' 1926 essay, "The Negro Artist and the Racial Mountain"—a fact that may justify Hughes' support of the novel itself. And so Mary offers a new vision of the black intellectual, which is central to truly understanding Van Vechten's work.

Engaging a relatively new context for the word *savage* outside of its negative history, Van Vechten is less likely referencing the image of the uncivilized tribesman or the jungle stereotype; rather, he may be celebrating the characteristics of black life in a language not altogether different from the language of primitivism simultaneously celebrated and condemned in black-authored texts. His praise of jazz and spirituals as savage thus anticipates the work of authors, like Claude McKay, who evoke similar themes in their fiction. In his debut novel, *Home to Harlem* (1928), McKay writes, "Far, far away from music-hall syncopation and jazz, he was lost in some sensual dream of his own. No tortures, banal shrieks and agonies. Tum-tum . . . Like black youth burning naked in the bush. Love in the deep heart of the jungle" (181). Here, McKay describes a similar internal debate brewing within the character of Ray, pulled toward the passion of jazz, while also maintaining his pursuit of the intellectual mind. Together, both works express the difficulty (and virtual inability) of assuaging these two points of view. Both characters seem to have lost that vital connection to the tum-tum of jazz—a fact that, contrary to Leon Coleman's contention, does not in fact suggest "Mary has become too civilized, in Van Vechten's view," but acknowledging that she "can only look on from its periphery" (116) until she rediscovers that valuable side to herself. In this sense, Van Vechten anticipates one of the central critiques of the Harlem Renaissance movement—a thread of inquiry that captivates the artistic and intellectual attention of writers, like McKay, who are eager to trace the role of the black intellectual—a newly developed figure not only in the literature and artistic expression of the time, but also in American daily life.

In reconsidering the novel this way—as an amalgamation of the high and low projects of the Harlem Renaissance instead—it is evident that Van Vechten's *Nigger Heaven* does not in fact present a singular approach, contrary to the dominant point of view adopted in much criticism. In this widely contested scene, Mary rejects that self-imposed exile that Cornel West suggests of the black intellectual (302) and instead "cherishe[s] an almost fanatic faith in her race, a love for her people in themselves, and a fervent belief in their possibilities" (Van Vechten 89). Though Mary does not possess many of the "Negro characteristics" that she admires, "through no fault of her own" (89), this characterization of his protagonist proves vital to Van Vechten's overall critique. Here, he asserts that "she had lost or [less likely, given the previous passage,] forfeited her birthright which was so valuable and important an asset, a birthright that all civilized races were struggling to get back to—this fact explained the art of a Picasso or a Stravinsky" (89). On the one hand, such a passage is startlingly reminiscent of Alain Locke's 1925 "The Legacy of the Ancestral Arts," and his celebration of the African artistic legacy—a birthright, he claims, that served a noted influence "in French and German modernist art" (191) such as Picasso's iconic *Les Demoiselles d'Avignon*. At the same time, this passage reveals a deepening sadness within the character of Mary at having lost that vital connection to her cultural past—"all savages, she repeated to herself, all, apparently but me" (Van Vechten 90). His critique of assimilation and the sacrifices of Americanization, this passage then highlights the importance of that heritage—a theme flourishing in all forms of Harlem Renaissance art.

Group Imprisonment with a Group: *Nigger Heaven* and the Great Cultural Divide

In addition to this impulse at the heart of *Nigger Heaven*, consistent with Van Vechten's overarching support of African American art and his vital role in promoting some of the era's most noteworthy figures, the novel also engages the all-important cultural debate between the Negro intelligentsia and the Negro masses at large, which are both present in the experiences of Byron and Mary. In his 1937 autobiographical work, *A Long Way from Home,* Claude McKay describes the intra-racial split, noting that "there is little group spirit among Negroes" and that "Negroes do not understand the difference between group segregation and group aggregation" (350). Though his argument here primarily applies to the stagnant growth of black organizations, for McKay, this also manifests in the developing divide between the era's educated elite and the folk, contending that "[t]he Negro intelligentsia cannot hope to get very far if the Negro masses are despised and neglected" (McKay, *Long Way* 351). McKay, however, was not alone in this critique. In his 1940 work, *The Big Sea,* Langston Hughes addresses similar concerns of a divide in aesthetic and artistic point of view. "The Negro critics and many of the intellectuals"—those who at times disregarded the younger generation of Harlem Renaissance writers and their publication of *Fire!!*—"were very sensitive about their race in books. (And still are.) In anything that white people were likely to read, they wanted to put their best foot forward, their politely polished and cultural foot" (Hughes 267). Hughes, however, had a different motivation for his art, responding that "I felt that the masses of our people had as much in their lives to put into books as did those more fortunate ones who had been born with some means and the ability to work up to a master's degree at a Northern college" (267–268).

In *Nigger Heaven,* Carl Van Vechten—"the he-who-gets-slapped" or "the goat of the New Negro Renaissance" (271), as Hughes describes him, also vocalizes these concerns, particularly in the character of Byron—a bitter and biting black figure unable to realize the artistic prowess inside him. In one key passage of the novel, Van Vechten writes, "Byron flamed as he thought how the uneducated Negroes delighted in keeping their upper level as low as possible, pulling them down, maliciously, even with glee, when they were able to do so" (179). This group, described here as "the uncultured mob," is placed in direct opposition to "the young writers who were trying to set down on paper what they knew to be true" and who, as a result, "were branded . . . as faithless to their race, untrue to their trust" (179). In essence, these words reveal the ever-present divide within the black community—a seemingly mutual antagonistic relationship with mistrust emerging from the Negro masses and a bitter disdain from those same black intellectuals whom Coleman describes as a "pseudo-intellectual group" (117). According to Coleman, such a scene clearly depicts "the social stratification of African American society, and portrays the social distinctions that separate the classes" (117). This, however, is not aimed at only correcting the "myopic view" (117) held by white society. In interrogating the era's color politics and what Du Bois describes as "group imprisonment within a group" (*Dusk* 651), Van Vechten also explores the ways in which that destructive mindset has infiltrated and compromised the black community.

Surrounded by black faces aboard the subway train, Bryon notes that "I am no more like them than they are like me, than I am like any of my friends . . . yet we are forced by this prodigious power of prejudice to line up together. To the white world we are a mass" (Van Vechten 189). Again, the parallel to McKay's later *Home to Harlem* is quite striking. Here Ray, employed on the railway, reflects upon the black cooks sleeping around him, noting that "[m]an and nature had put them in the same race. He ought to love them . . . They were all chain-ganged together and he was counted as one link. Yet he loathed every soul in that great barrack-room, except Jake" (McKay, *Home to Harlem* 164–165). Both scenes reveal the psycho-social divide present within the black intellectual figure, at least those figures depicted in early fiction of the time, and the seemingly burdensome connections that keep them linked, "chain-ganged together" with the larger black race. The discussion evoked here is two-fold in nature. On one hand, Van Vechten and McKay seem to criticize the racial binary itself, one that not only separates black from white society, but that also forces people together based on the artificial categories of race. These scenes then reveal that artifice very much so felt by Byron and Ray. On the other hand, however, these scenes also critique an intra-racial prejudice working along class, color, and educational lines, for the rationale of their loathing is rarely (if ever) truly disclosed. Are these passages truly "satiriz[ing] members of the black middle class who seek to deny their racial heritage by assuming a transparent veneer of white culture" (Coleman 117) or by separating themselves from their race? Or do these scenes point to something larger, a rootlessness perhaps, created by a color line both oppressive and confining for blacks?

The resulting thinking is then significant in the Harlem Renaissance critique and the insight that Van Vechten offers on the era's great cultural divide. The narrator questions, for instance, the future of this racially constructed mass, essentially wondering whether it might "be possible that prejudice was gradually creating, automatically and unconsciously, a force that would eventually solidify, in outward opinion at least" (Van Vechten 189). But as Bryon's mindset seems to reveal, "this mass, under this pressure of prejudice [is] dissipat[ing] and swe[eping] apart" (189)—a fate far removed from the more unified image of the New Negroes of the twentieth century. Here rests the value of *Nigger Heaven* outside of its engagement with primitivist thought. Like many novels of the era, this work offers a reflection upon the spirit of the time, and while "most of the novel's readers were less impressed by Van Vechten's attempts to educate, enlist sympathy, and to warn, than they were by the more sensational aspects of the book" (Coleman 118), *Nigger Heaven* was still valuable in evidencing the era's core values, while also calling attention to the limitations that impacted everyday social and racial life. The fact that (white) readers and critics alike then focused on "the exotic scenes of Harlem night life" (118) and the controversial "murder" at the conclusion of the text is somehow less relevant. In its attempt to capture a portrait of the different aspects of that "Negro society [that] existed apart from the rest of New York" (118), his intention was far from exploitation. In this sense, perhaps Hughes describes it best: "Carl Van Vechten . . . captured some of the bitterness and frustration of literary Harlem that Wallace Thurman later so effectively poured into his *Infants of the Spring*"—two significant novels that directly engaged the highs *and* the lows of "that fantastic period when Harlem was in vogue" (227).

Combating Erasure: *Nigger Heaven* and the Pursuit of a Black Aesthetic

From a critical perspective moving forward, the position that Emily Bernard offers in her essay, "What He Did for the Race: Carl Van Vechten and the Harlem Renaissance," then makes the most sense. Here, she asserts that perhaps the consistent "efforts to downplay and even erase Van Vechten's role in the Harlem Renaissance reflect a widespread cultural anxiety about white influence on black culture" and inherently "assume that Van Vechten's relationship to the Harlem Renaissance was unidirectional, that he benefitted from the movement but did nothing in return" (Bernard 533). From a historical standpoint, this is simply not the case—a fact that reinforces the value of *Nigger Heaven* and the overall importance of Van Vechten to the rise of African American artistic expression that the Harlem Renaissance ushered in. In a series of letters from throughout the early to mid-twentieth century, Van Vechten seems a necessary sounding board for many authors of the younger generation, like Hughes, whose support for *Nigger Heaven* allows them to forge a distinct artistic philosophy than that purported by earlier figures, like Locke and Du Bois. Similar to Van Vechten, these authors, from Hughes to Thurman to McKay, were not interested in the New Negro, a very specific middle-class and educated figure too far removed from the New masses—perhaps a representative of Du Bois' Talented Tenth. Rather, they were ready to unearth a very new New Negro defined by a pluralism of sorts—educated, but not isolated from the masses, working to find that necessary balance between the ethnic and intellectual selves.

As Bernard suggests, "They used the controversy surrounding Van Vechten and *Nigger Heaven* to sharpen and publicize their own views about black aesthetics, censorship, and literary responsibility in a way that helped them to distinguish themselves from the previous generation of black intellectuals" (540)—a fact that should seemingly place Van Vechten at the forefront, among others, of a critical dividing line in the Harlem Renaissance critique.[3] Ultimately, by approaching the subject of the black intellectual through the imperfect characters of Mary and Byron, he does in fact accomplish that realistic portrait of a sector of black life and the many Negroes whom Du Bois claims rarely frequented Harlem's cabarets. And yet, even today, many readers still refuse to read the novel for its title and supposed racist sensibility.[4] The discussion that emerges is thus vital. As Van Vechten declares through his response to *The Crisis* questionnaire entitled, "The Negro in Art: How Shall He Be Portrayed?," such works call into question "when the artist, black or white, portrays Negro characters is he under any obligations or limitations as to the sort of character he will portray? Can any author be criticized for painting the worst or best characters of a group?" (qtd. in Helbling 40). For some artists of the era, the answer is a definitive yes, as evidenced through the specific type of New Negro that earlier figures ultimately sought to portray. However, for Van Vechten, the answer would be quite different, pointing to the need for a multiplicity of diverse representations, not just the high and the low, but the rising masses in between.

In truth, Van Vechten believed that "the [true] artist must not be encumbered by external considerations, whether they be political or moral" (Helbling 42)—a claim that directly strikes the demand for propaganda emphasized in the Duboisian conception of black art. "Considerations of taste and propriety," after all, "were no less inhibiting and debilitating" to figures like Van Vechten "than speculation which attempted to assess whether what was said would or would not be helpful to the race" (Helbling 42). Under this lens, both Van Vechten's interest in the intellectual and the primitive of the African American condition are then valuable to the mounting conversation on the politics and aesthetics of the Harlem Renaissance era. Offering insight into different facets of African American life, both aspects of his text delved into the realities of the present day, calling attention to the fast-paced jazz of his beloved cabarets as well as the very real struggles the black intellectual faced—a veritable oxymoron in an American society still defined by the Confederate romance and its resulting racial hierarchy. The failure of his protagonists to successfully achieve the life of the mind is significant as well, highlighting an unfinished project and an everyday reality for authors thereafter to pick up. With this in mind, as Mark Helbling asserts, "Van Vechten, the precious dilettante with an eye and an ear for the bizarre and the exotic, has created a novel whose singular purpose is to delight the senses and arouse the emotions" (43). One might certainly add, though, one final endeavor to what should prove a limited and uncritical list, for Van Vechten was also writing in order to interrogate, to question, and to stimulate the American socioracial mind, perhaps his most significant, yet most misunderstood, contribution.

Notes

1. Like *Nigger Heaven, Seraph on the Suwanee* also received a negative critical reception from some of Hurston's readers upon its publication. Hurston's earlier novels, after all, focused on the lives and experiences of the black community—figures pulled from the porches of Eatonville and other diasporic communities Hurston encountered on her travels down South. Because Hurston chose to deviate from that project—a project consistent with the zeitgeist of the larger Harlem Renaissance and its developing thread of negritude—some critics were disconcerted by this shift in focus with her final novel. Still, *Seraph on the Suwanee* proves integral to Hurston's artistic and intellectual project—an attempt to heighten awareness of the skill of the black artist, capable of describing the everyday realities of both blacks and whites alike.

2.   Professor and critic Sterling Brown would disagree with this reading of *Nigger Heaven*. In the same essay where he outlines the multiplicity of stereotypes constructed by white authors from the antebellum age, he also openly confronts Van Vechten as "one of the pioneers of the hegira from downtown to Harlem," describing him as "one of the early discoverers of the cabaret," while also suggesting that *Nigger Heaven* is "to the exotic pattern what *Swallow Barn* was to the contented slave" (81). His interpretation, however, fails to recognize the inquiry that Van Vechten proposes beyond that of the exotic primitive—one that, although temporary, interrogates its characters not as primitive, but intellectual figures eager to harmonize the life of the soul-body with the life of the mind.

3.   Thurman, for instance, used his critique of *Nigger Heaven* as a platform to advance his artistic philosophy, also seen often as occupying that isolated space on the outskirts of Harlem society. He writes, "I would not be surprised should some of our uplift organizations and neighborhood clubs plan to erect a latter-day abolitionist statue to Carl Van Vechten . . ., for the author has been most fair, and most sympathetic in his treatment of a long mistreated group" (279). His statement differs greatly from Du Bois' more biting critique—a fact that points to an apparent intellectual divide between the older generation Harlem Renaissance thinkers and the era's young Turks. While his review is not entirely positive, noting that "some of his individual characters may seem tarnished" (279), Thurman's statements point to the central divide that hindered the Harlem Renaissance from ever becoming a cohesive movement; each author, after all, had a separate intellectual project he sought to explore, often with a unique set of artistic and real world goals.

4.   As Langston Hughes contends in *The Big Sea*, much of the overwhelming negative reaction to *Nigger Heaven* stemmed from the title itself, as "[t]he word *nigger* to colored people of high and low degree is like a red rag to a bull" (268), representing "all the bitter years of insult and struggle in America: the slave-beatings of yesterday, the lynchings of today" (269). Despite its negative associations, however, Van Vechten's decision to use this word is purposeful. For him, *Nigger Heaven* was intended to represent Harlem, that part of Negro society isolated from not only the rest of New York, but from the rest of the world. As Hughes posits, "[t] o Mr. Van Vechten, Harlem was like that, a segregated gallery in the

theater, the only place where Negroes could see or stage their own show" (270–271). The novel then maneuvers that cultural gallery from the troubles of Harlem's cabarets to the "whole rainbow of life above 110th Street that had never before been put into the color of words" (271).

Works Cited

Bernard, Emily. Introduction. *Remember Me to Harlem: The Letters of Langston Hughes and Carl Van Vechten*. Ed. Emily Bernard. New York: Vintage, 2002. xiii–xxvii.

_____. "What He Did for the Race: Carl Van Vechten and the Harlem Renaissance." *Soundings: An Interdisciplinary Journal* 80.4 (1997): 531–542.

Brown, Sterling. "Negro Character as Seen by White Authors." 1933. *Callaloo* 14/15 (1982): 55–89.

Coleman, Leon. *Carl Van Vechten and the Harlem Renaissance: A Critical Assessment*. New York: Garland, 1998.

Du Bois, W. E. B. *Dusk of Dawn: An Essay Toward an Autobiography of a Race Concept*. 1940. *Writings*. New York: Library of America, 1986.

_____. Rev. of *Nigger Heaven* by Carl Van Vechten. *The Crisis* 33 (December 1926): 81–82.

Fauset, Jessie Redmon. "The Gift of Laughter." *The New Negro: Readings on Race, Representation, and African American Culture, 1892–1938*. Eds. Henry Louis Gates, Jr. & Gene Andrew Jarrett. Princeton: Princeton UP, 2007. 515–518.

Gloster, Hugh M. "The Van Vechten Vogue." *Phylon* 6.4 (1945): 310–314.

Helbling, Mark. "Carl Van Vechten and the Harlem Renaissance." *Negro American Literature Forum* 10.2 (1976): 39–47.

Huggins, Nathan Irvin. *Harlem Renaissance*. 1971. Oxford: Oxford UP, 2007.

Hughes, Langston. *The Big Sea*. 1940. New York: Hill and Wang, 1993.

Hurston, Zora Neale. "What White Publishers Won't Print." 1950. *Within the Circle: An Anthology of African American Literary Criticism from the Harlem Renaissance to the Present*. Ed. Angelyn Mitchell. Durham: Duke UP, 1994. 117–121.

Kellner, Bruce. *Letters of Carl Van Vechten*. New Haven, CT: Yale UP, 1987.

Locke, Alain. "The Legacy of the Ancestral Arts." 1925. *The Works of Alain Locke*. Ed. Charles Molesworth. Oxford: Oxford UP, 2012. 188–193.

McKay, Claude. *A Long Way from Home*. 1937. San Diego: Harvest/HBJ, 1970.

_____. *"Home to Harlem."* 1928. *Classic Fiction of the Harlem Renaissance*. Ed. William L. Andrews. Oxford: Oxford UP, 1994. 105–237.

Schuyler, George. "Views and Reviews." *Pittsburgh Courier* 6 Nov. 1926: 14.

Thurman, Wallace. "A Stranger at the Gate." *Messenger* 8 (October 1926): 279.

Van Vechten, Carl. *Nigger Heaven*. 1926. Urbana: U of Illinois P, 2000.

West, Cornel. "The Dilemma of the Black Intellectual." 1985. *The Cornel West Reader*. New York: Basic Civitas, 1999. 302–315.

Worth, Robert F. "*Nigger Heaven* and the Harlem Renaissance." *African American Review* 29.3 (1995): 461–473.

Dancing Between Cultures: Claude McKay and the Harlem Renaissance_____

Lisa Tomlinson

Claude McKay was a Jamaican poet who migrated to the United States in the early nineteenth century and later emerged as a leading figure in the Harlem Renaissance. Prior to migrating to the US, McKay was an established poet. In his native country, McKay published two books of poetry, *Constab Ballad* (1912) and *Songs of Jamaica* (1912). Growing up in colonial Jamaica, where Africanized culture was demonized and berated, mimicking the British literary form would have been the standard aspiration for many writers of the period. McKay's books of poetry would have been considered groundbreaking at the time for his use of the Jamaican language, his handling of topical issues of race and class, and the way he gave voice to black rural and urban working-class Jamaicans. Sadly, McKay did not remain in Jamaica to advance the cause of championing a national literature, a literary culture that would finally affirm the African-Jamaican presence on the island. McKay's writing, however, became the template in his native country for later writers who shared the same desire of promoting black awareness and identity through poetry and/or fiction.

Nonetheless, following his migration to the United States, McKay's work remained grounded in black vernacular culture and, before long, became a part of a global discourse of black writing. As McKay drew from his African Caribbean roots and borrowed African American literary aesthetics, his writing style shifted between Harlem and the Caribbean. Indeed, this negotiation between cultures uniquely distinguished McKay's work among his African American peers, who wrote primarily of black American struggles. McKay's themes are multiple. His creative work speaks to the social reality of the black underworld in Harlem, challenges white racism, and affirms black cultural aesthetics and voices. Arguably, McKay's Jamaican roots allowed him to explore his subject matter from diverse perspectives. His novels are expressive of his experience as a colonial and diasporic subject writing in exile, the quest for individual identity, the Caribbean relationship with the African American community, and his extensive travels outside the US.

Hence, a close reading of McKay's life and writing reveals his Caribbean sensibilities and how this supports a transatlantic link beyond Harlem, thus opening up conversations between African American and Caribbean culture. Although critics and his biographers are aware of McKay's Jamaican background, they tend to give little emphasis to his distinct Caribbean roots and how they significantly informed his treatment of themes, settings, and characterization in his expansion of the Harlem Renaissance. Hence, McKay's work tends to be contextualized in a singular way as either Caribbean literature or as a literary body belonging to the Harlem Renaissance.[1] By surveying McKay's earlier poems, written in Jamaica; poetry from the Harlem Renaissance; and his novels *Home to Harlem* (1928), *Banjo* (1929), and *Banana Bottom* (1933), we can merge McKay's Caribbean aesthetics into a larger discourse of the Harlem Renaissance.

Claude McKay and the Folk: *Songs of Jamaica* and *Constab Ballad*

A close reading of Claude McKay's poems written in Jamaica helps to provide readers with a holistic understanding and a better appreciation of how McKay's rural upbringing and African Jamaican roots largely helped to shape his creative work throughout his career. McKay was born in the hills of Nairne Castle, Clarendon, Jamaica, to peasant farmers. He was tutored by his older brother Uriah Theodore McKay who was an elementary school teacher. It was through his brother's teaching that McKay was introduced to a diverse world of literature and radical political thoughts—an early influence that later led to his characterization as rebel sojourner. In his young adult years, McKay moved to the urban area of Jamaica and worked as a constable. His time spent in Kingston led him to Walter Jekyll, a British aristocrat and anthropologist who also helped to broaden McKay's literary exposure. Jekyll also became his mentor and is said to have been an early supporter of his literary effort in his choice to use African Jamaican folk aesthetics, particularly the African Jamaican language (Wagner 199).

In 1912, McKay published his first two collections of poetry, *Constab Ballad* and *Songs of Jamaica*. McKay's publications marked the evolution of a national literature and a literary movement that would span beyond the shores of his native country. McKay's folk poems would also spark a regional quest for self-identity and self-determination (Dance 290), which we witness many decades later in the Négritude movement[2] of the French colonies of Africa and the Caribbean as well as future nationalist efforts emerging from the region and its diaspora. Indeed, both collections were literary breakthroughs as they were written in the Jamaican "nation language,"[3] and they gave significant exposure and coverage to the African Jamaican folk culture. Correspondingly, both collections of poems spoke to the social realities of working class rural and urban African Jamaican people. In one letter in particular, McKay vividly recounts, "I remember when my first poem came out, the market women stopped me by the roadside and asked me to read them. Those were the happiest readings I ever gave" (qtd. in James 44).

Hence, in his poetry collection *Songs of Jamaica*, McKay pulls from his pastoral and agrarian roots to articulate the suffering of the rural folks in relation to the land on which they lived and toiled, but received no profits. For instance in the poem "Quashie to Buccra," McKay employs the work-song tradition of enslaved Africans to narrate the grievance of the rural peasants. In the poem, the speaker relates the difficulty of having to labor on the land in the scorching sun: "De sun hot like when fire ketch a town" (line 9). As Winston James remarks, "Quashie and buccra are antipodes of Jamaica's social world: the black country bumpkin, the peasant, the subaltern, and the symbol of power, superordination, the oppressor, the white man" (59). In this way, McKay attempts to empower Quashie by allowing him to speak against the systematic labor exploitation in his local language: "You tas'e petater an' you say it sweet, / But you no know how hard we wuk fe it" (lines 1–2). As such, Cooper reminds us that "Quashie is very much his own man . . . When writing of country life, [McKay] invariably took the point of view of the small, independent farmer who produced for both the local and the export markets" (38).

Similarly in the poem, "Hard Times," also from the collection *Songs of Jamaica*, the speaker is given the opportunity to politicize his dissatisfaction with his social conditions. In "Hard Times" the persona grumbles over unfair taxes, poverty, and the day-to-day struggle of barely meeting growing domestic needs:

> De picknies hab to go to school
> Widout a bite fe taste,
> An I am working like a mule
> While buccra, sittin' in de cool,
> Hab' nuff nenyam fe waste. (lines 9–13)

The poem also points to McKay's class awareness and understanding. The economic disparity that underlined colonial Jamaica framed and informed the existence of "the wretched of the earth." Embedded within the racial inequality of colonial Jamaica was the unequal distribution of wealth denied to Jamaica's black population, a topic rarely, if ever, addressed in the literature of predominately white expatriates. Class inequality and exploitation would later become a common theme of black and mixed-raced writers in their attempt to shed light on the struggles of Jamaica's black working class in urban and rural communities.

While Walter Jekyll may have initiated McKay's path to writing in Jamaican, by the time of McKay's ensuing volume of poems in the vernacular, he was working on his own. *Constab Ballad* found its genesis in McKay's profession as a police constable in Jamaica. Like *Songs of Jamaica*, *Constab Ballad* ushered into black poetry a commitment to the folk and the voice of his country's disenfranchised black population. Dissimilar from his previous collection, many of the poems in this volume critique the relationship between the police and the community as well as their struggle to survive in urban centers. In the "The Apple-Woman's Complaint," for instance, McKay uses the market woman's tongue-lashing against the police to attack the pervasive abuse of power aimed at the common black folks by the police and judicial system, in addition to the poverty that is perpetuated by the colonial system. In defense of her only means of survival, unauthorized street vending, the woman protests:

> Ef me no wuk, me boun' fe tief;
> S'pose dat will please de police chief!
> De prison dem mus' be wan' full,
> Mek dem's 'pon we like ravin' bull. (lines 5–8)

In the poem "Bobby to the Sneering Lady," another work from *Songs of Jamaica*, McKay depicts a more sympathetic police officer. Here, McKay has the constable side with a Black servant woman who has been abused by her White or "light-skinned" middle-class employer. Refusing to arrest the girl, the constable insists:

> Our soul's jes' like fe you,
>   If our work does make us rough
> Me won't 'res' you servant-gal
>   When you've beaten her enough. (lines 5–8)

In effect, many of the poems in Claude McKay's earlier collections give agency to the marginalized black Jamaican peasants and urban working class. This is in contrast to the belief of some critics, who attributed McKay's race and class consciousness solely to his migration to the United States. To some extent, this critique might hold some truth because McKay did not fully link the economic struggles of the Jamaican peasants to race, and he instead saw the social division between black and whites in Jamaica mainly from a class perspective (Tillery 16). However, it should be highlighted that in addition to a colonial-informed British education, McKay was fortunate to have been raised with racial pride and a strong sense of his African heritage (Wagner 198), which unsurprisingly appears in his Jamaican poems.

Unaware of his imminent poetic influence, McKay's earlier collection of poems penned in his native home later become the springboard for the future black renaissance movement(s) that strove to create a distinctive black literary and cultural model: a movement that would also open up dialogue between the African diaspora.

As Winston James asserts, "The respect, beauty and integrity with which black people especially the Jamaican peasantry are portrayed in these early poems make *Songs of Jamaica* and *Constab Ballad* founding texts in Négritude even before this ideology had a name" (130). By relying on the indigenous languages and local cultures of ordinary Jamaicans to shape a distinctively Jamaican expression on the island, McKay offered an early frame for black aesthetics that could be shared among writers of African descent seeking to assert creative and political agency.

Indeed, Claude McKay's various experiences on the island journeyed with him into his poetic work abroad. McKay migrated to the United States in 1912 to study agronomy at Tuskegee Institute in Alabama. However, after transferring to Kansas University, McKay soon realized his purpose in the US awaited within a literary pursuit. Thus, McKay's migration to America signaled a much larger role he was set to play in shaping a poetic expression for the new Negro voices via the Harlem Renaissance. Although McKay never returned to his native island, his childhood spent in the lush countryside of Clarendon Parish, colonial education, and the conflicts he witnessed in the city life of Kingston and Spanish Town would develop into a major feature in the emergence of a new black literary expression.

Writing in Exile: Selected Poems by Claude McKay

McKay's candid writing of black life in Harlem and militancy against social injustices in the United States in no time located his work among key players of the emerging Harlem Renaissance. However, while his collection of poems published as *Harlem Shadows* (1922) takes on newer themes and was illustrative of his new environment, there are often nuanced expressions of his Caribbean roots. In his poem "Harlem Dancer," he focuses on the life of a sex worker. Here McKay attempts to humanize the female dancer, while cynically depicting her "swaying body" through the male gaze as it is objectified by male onlookers:

> Applauding youths laughed with young prostitutes
> And watched her perfect, half-clothed body sway;

Her voice was like the sound of blended flutes
Blown by black players upon a picnic day. (lines 1–4)

Claude McKay's allusion to the musical rhythm of jazz and the hustling and pulsating night life of Harlem situates the poem skillfully into the aesthetic forms of the Harlem Renaissance. The "black players" (line 4) are presumably men, and they and their male friends are seemingly desirous of feasting on the very fetching body during the picnic. Similarly in "Harlem Shadows," McKay invites the reader into the dire reality experienced by black female sex workers wandering along the dim city streets of Harlem and the poverty he also observes:

I hear the halting footsteps of a lass
    In Negro Harlem when the night lets fall
Its veil. I see the shapes of girls who pass
    To bend and barter at desire's call.
Ah, little dark girls who in slippered feet
Go prowling through the night from street to street! (lines 1–6)

Unmistakably, McKay's theme of the exploitation of women in big cities like Harlem resounds with his fictitious sex workers in his Jamaican poems "Country Girl" and "Midnight to a Bobby," wherein both women are exposed to the cruelty and harshness of city life and are regrettably forced to escape the poverty of their rural areas by taking up exploitative work. McKay's themes are also expressive of his earlier or formative engagement or experience with the cityscape because of how he contrasts the unkindness of the metropolis against his idyllic views of his rural settings. Despite McKay's reproach of the impoverishing conditions of the rural area in his first collection of poems, he still clings to the serenity and freedom that the country landscape offered him.

Additionally, the Jamaican landscape remains a persistent backdrop for many of his other poems, such as "Flame Heart," "The Tropics of New York," and "I Shall Return"; these are just some of the poems that drew on the tropical topographies of the island to articulate McKay's yearning for home. In "Flame-Heart," Claude

McKay reminisces on the nature he relished from his childhood. His references to tropical fruits, climatic conditions in the tropics, images of nature, and selected memories all reveal his nostalgic attitude toward the place that nurtured his earlier development:

> So much have I forgotten in ten years?
> So much in ten brief years! I have forgot
> What time the purple apples come to juice,
> And what month brings the shy forget-me-not.
> I have forgot the special, startling season
> Of the pimento's flowering and fruiting;
> What time of year the ground doves brown the fields
> And fill the noonday with their curious fluting.
> I have forgotten much, but still remember
> The poinsettia's red, blood-red in warm December. (lines 1–10)

The poem was written in England at the time when McKay was overcome with bitterness because of the alien treatment and cultural shock he experienced in the colonial motherland. As a British subject, McKay's ill treatment at the hands of imperial Britain would have been a great cultural shock, if not devastating for him. On his arrival to the assumed motherland, England, McKay expected to be treated as a British citizen. However, he is met with racial discrimination and treated like an outsider (*Long Way* 304). Therefore, McKay's "Flame-Heart" signifies his reaction to clinging to his idyllic images of Jamaica's countryside for security. Hence, the speaker concludes, stressing, "We were so happy, happy, I remember, / Beneath the poinsettia's red in warm December" (lines 29–30). Ironically, although he uses his poem to offer consolation to the exile subject writing away from home, traces of the romantic literary style are present, which is, no doubt, a reflection of his colonial education. "Flame-Heart" contains parallel to Keats' "To Autumn," as both poems are structurally and thematically alike; both are written in the same meter and divided into three stanzas. McKay's ripening imagery and mouthwatering juicing of "purple apples" (line 3) and the blossoming of pimento and poinsettia conjure images similar to that in Keats' poem, but the details are specific to McKay's pastoral Jamaica.

Likewise, "The Tropics of New York" portrays his longing for the absent landscape of Jamaica. In the poem, the Jamaican-born speaker finds himself in a new environment, feeling lonely and isolated, but recalling old memories provoked by the discovery of the exotic fruits displayed on his windowsill:

> Bananas ripe and green, and ginger root
> Cocoa in pods and alligator pears,
> And tangerines and mangoes and grape fruit,
> Fit for the highest prize at parish fairs,
>
> Sat in the window, bringing memories
> of fruit-trees laden by low-singing rills,
> And dewy dawns, and mystical skies
> In benediction over nun-like hills. (lines 1–8)

Like, the speaker in "Flame Heart," the persona finds great comfort in the indigenous fruits of his native country. The bucolic landscape that the poet left behind in Jamaica (the hills, climate, etc.), however, is not as pronounced in this poem, as the speaker instead transports the tropical fruits to the cityscape of Harlem. The use of food imagery by McKay to trigger such an emotional response has a significant association with the diasporic subject. Literary writers from outside of the Caribbean often employ food as a salient motif to symbolize the exile's longing for home. In this way, food often acts as a gateway for immigrant writers to engage with collective memory, and, as Hathaway points out, food similar to language can serve as an armor for migrants living in an unfriendly diasporic environment (102–103).

The last poem in the section, "I Shall Return," embodies McKay's countryside upbringing as well as symbolically gesturing toward another crucial theme for the exile writer: the theme of the exile's promise and/or wish to one day return to his or her homeland. Thus, McKay once again finds his muse in the pastoral landscape of Jamaica to express his desire to one day go back to his native country: "I shall return again / I shall Return . . . To ease my mind of long, long, years of pain" (lines 1, 14). As McKay never fulfills the desire of ever seeing the land of his birthplace again, his longing to return to Jamaica is actualized "only through flights of his imagination" (Ramesh 83). McKay's writing, in the end, becomes a "battling ground for reconciling these warring identities" (83), which was misread by African American critics, his contemporaries, and later scholars who expected him to submerge himself in the African American culture (83).

It is worth noting that McKay's theme of "return" did not always gaze toward a symbolic return to Africa as would have been the impulse articulated in some of the other poetic and fictional writings of the Harlem Renaissance. McKay's exile and diasporic status, however, introduced a dual meaning to the symbolic theme of return. In his Jamaican poem "My Native Land, My Home" from the *Songs of Jamaica* collection, for instance, the speaker proudly asserts his nationalism, declaring that "Jamaica is de nigger's place . . . Although dem call we 'no-land race,' / I know me home is right here" (lines 5, 7–8). This is contrary to his compatriot Marcus Garvey, who envisioned Africa as the home for the black diaspora, regardless of nationality.

Finally, McKay's militant sonnets, "If We Must Die" and "America," first published in 1919, build on the unbending voice he developed in his native country. Equally, the poem begins to thematically connect more with the impulses of the African American writers of the Harlem Renaissance. His racial awareness and desire for justice are thus shifted from his Jamaican environment and relocated within the context of racialized America in "If We Must Die":

> If we must die, let it not be like hogs
> Hunted and penned in an inglorious spot,
> While round us bark the mad and hungry dogs,
> Making their mock at our accursed lot.
> If we must die, O let us nobly die,
> So that our precious blood may not be shed
> In vain; then even the monsters we defy
> Shall be constrained to honor us though dead! (lines 1–8)

Although Claude McKay mirrored the British literary sonnet in this poem, his content transgressed the thematic expectations of love and nature as was conveyed in his nostalgic poems. McKay reworks the sonnet form to express racial struggle, violent retaliation, and defiance. Not surprisingly, historian Tyrone Tillery critiques the sonnet as being problematic because of the way McKay failed to name the black race as the subject and rather invokes a universal experience of social injustice (33). While this claim might have had some merit, it is arguable that McKay's cultural dualism of embracing a wider cultural experience is again being overlooked. Even the reference to "hogs" is a reflection of the term that is most popularly used among the rural population in Jamaica instead of the American category "pigs."

Claude McKay's poem "America" resonates with Du Bois' notion of double-consciousness, which psychologically describes how black people are caught between being black and being American. This was a central trope in the writings of many Harlem Renaissance intellectuals and authors who struggled to reconcile with the culture that made up both their identities. Unlike McKay's poems that evoke homesickness and displacement within his new settlement, "America" evinces a firm leaning toward his embrace of the United States as his new identity:

> Althoughshe feeds me bread of bitterness, And sinks into my throat her tiger's tooth, Stealing my breath of life, I will confess I love this cultured hell that tests my youth! Her vigor flows like tides into my blood, Giving me strength erect against her hate. Her bigness sweeps my being like a flood. (lines 1–7)

Notwithstanding the disgust McKay harbors toward America for causing such bitterness and pain, he still holds great admiration and love for her because it is this country that has allowed him to grow and cultivate his potentials as a writer. Even though the poem is constructed as a sonnet, McKay imaginatively adapts this form to juxtapose the love and hate relationship as well as the pain and pleasure of the black American experience of the time. Ironically, like Du Bois' double-consciousness, the two-sided identity that

McKay demonstrates throughout much of his literary and political career is often criticized (as a diasporic and colonial subject) by some of his African American peers (Cruse 435).

Though many of Claude McKay's poems written during the Harlem Renaissance period reveal strong Caribbean sensibility, it is crucial to highlight that as we survey his work as a whole, readers must also recognize McKay's evolution as a writer. His novels, for example, best represent this growth as McKay began to connect his work to a larger black world and similar to many of his poems, his thematic approaches are more complex and diverse, hence giving the Harlem Renaissance a global reach to the African diaspora's creative and intellectual community.

The Global African Diaspora: Claude McKay and His Novels

In the period between 1923 and 1933, McKay had three novels published, *Home to Harlem* (1928), *Banjo* (1929), and *Banana Bottom.* (1933). Similar to some of his poems, McKay's first novel *Home to Harlem* drew on common threads from the Harlem Renaissance (the language, jazz nightclub, etc.), and he used the ghetto as his primary setting. The novel *Home to Harlem* captures the literary and cultural aesthetics of the Harlem Renaissance movement and was well received by writers of the time. However, like some of his poems, McKay's novel was met with criticism. W. E. B. Du Bois and Marcus Garvey, for instance, both believed that his portrait of Harlem worked against black respectability and catered to white stereotypes of African Americans. Indeed, the novel depicts a graphic and unembellished look at the underworld of black life in Harlem and evokes the energy and vitality of the African American jazz night scene. However, Du Bois and Garvey's criticism overlooked deeper layers of the novel, particularly the way McKay allowed his characters to open up a cross-cultural dialogue between African American and black Caribbean culture.

In this way, McKay engages Jake, the protagonist, and Ray in revelatory conversations, which become instructive in the way both characters attempt to use the opportunity to understand each other. When, the Haitian character, Ray, informs Jake that French is his native language, the bewildered African American asks a reflective question that further helps the two to explore their cultural differences: "Ain'tchu one of us too?" (131). Ray's response to this question opens up to Jake a whole new world of black culture that dispels his own stereotypes about Africans and Caribbean people (134). Arguably, both Du Bois and Garvey "failed to recognize the ways in which McKay built upon a collective Pan-Africanist consciousness, using his texts to imagine the possibilities of a global Black community informed by indigenous African (influenced) knowledges and a shared history of imperialism and slavery" (Tomlinson 204).

Similarly in the novel *Banjo*, Claude McKay continues to use his Caribbean character Ray as a mouthpiece to bridge the experiences of black people in the African diaspora; this time, however, he uses this opportunity to disclose and connect their lived realities beyond the shores of the Americas. He also includes characters from the continent. In doing so, McKay introduces the reader to African and Caribbean migrant seamen as they struggle to survive racism and unemployment in Marseilles, France. Here, the narrator establishes comradeship between these men: "All shades of Negros came together there. Even the mulattoes took a step down from their perch to mix in. For as British West Indies, South Africa, the mulattoes of the French colonies do not usually intermingle with the Blacks" (McKay, *Banjo* 46). As his characters represent a diverse range of black intellectuals and artists from Africa and different diasporic points, McKay uses their interaction to address varied social and political topics, ranging from the effects of British colonialism to what might be seen as his own critique of the African American bourgeois class. He does this purposefully through the voices of specific characters or chapters that touch on topical issues affecting blacks universally.

Banana Bottom, McKay's third novel, takes up the common theme (found in the Harlem Renaissance and Black Arts Movement) of the individual search for black identity in the face of having to struggle between cultures. McKay, however, returns the reader to his native rural Jamaica so as to tease out the dilemma of double-consciousness and cultural tensions in colonial Jamaica. The novel recounts the experience of Bita Plant, the protagonist who abandons her British grooming (imposed by her foster parents) in an effort to reclaim her African Jamaican culture. In this way, Bita rejects Western cultural values and Christianity in favor of her African-centered religion. She embraces the peasant folk culture of her Jamaican heritage. McKay relies solely on the indigenized, African-centered religion of Obeah,[4] the local African Jamaican language, and other folk traditions to develop his plot, further responding to the urgent need to restate black cultural aesthetics in literature.

In spite of the fact that McKay's novels are written outside of the US, it is only expected that his travels would inform his literary development. *Home to Harlem,* situated in Harlem, bridged the gap between the African American and Caribbean migrant communities that were key supporters in the shaping of the Harlem Renaissance. *Banjo* portrays a more expansive vision of McKay's diasporic sensibilities, wherein he was more inclusive of the lived realities of Black people globally and forming possible allegiances among people of African descent. Also, Claude McKay used the opportunity to widen the dialogue of black aesthetic forms among its people. Aimé Césaire and Leopold Senghor have both cited McKay as an inspirational source for the development of the Négritude Movement because of his text (James 130, Césaire 44). Interestingly, North Africa became an inspirational source in McKay's production of *Banana Bottom*. McKay states that Marrakesh was "like a big West Indian picnic with flags waving and a multitude of barefoot black children dancing to flourish drum, fiddle and fife" (*Long Way* 304). He also claimed that while in Africa, he "gravitated instinctively to the native element because physically and psychically [he] felt more affinity with it" (301). Although all the novels strikingly differed in setting, all three texts effectively handled the principle themes of the Harlem Renaissance, and they all contributed to the valorization of black aesthetic forms in literature.

An Internationalist

In many ways, Claude McKay departs from the typical Harlem Renaissance writer. He uniquely weaves the memory of his Jamaican past with that of his experience in the United States and his travels around the world. McKay's work, therefore, represents the complexity and versatility of having to negotiate cultural identities. Having grown up in the early nineteenth-century colonial Jamaica, British influence was inescapable, which clearly explains the writer's perceived double-consciousness of swaying between two cultures, his African Jamaican and his disillusioned Britishness. At the same time, Claude McKay's extensive journey around the world situates his work as an internationalist and it allowed him to engage with various social and political issues affecting the wider black diaspora. In the course of his travels, McKay also became acquainted with other literary models that shared similar quests to self-redefinition, namely the Irish and Russian renaissance. As such, McKay exploited his international consciousness as an outlet to seek social equality, which enabled him to broaden the scope of black artistic expressions and to view the diaspora from a wider perspective.

In spite of having to sway amid his cultural experiences and/or identity, he never compromised his Caribbean heritage and, at the same time, McKay remained steadfast in his commitment to developing a black literary canon that not only valorized black cultural expressions, but also represented the everyday realities of Africans throughout the diaspora. Indeed, McKay's unique background as a writer helped to nurture the diverse ways he expressed his craft.

Notes

1. Only a few writers have provided a detailed analysis of Claude McKay's Caribbean influence as it relates to the Harlem Renaissance. See, for instance, A. B. Rose's *Critical Nostalgia and Caribbean Migration*.

2. Négritude is a cultural movement started in 1930s Paris by French-speaking black graduate students from France's colonies in Africa and the Caribbean. Their goal was to combat French imperialism

through affirming self-pride in their African heritage and reclaiming black cultural identities destroyed through the transatlantic slave trade. McKay, whose writing recalibrated black cultural aesthetics and lived experiences, was celebrated by Négritude poet and politician Léopold Sédar Senghor as the spiritual founder of Négritude values.

3.   "Nation language" is the term coined by Caribbean historian and poet Kamau Braithwaite. The term is now commonly preferred to describe the work of writers from the Caribbean and the African diaspora in non-standard English, as opposed to the traditional reference as "dialect."

4.   This is an African-centered religion involving the practicing of sorcery. It is found in Jamaica and other parts of the Caribbean.

Works Cited

Brathwaite, Edward Kamau. *History of the Voice: The Development of Nation Language in Anglophone Caribbean Poetry*. London: New Beacon, 1984.

Brown, Ethelred & Eugene Kinckle Jones. "West Indian-American Relations: A Symposium." *Opportunity* 4 (November 1926): 355–356.

Brown-Rose. *Critical Nostalgia ad Caribbean Migration*. New York: Peter Lang, 2009.

Césaire, Aimé. *Discourse on Negritude: Miami 1987*. Fort-de-France: Conseil général de la Martinique, Bureau de la Communication et des Relations avec la Presse, 2003.

Cooper, Wayne F. *Claude McKay: Rebel Sojourner in the Harlem Renaissance*. Baton Rouge: Louisiana State UP, 1987.

Cruse, Harold. *The Crisis of the Negro Intellectual*. New York: Quill, 1984.

Dance, Daryl Cumber. *Fifty Caribbean Writers: A Bio-bibliographical Critical Sourcebook*. New York: Greenwood P, 1986.

Du Bois, W. E. B. Rev. of *Home to Harlem* by Claude McKay and *Quicksand* by Nella Larsen. *Crisis* 35 (June 1928). 202. Rpt. in *Voices of a Black Nation: Political Journalism in the Harlem Renaissance*. Ed. Theodore G. Vincent. San Francisco: Rampart P, 1973. 359–360.

Goudie, Sean X. "New Regionalisms: US–Caribbean Literary Relations." *A Companion to American Literary Studies*. Eds. Caroline Levander

& Robert Levine Chichester. Malden, MA: Wiley Blackwell, 2011. 310–14.

Garvey, Marcus. *Philosophy and Opinions of Marcus Garvey*. Ed. Amy Jacques Garvey. New York: Atheneum, 1982.

Hathaway, Heather. *Caribbean Waves: Relocating Claude McKay and Paule Marshall* Bloomington: Indiana UP, 1999.

James, Winston. *A Fierce Hatred of Injustice: Claude McKay's Jamaica and His Poetry of Rebellion*. London: Verso, 2001.

_____. "Becoming the People's Poet: Claude McKay's Jamaican Years, 1889–1912." *Small Axe: A Caribbean Journal of Criticism* 13 (March 2003): 17–45.

McKay, Claude. *Banana Bottom*. 1933. New York: Harcourt Brace Jovanovich, 1961.

_____. *Banjo: A Story Without a Plot*. New York: Harcourt Brace Jovanovich, 1932.

_____. *Complete Poems*. Ed. William J. Maxwell. Urbana: U of Illinois P, 2004.

_____. *Constab Ballads*. London: Watts, 1912.

_____. *Harlem Shadows* 1922 New York: Harcourt, Brace, 1922.

_____. *Home to Harlem*. 1928. Boston: Northeastern UP, 1987.

_____. *A Long Way from Home*. 1937. New York: Arno, 1969.

_____. *My Green Hills of Jamaica*. 1975. Jamaica: Heinemann Caribbean, 1979.

_____. "A Negro Writer to His Critics." *The Passion of Claude McKay: Selected Poetry and Prose, 1912–1948*. Ed. Wayne F. Cooper. New York: Schocken, 1973. 132–139.

Paquet, Sandra Pouchet. *Caribbean Autobiography: Cultural Identity and Self-Representation*. Madison: U of Wisconsin P, 2002.

Ramesh, Kotti Sree & Kandula Nirupa Rani. *Claude McKay: The Literary Identity from Jamaica to Harlem and Beyond*. North Carolina: McFarland, 2006.

Tillery, Tyrone. *Claude McKay: A Black Poet's Struggle for Identity*. Amherst: U of Massachusetts P, 1992.

Tomlinson, Lisa. "African Jamaican Aesthetics: Cultural Retention and Transformation Across Borders." Diss. York University, 2013.

"Blue Smoke" and "Stale Fried Fish": A Decadent View of Richard Bruce Nugent

Tiffany Austin

"He sits around helpless, possessed of great talent, doing nothing [. . .] Being a Negro, he feels that his chances for notoriety *á la Wilde* are slim." In the above, the narrator in Wallace Thurman's *Infants of the Spring* sardonically describes fellow Harlem Renaissance artist Richard Bruce Nugent through the character Paul Arbian. Arbian is viewed as destined for futility even though he is marked by genius because of his choice of Oscar Wilde as guiding artistic influence. Richard Bruce Nugent, previously lesser known than other Harlem Renaissance participants, is a notable artist/writer in recent scholarship because he is considered the "only openly gay writer of the Harlem Renaissance" (Schwarz 3). Regarded as a "bohemian" artist, he also looked towards European aestheticism and decadence, literary and artistic movements presumably associated with figures like Oscar Wilde and Aubrey Beardsley.[1]

Nugent's literary kinship with these artists raises important questions about decadence's influence on the Harlem Renaissance, especially by those who considered themselves the Niggeratti and who desired to break from the Old "New Negro" towards a newer "New Negro" in his or her modernist manifestations. Nugent's decision to create the *Salome* visual series (influenced by Beardsley's illustrations for Wilde's work), Nugent's unpublished biblical story of Salome, and the publication of his short story "Smoke, Lilies and Jade" in the only publication of the Niggeratti's *Fire!!* showcase an affinity for decadence that is colored by a more open "male desire" sensibility. The space within the Harlem Renaissance that conflated primitiveness with overt sexuality allowed Nugent to perform more ambiguous possibilities of a New Negro identity. Nugent appropriated primitive language to promulgate works that idealized beauty—a decadent imaging much closer to the enlivened versus decaying body—a Niggeratti inflected decadence with its "stale fried fish" smells.

A. B. Christa Schwarz, in *Gay Voices of the Harlem Renaissance*, provides a nuanced view of the era as one embodying the familiar, euphonious descriptions, "Jazz Age" and the "roaring twenties," but also one that could be described in terms of is continual "anxiety" about race as well as sexuality (6).[2] As blacks migrated to the community, Harlem developed into what Claude McKay described as the "'Negro capital of the world'" where New Negroes desired to assert racial uplift as espoused by leaders like W. E. B. Du Bois and the black bourgeoisie by alleviating racial stereotypes through cultural contributions (Schwarz 8). But as Schwarz explores throughout his work, the physical and literary spaces came to be (sometimes opportunistically, sometimes freeingly by the Niggeratti, but negatively by the Renaissance leaders and black bourgeoisie) viewed as a space of exoticism and primitivism visited by whites. Although the Harlem Renaissance luminaries attempted to draw attention to the positive cultural contributions of blacks, Thomas H. Wirth asserts that the white elites ended up "touring" Harlem for the "alcohol," "jazz" and "easy access to sex partners" (Introduction 20). These conflicting desires and rejections for racial uplift and primitivism by both the white visitors and black participants could be perceived as a latticed space that the Niggeratti simultaneously delved into and attempted to free itself from.

The Niggeratti's endeavors can be examined through Linda Dowling's view that Wilde and others within the Oxford School, celebrating Hellenism, appropriated Buchanan's attack on "fleshly poetry" in order to assert a "counter-discourse" of "male love" (26). In *Hellenism and Homosexuality in Victorian Oxford*, she views Wilde's defense of "male love" within its Greek origins concerning "mind" and "spirit" at his criminal trial at the Old Bailey as a "cultural discontinuity or rupture" that provides the impetus for a homosexual identity (Dowling 2). Similarly, the self-named Niggeratti younger artists' publication of *FIRE!!* signals an eruption, one of continuity and disruption of the older participants' vanguard of positive contributions to art made by blacks.[3] The publication provided an outlet for Nugent's expression of "same-sex" desire in his short story "Smoke, Lilies and Jade." Wirth believes that the Niggeratti of *FIRE!!* desired to posit a "truth," countering older ideas about racial uplift wanted by civil rights sponsored publications like *The Crisis* and *Opportunity* (Introduction 13–14). Hughes expresses this desire in *The Nation* on June 23, 1926 in "The Negro Artist and the Racial Mountain":

> We younger Negro artists who create now intend to express our individual dark-skinned selves without fear or shame. If white people are pleased we are glad. If they are not, it doesn't matter. We know we are beautiful. And ugly, too. The tom-tom cries and the tom-tom laughs. If colored people are pleased we are glad. If they are not, their displeasure doesn't matter either. We build our temples for tomorrow, strong as we know how, and we stand on top of the mountain, free within ourselves. (qtd. in Wirth, Introduction 14)

But still, many of the works within *FIRE!!* "can be interpreted as reinforcing racial stereotypes" (Wirth, Introduction 14). Wirth points to Thurman's "Cordelia the Crude" concerning prostitution, Hughes' "Elevator Boy" about the speaker quitting his job, Hurston's *Color Struck* about skin color within the black community, and "Sweat" referring to abusive black relationships (Introduction 14). Within these stereotypes is the aspect of laziness akin to the languidness expressed in decadence. But while the egotism within languidness of the European decadent refers to the inversion of beauty, the languidness of decadent blackness is aligned with ugliness. Yet, the decadence expressed in the works of the Niggeratti allowed for a "truth" for the artists beyond the moralist standards of the early Harlem Renaissance vanguard akin to European decadence countering Victorian morals.

Nugent's work within the Harlem Renaissance appeared as another rupture, one made up of decadent materials that disrupted the racialized Negro subject. Eric Garber notes that during the Harlem Renaissance, "black lesbians and gay men were meeting each other on street corners, socializing in cabarets and rent parties, and worshiping in church on Sundays, creating a language, a social structure, and a complex network of institutions" (318). Nugent may be best known for his contribution to *FIRE!!* in November of 1926, but Wirth considers Nugent to be the first black writer to "write from a self-declared homosexual perspective," although, as has been often noted, many of the participants of the Harlem Renaissance displayed overtly or covertly "same-sex" desire (Introduction 1). Nugent chose to counter the discourse of racial uplift, not only by deciding to write about homosexuality, but also by explicitly pointing to Wilde as artistic influence, positing himself as a metaphoric expatriate, not physically but psychically departing from the aesthetic framework of the Harlem Renaissance.

Nugent, born in Washington, DC, in 1906, returned to New York with Hughes in 1925 after living there earlier with his mother (Wirth, Introduction 1). He published his first story "Sahdji" after being asked for a contribution to *The New Negro* by Locke (3). In New York during the Renaissance, Nugent lived with fellow friend and artist Wallace Thurman at 267 West 136th Street, known as "Niggeratti Manor" (14). Although Nugent is considered a "bohemian" artist by not pursuing a career, often "writing on 'paper bags and toilet paper'" (Schwarz 121), Nugent's art was published in *Opportunity* and in the *Opportunity*-sponsored anthology *Ebony and Topaz*; it was also featured in a 1931 traveling exhibition sponsored by the Harmon Foundation (Wirth, Introduction 30–31). During the Renaissance, Nugent danced with Hemsley Winfield, who performed the role of Salome at the Cherry Lane Theater in 1920 (31). Nugent also danced with Asadata Dafora and in Hall Johnson's *Run, Little Chillun* (31). Along with working as a "freelance artist and portraitist" and at one time working for the Federal Writers' Project in the 1930s, Nugent also held "regular" jobs, like employment at a night desk and at a hardware supply company in the 1950s and 1960s (35–36). But Wirth notes that "he was left to survive on the wages of his wife and the kindness of friends" (36).

Not until the 1970s was Nugent the subject of scholarly study for the Harlem Renaissance, informing the works of Robert Hemenway, David Levering Lewis, Arnold Rampersad, and Jeff Kisseloff (Wirth, Introduction 39). In the 1980s, he aided the scholarly work in gay history, appearing in the 1986 documentary *Before Stonewall*, contributing an interview to the work of Joseph Beam, and Isaac Julien made use of his prose piece "Smoke, Lilies and Jade" for his 1989 film *Looking for Langston* (Wirth, Introduction 39–40). Nugent was also the center subject of the 2004 film by Rodney Evans titled *Brother to Brother*. But Wirth notes that "because Nugent did not pursue a conventional career as a writer or artist, and because his work profoundly subverted sexual, racial, and religious norms, most of it was never published" (61). Wirth, in his work *Gay Rebel of the Harlem Renaissance*, published for the first time many of Nugent's works, which include short stories, poems, excerpts from a novel, Bible stories, essays on Harlem and Harlem Renaissance personalities, and varied drawings. He further notes, "Bruce was an unregenerate Bohemian to the very end. His unkempt apartment was more than some visitors could take. His sexual interests never flagged. Young men from the neighborhood were always welcome, and many took advantage of his open door" (Wirth, *Gay Rebel* 40). Nugent later died of congestive heart failure on May 27, 1987, as source of developing interest (40).

In terms of his artistic and literary work, Nugent was greatly influenced by European decadence, especially Joris-Karl Huysman's *À rebours* and Oscar Wilde (Wirth, Introduction 41). Wirth states:

> Wallace Thurman's *Infants of the Spring* explicitly sets forth Nugent's awareness of and enthusiasm for the work of Huysmans and Wilde. Paul Arbian (the character based on Nugent) wrote a novel entitled *Wu Sing: The Geisha Man* dedicated to: Huysman's Des Esseintes and Oscar Wilde's Oscar Wilde/Ecstatic Sprits with whom I Cohabit/ And whose golden spores of decadent pollen/I shall broadcast and fertilize. (41–42)

With this influence, Nugent was able to broaden the "concept" of blackness within a discourse of blackness as "primitive," as can be seen in his prose piece "Smoke, Lilies and Jade." Instead of centering the "wealthy, effete young men drifting indecisively through life without emotional ties to anyone but themselves" with "lengthy catalogs of exquisitely described fabrics, flowers, furnishings, books, jewels, and perfumes" (Wirth, *Gay Rebel* 42), Nugent is able to posit decadence within an ambiguously racialized body.

Nugent's short story "Smoke, Lilies and Jade" was the most criticized of *Fire!!*'s works because of its open "homosexuality" (Wirth, Introduction 14). In a stream-of-consciousness style that greatly utilizes ellipses, it showcases bisexual and same sex desire through the story of Alex's love for Adrian/Beauty. Notably, Locke was critical of the inclusion of Nugent's work in *Fire!!* He states:

> If Negro life is to provide a healthy antidote to Puritanism, and to become one of the effective instruments of sound artistic progress, its flesh values must more and more be expressed in the clean, original, primitive but fundamental terms of the senses and not, as too often in this particular issue of Fire [sic], in hectic imitation of the 'naughty nineties' and effete echoes of contemporary decadence. Back to Whitman would have been a better point of support than a left-wing pivoting on Wilde and Beardsley. (qtd. in Wirth, Introduction 49)

Locke desired a "clean, original, primitive," but the view of the primitive through a focus on the senses as argued for by Locke is what seems to allow Nugent to point to the sexuality of male desire—as part of the flesh of primitive bodies. In regards to the story, Schwarz notes that "explicitly mentioned or described sexual contacts remain absent. In this context, it is noteworthy that while Nugent enjoyed sexual affairs with men, he described himself as 'sensual rather than sexual'—an evaluation that seems reflected in his texts" (133). Schwarz further states, "Focusing on sensuality through his detailed depiction of desirous looks and touches, Nugent seems to assign sex a subordinate position in his work" (133). Instead, Nugent conflates discourses of sexuality and race within the primitive, and this allows for an ambiguous performance. Judith Butler, in *Gender Trouble*, speaking of the performance of gender, notes that "drag fully subverts the distinction between inner and outer psychic space and effectively mocks both the expressive model of gender and the notion of a true gender identity" (174). Nugent acts out or presents desire surrounded by and through artifice that goes beyond even drag. The performance's ambiguity does not surface from the ambiguity surrounding race, gender, and sexuality that exists in the text. Butler explains further, "In imitating gender, drag implicitly reveals the imitative structure of gender itself—as well as its contingency" (175). Within the discourses about race and sex as primitive, Nugent wants us to focus on the "contingency."

Yet the "contingency" in Nugent's prose is not focused on race, gender, and sexuality. Rather, the prose posits a racialized, gendered, and sexualized androgyny that centralizes the imagination and its possibility for subversion: *He wanted to do something…*to write or draw…or something…but it was so comfortable just to lie there on the bed…his shoes off…and think…think of everything… short disconnected thoughts….to wonder…to remember…to think and smoke" (Nugent, "Smoke" 75). The passage, referring to the thoughts of central character, Alex, reminds one of Wilde's epigram that "to do nothing at all is the most difficult thing in the world, the most difficult and the most intellectual" (1136). Like Wilde, Nugent focuses on the identity of the individual as artist. Alex relates that "anyway people never cried for beautiful sunsets…or music…and those were the things that hurt…the things to sympathize with" (Nugent, "Smoke" 75). Nugent turns the critical eye within the Harlem Renaissance from the racialized body and "sympathies" for the abilities of a black artist to contribute artistically to a full embodiment of an artist who has "sympathies" for art. Remembering his father's death, the narrator once again refers to the art of imagination: "Alex puffed contentedly on his cigarette… he was hungry and comfortable…and he had an ivory holder inlaid with red jade and green…funny how the smoke seemed to climb up that ray of sunlight…went up the slant just like imagination… was imagination blue" (76). Alex asks himself, "[W]as all life like that…smoke…blue smoke from an ivory holder"? (78). The blue smoke represents his own self-conscious imagination contouring his life. Rather than withdrawing from the realness of life that does not accept his racial, gendered, and sexual body, he envelops within the imagination, an imagination that will then color the life of that body. Thus, Alex can be hungry and comfortable at the same time. Alex's form of aestheticism is filled more with quest and mediation rather than of the seemingly self-confident irony of Wilde:

> [W]as he sophisticated…no because he was seldom bored…seldom bored by anything…and weren't the sophisticated continually suffering from ennui…on the contrary…he was amused…amused by the artificiality of naiveté and sophistication alike…but maybe that in itself was the essence of sophistication or…was it cynicism…or were the two identical…he blew a cloud of smoke…. …truly smoke was like imagination. (Nugent, "Smoke" 78)

As the narrator alludes to, imagination is not mere artificiality, but with smoke as its metaphor, imagination embodies artistic practice—material but elusive. The important point is the amusement enjoyed by Alex—to be present in the blue smoke.

Nugent's prose is akin to Wildean aestheticism in its descriptions of objects, experiences, and feelings as color and music—"color music"—and Alex experiences them as momentary—"but he no longer felt that urge" (Nugent, "Smoke" 80). But Alex also posits archetypal decadence beside the realism of his material life: "[H]e climbed the noisy stair of the odorous tenement…smelled of fish… of stale fried fish and dirty milk bottles…he rather liked it…he liked the acrid smell of horse manure too…strong…thoughts…yes to lie back among strangely fashioned cushions and sip eastern wines and talk…" (Nugent, "Smoke" 80–81). Nugent combines decadence with "uncoded" touch, allowed by blackness' link to bodies within the primitive. So, while Nugent can point to aestheticism in describing Alex meeting a stranger upon the nightly street—"Alex walked music" and "he walked music also" "and their echoes mingled" (81)—he could also describe their touching within a bedroom: "as they undressed by the blue dawn…Alex knew he had never seen a more perfect being…his body was all symmetry and music… and Alex called him Beauty…long they lay…blowing smoke and exchanging thoughts…and Alex swallowed with difficulty…he felt a glow of tremor…and they talked and…slept" (82). Descriptions of explicit sex are absent, and the focus is more on Alex's quest for Beauty—within Adrian's body and the imagination. In this quest,

Alex is attracted to both Melba and Adrian, but as Schwarz notes, the positing of these characters is less about androgyny or sexual confusion: "The number—not the gender—of his lovers is troubling Alex, who solves his problem by concluding: '[O]ne can love two at the same time.' Against all expectations of critics, Nugent in 'Smoke, Lilies and Jade' presents neither homosexuality, heterosexuality, nor bisexuality as areas of conflict" (135).

Yet, Nugent is not even referring to a number, but rather he seems more concerned with the range of sexual experiences, a view that aligns with Alex's decadent view of the imagination. Amongst the two physical images of Melba and Adrian in a dream, Alex searches in a "field of blue smoke and black poppies and red cala lilies" and in the end, "suddenly he stood erect...exultant...and in his hand he held...an ivory holder...inlaid with red jade...and green" (Nugent, "Smoke" 83). Again, Nugent refers to Wilde: "Alex wondered why he always thought of that passage from Wilde's Salome...when he looked at Beauty's lips...I would kiss your lips...he *would* like to kiss Beauty's lips" (83). Simultaneously, Nugent refers to Langston Hughes' spiritual: "f-ah-fy-ah-Lawd...fy-ah's gonna burn ma soul," repeated as Alex thinks about Beauty throughout the story (84–85). Again, Nugent places artifice and the body in mediation with one another (Wilde's lips and Hughes' spiritual) without focusing on the black color as racial. Instead, Nugent presupposes the black body as a valid site of experience. Beside the avant-garde encroachment of homosexuality, Nugent posits an artistic body in the Harlem Renaissance. As Alex walks in the blue of night towards the stars to meet Adrian/Beauty and walks in the blue of night towards the moon with Melva, he says, "[O]ne can love two at the same time" (87). Situated in the middle are the words "blue smoke from an ivory holder" and the prose ends with "one *can* love" (87). This spacing of the phrase in the middle and italicizing of "can" center the love and the ways one can love the imagination. More important than the identities of Adrian and Melva as desired characters or even Alex as central character is the praxis of the imagination. In the prose, Nugent centralizes the horizon filled with blue smoke, a horizon suggesting a range of identities versus identity as delimiting boundary, made possible through a focus on art.

As a visual artist, Nugent can be perceived as original by employing African motifs in his work (Wirth, Introduction 57). Nugent was influenced by Aaron Douglas (in terms of the use of African motifs) and Winold Reiss (Bavarian artist who used a German folk technique of drawing with black cut silhouettes— Scherenschnitte) (57). Dance becomes Nugent's "praxis" to implode the meanings and performances of the body. Wirth believes that "Nugent employed dance as a trope to express primitive vitality and freedom from sexual inhibition" (57), but "[t]o Nugent, the forms and movements of dance were of importance in themselves, not just as symbols of the primitive" (58). Moreover, overtly influenced by the visual milieu of Beardsley, Nugent participated in the "grotesqueness" of the silhouette. He again embraced aestheticism as informing his own visual works. By focusing on the artistic body obliquely linked to the primitive, he provides a subversive perspective within the Harlem Renaissance.

Nugent continued his link with Wilde and Beardsley and the subversive possibilities for gender, sexual, and racial identity through creating the *Salome series* after their works. In "Biblical Gender Bending in Harlem: The Queer Performance of Nugent's *Salome*," Ellen McBreen explores Nugent's *Salome* illustrations as Nugent's expression of gay culture within the racially identified Harlem Renaissance. Wirth and McBreen point to the drawings as part of Judith Butler's drag performative. Certainly, the drawings remind one of drag performance in relation to the androgynous subject matter of Wilde's *Salome* and Beardsley's even more androgynous illustrations, but by making the figures more voluptuous, again, Nugent was attempting to posit a primitive corporeality into the artifice of racial, gender, and sexual ambiguity. More than a drag performance, the curvy and curving bodies allow a focus on the dance, whereby the body becomes the most elevated artifice. While the erect nipples, bi-and inverted triangulated genitals, and make-up could be masks, they also embody an androgynous crossing that results in a mulatto body, not unlike the figures Nugent created for the *Drawings for Mulattoes*.

Disagreeing with McBreen, the mulatto body appears as an enveloping of a racial, gender, and sexual ambiguity that relates inclusiveness within the "primitive." This is most seen in the drawing of the two women, who appear to be the same woman crossing one another. This doubling implodes considerations of certainty regarding identities and desire as will be discussed further below. The women cross with their alternating aqua and blond bodily outlines and hair. As will be discussed in relation to "Slender Length of Beauty," the primitive can be reinterpreted as a concentration on the individual body—an imaginative narcissism. Also in *Naomi and Ruth*, two women appear (more so move with the curvatures of the drawing), one's front facing the viewer and the other's back facing the viewer. The one facing the viewer holds the breast of the other, swayed to our vision, offering the curved out parcel of the body to the viewer. Within the discourse of primitiveness, where black women "symbolized the exotic, erotic, and sexually lascivious" (Krasner 196), Nugent appropriates the space of the primitive black woman's body to erase the black, offering a pure, primitive body that is primitive no longer. Decadence's link to the primitive has its historicity, but in Nugent's work, it is informed by Nugent's participation in the Harlem Renaissance, whereby his work is associated with the primitiveness of blackness. Nugent will intersect these conversations about decadence and the primitive pouring from European decadence and Harlem Renaissance decadence in choosing to write about, as well as draw, Salome. The written work allows for the duplicity of the primitive aesthetic by replacing it with the language of beauty—the unsophisticate becomes the sophisticate.

Nugent's "Slender Length of Beauty" provides a version of Salome that converses with previous works on Salome; especially Wilde's, but also reveals his nuanced view of the imagination with its relation to the primitive body. As in Wilde's *Salome*, Nugent's use of decadent language, of the sensual, and of artifice is reminiscent of the biblical language of *Song of Solomon*. The notable difference is that while Wilde's language of love and beauty centers on the interchange between Salome and Iokanaan, Nugent focuses on the "lover language" between Salome and Narcissus (a shepherd), Iokanaan's twin. In between exchanges of compliments of beauty, Narcissus tells Salome, "'I am a twin, Sa-la-ma'" ("Slender" 131) and to counter Salome's jealousy, "'My twin is a brother'" (131). Instead of the subtext of same-sex desire between the young Syrian and the page of Herodias in Wilde's *Salome*, Nugent seems to posit an ambiguous and incestuous sexuality around the characters of Narcissus and Iokanaan as twins and their relationships with Salome. Once again, as in Nugent's short story, functioning is a doubling that broadens in its link to the imagination. Adhering to the importance of the dance motif, Nugent also focuses on Salome's preparations before the dance performed for Herod. Preparations of the bath, make-up, and dress point to the dance as a drag performance. Specifically, the descriptions of the make-up remind one of Nugent's *Salome* series:

> The lids of her eyes she carefully painted blue. Her lips and the nipples of her breasts she drew crimson with a paste made of cochineal and the oil from lotus-blooms. The nails on her fingers and toes were likewise made crimson with lacquer. Her lashes she weighted with gold paint smelling of the oil of oranges. Over her whole body she dusted pale purple powder. Into her hair she sifted gold and sparkling dust. From her ears were hung tiny silver bells, and on the first finger of each hand she wore a great ruby ring. ("Slender" 134)

Again, Nugent self-consciously points to Wilde. Iokanaan says to Herod of Salome, "'Thy daughter, thy niece, shall kill the thing she loves, and also shall this Salome—'" ("Slender" 137), referencing Wilde's The "Ballad of Reading Gaol." But, here, as with the drawings, Nugent focuses on the dance when Salome becomes "contortionist" and "courtesan" (138), throwing her veils of sexuality to her audience, mirroring the veils of their religion. When she sees Iokanaan, who she believes is Narcissus, "[h]er breasts hardened. Her lips grew soft, and her hips more seductively sexual as she twirled into a final passion—spasm and threw to the prophet the blood-red veil. It was scented with lotus" (138). Again, Nugent is able to "uncode" the body coded through Salome's confusion about the number and "objects" of her desire alongside rendering beautiful languages and images. This turn moves the work beyond drag performance, doubling as drag and praxis of the imagination. The work showcases the decadent imagining of desire.

As in Wilde's work, death ensues. But in Nugent's work, the death is a product of illusion rather than overladen desire. Eliot L. Gilbert notes, in "'Tumult of Images': Wilde, Beardsley, and Salome, "[I]f as a radical and homosexual he attacks the patriarchal establishment by showing uncommon sympathy for Salome and her subversive self-absorption, as an artist and male homosexual he recoils from the full implications of an uncontrolled and murderous female energy" (154) in aligning with Iokanaan as victim and Herod as announcer of death. In Nugent's work, Salome remains a sympathetic character who does not display unbridled desire. When the Tetrarch promises Salome anything she desires after watching her dance, "Salome stood shamed and still, for now she recognized Iokanaan. And, turning to hide her nakedness and fleeing the banquet hall, she answered over her trembling shoulder, 'My mother will ask my reward.' And the voice of Herodias followed her faintly, saying, 'Give me the head of Iokanaan'" (Nugent, "Slender" 138). Unlike in Wilde's version, Salome is shamed and finally willed by Herodias. Salome's shame derives from the illusion surrounding her desire. Is it for Narcissus, Iokanaan, or herself? When Salome returns to her shepherd, Narcissus, she once again espouses his beauty: "'[T] hy lips are so beautiful, Narcissus, it is a pity I cannot kiss them and see them together'" (139). The imagery and the subtext are masturbatory and within Salome's inability to perceive the illusion, she kills Narcissus by allowing his twin, Iokanaan, to be killed: "the bells in her ears tinkled as she kissed him. But Narcissus was dead" (139). Even though Salome desired to kiss Iokanaan, it is because of his likeness to Narcissus, who is like Salome. Again, Nugent paints androgyny with his prose, but stroked within is the contemplation on narcissist imagination and is the centering of beauty. The title of the short story is derived from Salome's description of Narcissus' lips as "a slender straight line" (133), and this is where beauty is located, within a "line," within a horizon that can look towards the primitive body, towards the lips. Yet the primitive body becomes a quivering line concerning desire, making it a naïve and sophisticated argument.

Insofar as Nugent looked towards Wilde as literary ancestor, one could presume that Nugent attempted to erase race and embolden his art within an "effete, white" tradition. However, as Nugent's works show, Nugent participated in the primitive discourse surrounding the Harlem Renaissance. It became a vicissitude for writing about and drawing the body. His literary and visual works become instances of dancing—the embodiment of art's movement. This movement not only involves one from primitive to non-primitive, but also a movement from ideological concerns of a racialized body in the Harlem Renaissance. His works assert not that the black body can achieve art—can dance—but the positioning of the black artist relegating art—is dance. The older vanguard of the Harlem Renaissance may have desired climbing to obtain racial uplift, but as Hughes decried, Nugent stood on top of the mountain—a mountain made up of contents of race, sex, and gender discourses and contexts of primitiveness and decadence—free within his beauty emboldened imagination. Combining the efficacy of decadent and primitive beauty, Nugent reveals a primary concern with the individual artist interpreting the body. Yet, aware of the inadequacy of decadent and primitive language to express body's meaning—as racial, gendered, and sexed, his works privileged the language of the body's intimacy with beauty instead.

Notes

1. The European Aestheticism Movement, generally termed "art for art's sake" and Decadent Movements, historically aligned with depravity and perversity with its focus on artifice, developed in the nineteenth century as a critique of the Industrial Revolution and bourgeois morality.

2. Siobhan B. Somerville, in *Queering the Color Line: Race and the Invention of Homosexuality in American Culture*, specifically probes the policing and intersecting discourses concerning racial and sexual identity in the late nineteenth-century.

3. The November 1926 premiere and only issue of an art quarterly "devoted to younger Negro artists" featured Langston Hughes, Zora Neale Hurston, Aaron Douglas, Wallace Thurman, Gwendolyn Bennett, John P. Davis, and Nugent as the contributors.

Works Cited

Butler, Judith. "Bodily Inscriptions, Performative Subversions." *Gender Trouble: Feminism and the Subversion of Identity*. New York: Routledge, 1999. 163–180.

Dowling, Linda. "Aesthete and Effeminatus." *Hellenism and Homosexuality in Victorian Oxford*. 1994. Ithaca: Cornell UP, 1996. 1–31.

Garber, Eric. "A Spectacle in Color: The Lesbian and Gay Subculture of Jazz Age Harlem." *Hidden from History: Reclaiming the Gay and Lesbian Past*. Eds. Martin Duberman, George Chauncey, Jr. & Martha Vicinus. New York: Meridian, 1990. 318–331.

Gilbert, Elliot L. "'Tumult of Images': Wilde, Beardsley, and *Salome*." *Victorian Studies* 26.2 (1983): 133–59.

Krasner, David. "Black Salome: Exoticism, Dance, and Racial Myths." *African American Performance and Theater History: A Critical Reader*. Eds. Harry J. Elam, Jr. & David Krasner. Oxford: Oxford UP, 2001. 192–211.

McBreen, Ellen. "Biblical Gender Bending in Harlem: The Queer Performance of Nugent's *Salome*." *Art Journal* 57.3 (1998): 22–28.

Mishkin, Tracy. *The Harlem and Irish Renaissances: Language, Identity, and Representation*. Gainesville: UP of Florida, 1998.

Nugent, Richard Bruce. "Slender Length of Beauty." *Gay Rebel of the Harlem Renaissance: Selections from the Work of Richard Bruce Nugent*. Ed. Thomas H. Wirth. Durham: Duke UP, 2002. 130–138.

_____. "Smoke, Lilies and Jade." *Gay Rebel of the Harlem Renaissance: Selections from the Work of Richard Bruce Nugent*. Ed. Thomas H. Wirth. Durham: Duke UP, 2002. 75–86.

Schwarz, A.B. Christa. *Gay Voices of the Harlem Renaissance*. Bloomington: Indiana UP, 2003.

Somerville, Siobhan B. *Queering the Color Line: Race and the Invention of Homosexuality in American Culture*. Durham: Duke UP, 2000.

Thurman, Wallace. *Infants of the Spring*. 1932. New York: Random, 1999.

Wilde, Oscar. "The Critic as Artist." *Collins Complete Works of Oscar Wilde.* 1999. Glasgow: Harper, 1999. 1108–1155.

Wirth, Thomas H., ed. *Gay Rebel of the Harlem Renaissance: Selections from the Work of Richard Bruce Nugent.* Durham: Duke UP, 2002.

_____. Introduction. *Gay Rebel of the Harlem Renaissance: Selections from the Work of Richard Bruce Nugent.* Ed. Thomas H. Wirth. Durham: Duke UP, 2002. 1–61.

Going Back to Work Through: The Return to Folk Origins in the Late Harlem Renaissance____

Karl Henzy

Until the US stock market crashed on October 24, 1929, Harlem Renaissance writing had been overwhelmingly focused on the emergence of "the New Negro" from the "Negro migration, northward and city-ward . . . from the cotton-field and farm to the heart of the most complex urban civilization" (Locke 629–30). But between the Crash in 1929 and the Harlem Race Riot of March 19, 1935, four important novels were published by Harlem Renaissance authors returning to black folk origins: Langston Hughes' *Not Without Laughter* (1930), Arna Bontemps' *God Sends Sunday* (1931), Claude McKay's *Banana Bottom* (1933) and Zora Neale Hurston's *Jonah's Gourd Vine* (1934). These works might be seen as abandoning the Harlem Renaissance project, but that would be based on the mistaken notion that the Renaissance had ever been about a few square miles in northern Manhattan. The Renaissance was never really about *Harlem*, the physical space; it was about "Harlem," the idea of a black utopia.

From about 1917 to 1929, that idea largely coincided with the physical space of the actual *Harlem*, but after the Crash, the once-thriving neighborhood degenerated rapidly into a slum (Gates 47). The Renaissance idea was then in need of new spaces. Hughes, Bontemps, McKay, and Hurston found those spaces in the folk cultures of their pasts, but they never stopped examining, through their art, what had happened in the actual Harlem, New York: the birth and death of the idea of a black utopia. This is why their return-to-folk-origin novels between the Crash and the Riot are not, conversely, to be valorized simply for their ethnographic content. There is plenty of it: the reader can learn of roadhouse blues in Hughes, Mississippi River sporting life in Bontemps, Jamaican Obeah practices in McKay, and southern black church politics in Hurston, among many other features of black folk life. But the authors considered here are interested in more than folk customs. They return to folk origins in order to continue to work through, by way of narrative, their thoughts and feelings about "Harlem" (not *Harlem*), what it was, why it ended, and how to survive its collapse. Their results are as various as their temperaments, as we shall see.

Langston Hughes' *Not Without Laughter* and Negative Capability

In the last two months of 1817, British romantic poet John Keats wrote letters to family and friends in which he worked out his theory of negative capability. In a November 22 letter to his friend Benjamin Bailey, Keats writes of his conviction that arguments happen only because the minds of contestants have not had sufficient time to enter into each other's points-of-view (31). Similarly, in a December 22 letter, he proclaims that the intensity of art makes "all disagreeables evaporate" (Keats 33). The logical handling of propositions and deductions, which Keats calls "consecutive reasoning" (32), cannot allow that both *A* and *not A* be true. Philosophers need to separate valid from faulty arguments, but Keats sees all ideas in terms of their beauty and imagination, and "what the Imagination seizes as Beauty must be truth—whether it existed before or not" (31). *A* and *not A* might both be "truth" in this sense. Whenever abstraction leads Keats astray, as it sometimes does, he assures Bailey that "[t]he Setting Sun will always set me to rights, or if a Sparrow come before my Window, I take part in its existence and pick about the gravel" (32). The poet, through imagination, enters into the existence of beings, moments, or even ideas, avoiding the opposition of "disagreeables" or the claims of contending parties.

In the Harlem Renaissance, though Countee Cullen worshipped Keats, it was Langston Hughes who was the true poet of negative capability. That is why Hughes could, for instance, be an atheist and yet make use of the language of the black church in some of his poems (and celebrate the language of "sinners" just as much in other poems). He was not concerned with the truth-value of Christian theology as a statement about the nature of existence, but with the "truth" of certain religious experiences as expressions of black lives, their longing for love, their refusal to be defined by past frustrations, and the poetry of their language.

Hughes' intention to poeticize all of black life regardless of any oppositions within it put him in a somewhat difficult position during the Harlem Renaissance, for the movement was fracturing into contending parties almost from its inception. The older generation of Harlem Renaissance luminaries, led by W. E. B. Du Bois, James Weldon Johnson, Alain Locke, and Jessie Redmon Fauset, conceived of the Renaissance as a means of improving the lives of black Americans through achievement in the arts, which would depict black people "of the higher type," Du Bois' Talented Tenth, refined, cultured, and articulate in Standard English. This high-culture product of the Harlem Renaissance was supposed to convince white America to embrace blacks as equals, with measurable results, such as a reduction and eventual elimination of lynchings. Already by the beginning of 1926, however, Hughes was leading the charge of the movement's young Turks, rejecting the dignified respectability of the NAACP crowd in the name of artistic freedom and celebrating the vitality of what he referred to as "the low-down folks, the so-called common element" (Hughes, "Negro Artist" 92)—their jazz, blues, dialect, the numbers games, Harlem nightlife, sexual exuberance. What was at stake was who would be included in the new black utopia.

With the Crash in 1929 and the economic pressures of the Great Depression, the oppositions within black life had the potential to pull apart the Renaissance. However, the next year, in his novel *Not Without Laughter*, Hughes explores the possibility of unifying contending forces through the love that dreamy, young, incipient poet Sandy has for his grandmother, mother, and aunt in spite of the acrimony between them. In effect, *Not Without Laughter* is a novel of negative capability. Aunt Hager, the grandmother who washes white people's clothes, values hardworking respectability. The black church is her rock, and she is proud that white folk trust her, but she drives away her daughter Harriett, who hates white people and feels that life is too short to forego any opportunity to have fun. Harriett loves blues, jazz, and dancing and eventually ends up living as a prostitute in the Bottoms, the red light district, before restarting her career as a blues singer. Sandy's mother Anjee, domestic servant in white women's homes, is hopelessly in love with Sandy's father Jimboy, who is great at picking blues on a guitar, but is mostly gone from home, supposedly looking for work in different parts of the country from where he rarely writes back or sends money. Anjee's distraction over Jimboy often makes her at best a neglectful mother to Sandy, who by default is really raised by his grandmother Hager.

Hager, Harriett, and Anjee: Sandy "loved all three of them" and so "he didn't carry tales on any one of them to the others" (Hughes, *Laughter* 115). Sandy always "wanted to make everything all right" (95). But it is Aunt Hager who spells out what is needed:

> I's been livin' a long time in yesterday, Sandy chile, an' I knows there ain't no room in de world fo' nothin' mo'n love. I knows, chile! Ever'thing there is but lovin' leaves a rust on yo' soul. An' to love sho 'nough, you got to have a spot in you' heart fo' ever'body—great an' small—'cause love ain't got no crowded-out places where de good ones stays an' de bad ones can't come in. When it gets that way, then it ain't love. (Hughes, *Laughter* 183)

It is a measure of Hughes' art that this great speech, which theoretically could tie together the different parts of Sandy's world and ultimately of the Harlem Renaissance—black and white, church people and sinners, country and city, women and men, high culture and low culture—is spoken by a character who is at least slightly a female "Uncle Tom" and who has already driven away one daughter, has another who is ashamed of her for her country ways, and is constantly attacking a third daughter's husband. Yet the speech she makes on the necessary unifying power of love clearly has the imprimatur of the author, of Langston Hughes himself, even if, by giving the speech to Hager, he knows how difficult it is for the speech to find its proper place in the world. But Hughes is like the composer Charles Ives, who in *Putnam's Camp, Redding, Connecticut*, the second of his *Three Places in New England (Orchestral Set No.1)* (1912), has the orchestra recreate the effect, on a July 4 celebration, of two marching bands approaching each other from different directions, their music mingling. Hughes reports that on the evening of the carnival "mourning songs of the Christians could be heard rising from the Hickory Woods [where they are holding a revival] while the profound syncopation of the minstrel band blared from Galoway's Lots, strangely intermingling their notes of praise and joy" (*Laughter* 109). The listener who must be "irritabl[y] reaching after fact and reason" (Keats 33) would want to shut out one or the other, the minstrel band or the Christians, one or the other marching band, but Hughes, like Ives, hears a third music rising above the two, the cacophony of a new inclusive American music.

That is why Sandy affirms the singing at the end of the novel, in Chicago, coming from "a little Southern church in a side street," by "some old black worshippers" (Hughes, *Laughter* 298). Anjee seems ready to mock them as remnants from black country life, out of place in the big city, but Sandy, who is not even particularly religious (like Hughes), thinks it is beautiful because they sing that "Saints an' sinners *all* are gathered home" [emphasis added]. And that is why, when Sandy is stuck in his Aunt Tempy's respectable Harlem Renaissance home (and assigned to read W. E. B. Du Bois), Hughes gleefully affirms the irony that "the Bottoms should be the only section of Stanton where Negroes and whites mingled freely on equal terms" (239), for it is in the whorehouses of the red light district that "people of all colors came together for the sake of joy" (217). It is there that Hughes, ultimately, finds his preferred image of a black utopia. Hughes seeks unification, not separation. The negative capability of his *Not Without Laughter* gives him a way of examining all the contending forces at work in the Harlem Renaissance after the start of the Depression, ignoring their competing claims, and seeing them all as expressions of the lives of black people and even of America as a whole.

Arna Bontemps' *God Sends Sunday* and Mock Epic

Although mock epic became a popular form in eighteenth-century British literature, the first mock epic was composed by the first and greatest epic writer, Homer. In the *Odyssey*, Odysseus' great adventures are only *told* by Odysseus (not narrated by Homer directly) to the Phaeacians: his victory over the Cyclops Polyphemus, entrapment by the witch Circe, and journey into the underworld are all narrated second-hand. For all the reader knows, these may be just the fanciful ravings of an old wanderer, dependent on the hospitality of strangers. In the conflict in which the reader first *sees* Odysseus fight (i.e., reads Homer describe it directly), he is dressed as a beggar and forced to fight a fellow beggar, the fat Irus, for panhandling turf back home in Ithaca. The great Odysseus is reduced to the petty territorial claims of raggedy mendicants. And even after Odysseus vanquishes the usurpers, Homer turns from the heroic to the farcical. The old men of the island, fathers of the suitors Odysseus has slain, gather for revenge in Book XXIV, and are met by Odysseus with a little army of old men of his own, "warriors at a pinch despite their white hair" (Homer 519). A full scale skirmish between seniors threatens until Athena, exasperated, calls a halt to the deadly hijinks (552–3), and the epic is allowed finally to end without quite descending into pure farce.

Just as Homer punctuates the epic struggle of *The Iliad* and *The Odyssey* with the mock epic burlesque of *Odyssey* Book VIII and ends it with the same in *Odyssey* Book XXIV, so Arna Bontemps depicts the Harlem Renaissance's aspirational struggle in mock-epic style in *God Sends Sunday* (1931). He does that, first of all, by his choice of protagonist, Little Augie. Though Augie rises to prominence in his life as a jockey, kills two men in fights, and sleeps with many women, and though Bontemps at times drops the epithet "Little," the author also reminds us, whenever Augie loses himself in dreams of grandeur, that he is after all just a little man who looks "as absurd as an infant" with "dreams of heroism too big for his body" (Bontemps 179). Though Augie has ridden real horses, beautiful winners, he himself is more like the merry-go-round horses of Part Two, section V: "one horse lacked a tail and one a foreleg and . . . others were losing their manes" (149).

All of these humbling elements connected to Augie would be fine if there was not an uncomfortable association of Augie with the Harlem Renaissance, that first glorious time of self-proclamation for African Americans. But Augie *is* a New Negro. When his winnings give him spending money, he buys expensive clothes and goes for what he thinks of as an elegant look, just as the New Negroes of the Harlem Renaissance aspired to look the part of gentlemen. The fact that Augie's taste is grotesque and tawdry only serves Bontemps' mock-epic purposes and raises the question of whether any form of preening, be it Augie's silk shirts with "two inch candy-stripes of purple, pink, or orange" (Bontemps 25) or Du Bois' famous dandified, if more tasteful, look, is faintly ridiculous.

Augie, like the Renaissance writers, has his ideal, and her name is Florence Dessau. Florence, of course, was the capital city of the *first* Renaissance, the Italian Cinquecento. And Dessau, which after all is just a common family name among the French creoles of Louisiana, was *also* the capital of another artistic renaissance, the modernist flowering of the Bauhaus school, centered in Dessau, Germany, from 1925 to 1932, during which *God Sends Sunday* was published. So Florence Dessau is twice over a reminder of renaissances ancient and modern. She also happens to be a white man's whore, as Augie discovers. Again, Bontemps was fully aware of the contention of critics that the Harlem Renaissance, for all its celebration of black artistic talent, was largely owned by whites— white revelers in whites-only Harlem nightclubs; white sponsors, like Charlotte Osgood Mason; and white publishing houses. But white proprietariness did nothing to diminish the vitality of the Harlem Renaissance's "social dreaming" (Sargent 5) about black utopias, any more than it sullied Florence Dessau's allure for Augie: "Florence's beauty fascinated Augie more than ever. It seemed more unreal, more unattainable" (Bontemps 41).

Like the Harlem Renaissance, Augie has his own Great Migration north, though in his case, it is from New Orleans to Saint Louis. It is there that Augie "met his own conception of fine living" (Bontemps 53), his black utopia. It is there, he feels, that black men really know how to express the most joyful possibilities of life. As for the women, they "could not fail to [help him] forget Florence Dessau" (53). He even finds a substitute for Dessau in Della Green (*of the green, of nature*). And he takes on and vanquishes the Natural Man, Biglow (*big* and vital in the *low* culture world). St. Louis, then, is Augie's complete Harlem Renaissance, but having gotten everything he thought he wanted there, it ceases to please him because it all feels like a pale imitation of what the white man has. Della Green might "look . . . for all the world like Florence . . . But she [is] not Florence" (73).

The Harlem Renaissance, Bontemps appears to suggest, was destined to fail to the extent that it imitated a white ideal. For Augie, that imitation does not work, even when he attains the white man's woman, for he finally moves in with Florence upon his return to New Orleans, flush with money, only to find that the neighbors cast him and Florence out of the fine house in the white neighborhood. Thus Augie lives with his dream woman, but only in a shack on the outskirts of town and then just until his luck at the track ends, after which Florence unsentimentally leaves him. As Augie leaves the scene of his renaissance for good, Bontemps constructs one of those scale reversals that remind his readers that, however grand Augie appears in moments, mostly in his own eyes, he is a small man in an uncaring world: "In the distance, he suggested an insect crawling toward the ultimate needle-point where the rails converge. Curiously, as his figure diminished, the ironic silk hat seemed to wax larger and larger. In the end it swallowed both man and luggage" (Bontemps 112).

Bontemps, like Homer, ends his "epic" with the battles of old men (Augie and Lissus), sad repetitions of more glorious origins. And as post-Crash writers were going back to southern folk origins, Bontemps has Augie go back, not to the south, but to a place just like it: the Mudtown section of Watts, California. But Augie is a dozen years past his prime, and though he repeats his pursuit of the young black beauty and his battle with the natural man, it is all simply too pitiful. Augie's nephew Terry "could almost cry looking at Augie in his ridiculous mashed-up hat" (Bontemps 162). "The sizes of things become temporarily adjusted" only by Augie's drinking liquor at this point (179), but he is "a hopeless old wreck" . . . "absurd as an infant," forced to move on yet again because he cannot leave well enough alone and remember who he is.

Critical Insights

The question is, why does Bontemps take such a mocking attitude towards the Harlem Renaissance through Little Augie? Why did Homer turn the great epics of *The Iliad* and *The Odyssey* into mock-epics? It is about *coming home*. About finding peace after the glory days have passed. The mock epic performs a readjustment of scale. Odysseus cannot be a husband and father if in his head he is forever the great Odysseus, warrior on the plains of Troy. He must be cut down from heroic to human size and reminded of his age in order to take possession of Ithaca. The glory days of the Harlem Renaissance ended with the Crash of 1929. Prior to that catastrophe, it was the "New Negro's" day—he had his Civic Club dinners, his *Opportunity* Awards, his press, his white patrons fascinated by his every move. With the crash and the ensuing Depression, that would all go away; black people might have their heads ringing with memories of the clink of champagne glasses and the rustle of flattering press clippings, but they might have to live in the dust.

Bontemps' mock epic readjusts scales in the service of living on through the hard times ahead. The glory days of the Harlem Renaissance, of Augie's Saint Louis, were fine because of the glimpses of some ideal they offered, but they were also faintly ridiculous (from the mock-epic point of view), much ado about nothing. If that were not the case, maybe it would be too painful to carry on post-Crash. But we are not fallen giants; we are human beings whose dreams, like all dreams, are like "toy balloons at a fair when suddenly, [they are loosed and] the sky [is] full of bright lovely things, gradually ascending on the wind" (Bontemps 66). The road lies ahead, and "there [is] no need to turn back" (196). Better get on up the road.

Claude McKay's *Banana Bottom* and the Imp in Utopia

In D. H. Lawrence's novel *The Rainbow* (1915), Will and Anna Brangwen visit Lincoln Cathedral, in England's East Midlands. Will seeks in the cathedral a consummate image of transcendence. His wife Anna is also struck by the cathedral's majesty, but she and Will are always in a state of tension, and so she balks at his ecstasy over the great church and gleefully seizes on the famous Lincoln Imp and other assorted gargoyles in the building, "wicked, odd little faces carved in stone" (Lawrence 195), calling his attention to them:

> These sly little faces peeped out of the grand tide of the cathedral like something that knew better. They knew quite well, these little imps that retorted on man's own illusion, that the cathedral was not absolute. They winked and leered, giving suggestion of the many things that had been left out of the great concept of the church.

Outwardly, Will denies his wife's interpretation of the figures, but his experience of the cathedral is ruined (it had "become to him . . . a shapely heap of dead matter" [196]). For Anna, the imps free her from the cathedral's impact and, therefore, from her husband's domineering hold on her.

Claude McKay "had a profound and lasting admiration" for Lawrence (Cooper 208). And in *Banana Bottom*, his post-Crash Harlem Renaissance novel that returns to his folk roots in the Jamaican highlands, he makes use of a device similar to the Lincoln gargoyles as a way of giving his response to the Renaissance's utopian aspirations. The Renaissance of Talented Tenth elevation is present in *Banana Bottom* as the Mission, the protestant Church and school run by the descendant of white colonizers, Malcolm Craig, and his wife Priscilla, as so much of the Harlem Renaissance was sponsored by white New Yorkers. The Craigs want to sponsor "the right sort" of black Jamaican to take over the mission and eventually redeem a primitive local population. But McKay has a wicked—some would say even juvenile—sense of humor, and the novel keeps returning to crude and often sexual jokes. McKay allows Tabitha "Bita" Plant, the young Jamaican woman returned from an elevating education in England and adopted by the Craigs, to escape from an unwanted marital engagement when her fiancée, a pedantic bore the Craigs have slotted for inheriting the Mission, inexplicably shames himself by getting caught having sex with a goat, apparently a childhood habit that he has been unable to shake even after becoming educated and respectable. In language humorously incommensurate with the act, McKay refers to it as "one of those strange, unaccountable phenomena that sometimes startle with impish ingenuity even the most perfect Utopia" (175).

The imps in utopia, as the imps in the cathedral do for Will, spoil for Priscilla Craig her confidence in the Mission. She had been staring at the West African figurines and masks in the collection of a recently transferred English missionary, who uses the art objects to illustrate his lectures on "The Primitive Customs and Superstitions of the Primitive African" (McKay 197). Mrs. Craig is appalled by the objects, yet transfixed by them, until her long gazing at them produces a reverie in which the masks seem to come to life and dance around her, "hideously grinning . . . circling and darting towards her . . . with that mad grinning" (199). The face of her own intellectually disabled son, called "Patou" or screech-owl by the locals, merges with the "bodiless barbaric faces" of the African objects, thus reminding her that the imp in utopia is of the same flesh and blood as herself and cannot be easily dismissed. And later that night, she has a similar vision of Bita (sneaking home from a rendezvous with a young man of whom Mrs. Craig disapproves), her adopted daughter and the embodiment of her aspirations to elevate the black "natives." In Mrs. Craig's sleepy disorientation, combined with the moonlight, Bita appears to her as a "dark nymph" confused with her memories of the "African masks and Patou gyrating around her" (201). It is not long before Bita leaves the Mission in disgrace (at least as far as Priscilla Craig is concerned), and Mrs. Craig despairs entirely of her life's work, as Will Brangwen despairs of Lincoln Cathedral in Lawrence's novel.

But just as the imps have a contrasting and liberating impact on Will's wife Anna, so a vision of the imp in utopia later frees Bita of the pressure she has felt to reconcile her English education, the disappointed hopes the Craigs had for her, and her need to take pride in herself as a black woman and a Jamaican. Exiled from the Mission back to her childhood home in the nearby town, Bita is sexually harassed and racially insulted by the half-white, spoiled aristocrat Marse Arthur. Though rescued by the family friend, Jubban (her eventual husband), she remains disturbed by the incident and seeks equanimity in meditating on some of her favorite poetry from her school days. Unfortunately, Marse Arthur's racial insult comes back to her "like a wicked imp . . . darting down into her deepest thinking and spoiling it" (McKay 268), as the imps had spoiled Will's experience of the cathedral and vitiated Priscilla Craig's pride in the Mission. But Bita, like Anna, experiences a positive side to the imp: "The constant image of the ugly little thing so insignificant and yet so insistent brought sharply home to Bita the sense and humour of the ridiculous in all things and she exploded with laughter" (269). The cathedral, the mission, of the Harlem Renaissance had aspired to raise black people to the highest possible level. With the Crash in 1929, the black utopia of the Renaissance was brought down to some extent into the dust of the Depression. McKay, like Hughes and Bontemps, turns from the city streets of Harlem to the black folk life of his past—in McKay's case, that of highland Jamaica—and finds no cause for despair, but laughs with the imps, who always knew of the "many things that had been left out of the great concept of the church" (or mission, or renaissance).

McKay ends *Banana Bottom* with Bita meditating with relish on a passage from Pascal's *Pensées*: "la vraie morale se moque de la morale; la morale du jugement se moque de la morale de l'esprit" (314). In other words, authentic, instinctual morality makes a mockery of intellectually conceived, rules-based morality. McKay is ironic in having Bita explicate one of the masters of European thought, even as she "descends" from her English education and her expected position as mistress of the Mission into the folk life of the uneducated and superstitious highland peasants. Just as Bita's friend Squire Gensir had found a Mozart melody hidden in a local peasant song (McKay 123–124), so Bita (and McKay) find the highest of thoughts in ordinary folk life and reaffirm the truth of a seventeenth-century French philosopher in twentieth-century rural Jamaica that the mocking laughter of the imps allows one to outlive the end of utopia.

Zora Neale Hurston's *Jonah's Gourd Vine* and the Power of *Vergessen*

In 1874, a young, thirty-year-old German professor at the University of Basel (Switzerland), Friedrich Nietzsche, published the second of his *Unzeitgemässe Betrachtungen* [Thoughts Out of Season], "The Use and Abuse of History." Nietzsche argues in the essay that there is such a thing as *too* much historical knowledge and warns the Germans of his era that they must learn the power of *Vergessen*, or forgetting, if they want to live as fully as possible (8). Too much historical memory weighs down human beings and impedes action. Of course, society cannot do entirely without knowledge of the past, but "history must solve the problem of history" (Nietzsche 69), and the hero "will always rise against the blind force of facts, the tyranny of the actual" (74). Nietzsche praises the ancient Greeks for knowing history, but ultimately overcoming its paralyzing effect, from which he discovers "a parable for each one of us: he must organize the chaos in himself by 'thinking himself back' to his true needs" (99), an observation that could readily apply to the Harlem Renaissance's return-to-folk-origin novels between the Crash and the Race Riot.

Zora Neale Hurston's first novel, *Jonah's Gourd Vine*, published one year after McKay's *Banana Bottom* and one year before the Harlem Race Riot, is virtually an extended meditation on the "use and abuse" of forgetting for the Harlem Renaissance project, both before and after the Crash. Like Bontemps, she goes back after the Crash to her family history, in her case to the history of her father and mother, and to the pre-Migration folk roots of African American culture. But as for Bontemps before her, and also for Hughes and McKay, she continues to examine the "Harlem Renaissance" utopian project, even as she plumbs the depths of its folk pre-history. Her "Harlem" (all black community) is there in Eatonville. But the "Harlem Renaissance" is also there in *Jonah* in the relationship between John and Lucy, between the "natchel man" (Hurston 122) and *light* (by which *Lucy* is derived from Latin). John is body, instinct, a "walking orgasm" (50); Lucy is not only light, but also ambition as well as the elicitor of words not just action (32), the mate who would put *any* husband on the ladder of uplift (110).

That relationship, between the higher consciousness of the New Negro and the instinctive vitality of the natural man (or woman), had been central to the Harlem Renaissance since the beginning, as for instance in McKay's "Negro Dancers" (1919) in which the McKay-like narrator *contemplates* the deep significance of the blithe dancers in the dingy Harlem basement club, dancers unconscious of anything special in their brilliant movements. The Renaissance was producing black thinkers, articulate, refined, educated, but feeling in themselves the beginnings of deracination, of alienation from the energy and natural grace of the folk. The natural men and women of those folk know the power of *Vergessen*, of forgetting their humiliations and obstacles in an oppressive, racist society, to live in the moment with energy and joy. Or rather, they do not *know* this power (knowing is the province of the New Negroes); they *live* it.

Under the influence of Lucy pulling the words out of him, drawing him towards articulation, John reiterates again and again his real strength, the power of forgetting. His very first prayer is an appeal to this power: "O Lawd . . . if you find any sin lurkin' in and about mah heart pleast pluck it out and cast in intuh de sea uh forgitfulness whar it'll never rise" (Hurston 25). Though, like his people, John knows hardship and misery, "he only remembered his misery in short snatches, while glory lay all over him for hours at a time" (104). John knows that he messes up, violates, for instance, Lucy's faith in him, or his church's expectations for their minister, but, he says, "Ah ain't got no remembrance. . . . when de sun . . . go intuh his house at night, he takes all mah remembrance wid 'im" (122). John plunges into the present again and again, never burdened by memory, even memory of his own faults.

Of course, there *is* memory within John, but it is an unconscious one, the race memory of Africa, of the drum. Thus he is a natural at prayer only because "he rolled his drum up to the altar, and called his Congo Gods by Christian names" (Hurston 89), and thus he resonates so powerfully with his people, who "had brought to America in their skins . . . the dance drums of Africa" (29). But this skin (body, not mind) memory of Africa, of the African rhythm, is not a conscious memory, and so it, too, is a kind of forgetting, awaiting its light, it *luce*, Lucy, to direct it in the New World. And though Lucy is often disappointed or even betrayed by John, she reminds him that "ignorance is de hawse dat wisdom rides" (128);

i.e., John's ignorance, his power of forgetting, is the horse. It is the energy that wisdom, light (Lucy) rides to make her man a "sho 'nuff big nigger" (112, 116). The vitality of the folk, the natural men and women, is the source of energy that the New Negro intellectuals must harness in order to create a Renaissance, a black utopia of recognition for the greatness of the African American people.

But the glory days of the Harlem Renaissance end with the Crash, and Lucy dies. And subsequent to the Crash, Hughes, Bontemps, McKay, and now Hurston *do* recall what the Renaissance was, even as they appear to be abandoning it by leaving the streets of Harlem and returning to the black belt in their writings. Likewise, John, the great forgetter, after Lucy's death for the first time in his life must live under the grip of *memory*: "[H]is daily self seemed to be wearing thin, and the past seeped thru and mastered him for increasingly longer periods. He whose present had always been so bubbling that it crowded out past and future now found himself with a memory" (Hurston 141–142). Like Nietzsche's over-historical German, John's past "presses him down, and bows his shoulders" (Nietzsche 7).

What of this project of Hughes, Bontemps, McKay, and now Hurston to return, to go back, to *remember* the forgetting in black folk culture before the Renaissance, yet all the while reflecting on the Renaissance's lessons? It is typical of Hurston—the anthropologist with a graduate-level education repeatedly mistaken by others for a mere prankster or even minstrel performer—that she is the one to reflect *as a whole* in *Jonah's Gourd Vine* on this particular project of a return to roots, to assess and evaluate it, just as she would finally sum up the entire Renaissance in its final novel, *Their Eyes Were Watching God*. And the answer to the question of the value of the return to roots is, for Zora, that it depends on how it is done. When John accepts Sally's love in Plant City, it appears as a positive return in a world that only does revolve in cycles after all, the world of "[t]he Lord of the wheel that turns on itself" (Hurston 141).

John has an opportunity to use, but not abuse, the past in loving again, in loving Sally with the forgetfulness of misery that love is, but without forgetting the mistakes he made with Lucy. He prays that "Lucy see it too, Lawd, so she kin rest," but he again asks his God "to cast certain memories in duh sea of fuhgitfulness" (Hurston 191). John returns in mind and spirit to Eatonville, but in a new place and with a new love. Yet, when he actually, physically returns to Eatonville, to the place of his past, he becomes again the same John as before, the John of *stupid* forgetting, seduced into betraying Sally as before he had been seduced into betraying Lucy. If the going back of the return-to-folk-origin novels between the Crash and the Race Riot is simply a retreat from the Renaissance, a forgetting of the Renaissance's light (Lucy) in mere ethnographic accumulation, then it is simply "de same ole soup-bone—jus' warmed over" (194). However, if the going back in these works is not a mere return, but a means of working through in the mind the problems of the Harlem Renaissance project, of black utopia, then the result might be "a song for [the] heart," as Sally's memory of John is after he is hit by the train, like Harlem in its glory was hit by the trainwreck of the Crash. *Jonah's Gourd Vine*, like *Not Without Laughter*, *God Sends Sunday*, and *Banana Bottom*, is no mere retreat to ethnography, but a "thinking . . . back to . . . true needs" as Nietzsche says (99), by organizing the chaos left in the wake of the Crash. It is a going back to work through.

Works Cited

Bontemps, Arna. *God Sends Sunday*. New York: Washington Square P, 2005.

Cooper, Wayne F. *Claude McKay: Rebel Sojourner in the Harlem Renaissance*. Baton Rouge, LA: Louisiana State UP, 1987.

Gates, Skip G. "Of Negroes Old and New." *Transition* 46 (1974): 44–58.

Homer. *The Odyssey*. Tr. Stanley Lombardo. *The Norton Anthology of World Literature*, Volume 1. Shorter 3rd ed. New York: W. W. Norton, 2013.

Hughes, Langston. "The Negro Artist and the Racial Mountain." *The Portable Harlem Renaissance Reader*. Ed. David Levering Lewis. New York: Penguin, 1994. 91–95.

_____. *Not Without Laughter*. New York: Simon & Schuster, 1969.

Hurston, Zora Neale. *Jonah's Gourd Vine*. New York: HarperCollins, 1990.

Keats, John. *The Letters of John Keats to His Family and Friends*. Ed. Sidney Colvin. London: Macmillan, 1925.

Lawrence, D. H. *The Rainbow*. New York: Modern Library, 2002.

Lewis, David Levering, ed. *The Portable Harlem Renaissance Reader*. New York: Penguin, 1994.

Locke, Alain. "Harlem." *Harlem: Mecca of the New Negro*. Spec. issue of *Survey Graphic* VI.6 (March 1925): 629–30.

McKay, Claude. *Banana Bottom*. New York: Harcourt Brace Jovanovich, 1961.

Nietzsche, Friedrich. "Thoughts Out of Season." Trans. Adrian Collins. *The Complete Works of Friedrich Nietzsche*, Vol. 2, Pt. 2. Edinburgh, Scotland: Morrison and Gibb, 1909. Web. 4 Apr. 2015.

Sargent, Lyman Tower. *Utopianism: A Very Short Introduction*. New York: Oxford UP, 2001.

RESOURCES

Chronology of the Harlem Renaissance_____

Christopher Allen Varlack & Karl Henzy

The Precursor to the Harlem Renaissance: 1903 to 1919

1903	April, W. E. B. Du Bois publishes *The Souls of Black Folk*. September, W. E. B. Du Bois publishes "The Talented Tenth."
1905	Thomas Dixon publishes *The Clansman: An Historical Romance of the Ku Klux Klan*, which contributes to a rise in Klan membership and the negative stigmatization of the African American community post-Reconstruction. Jessie Redmon Fauset also graduates from Cornell University with a Bachelor of Arts in classical languages.
1906	September, the Atlanta Race Riots occur, resulting in the deaths of twenty-five to forty African Americans.
1907	Alain Locke graduates from Harvard University with degrees in literature and philosophy, becomes the first African American Rhodes Scholar, and attends Hertford College, unable to obtain admission to several colleges at Oxford University due to racial discrimination.
1909	February, the National Association for the Advancement of Colored People (NAACP) is founded.
1910	November, Du Bois publishes the first issue of *The Crisis*, originally titled *The Crisis: A Record of the Darker Races*. Throughout the year, the Great Migration begins as approximately 1.6 million African Americans begin to migrate from the South by 1930.

1912	May, James Weldon Johnson anonymously publishes *The Autobiography of an Ex-Colored Man.*
1914	March through April, Locke delivers a series of five lectures at Howard University entitled, *Race Contacts and Interracial Relations.*
1915	March, D. W. Griffith produces the film *The Birth of a Nation*—an adaptation of Dixon's *The Clansman* that sparks the founding of a second incarnation of the Klan. May, Du Bois publishes *The Negro.* Nella Larsen graduates from the nursing school at NYC's Lincoln Hospital and Nursing Home.
1916	March, Angelina Weld Grimké's anti-lynching play *Rachel* opens in Washington, DC. Walter White also graduates from Atlanta University.
1917	May, Marcus Garvey founds the Universal Negro Improvement Association (UNIA). July, Du Bois organizes the Silent Protest Parade in New York—a march of between eight thousand and fifteen thousand African Americans protesting the rise in lynchings and violence toward blacks. August, Chandler Owen and A. Philip Randolph found *The Messenger*—an independent magazine devoted to promoting the work of the era's black intellectuals and political leaders.
1918	Locke receives his PhD from Harvard University.

The Harlem Renaissance in Its Infancy: 1919 to 1923

1919	February, Du Bois organizes the first Pan-African Congress in Paris. May, Du Bois publishes "Returning Soldiers" (May). July, McKay publishes "If We Must Die" in response to the Red Summer—a series of race riots that occurred from June to September in more than three dozen US cities. Between 150 and 250 blacks were killed and tens of thousands were

forced to flee their homes. He also publishes "Negro Dancers" to reflect the collective joy of the black community. Fauset receives her Masters in French from the University of Pennsylvania. Rudolph Fisher graduates from Brown University with a dual major in biology and English. November, Fauset is named the literary editor of *The Crisis.*

1920	August, the UNIA holds its First International Convention of the Negro Peoples of the World at Madison Square Garden. November, Eugene O'Neil's *The Emperor Jones* opens. Fisher receives his Masters in biology from Brown University.
1921	March, *Shuffle Along*, a musical comedy noted for its all black cast, opens in Washington, DC, before opening on Broadway. June, Langston Hughes publishes "The Negro Speaks of Rivers." August, McKay publishes "Africa." October, T. S. Stribling publishes *Birthright*, which serves as a catalyst for works such as White's *Fire in the Flint* and Fauset's *There is Confusion.* During this time, the second Pan-African Congress is held.
1922	March, James Weldon Johnson edits *The Book of American Negro Poetry.* April, McKay publishes *Harlem Shadows.* Sterling A. Brown also graduates from Williams College.
1923	January, *Opportunity* begins publication under Charles S. Johnson, and Alain Locke publishes "The Problem of Race Classification." February, Bessie Smith makes her first recordings, such as "Downhearted Blues," which marks the beginning of her rise as one of the nation's most famous blues singers. September, Jean Toomer publishes *Cane.* Larsen becomes the first black woman to graduate from NYPL library school. Brown also receives his Master's degree from Harvard

University, and Arna Bontemps graduates from Pacific Union College.

The Zenith of the Harlem Renaissance: 1924 to 1929

1924   February, Du Bois publishes "The Younger Literary Movement." March, Charles S. Johnson hosts his Civic Club dinner to join black writers and white publishers; one week later the *New York Herald Tribune* refers to the development of a "Negro Renaissance." Fauset also publishes *There is Confusion*. Fisher graduates from Howard University's medical school. June, Locke publishes "The Concept of Race as Applied to Social Culture." September, White publishes *The Fire in the Flint*.

1925   March, Locke edits the *Survey Graphic* special issue, *Harlem: Mecca of the New Negro*, which includes key works such as Hughes' "I, Too" and Countee Cullen's "Heritage." May, the first *Opportunity* Award banquet is held. Cullen graduates from NYU. June, Du Bois publishes "The Negro Art Renaissance." October, Cullen publishes *Color.* November, Louis Armstrong's Hot Five, inc. completes its first recordings. December, Locke edits *The New Negro: An Interpretation.*

1926   January, Hughes publishes *The Weary Blues.* April, White publishes *Flight* and the second *Opportunity* awards banquet is held. May, Fauset ends her tenure as literary editor of *The Crisis.* W. C. Handy also publishes *Blues: An Anthology*. June, George Schuyler publishes "The Negro-Art Hokum," and Hughes publishes "The Negro Artist and the Racial Mountain." August, Carl Van Vechten publishes *Nigger Heaven*. October, Eric Walrond publishes *Tropic Death*, and Du Bois publishes "Criteria of Negro Art." November, Wallace Thurman edits the sole issue of *Fire!!*, which includes works such as Hurston's *Color Struck* and

"Sweat" as well as Richard Bruce Nugent's "Smoke, Lilies, and Jade." William Grant Still's *Darker America*, performed by the International Composers Guild, premieres. Armstrong records songs such as "Jazz Lips" and "Skid-Dat-De-Dat."

1927	February, Hughes publishes *Fine Clothes to the Jew*. May, James Weldon Johnson publishes *God's Trombones: Seven Negro Sermons in Verse*. June, Cullen publishes *Ballad of the Brown Girl*. July, Cullen publishes *Copper Sun*. August, James Weldon Johnson republishes *Autobiography of an Ex-Colored Man*. October, the first sound film, *The Jazz Singer*, is released, starring Al Jolson and expanding the tradition of blackface minstrelsy in the American film industry. Alain Locke and Gregory Montgomery edit *Plays of Negro Life*, which includes Nugent's "Sahdji, an African Ballet." During this time, Cullen also edits *Caroling Dusk*. December, Marcus Garvey is deported and returns to Jamaica. Charlotte Osgood Mason, otherwise known as the "Godmother," becomes a patron of the New Negro, financially supporting black writers, such as Hurston and Hughes.
1928	March, McKay publishes *Home to Harlem*, and Nella Larsen publishes *Quicksand*. April, Du Bois publishes *Dark Princess*. May, Hurston publishes "How It Feels to be Colored Me" and receives her Bachelor of Arts in anthropology from Barnard College, Columbia University, after working with Franz Boas and conducting ethnographic research throughout the South. August, Rudolph Fisher publishes *The Walls of Jericho*. November, Thurman edits *Harlem*, the successor to *Fire!!*
1929	February, Thurman publishes *The Blacker the Berry*. February, Fauset publishes *Plum Bun: A Novel without*

a Moral and *Harlem: A Melodrama of Negro Life in Harlem*—a collaboration by Thurman and William Jourdan Rapp—opens on Broadway. April, Larsen publishes *Passing*. May, McKay publishes *Banjo: A Story without a Plot*. Hughes graduates from Lincoln University. October, the Stock Market crashes, sparking the Great Depression—a period that some mark as the end of the Harlem Renaissance. November, Cullen publishes *The Black Christ*.

The Later Years of the Harlem Renaissance: 1930 to 1935

1930   March, Hurston and Hughes begin planning to collaborate on the comic play, *Mule Bone*, based on Hurston's short story, "Bone of Contention." May, Hughes dissolves his relationship with Mason. July, James Weldon Johnson publishes *Black Manhattan*, and Hughes publishes "Afro-American Fragment" as well as *Not Without Laughter*. October, Du Bois publishes *Africa*. October, Hurston submits for a copyright for *Mule Bone* without telling Hughes.

1931   January, Schuyler publishes *Black No More*. February, Hurston and Hughes break over tensions surrounding *Mule Bone*. March, Arna Bontemps publishes *God Sends Sunday*, and the Scottsboro incident occurs in which nine African American teenagers were accused of raping two white women in Alabama, setting in motion widespread discussions of racism in the US legal system as well as politicized texts, such as Sterling A. Brown's "Convict" and Hughes' "Christ in Alabama." May, Still's *Sahdji*—a ballet based on Nugent's *Sahdji* in *The New Negro* premieres. October, Still's Symphony No. 1, "Afro-American," premieres. November, Hughes publishes *Scottsboro, Limited*. December, Fauset publishes *The Chinaberry Tree*.

1932	January, Thurman publishes *Infants of the Spring*. February, Cullen publishes *One Way to Heaven*. Duke Ellington also records "It Don't Mean a Thing (If it Ain't Got That Swing)" and "Lazy Rhapsody." March, McKay abandons his unpublished manuscript "Romance in Marseilles" in order to publish *Gingertown*. May, Sterling A. Brown publishes *Southern Road*. June, Hughes, Dorothy West, and eighteen other African Americans travel to the Soviet Union to play roles in the film, *Black and White*. July, Fisher publishes *The Conjure-Man Dies*.
1933	March, McKay publishes *Banana Bottom*. April, Brown publishes "Negro Character as Seen by White Authors." August, Hurston publishes "The Gilded Six-Bits." October, James Weldon Johnson publishes *Along This Way*. November, Fauset publishes *Comedy: American Style*. This period is also marked as the low point of the US economy during the Great Depression. Many writers and artists of the Harlem Renaissance seek employment with the Works Project Administration.
1934	February, Hurston publishes "Characteristics of Negro Expression" in Nancy Cunard's *Negro: An Anthology*. March, Hurston publishes *Jonah's Gourd Vine*. June, Hughes publishes *The Ways of White Folks*. December, Thurman and Fisher die. Du Bois resigns from *The Crisis* and the NAACP after disputes regarding his platform of black separatism.
1935	March, the Harlem Riot occurs—another event that many cite as the end of the Harlem Renaissance. April, McKay publishes "Harlem Runs Wild."

The Harlem Renaissance in Retrospection: 1935 and Beyond

1935	June, Du Bois publishes *Black Reconstruction in America*. August, Cullen publishes *The Medea and Some Poems*. September, Hurston publishes *Mules and Men*. That same month DuBose Heyward and George Gershwin produce the infamous opera *Porgy and Bess*. October, Hughes' *Mulatto* opens on Broadway. Throughout this time, the Federal Writer's Project begins, and Brown composes *No Hiding Place*, which is rejected by publishers for economic reasons.
1936	January, Bontemps publishes *Black Thunder*. February, Ellington records "Echoes in Harlem." July, Hughes publishes "Let America be America Again." November, Toomer publishes *Blue Meridian*.
1937	March, McKay publishes *A Long Way from Home*. September, Hurston publishes *Their Eyes Were Watching God*. Ellington records songs such as "Diminuendo in Blue" and "Crescendo in Blue." Mid-year, the US economy takes a sharp downturn with production plummeting and unemployment further spiking. December, Still's Symphony No. 2, "Song of a New Race," premieres with the Philadelphia Orchestra.
1938	August, Brown publishes *The Negro in American Fiction* as well as *Negro Poetry and Drama*. September, Hurston publishes *Tell My Horse*.
1939	October, Hurston publishes *Moses, Man of the Mountain*.
1940	August, Hughes publishes *The Big Sea*. September, Du Bois publishes *Dusk of Dawn: An Essay Toward an Autobiography of a Race Concept*. October, McKay publishes *Harlem: Negro Metropolis*.

| 1942 | October, Hurston publishes *Dust Tracks on a Road*. |

| 1943 | Bontemps receives a Masters in Library Science from the University of Chicago. |

| 1948 | April, Dorothy West publishes *The Living is Easy*. October, Hurston publishes *Seraph on the Suwanee*. |

| 1956 | Hughes publishes *I Wonder as I Wander*. |

New Discoveries in the Harlem Renaissance: 1990 to the Present

| 1990 | McKay's *Harlem Glory: A Fragment of Aframerican Life*, written in the later 1940s, is published. |

| 2008 | Nugent's *Gentleman Jigger: A Novel of the Harlem Renaissance*, written in the 1930s, is published. |

| 2009 | Jean-Christophe Cloutier discovers McKay's previously unknown 1941 manuscript, "Amiable with Big Teeth: A Novel of the Love Affair Between the Communists and the Poor Black Sheep of Harlem." |

Works of the Harlem Renaissance_____

Autobiographies

Du Bois, W. E. B. *Dusk of Dawn: An Essay Toward an Autobiography of a Race Concept.* 1940.

Hughes, Langston. *I Wonder as I Wander.* 1956.

_____. *The Big Sea.* 1940.

Hurston, Zora Neale. *Dust Tracks on a Road.* 1942.

McKay, Claude. *A Long Way from Home.* 1937.

Drama

Bonner, Marita. *Exit: An Illusion.* 1929.

_____. *The Purple Flower.* 1928.

Grimké, Angelina Weld. *Rachel.* 1916.

Hughes, Langston. *Mulatto.* 1935.

_____ & Zora Neale Hurston. *Mule-Bone: A Comedy of Negro Life.* 1930.

Hurston, Zora Neale. *Color Struck: A Play in Four Scenes.* 1926.

Thurman, Wallace & William Jourdan Rapp. *Harlem: A Melodrama of Negro Life in Harlem.* 1929.

Poetry

Brown, Sterling. *Southern Road.* 1932.

Cullen, Countee. *Ballad of the Brown Girl.* 1927.

_____. *Color.* 1925.

_____. *Copper Sun.* 1927.

_____. *The Black Christ.* 1929.

_____. *The Medea and Some Poems.* 1935.

Hughes, Langston. *Fine Clothes to the Jew.* 1927.

_____. *The Weary Blues.* 1926.

Johnson, James Weldon. *God's Trombones: Seven Negro Sermons in Verse.* 1927.

McKay, Claude. *Harlem Shadows*. 1922.

Toomer, Jean. *Blue Meridian*. 1936.

Nonfiction

Du Bois, W. E. B. *Africa*. 1930.

_____. *Black Reconstruction in America*. 1935.

_____. *The Negro*. 1915.

_____. *The Souls of Black Folk*. 1903.

Hurston, Zora Neale. *Mules and Men*. 1935.

_____. *Tell My Horse*. 1938.

Johnson, James Weldon. *Black Manhattan*. 1930.

McKay, Claude. *Harlem: Negro Metropolis*. 1940.

Essays/Journalism

Du Bois, W. E. B. "Criteria of Negro Art." 1926.

_____. "The Talented Tenth." 1903

Hughes, Langston. "Negro Artist and the Racial Mountain." 1926.

Hurston, Zora Neale. "Characteristics of Negro Expression." 1934.

_____. "How It Feels To Be Colored Me." 1928.

_____. "What White Publishers Won't Print." 1950.

Locke, Alain. "The Problem of Race Classification." 1923.

McKay, Claude. "Harlem Runs Wild." 1935.

Schuyler, George. "The Negro-Art Hokum." 1926.

Novels

Bontemps, Arna. *Black Thunder*. 1936.

_____. *God Sends Sunday*. 1931.

Cullen, Countee. *One Way to Heaven*. 1932.

_____. *The Black Christ and Other Poems*. 1929.

Du Bois, W. E. B. *The Dark Princess*. 1928.

Fauset, Jessie Redmon. *Comedy, American Style*. 1933

_____. *Plum Bun: A Novel without a Moral*. 1928.

_____. *The Chinaberry Tree.* 1931.

_____. *There is Confusion.* 1924.

Fisher, Rudolph. *The Conjure-Man Dies.* 1932.

_____. *The Walls of Jericho.* 1928.

Hughes, Langston. *Not Without Laughter*, 1930.

Hurston, Zora Neale. *Jonah's Gourd Vine.* 1934.

_____. *Moses, Man of the Mountain.* 1939.

_____. *Seraph on the Suwanee.* 1948.

_____. *Their Eyes Were Watching God.* 1937.

Johnson, James Weldon. *The Autobiography of an Ex-Colored Man.* 1912.

Larsen, Nella. *Passing.* 1929.

_____. *Quicksand.* 1928.

McKay, Claude. *Banana Bottom.* 1933.

_____. *Banjo: A Novel without a Plot.* 1929.

_____. *Harlem Glory.* 1990 (posthumously).

_____. *Home to Harlem.* 1928.

Nugent, Richard Bruce. *Gentleman Jigger: A Novel of the Harlem Renaissance.* 2008 (posthumously).

Schuyler, George. *Black No More.* 1930.

Thurman, Wallace. *Infants of the Spring.* 1932.

_____. *The Blacker the Berry.* 1929.

Toomer, Jean. *Cane.* 1923.

Van Vechten, Carl. *Nigger Heaven.* 1926.

White, Walter. *Flight.* 1926.

_____. *The Fire in the Flint.* 1924.

West, Dorothy. *The Living Is Easy.* 1948.

Short Story Collections

Hughes, Langston. *The Ways of White Folk.* 1934.

McKay, Claude. *Gingertown.* 1932.

Walrond, Eric. *Tropic Death.* 1926.

Bibliography

Allen, Carol. *Black Women Intellectuals: Strategies of Nation, Family, and Neighborhood in the Works of Pauline Hopkins, Jessie Fauset, and Marita Bonner.* New York: Garland, 1998.

Baker, Houston A., Jr. *Modernism and the Harlem Renaissance.* Chicago: U of Chicago P, 1987.

Baldwin, Davarian L. & Minkah Makalani, eds. *Escape from New York: The New Negro Renaissance Beyond Harlem.* Minneapolis: U of Minnesota P, 2013.

Bloom, Harold, ed. *Langston Hughes.* New York: Chelsea House, 1989. P

_____. *The Harlem Renaissance.* Philadelphia: Chelsea House, 2004.

_____. ed. *W.E.B. Du Bois.* New York: Chelsea House, 2002.

_____, ed. *Zora Neale Hurston.* New York: Bloom's Literary Criticism, 2008.

Bone, Robert A. *The Negro Novel in America.* 1958. New Haven: Yale UP, 1969.

Bontemps, Arna, ed. *The Harlem Renaissance Remembered.* New York: Dodd & Mead, 1972.

Egar, Emmanuel E. *The Poetics of Rage: Wole Soyinka, Jean Toomer, and Claude McKay.* Lanham: UP of America, 2005.

Fabre, Michel. *From Harlem to Paris: Black American Writers in France, 1840–1980.* Urbana: U of Illinois P, 1991.

Favor, J. Martin. *Authentic Blackness: The Folk in the New Negro Renaissance.* Durham: Duke UP, 1999.

Gates, Henry Louis, Jr. & K. A. Appiah, eds. *Langston Hughes: Critical Perspectives Past and Present.* New York: Amistad, 1993.

Helbling, Mark. *The Harlem Renaissance in Black and White.* Cambridge: Belknap P, 1995.

_____. *The Harlem Renaissance: The One and the Many.* Westport: Greenwood Press, 1999.

Hodges, Graham Russell, ed. *Carl Van Vechten and the Harlem Renaissance: A Critical Assessment.* New York: Garland, 1998.

Huggins, Nathan Irvin. *Harlem Renaissance*. 1971. Oxford: Oxford UP, 2007.

Hutchinson, George, ed. *The Cambridge Companion to the Harlem Renaissance*. Cambridge: Cambridge UP, 2007.

Ikonné, Chidi. *From Du Bois to Van Vechten: The Early New Negro Literature, 1903–1926*. Westport: Greenwood Press, 1981.

Jones, Sharon L. *Rereading the Harlem Renaissance: Race, Class, and Gender in the Fiction of Jessie Fauset, Zora Neale Hurston, and Dorothy West*. Westport: Greenwood Press, 2002.

Kramer, Victor A. & Robert A. Russ, eds. *Harlem Renaissance Re-examined: A Revised and Expanded Edition*. Troy, NY: Whitston, 1997.

Lewis, David Levering. *When Harlem Was in Vogue*. 1981. New York: Penguin, 1997.

Maxwell, William J. *New Negro, Old Left: African-American Writing and Communism Between the Wars*. New York: Columbia UP, 1999.

McLendon, Jacquelyn Y. *The Politics of Color in the Fiction of Jessie Fauset and Nella Larsen*. Charlottesville: UP of Virginia, 1995.

O'Daniel, Therman B., ed. *Langston Hughes: Black Genius, A Critical Evaluation*. New York: William Morrow, 1971.

Ogbar, Jeffrey O. G., ed. *The Harlem Renaissance Revisited: Politics, Arts, and Letters*. Baltimore: Johns Hopkins UP, 2010.

Pochmara, Anna. *The Making of the New Negro: Black Authorship, Masculinity, and Sexuality in the Harlem Renaissance*. Amsterdam: Amsterdam UP, 2011.

Posnock, Ross. *Color & Culture: Black Writers and the Making of the Modern Intellectual*. Cambridge: Harvard UP, 1998.

Roses, Lorraine Elena & Ruth Elizabeth Randolph, eds. *Harlem Renaissance and Beyond: Literary Biographies of 100 Black Women Writers, 1900–1945*. Cambridge: Harvard UP, 1990.

Sherrard-Johnson, Cherene. *Portraits of the New Negro Woman: Visual and Literary Culture in the Harlem Renaissance*. New Brunswick: Rutgers UP, 2007.

Singh, Amritjit. *The Novels of the Harlem Renaissance: Twelve Black Writers 1923–1933*. University Park: Pennsylvania State UP, 1976.

_____, William S. Shiver, & Stanley Brodwin, eds. *The Harlem Renaissance: Revaluations*. New York: Garland, 1989.

Smith, Katharine Capshaw. *Children's Literature of the Harlem Renaissance*. Bloomington: Indiana UP, 2004.

Tarver, Australia & Paula C. Barnes, eds. *New Voices on the Harlem Renaissance: Essays on Race, Gender, and Literary Discourse*. Madison: Fairleigh Dickinson UP, 2006.

Thaggert, Miriam. *Images of Black Modernism: Verbal and Visual Strategies of the Harlem Renaissance*. Amherst: U of Massachusetts P, 2010.

Tidwell, John Edgar & Steven C. Tracy, eds. *After Winter: The Art and Life of Sterling A. Brown,* Oxford: Oxford UP, 2009.

Vogel, Shane. *The Scene of Harlem Cabaret: Race, Sexuality, Performance*. Chicago: U of Chicago P, 2009.

Wall, Cheryl A. *Women of the Harlem Renaissance*. Bloomington: Indiana UP, 1995.

Watson, Steven. *The Harlem Renaissance: Hub of African-American Culture, 1920–1930*. New York: Pantheon, 1995.

Wintz, Cary D., ed. *Analysis and Assessment, 1940–1979*. New York: Garland, 1996.

_____. *Analysis and Assessment, 1980–1994*. New York: Garland, 1996.

_____. *Black Culture and the Harlem Renaissance*. College Station: Texas A&M UP, 1996.

About the Editor

Christopher Allen Varlack is a lecturer in the Writing and Rhetoric Division of the Department of English at the University of Maryland, Baltimore County, where he teaches courses in composition and creative writing. He earned a BA in communications from Loyola University Maryland and his MFA in creative writing from the University of Southern Maine's Stonecoast MFA Program. He is also a PhD candidate at Morgan State University, where he is now writing his dissertation on the alternative intellectual projects of the Harlem Renaissance with particular attention to the fiction works of the rebel sojourner and *l'enfant terrible*, Claude McKay. As a writer and scholar, Varlack is interested in how literature can preserve or reclaim the voices of the past, shedding new light on the struggles and the people who define who we are today. Much of his scholarship thus focuses on the literature of the Harlem Renaissance—arguably the most important movement in the burgeoning African American literary tradition. Always in search of his next major project, his recent publications include chapters in *Critical Insights: Zora Neale Hurston* (2013), *Critical Insights: The Slave Narrative* (2014), *Baby Boomers and Popular Culture: An Inquiry into America's Most Powerful Generation* (2014), and *Critical Insights: Virginia Woolf & 20th Century Women Writers* (2014).

Contributors

Carolyn Kyler holds a PhD from the State University of New York at Buffalo. She is a professor of English at Washington & Jefferson College, where she also directs the Gender & Women's Studies Program. She has taught a variety of courses in African American fiction, poetry, and autobiography as well as a senior seminar on the Harlem Renaissance. In addition to African American literature, her research interests include historical fiction and graphic memoir. She has published articles in those areas as well as articles on illustration in the stories of Louisa May Alcott. Selected presentation topics include James Weldon Johnson, African American autobiography, and teaching the Harlem Renaissance.

Gerardo Del Guercio holds a BA from Concordia University, an MA from Université de Montréal, and a TESOL (Teaching English as a Second Language) certificate from York College, CUNY. At present, he is teaching English in Montréal, Canada. He is the author of *The Fugitive Slave Law in The Life of Frederick Douglass, an American Slave and Harriet Beecher Stowe's Uncle Tom's Cabin: American Society Transforms Its Culture* (2013). His essays have been published by *Southern Studies,* the *College Language Association Journal,* and Oxford University Press.

Allyson Denise Marino holds a BA in English from SUNY Fredonia, an MA in English from SUNY College at Buffalo, and a PhD from Indiana University of Pennsylvania. She is an assistant professor of English and the director of fine arts events in the School of Arts and Sciences at Saint Leo University. Marino's research interests include women's literature and food politics, environmental justice, US multiethnic literature, and postcolonial and third world studies. At Saint Leo University, she teaches courses on love and desire in literature, Caribbean literature, multiethnic US literature, critical theory, and composition.

Cheryl Lester holds a PhD in English and comparative literature from the State University of New York at Buffalo. She is an associate professor of English and American studies at the University of Kansas, publishing journal articles and book chapters on twentieth century US literature and culture with a focus on modernism and modernity, William Faulkner, African American literature, and the literature and culture of twentieth century mobility, migration, and immigration. She is collaborating editor for *Digital Yoknapatawpha*, an NEH-funded digital humanities project housed at the University of Virginia. She is also co-editor of *Social Work Practice with a Difference: A Literary Approach* (2003) as well as coeditor and cotranslator of Philippe Lacoue-Labarthe and Jean-Luc Nancy's *The Literary Absolute: The Theory of Literature in German Romanticism* (1988).

Jericho Williams holds a BA in English from Winthrop University and an MA in English from the University of Alaska Fairbanks. He is currently a PhD candidate in English at West Virginia University. His primary research interests are nineteenth- and twentieth-century American literature with an emphasis on how environment and culture influence education. Outside of his scholarly work, he serves as an assistant cross-country, basketball, and track and field coach for middle school students.

Seretha D. Williams holds a PhD in comparative literature from the University of Georgia. She is a professor of English at Georgia Regents University and teaches courses in world humanities, women's and gender studies, literature, and composition. Her scholarship focuses on African and African diaspora literatures. She has published book chapters on Zakes Mda and Lalita Tademy; coedited the critical collection, *Afterimages of Slavery: Essays on Appearances in Recent American Films, Literature, Television and Other Media (2012)*; and presented numerous scholarly papers at national and international conferences. She has a forthcoming book chapter on Chimamanda Ngozi Adichie, and her current research project is a study of the poet Margaret Walker.

Holly Simpson Fling is working toward her PhD in English at the University of Georgia. In addition to studying British romantic and Victorian literature and working toward a graduate certificate in women's studies, she teaches first-year composition. She grew up in Northeast Missouri and graduated *summa cum laude* from Truman State University, where she also earned an MA in English. Though her focus is on applying new materialist methodologies to texts by nineteenth-century British women writers, she also enjoys nineteenth- and twentieth-century American literature with an interest in passing texts, such as Nella Larsen's *Passing* and James Weldon Johnson's *The Autobiography of an Ex-Colored Man.*

Charlotte Teague holds an MEd from Alabama A&M University and her MA from the University of Alabama in Huntsville. She is currently a graduate student in the PhD program at Morgan State University in Baltimore, MD. Outside of her studies, Teague is an assistant professor of English at Alabama A&M University. Her research interests include African American female writers, the Harlem Renaissance, theories of composition, and technical and professional writing.

Holly T. Baker holds a PhD in English literary studies from the University of South Dakota, where she also teaches composition, literature, and critical thinking courses. Her critical interests include twentieth- and twenty-first-century American literature with a particular focus on masculine and feminine representations in the postmodern novel. She has received a Fulbright Scholarship for research and writing in Bucharest, Romania, in support of her first book.

Joshua M. Murray is a PhD candidate in English at Kent State University. His areas of focus are African American literature, transnational studies, twentieth-century American literature, and writings of the Black diaspora. At Kent State University, he teaches courses in the English Department, and he also contributes to the interdepartmental Transnational Studies Reading and Working Group as well as the biannual Pan-African Studies Conference. He currently has multiple ongoing projects, the greatest of which is his dissertation, which examines the Harlem Renaissance through a historical and transnational lens.

Lisa Elwood-Farber is working toward her PhD in literature and criticism at Indiana University of Pennsylvania. She is an associate professor of English at Herkimer College, where she teaches writing and literature courses, including African American literature. In these courses, she covers slave narratives, the Harlem Renaissance, and at least one modern novel. Similarly, her research examines American literature as it expands or contests specific literary genres. She has published on Harriet

Wilson's *Our Nig* in *Women's Studies: An Interdisciplinary Journal*, and her most recent work about historical representations of black motherhood in fiction is being published in an anthology entitled *Black Motherhood*.

Brandon L. A. Hutchinson holds a PhD from the University of Massachusetts at Amherst. She is an associate professor of English at Southern Connecticut State University, where she teaches a range of courses, most of which focus on the scholarship of black women writers.

Michelle J. Pinkard holds a PhD from Arizona State University and is a poet, writer, and educator living in Nashville, Tennessee. She is also an assistant professor of African American literature at Tennessee State University, and her scholarly interests explore the intersections of race, gender, and literature. Pinkard is the author of one collection of poetry; her work has most recently been published in *Callaloo* and *The African American Review.* Her essays, short stories, and poems have appeared in several anthologies, and she is working on a forthcoming study on women poets of the Harlem Renaissance.

Lisa Tomlinson is a Jamaican researcher and scholar residing in Toronto, Canada, who holds a PhD from York University. She works as a lecturer in English literature at the University of the West Indies, Mona Campus, and she has taught courses in Caribbean studies, the humanities, and community research. Her areas of specialization include literary and cultural studies of the Caribbean, black literary criticism, and diaspora and anti-colonial studies. Some of her publications include book chapters on Jamaican popular music and Caribbean diaspora literature. Tomlinson recently completed her forthcoming book on the literary history of Jamaica entitled *African Jamaican Aesthetics: Cultural Retention and Transformation across Borders (A Literary Journey).* Her writing has also been featured in popular online newspapers, the *Black Agenda, Feminist Wire,* and *Huffington Post Canada.*

Tiffany Austin holds a BA in English from Spelman College, a JD from Northeastern, an MFA in creative writing from Chicago State, and PhD in English from Saint Louis University. Austin has published poetry in *Callaloo, Obsidian III, Coloring Book: An Anthology of Poetry and Fiction* by *Multicultural Writers*, and *Warpland*. Her poetry chapbook, Étude, was recently published by Finishing Line Press. She has also attended a summer workshop at Fine Arts Work Center in Provincetown, MA, received a fellowship at the Virginia Center for the Creative Arts, and the Gwendolyn Brooks Poetry Award in Chicago, IL. She presently teaches at Florida Memorial University, and her major research interest is African diaspora literature, including African American, Afro Latin American, and Caribbean literature.

Karl Henzy holds a PhD from the University of Delaware. He has been on the faculty of Morgan State University since 1993 and earned tenure there in 2001. Henzy researches and publishes on twentieth-century literature. He has published in *The Chronicle for Higher Education, Callaloo,* and *The D.H. Lawrence Review,* among other journals. His current research project is focused on the broad connections between modernism and the Harlem Renaissance.

Index

Abbott, Robert 105
absence 108, 109, 111, 157, 162, 164, 213
accomodationism 94
Aesthetics x, xxx, 100, 103, 264, 324
African diaspora 37, 38, 49, 252, 259, 260, 263, 322, 325
alienation 132, 180, 294
Allen, James S. 126
American Dream, The 112, 126, 134, 197
Anderson, Robert 181
androgyny 271, 273, 277
anti-lynching play 302
Arbian, Paul 265, 269
Armstrong, Nancy 184, 185
Arthur, Marse 291, 292
artifice 100, 241, 270, 273, 274, 275, 278
Assimilation xi, 135, 143, 167
Association of Southern Women for the Prevention of Lynching (ASWPL) 204
Aunt Hager 145, 148, 283, 284
Aunt Harriet 145, 146
Aunt Tempy 285
autonomy 157

Bahktin, M. M. 144
Bailey, Benjamin 282
Barndt, Deborah 41
Barnes, Paula C. vii, 317
Barthé, Richmond 3
Beam, Joseph 269
Beardsley, Aubrey 265

Bellew, John 158, 162
Bennett, Gwendolyn 4, 15, 279
Bennett, Juda 120
Bernard, Emily 242, 246
Bethune, Mary McLeod 12
Black Arts Movement 22, 260
black bourgeoisie 60, 266
black liberation struggle xv
blues xxi, xxii, 24, 50, 105, 106, 145, 281, 283, 284, 303
Blue Vein Society 152
Bohanan, Otto Leland 7
Bontemps, Arna xiii, xxviii, 14, 228, 281, 285, 286, 304, 306
Bourdieu, Pierre 53
bourgeois 57, 60, 142, 172, 236, 260, 278
Braithwaite, Kamau 263
Braithwaite, William S. xxv
Brangwen, Anna 289
Brangwen, Will 291
Brown, Jake 72, 73, 74
Brown, John 104
Brown, Sterling A. xxviii, xxix, xxx, 106, 303, 306, 307, 317
Brown, William Wells 96
brute Negro xxi, xxiii, 234
Bryd, Rudolph P. 33
Burne-Jones, Edward 187
Burrill, Mary P. 202
Butler, Judith 270, 274

cabaret 317
Campbell, Mary Schmidt 3
Canaday, Nicholas, Jr. xxii
Cape, Jonathan 54

capitalism 40, 41, 101
Carey, Mariah 34
caricature xxi, 89, 96
Césaire, Aimé 261
Chesnutt, Charles W. 152, 153
Chinese Communist Revolution
    115
chronotope xi, 121
Civil Rights Act of 1964 115
civil rights movement 38
Civil War xvi, 46, 63
class consciousness 252
Cloutier, Jean-Christophe viii, 309
code-switching 180
Coleman, Leon 238
Collier, Eugenia 140
Collins, Addie 114
Collins, Patricia 230
colonialism 175, 260
colonization 38
Color consciousness 100
color line xi, 34, 98, 125, 126,
    132, 148, 233, 235, 236, 241
color prejudice 61, 63, 72, 175
commodity 37, 45, 47, 48, 50, 96
Compson, Caroline 64
Compson, Jason 68
Compson, Quentin 56, 63
Confederacy 65, 109
Connor, Eugene "Bull" 114
contented slave xx, 245
Cooper, Wayne F. xxvi, 77, 264
Craig, Malcolm 290
Craig, Priscilla 291, 292
Crane, Helga 55, 57, 67, 169, 180,
    236
Crenshaw, Kimberlé 219
Crookman, Junius 96, 97, 236
Cross, Anthony 176, 178

Cruse, Harold 99, 102
Cullen, Countee xvi, xxii, xxvi,
    xxviii, 12, 16, 20, 35, 106,
    108, 282, 304
cultural production 53, 66
cultural racialism 57

Dafora, Asadata 268
Daquin, Mimi 169, 174
Davis, David A. 95
Davis, John P. 279
Dawahare, Anthony 109
decadence 265, 266, 267, 269,
    270, 272, 275, 278
Decadent Movements 278
de Certeau, Michel 179
de Jongh, James 117
Dessau, Florence 287
de Zarraga, Miguel 104
dialect xx, xxv, xxvi, 27, 28, 29,
    35, 93, 263, 283
diaspora 37, 38, 49, 91, 168, 250,
    252, 257, 259, 260, 262,
    263, 322, 323, 324, 325
discrimination xxii, xxvi, 7, 9, 60,
    76, 89, 140, 149, 153, 182,
    191, 192, 196, 255, 301
disenfranchisement 7, 106, 121
Disher, Max 97
disillusionment 132, 170, 218, 221
displacement 110, 180, 181, 258
Dixon, Melvin 143
Dixon, Thomas, Jr. xv, 89, 234
domesticity 221
double-coding 229
double-consciousness 131, 132,
    137, 139, 258, 261, 262
double-directed discourse 144

Douglas, Aaron 3, 10, 13, 14, 15, 16, 17, 20, 103, 274, 279
Douglass, Frederick 108, 129, 130, 131, 133, 199, 321
Dowling, Linda 266
Du Bois, W. E. B. x, xv, xxix, 11, 12, 18, 22, 31, 71, 74, 75, 86, 102, 127, 137, 148, 187, 189, 191, 234, 259, 266, 283, 285, 301
Dunbar, Paul Laurence xx, 28
Dyer Anti-Lynching Bill 150
Dyja, Thomas 95

Eastman, Max xxvi
economic politics 45
Edwards, Brent Hayes 174
elite x, xxvii, 44, 57, 58, 59, 60, 85, 86, 87, 96, 98, 229, 236, 237, 239
Esseintes, Des 269
Evans, Rodney 269
Exile 253
exoticism xxiii, 234, 266
exploitation x, 25, 38, 41, 46, 51, 99, 106, 111, 116, 123, 191, 234, 242, 250, 251, 254

Fabi, Giulia M. 132
Farmer, Paul 42
Faulkner, William 54, 322
Fauset, Jessie Redmon xi, 8, 101, 168, 233, 283, 301
Favor, J. Martin viii
Federal Writers' Project 268
Feminism xii, 167, 184, 197, 199, 200, 279
Ferguson, Jeffrey B. 98, 135
Fielding, Roger 176

Fleming, Robert 137
folk origins xiii, 281
Ford, Karen xix
Forrester, Jimmie 172
fragmentation 143, 180, 181
Frank, Waldo 23, 25, 27, 36
Fuller, Meta Vaux Warrick 3

Gains, Kevin 219
Garber, Eric 267
Garner, Margaret 214
Garvey, Marcus 5, 257, 259, 264, 302, 305
Gates, Henry Louis, Jr. xxix, 5, 19, 20, 33, 34, 36, 38, 102, 103, 118, 198, 232, 246
gendered identity xii, 37, 38, 44, 45, 46, 47, 48, 50, 51, 117, 159, 186, 218, 219, 222, 223, 226, 227, 229, 230, 231, 271, 278
Gensir, Squire 292
Gibson, Dilsey 63
Gilbert, Eliot L. 277
Gloster, Hugh M. 234
Goellnicht, Donald 141
Goeser, Caroline 13
Goldsby, Jacqueline Denise 128
Graham, Maryemma 104
Grant, James 80
Great Depression 283, 306, 307
Great Migration 56, 287, 301
Green, Della 287, 288
Green, Ernest 110
Green, Pleasant 181, 236
Gregory, Montgomery 29
Grey, Tom 210
Griffin, Farah Jasmine 123
Griffith, Rachel Eliza 108